Webster's New World
Guide to
Current American Usage

Webster's New World
Guide to
Current American
Usage

Bernice Randall

Webster's New World
New York

A WORD ABOUT OUR CHANGING LANGUAGE

If only language would stay put. Why take the trouble to learn that an infinitive cannot be split, that *exquisite* is stressed on the first syllable, that *data* is the plural of *datum* and must therefore be used with a plural verb, that *continuous* means one thing and *continual* another, only to find, years later, that hardly anyone knows or cares about those rules?

Surely the laws governing the way a language is spoken and written ought to be as immutable as the laws of science. Archimedes' Principle does not say that the loss of weight of a body immersed in water sometimes equals the weight of the water it displaces. Newton's Third Law of Motion does not say that to every action there is likely to be an equal and opposite reaction. And, in explaining mass and energy, Einstein's Special Theory of Relativity does not say that $E = MC^2$ and in leap year MC^3.

But only dead languages like ancient Greek and classical Latin are static. Everything that makes up a living language changes over time: the word stock and the meanings of words, the ways words are formed and put together in phrases and sentences, how words are spelled and pronounced, and notions of what is acceptable and unacceptable.

If we still spoke Old English—as inhabitants of the region now called England did roughly between the years 400 and 1100—our language would be very different from the one we know.

We would have one-tenth of the words to draw on that we have today.

We would treat every noun as masculine, feminine, or neuter, regardless of the sex or sexlessness of what we were talking about. For instance, *hnecca* ("neck") would be masculine; *heorte* ("heart") would be feminine; and *cneow* ("knee") would be neuter. A far more complicated business, this, than considering, as we do today, that *boy* and *colt* are masculine and *girl* and *filly* feminine because they refer to people or animals that are really of one sex or the other.

For the definite article we would have twenty grammatical forms to indicate gender, number, and case. We now have a single word: *the*.

We would not show the relationship of words in a sentence by arranging them in a certain order, as we do today (for instance, "Hank sent Sara flowers." "Did she thank him?"). Instead, under an elaborate case system, we would constantly change the forms of nouns, pronouns, adjectives, and articles, depending on their grammatical relation to other words in the sentence. So *guma*, a noun meaning "man," would have that form when it was used as a singular masculine subject. But the form for the plural possessive would be *gumena;* the form for the plural indirect object would be *gumum*; and the form for either a singular or a plural direct object would be *guman*.

In writing, we would use one letter (þ) for the t*h* sound in the word for *thief* and another letter (ð) for the t*h* sound in the word for *further*.

The pronunciation of many words, especially those with long vowels, would be very different from what it is today. For example, *her* ("here") would be pronounced hār; *wif* ("wife") would be pronounced wēf.

Clearly, then, the variations that we observe in our own lifetime do not begin to compare to the radical transformations that have shaped the language over centuries. So why the acute distress today? Is it, as the alarmists warn, that the recent changes are signs not of gradual development but of headlong decline; that unless the line is drawn now, there will be no stopping the deterioration?

The Back to Good English proponents are determined to set today's slipshod grammar and usage to rights. With *Webster's New International Dictionary* (second edition, 1934) open on its stand in the family room and Fowler's *Dictionary of Modern English Usage* (first edition, 1926) on the bedside table, these nostalgics want to restore the language not to the state it was in during, say, the ninth century but to that of the period when they learned the rules.

The greater the insistence on correctness, the greater the need for authority, since without the standards that authority sets, how can deviations from proper grammar and usage be measured and judged? From about the middle of the eighteenth century until well into the twentieth, most grammar books laid down the law on what is right and what is wrong in English, imposing rules based mainly on classical Latin models but partly on pure invention. Thus the injunctions against split infinitives and prepositions at the ends of sentences.

In the past, dictionaries, usage guides, and commentaries, too, reflected an ideal language that had to be saved from those who spoke and wrote it. True, virtually all lexicographers and scholars try to be more objective today, recording usage instead of legislating it. But what defenders of linguistic law and order want are books that deplore the state of the language and, at the same time, exhort their readers to avoid words and constructions seen and heard every day.

Prescriptive grammar books, dictionaries, and usage guides are the next best thing to an Academy of the English Language. Like the reassuring advertisement that proclaimed Blue Nun white wine to be "correct with any dish," they take the worry out of acting on one's own. Why say or write *hopefully* or *the reason why* and risk being criticized? A Nuits-Saint-Georges might taste better with a roast fillet of beef, but Blue Nun is safer.

There is, of course, nothing wrong with wishing that English-speakers paid attention to their language. Even today, when more and more people do what makes them feel good, there are limits to our tolerance of indifference to the marvel of language, of laziness or carelessness in putting together a thought or a sentence, of refuge in words and phrases that sound grand but have next to no meaning, of insensitivity to occasion. We remember a time when:

> Friends invited friends for an evening of conversation, not to play electronic video games.

> Secretaries of state did not "caveat it that way" or push a troublesome topic "to a lower decibel of public fixation."

> In recounting earlier conversations, people used verbs like *say*, in the past tense, not *go* in the present.

> When I got home, Mother goes, "Where have you been?"
> I go, "Out."
> She goes, "Well, call me next time."

> Weather forecasters talked about "heavy rain," not "major precipitation events."

> Those who felt the least possible interest in something said that they couldn't care less, not that they could.

Without reimposing rigid eighteenth-century rules, we ought to expect educated people to choose, order, spell, and pronounce words with care, taste, common sense, and an awareness that appropriateness in context is more important than absolute "correctness." We may tell a friend that we'll "drop in on our way back from the vet's," but does that mean we must always use the informal expression *drop in* when we talk about paying a casual or unexpected visit? That every time we find such relation words as *in* and *on* in the same sentence we are required to run them together? That we may never use the entire word *veterinarian,* only its clipped form?

The words we select and the way we put them together depend on the purpose of our communication and on who our listeners or readers are. A list of Saturday chores that we scribble to ourselves is not the same as a carefully written job application, a thoughtfully composed magazine article, a meticulously edited textbook, or a polished lecture delivered before the American Philosophical Association.

To those who see Modern English not as a comatose patient being kept alive by an artificial life-support system but as a living, growing body with both a memory and a sensitivity to its environment, linguistic change is natural and inevitable. Though the variations may seem chaotic when viewed in the short run, they follow certain linguistic principles that have to do with sound, word form, syntax, vocabulary, and acceptance by various groups in the society. And, regardless of what the hand-wringers and forehead-slappers say, the body and structure of English have not undergone fundamental change in the past five hundred years or so. If they had, how would the more than 300 million first-language speakers of English throughout the world, as well as the more than a billion other people for whom English is a second language, be able to understand one another? How would today's college students be able to read the sonnets of Sir Thomas Wyatt, who died in 1542?

Not all coinages, elliptical constructions, slang expressions, buzzwords, euphemisms, and the like find a permanent place in the language. Those that fill a need or satisfy a large number of people over time will last; those that don't, won't. *Smog* will probably be around long after a newspaper columnist's *untrumors* has been forgotten; *Oval Office,* long after Alexander Haig's verb *caveat* has been buried in Foggy Bottom.

On the other hand, purists of the past were unable to keep *thee* and *thou* from becoming *you; everyone's else* from becoming *everyone else's; a remarkable fact* from becoming *a curious fact;* and the adjective *human* from becoming the noun *human.* It is no more likely that today's purists will be able to keep *center on* from becoming *center around; it is to be hoped* from becoming *hopefully;* and *whom did you see?* from becoming *who did you see?*

Anyone who prefers not to, need not adopt every change that comes along; in fact, established usage is sometimes preferable to current fashion. The trouble is that those who resist all change can't hold out forever and still expect to be understood, for, unlike Humpty Dumpty in *Through the Looking-Glass*, they can't make a word mean just what they "choose it to mean—neither more nor less." Usage cannot be so private that it fails to take into account how others speak and write.

There is a Spanish saying that applies to the attempts—well-meaning or presumptuous, but ultimately futile—to stop linguistic change: "One cannot cover the sun with a finger" (*"No se puede tapar el sol con un dedo"*). Those who long to preserve what they consider to be the purity of the language may close one eye and hold a finger up to any practice that they believe deviates from the established rules of grammar and usage. Sure enough, they are able to blot out the offending word or construction. But as soon as they lower their finger they discover that the new form is still there.

Webster's New World
Guide to
Current American Usage

A

a or *an*?

It's a wonder we don't say and write "*A napple* a day keeps the doctor away" and "Reporters must have *an ose* for news." *Apple* has always begun with *a* and *nose* with *n*, but there are other English words that, through the twin processes of faulty word separation and syllabic merging, have either passed on their initial *n* to the preceding *a* form of the indefinite article or picked up the *n* from the *an* form of that article.

Some nine hundred to five hundred years ago—during the Middle English period—the cloth or leather garment worn over the front part of the body to protect one's clothes was called *a napron*. In time people began to think that the *n* was part of the article preceding the noun, so they redivided the two words into *an apron*.

About the same time, people in the British Isles began to hear *an oumpere* instead of *a noumpire* when someone chosen to render a decision in a dispute was being referred to. An even earlier form of the noun had been *noumpere*, from the Middle French *nomper*, whose elements *non* ("not") and *per* ("even") had given it the sense of "an uneven number, or third person." If the *n* had not got attached to the article, we would be shouting "Kill the nump!" at baseball games today.

The reddish-yellow citrus fruit whose juice we drink for breakfast was *naranga* in Sanskrit, *nārang* in Persian, and *nāranj* in Arabic before it became *naranja* in Spanish. Partly because of the influence of the Latin *aurum* ("gold") and partly because of the loss of the initial *n* through faulty separation of the article *un*, the spelling was changed to *auranja* in Provençal. The word became *orenge* in Old French and *orange* in Middle English.

Syllabic merging gave us *a nickname*, meaning an "additional or substitute name," from the Middle English *an ekename* (which, in turn, had come from *eken*, meaning "to increase," plus *name*). And the small salamander we call *a newt* got its name changed from *an eute* during that same busy Middle English period. (For some other things that were happening then, or had happened in the Old English period, see the table on pages 4–6.)

WHATEVER THE NOUN, it is its sound, not its spelling, that determines which form of the indefinite article—*a* or *an*—goes before it. *A* is used before words that begin with a consonant sound:

a bear   a coffeepot   a zebra

and before words that begin with the "yoo" sound:

a union   a European   a unique situation

An, on the other hand, is used before words that begin with a vowel sound.

an onion   an ambassador   an umbrella

Usage is not so uniform when it comes to words that are spelled with an initial *h.* Everyone agrees that in some words the *h* is sounded like a consonant; that is, one's breath is somehow obstructed as it passes from the lungs through the mouth. So before a sounded *h,* the appropriate indefinite form of the article is *a.*

a house   a heavy load   a hyacinth   a human being

Everyone agrees, too, that in other words the initial *h* is always silent, so the subsequent vowel sound requires the *an* form of the article.

an hour   an heir   an honest politician

What everyone does not agree about are words in which the initial *h* is sometimes fully sounded, sometimes lightly sounded, and sometimes not sounded at all. Most Americans pronounce *hotel, heroic, humble,* and *history* and its derivatives (*historic, historical, historian,* and the like) with a decided *h* sound, and therefore use the *a* form of the indefinite article.

a hotel   a history course

a heroic act   a historic event

a humble genius a historical novel

But Britons whose speech is the cultivated BBC variety tend either to drop the initial *h* or to pronounce it so faintly as to make *an* the more natural spoken, and thus written, form of the article. They do this especially when the *h* syllable is unstressed.

an hotel   an historical novel

an heroic act   an historian

Even though many of their compatriots consider them affected, some Americans follow the British practice. *An historic,* especially, often appears in print in the States.

There is an odd twist in the American and British pronunciations of *herb* and words that begin with those four letters. Most Americans do not sound the *h* in *herb* and *herbage,* so they would use the *an* form of the indefinite article; but they usually do sound the *h* in *herbaceous, herbicide, herbivore,* and the like, so here they would use the *a* form. Upper-class Britons sound the *h* in all those words and therefore use *a* before them. (For Cockneys like Eliza Doolittle, the heroine of George Bernard Shaw's play *Pygmalion* and its musical adaptation, *My Fair Lady,* the question of when the written initial *h* is silent never comes up: it always is. Ask Professor 'enry 'iggins.)

Sound, not spelling, determines also whether *a* or *an* is used before a symbol, an abbreviation, or an acronym (a word formed from the first, or first few, letters in a series of words). Whether pronounced as a whole word or by its individual letters, the shortened form takes *a* if it begins with a consonant sound, a "yoo" sound, or an *h* sound.

Consonant Sound

a lab technician
a Ph.D. candidate
a BBC broadcast
a radar wave
a FORTRAN tutorial

"Yoo" Sound

a U.S. (yo͞o′ es′) airline
a UN (yo͞o′ en′) commission
a UNICEF (yo͞o′nə sef′) fund-raiser
a u.c. (yo͞o′ sē′), or uppercase, letter

"H" Sound

a HOPE (hōp) medical team
a HUD (hud) survey

But if the shortened form begins with a vowel sound or with an *h* sounded by its letter name, it is preceded by *an.*

Vowel Sound

an i.o.u. (ī′ ō′ u′)
an NBC (en′ bē′ sē′) special
an UNRRA (un′rə) working party
an L.A. (el′ ā′) mailing address

"Aich" Sound

an HMO (āch′ em′ ō′) clinic

With phrases that begin with numbers expressed in figures, again it is the way the phrases are pronounced that determines whether *a* or *an* is used before them in speech and writing.

a 4-ply tire

an 11-pound turkey

For numbers over a thousand, the choice of the indefinite article sometimes depends on how the speaker or writer thinks of the numbers.

a $1100 (one thousand one hundred–dollar) balance

an $1100 (eleven hundred–dollar) balance

Centuries expressed in figures also take *a* or *an* according to the sound that follows the indefinite article.

a 21st-century space station

an 18th-century painting

MANY GRAMMAR AND USAGE BOOKS consider both forms of the indefinite article—*a* and *an*—superfluous in certain constructions. One such construction is a phrase like *what kind of, what sort of,* or *what type of* followed by a noun. So, according to those books:

What kind of a teacher is she?

What sort of an animal is that?

ought to be changed to:

What kind of teacher is she?

What sort of animal is that?

Yet the reason for the objection is hard to understand, for leaving the indefinite article out or putting it in can change the meaning of a sentence. In answer to the question "What kind of teacher is she?" one might expect to be told the teacher's level, field, or specialty, for example, "a kindergarten teacher," "a science teacher," or "an Arthur Murray dance instructor." On the other hand, the question "What kind of a teacher is she?" calls for an opinion about the teacher's qualities or attributes, so it might elicit an answer like "conscientious," "a thorough bore," or "first-rate."

Another construction in which either *a* or *an* is generally considered superfluous, especially in formal speech and writing, has to do with an adjective in the comparative form. Except in casual conversation, the indefinite article would ordinarily be dropped from these sentences:

There is no better a time to fish than when it rains.

The robber asked whether there was any faster an RV on the lot.

However, the indefinite article is required when the adjective is in the simple form.

Now is as good a time as any to hold the election.

I doubt that the platoon had ever faced as hostile an enemy.

This construction is sometimes heard in casual speech: an adjective in its simple form + *of* + *a* + a noun. A Chicago FBI spokesman used it when he told an Associated Press reporter that an explosive mailed to United Airlines president Percy Wood was contained in "not too big of a package." In formal speech and writing, the *of* is ordinarily dropped and only the *a* retained.

About the Time Old English and Middle English Were Being Spoken ...

Old English period (roughly A.D. 400–1100)

407 The Roman legions withdraw from Britain.

426 St. Augustine, of Hippo (North Africa), finishes *The City of God*.

432 St. Patrick arrives in Ireland to preach the Gospel.

450*   Germanic tribes (Angles, Saxons, and Jutes) invade Britain; Attila the Hun invades western Europe.

476   The Middle Ages begin, when the Western Roman Empire falls to the barbarians under Odoacer.

597   Augustine, a Roman monk, arrives in England to convert the people to Christianity.

622   The Muslim era begins, when Mohammed flees from Mecca to Medina.

700*   *Beowulf,* an Anglo-Saxon epic, is composed.

711   The Moors invade and conquer Spain.

800   Charlemagne is crowned emperor of the Holy Roman Empire.

855*   The Danes invade England.

871   Alfred the Great becomes king of Wessex (Anglo-Saxon kingdom).

1000   The Norwegian Leif Ericsson explores the North American coast.

1017   Canute becomes the first Danish king of England.

1042   Edward the Confessor restores the Saxon line.

1065   Westminster Abbey is consecrated.

1066   The Battle of Hastings; William I ("the Conqueror") becomes the first Norman king.

Middle English period (roughly 1100–1500)

1100   King Henry I unites the Normans and Saxons.

1150*   The University of Paris is founded.

1167*   Oxford University is founded.

1170   St. Thomas à Becket, archbishop of Canterbury, is murdered.

1189   Richard I ("the Lion-Hearted") sets out on the Third Crusade.

1194   Construction of the cathedral of Chartres begins.

1209   The University of Cambridge is founded.

1215   English barons force King John to sign the Magna Charta.

1230*   The University of Salamanca is founded.

1233   The Inquisition begins, under Pope Gregory IX.

1271   Marco Polo leaves Venice for Kublai Khan's court, in China.

1274   St. Thomas Aquinas dies, leaving his *Summa Theologica* unfinished.

*Approximate date.

1304* Giotto begins the frescoes in the Arena Chapel in Padua.

1318* Dante completes *The Divine Comedy*.

1325 Tenochtitlán, the Aztec capital, is founded.

1334 The plague (the "Black Death") spreads through Europe from Constantinople.

1337 The Hundred Years' War, between England and France, begins.

1353 Boccaccio completes the *Decameron*.

1400 Chaucer dies, leaving *The Canterbury Tales* unfinished.

1431 St. Joan of Arc is burned at the stake by the English.

1450* The Middle Ages end, as the Renaissance spreads throughout central and western Europe.

1452* Johann Gutenberg prints a Bible from movable type.

1453 The Turks capture Constantinople; the Hundred Years' War ends.

1455 The Wars of the Roses, between the houses of Lancaster and York, begin.

1477 The first dated book printed in England is brought out by William Caxton.

1485 The Wars of the Roses end; Sir Thomas Malory's *Morte d'Arthur* is published.

1486 The Portuguese navigator Bartholomeu Dias rounds the Cape of Good Hope.

1492 Columbus discovers America; the Moors and the Jews are expelled from Spain.

1498* Leonardo da Vinci completes *The Last Supper*.

1509 Henry VIII is crowned king of England.

*Approximate date.

---

abbreviations.   See **An LL.D. KO'd a Brig. Gen. at a BYOB party.**

about or *around*?

Some dictionaries and usage guides do not consider *about* and *around* interchangeable in the senses of "approximately," "approximately at," "nearby," and "here and there." Whereas they find *about* acceptable in both formal and informal speech and writing, they say that *around* is appropriate only in informal contexts.

Formal and Informal	Informal
Each box weighs about two kilos.	Each box weighs around two kilos.
The train is due about midnight.	The train is due around midnight.
Is there a salesperson about?	Is there a salesperson around?
Coffee cups and ashtrays were lying about the room.	Coffee cups and ashtrays were lying around the room.

Others relax the restriction on *around* in all senses except "approximately" and "approximately at." And still others make no distinction at all.

The fact is, educated Americans frequently use *around* constructions, and not only in conversation and informal writing. Far fewer educated Britons do. This, in fact, is the entire entry for *around* in Frederick T. Wood's *Current English Usage:*

> " 'He spent the whole afternoon sitting around doing nothing,' 'The papers were left lying around,' 'I shall be home around five o'clock.' This use of *around* is an Americanism and is to be deprecated in British English. Use *about*."

About the Time Old English and Middle English Were Being Spoken . . .   See table in *a* or *an*?

above; below

Writers sometimes wonder how to refer to a passage, table, or other matter that appears elsewhere in a book or article. They were probably told that, in the sense of "previously mentioned," "subsequently cited," or the like, *above* and *below* are incorrect.

As an adverb, *above* is now widely accepted, either alone or in hyphenated compounds.

> A Petrarchan sonnet appears above.

> See the sonnet above.

> Such a mood is conveyed in the above-cited Petrarchan sonnet.

It is often used as an adjective as well.

> See the above sonnet.

And even as a noun.

> This sonnet echoes the above.

In such references, *below* is used only as an adverb.

> The contours can be seen more clearly in the map below.

> For a sharper definition, see the photo given below.

Above need not refer only to matter that immediately precedes the reference or appears higher on the same page. For a span of more than a page or two, however, writers usually prefer to give a more precise cross-reference.

Similarly, *below* generally refers either to a lower place on the same page or to the page or two following.

absolute constructions.   See **Covered with onions, relish, and ketchup, I ate a hot dog at the ballpark.**

acronyms.   See **NASA's lox needs no bagels.**

A.D.   See *B.C.; A.D.*

adjectives and adverbs: in comparisons, see *as . . . as* or *so . . . as?*; **Excitinger times lie ahead; Kilimanjaro is taller than any mountain in Africa; misplaced,** see **"Electric shaver for women with delicate floral design on the handle."**

adverbs: **and predicate adjectives,** see **People who want to arrive safe don't drive drunkenly; in verb sets,** see **Washing down pillows takes a strong stomach.**

affixes.   See **Who needs a rabbit's foot more: an unlucky person or a luckless one?**

aggravate

In the sense of "to increase the gravity of, to make more grievous or burdensome; to make worse, intensify, exacerbate," *aggravate* is a useful word.

In many cities overcrowding is aggravated by inadequate public transportation.

The examples from literature that are given in *The Oxford English Dictionary* date from before 1600.

The *OED* traces another sense of *aggravate*—that of exasperating, incensing, or embittering a person—almost as far back, though some critics of this usage prefer to believe that it is quite new and can therefore still be driven off. They insist that the so-called traditional sense is the only legitimate one. That is, the verb may be applied to a disease or to a troublesome or unpleasant situation:

Cat dander aggravates Leslie's asthma.

The farmers' problems were aggravated by record heat and a four-month drought.

but not to a person:

Aggravated by a blaring radio, the bus rider shot its owner.

They also point out that, with so many other verbs around to convey the notion of moving someone to impatience or anger—*exasperate, annoy, vex, irritate, bother, provoke, nettle, peeve, irk,* and *rile* are, with varying degrees of formality, some of them—there is no need for yet another. But English is full of words that have either given up what is sometimes thought of as their "proper" or "basic" meaning or taken on another sense already available in other words, or both. Take *exasperate,*which is now rarely used in its earlier sense of "to intensify (a feeling, disease, etc.)" but, instead, is generally taken to mean "to irritate or annoy very much; make angry, vex." This is precisely the course that *aggravate* is following, and—the development of languages being what it is— the second meaning is likely to gain full acceptance, with the other one either being carried along or eventually dropped. Meanwhile, most current American and British dictionaries note that, at least in informal writing and speech, the verb is widely used in the sense of "to annoy."

The noun *aggravation* and the adjective *aggravating* get the same treatment as the verb they come from: denounced by some and used, especially informally, by others.

A daily aggravation to anyone who uses a phone nowadays is being put on hold.

Listening to on-hold music also causes some people aggravation.

What do you find more aggravating: missing a bus or catching one?

ain't

To many people, *ain't* doesn't bear discussion: it is simply a mark of illiteracy. Yet it was once a standard contraction of *am not,* and some authorities still defend this use as a proper informal construction in questions.

I'm invited too, ain't I?

They usually point out that the proposed alternatives have problems of their own. "I'm invited too, *am* I *not?*" is too formal for most occasions—though not nearly as stilted as "I'm invited too, *amn't* I?" And "I'm invited too, *aren't* I?" is awkward, especially since *aren't* is a contraction of *are not,* and nobody would say "I'm invited too, are I not?"

Many English-speakers go beyond defending *ain't,* for *am not,* in questions. They believe that in negative declarative sentences, too, *I ain't* sounds as natural as *I'm not,* and certainly less formal than *I am not.*

I ain't saying yes and I ain't saying no.

Yet, despite its defenders, *ain't,* for *am not,* is mainly limited to dialogue and humorous contexts nowadays. The risk of criticism or ridicule is too high a price to pay for using this handy contraction in formal speech or writing.

The use of *ain't* as a contraction of *is not, are not, has not,* and *have not* is even more restricted. It is generally regarded either as dialectal (peculiar to a certain region, community, social group, or the like) or as nonstandard (not conforming to the standards of the language variety of educated speakers). Occasionally, however, those who are certain of their status as cultivated speakers of standard English dare to use it. They do so usually in clichés like "And that ain't hay!" (meaning "That's not a trifling sum"), or to lighten the tone of their remarks. Senator Ernest F. Hollings, of South Carolina, used *ain't* in this way during the Senate's 1979 hearings on Senator Herman Talmadge, of Georgia.

> " 'People who know 'Hummon,' " Mr. Hollings said, emphasizing the way many Georgians pronounce the Senator's name, 'know he ain't no crook.' It was one of the few light moments in the proceedings, which were as solemn as any in the Senate in many months." (*New York Times*)

So did the television news correspondent Roger Mudd, on announcing that he was leaving NBC in 1987 to join public television's *MacNeil-Lehrer NewsHour*.

> " 'I must say I've found over the years that money and audience ain't everything.' " (*San Francisco Chronicle*)

all or *all of?*

At about the time they were forbidden to speak to strangers, many children were warned against using the phrase *all of*. When they grew up, they could count on authorities on usage to remind them to stay away from *of*. Rudolf Flesch, for example, says, in *The ABC of Style: A Guide to Plain English:* "A good writer or editor automatically changes *all of* to *all*."

A good writer or a good editor might wonder why. Is *all of* less idiomatic than *the whole of* (as in "The whole of Kansas could hear him")? Than *none of* ("None of the family came")? Than *some of* ("Some of the hikers brought their lunch")? Than *few of* ("Few of the birds survived")?

Besides, if *all* is followed by a pronoun instead of a noun, *of* cannot be dropped. That is, we must say "All of them received it," not "All them received it."

What the controversy comes down to is this: When it is a matter of choice, and if the sentence sounds or reads better without *of*, many speakers and writers do not use it. But they will not be bullied into dropping the preposition any more than they will stop putting bananas in the refrigerator just because they are told not to.

For the omission of other prepositions some people are attached to, see "SHOP MACY'S AND SAVE."

All right already!

When we mean "satisfactory," "satisfactorily," "unhurt," "correct," "yes," "certainly," and the like, we ordinarily use *all right*—written as two words and pronounced with equal stress on each word.

> Sandy does all right as a painter.

> Even though the bus rolled over, the passengers were all right.

> My tax return was all right, according to the IRS.

> All right, you can have the car tonight.

> You landed a cushy job, all right!

As an expression of approval, *all right* sometimes precedes the noun it modifies. In this slang usage, it is written with a hyphen and *all* is stressed in speech.

Sandy is an all-right painter.

Except in English subtitles of foreign films, *alright* seldom appears in print. That's because many people object to this variant spelling. Yet if *alright* follows the path of *all most → almost,* it will eventually replace *all right.* Or both forms might be used at the same time, with slightly different meanings.

That's what happened to the pairs *all together* / *altogether* and *all ready* / *already. All together* means "in a group."

The class went to the museum all together.

Altogether means "completely," "all being included," "everything being considered."

Do you believe that the referee was altogether right?

How many Oscars has she won altogether?

Altogether, it was a disappointing opera season.

All ready means "completely ready."

The set is all ready for the camera crew.

Already means "by or before the given or implied time" or "even now or even then."

By the time I got to the airport, the plane had already left.

I'm already late for lunch.

It is also used informally as an intensive, especially to express impatience.

All right already!

all-around; all-round. See *around* or *round?*

almost or most? See *most or almost?*

already. See **All right already!**

alternate or alternative?

Until around the middle of the twentieth century, dictionaries stressed a basic difference between *alternate* and *alternative.* They pointed out that *alternate,* as both an adjective and a verb, and the adverb *alternately,* referred to something occurring as every other one in a series, following by turn, rotating, or interchanging regularly.

Gym classes are held on alternate Fridays.

The casserole has alternate layers of ham and noodles.

The sky alternated between blue and gray.

Jody became alternately euphoric and morose.

On the other hand, *alternative,* as either an adjective or a noun, and the adverb *alternatively,* had to do with a choice between possibilities, things, or courses of action.

Opponents of nuclear power look to the sun as an alternative source of energy.

Who but the Sandinistas were the logical alternative to Somoza?

The speaker said that we must seek peace or, alternatively, prepare for nuclear war.

The breakdown of that long-held distinction probably came about as Americans began to use *alternate* as a noun referring to someone standing by to take the place of another if necessary, that is, a substitute. From the notion of a person designated as a stand-in for someone else (as in ''an alternate delegate'' to a political convention), it was not far to that of anything being a possible replacement in a series, and from there it was but a step to *alternate* and *alternative* sharing broader meanings. Nowadays *alternate* is so often used in the context of choices or possibilites that many current dictionaries show it as a synonym for *alternative,* especially as an adjective.

Highway signs, for example, point to alternate routes. *Bibliography and Footnotes: A Style Manual for Students and Writers* notes:

"An alternate form of reference places the title of the document within quotation marks and uses italics for the series notation. . . ."

In *American Usage: The Consensus* (1970), Roy H. Copperud said of the word *bugger:*

"Widely enough known in the sense of *sodomite* to be offensive in its alternate sense as a term of affection. . . ."

(However, in a 1980 version of that book, Copperud changed ''alternate sense'' to ''alternative sense,'' probably because he realized that his entry for *alternate(ly), alternative(ly)* upholds the traditional distinction between the two words.)

SOME TRADITIONALISTS BELIEVE that since *alternative* comes from a Latin word originally meaning ''one of two,'' it should be used only when there are two choices, possibilities, or courses of action. If there are three or more, they insist, *alternative* should be replaced by a word like *choices* or *possibilities.*

Yet *alternative* was extended to ''one of several'' by the middle of the nineteenth century. *The Oxford English Dictionary* gives this 1848 citation from John Stuart Mill:

"The alternative seemed to be either death, or to be permanently supported by other people, or a radical change in the economical arrangements."

And this 1857 one from William Gladstone:

"My decided preference is for the fourth and last of these alternatives."

Most American and British dictionaries and usage guides now set no limit on the number of possibilities between which an alternative is chosen.

although or *though?*   See *though* or *although?*

altogether or *all together?*   See **All right already!**

A.M.; P.M.

These abbreviations show which half of the day is meant. A.M., also written *a.m.* or AM, comes from the Latin *ante meridiem* ("before noon") and designates the time from midnight to noon. P.M., also written *p.m.* or PM, comes from the Latin *post meridiem* ("after noon") and designates the time from noon to midnight.

The formal abbreviation for *noon,* as in timetables, is M. or *m.,* from the Latin *meridies; 12:00 P.M.* stands for *midnight.*

A.M. and P.M. are ordinarily used with figures.

10:15 A.M.   8:00 P.M.

Phrases like *10:15 A.M. in the morning* and *8:00 P.M. tonight* are generally considered redundant, since either the abbreviation or the word or phrase is enough to denote the time of day. Both, however, are occasionally used for emphasis.

These abbreviations usually appear in small capitals in books and magazines:

10:15 A.M.   8:00 P.M.   12:00 P.M.

and in full capitals in newspapers and typescript:

10:15 A.M.   8:00 P.M.   12:00 P.M.

American English and British English.   See **There's no home like Eaton Place.**

among or *between?*

"Be sure to brush among your teeth" is the kind of foolishness we can expect if we blindly apply the rule that *among* must be used with three or more persons or things. The corollary of that rule—use *between* with two persons or things—presents no problem, since no native English-speaker would say "Lunch is served among noon and three o'clock" or "Among you and me, the play won't make it past New Haven."

In many constructions *among* is indeed appropriate with more than two:

The chemistry and physics prizes were shared among three Americans, a Pakistani, and a West German.

especially when the object is a group treated as a collective unit:

CARE distributes food among the needy.

What leads to unidiomatic usage—that is, usage that goes counter to the patterns of the language—is insisting on *among* when the three or more persons or things are thought of not in relation to all the other elements of the group but individually or one pair at a time. For centuries *between* has been used for this purpose. As *The Oxford English Dictionary* notes:

> "In all senses, *between* has been, from its earliest appearance, extended to more than two. . . . It is still the only word available to express the relation of a thing to many surrounding things severally and individually, *among* expressing a relation to them collectively and vaguely: we should not say 'the space lying among the three points,' or 'a treaty among three powers,' or 'the choice lies among the three candidates in the select list,' or 'to insert a needle among the closed petals of a flower.' "

When we say, for example, "Careful writers choose the most appropriate word from among those meaning 'laughable' or 'absurd,' " we are thinking of an indefinite number of near-synonyms as a group. But when we say "Careful writers distinguish between *ludicrous, preposterous,* and *ridiculous,*" we are thinking of each of these words individually, compared with each of the others.

Believing that they are observing a nicety of the language when in fact they are doing away with one of its long-standing useful distinctions, some speakers and writers cling to the wrongheaded notion that *between* can't be caught anywhere in the neighborhood of more than two. John Simon, for instance, writing in the *New York Times Book Review*, described James L. Clifford's *Dictionary Johnson* as "a worthy book that nevertheless falls among many stools." The sense of the expression calls for *between*, not *among*, since what a book might fall in is the space that separates one stool from another—just as "Be sure to brush between your teeth" refers to each tooth in relation to the one on either side of it, not to all the teeth in your mouth collectively. But perhaps Mr. Simon knew that and used *among* simply to camouflage the cliché "fall between two stools."

In a study on Virginia Woolf, Peter Salm clearly followed long-established usage governing *between*.

> "In *The Waves*, a novel which traces the lives of six friends from childhood to maturity, verbal exchanges between members of this close-knit group unobtrusively mark the progression of time."

amuse or *bemuse*?   See *bemuse* or *amuse*?

an or *a*?   See *a* or *an*?

and, at the beginning of a sentence.   See "And so it goes."

and etc.

The abbreviation *etc.* derives from the Latin *et cetera* (*et* meaning "and" and *cetera*, or *cætera*, meaning "the rest"). With *and* already included in the senses "and others," "and the like," "and the rest," "and so forth," *and etc.* is redundant. That is, in a sentence like:

Ermines, sables, minks, otters, and etc., are members of the marten family.

and might be omitted. However, the abbreviation *etc.* seldom appears in ordinary text (though it is often found in tables and other material where space must be saved). So *and etc.* might be replaced by a phrase such as *and the like, and so on,* or *and so forth.*

Like most abbreviations, *etc.* is pronounced as if it were spelled out. Usually infuriating at least one of their listeners, some people substitute a *k* sound for the *t* sound of *et.* That is, they say:

ek set'ər ə (or ek set'rə) instead of et set'ər ə (or et set'rə)

Research is underway to determine whether they are the same people who pronounce:

asterisk as as'tər iks (or as'tər ik) instead of as'tər isk

escape as ek skāp' instead of ə skāp' (or e skāp')

escapade as eks'kə pād' instead of es'kə pād'

and or *as well as*?   See *as well as* or *and*?

and or *or*?

The coordinating conjunctions most often used in joining two or more logically and grammatically equal elements in a series are *and* and *or.* Whereas *and* brings together elements of the same value or rank:

They went to Copenhagen, Stockholm, and Oslo.

or introduces an alternative, that is, any of the possibilities in a series (even though it usually appears only before the last element):

They wanted to go to Copenhagen, Stockholm, or Oslo.

A series introduced by a plural noun ordinarily takes *and.*

Boys usually amass a lot of information about such *subjects* as sports *and* cars.

Disillusion with Victorian values is apparent in twentieth-century English *novelists* like Conrad, Joyce, *and* Woolf.

On the other hand, a series introduced by a singular noun takes *or.*

Boys usually amass a lot of information about a *subject* like sports *or* cars.

Disillusion with Victorian values is apparent in a twentieth-century English *novelist* like Conrad, Joyce, *or* Woolf.

Or is more likely to be used in negative constructions or in statements that convey a negative sense. It would, for example, be more idiomatic than *and* in this sentence, from a United Press International article on the bugging of the Republican Party headquarters in 1980:

"But they [experts in a Washington security firm] had not yet looked at Crisp's phone <u>and</u> investigated a mysterious wire, running the length of the office and believed to be possible evidence of past bugging."

and or *to*, in infinitives of purpose.   See "Come up and see me sometime."

"And so it goes."

Some English-speakers cling to the superstitious belief that a sentence ought not to begin with *and* or *but*. Their teachers probably told them that these two coordinating conjunctions should be used to join independent clauses within a sentence, not divide them, and that a preceding period (actual or implied) only emphasizes the separation.

Yet many speakers and writers, today as in the past, start sentences with *and* and, even more often, with *but*.

"And I can just imagine what my grandmother would say if she knew." (Paul Leslie, "Exits")

"And they regret the absence of humor and gusto—with better reason, perhaps, in this gray world we have to live in." (Albert J. Guerard, "The Ivory Tower and the Dust Bowl")

"But it is sadism after the English fashion: that is to say, it is unconscious, there is not overtly any sex in it, and it keeps within the bounds of the law." (George Orwell, "Raffles and Miss Blandish")

"But this does not mean that they are not affected by the noise: part of the brain must be employed in sorting out the noises and discounting them." (Robert Graves and Alan Hodge, "The Present Confusion of English Prose")

In choosing a title for her memoirs, the television commentator Linda Ellerbee turned to the same catch phrase she had used as the sign-off on *NBC News Overnight:* "And so it goes."

and which, and who; but which, but who.   See **Tennis is a sport I enjoy but which I don't play well.**

and/or

Perhaps what makes *and/or* look like an entry in an accountant's ledger is the solidus, or slant line, which was originally the long *s* (ʃ) used to separate shillings from pence. The off-putting conjunction, meaning "either *and* or *or*, according to what is meant," is in fact usually found in business or legal texts.

The disposition of personal and/or real property is covered in article 12 of the will.

In other kinds of writing, either *and* or *or* will generally do.

On a windy day we can expect to see flat kites and bowed kites.

On a windy day we can expect to see flat kites or bowed kites.

If further clarification is needed, a phrase is usually added.

On a windy day we can expect to see flat kites or bowed kites, or both.

Yet, as a function word, *and/or* is sometimes useful in showing, in a kind of shorthand, the relation between words or phrases. These, for example, are the closing lines in Gilbert Highet's essay "Learning a Language":

"It is because of writing that there are no dead languages, except those that are spoken by illiterate tribes now vanished. The rest are either living (if spoken and/or read) or in suspended animation, waiting to be called back into life."

angry or *mad*?   See *mad* or *angry*?

anxious or *eager*?   See *eager* or *anxious*?

any

This word is not bound by its early sense of "one." As an adjective, it modifies both singular and plural nouns.

any child, any children

any ambition

any number of balloons

As a pronoun, *any* takes either a singular or plural verb, depending on the context. To convey the notion of "one"—that is, to set an item apart from a group—a singular verb is used.

Has any of Porter's stories been recorded?

Which of the salads do you prefer? Any *is* fine with me.

But if the sense is "some," a plural verb is used.

Have any of Porter's stories been recorded?

Which of the salads do you prefer? Are any on the table yet?

For more on the agreement between subjects and verbs, in number, see FISH AND CHIPS IS ON THE MENU AGAIN.

Any is also used as an adverb meaning "to any degree or extent; at all."

Won't this car go any faster?

any, in comparisons.   See **Kilimanjaro is taller than any mountain in Africa.**

anymore

In the sense of "now," "nowadays," "lately," or "from now on," *anymore* is generally used only in questions and negative constructions.

Do you see your nephew anymore?

Now that they're not making Edsels anymore, I take the bus.

Anymore is appropriate in positive statements as well, provided they convey a negative sense.

Few people write thank-you letters anymore.

It's hard to think anymore of a T-shirt without a message on it.

In certain regions, communities, and social groups in the United States *anymore* is heard in straightforward positive constructions, but this usage is far from universally accepted in speech or writing.

It rains a lot around here anymore.

Anymore it's expensive to go to the movies.

ALTHOUGH THE ADVERB can be spelled either *anymore* or *any more,* the solid form has become more common. Even the *New Yorker,* which still prefers *coöperate* to *cooperate,* has been won over to *anymore.* However, the two-word form is always used in constructions in which *any* is followed either by the noun or adjective *more* in the sense of "something additional" or "further."

The lawyer doubted that any more could have been done for her client.

Tell him that we simply haven't any more time.

anyone or *anybody*?

The pronouns *anyone* and *anybody* are used interchangeably in the sense of "any person." They are written as one word.

Anyone (or anybody) can come to the dance.

Can anyone (or anybody) tell me the time?

The two-word construction *any one* is used when the adjective *any* is followed by the pronoun *one.*

Take any one of the apples in the bag.

Any one of us might win first prize.

When used as subjects, the pronouns *anyone* and *anybody* are singular and take singular verbs.

Has anyone (or anybody) come in for an interview?

Anyone (or anybody) is welcome to my share of the pie.

However, like the pronouns *everyone, everybody, no one, nobody, someone, somebody,* and others, *anyone* and *anybody* can apply to more than one person, of either sex or both sexes. So the pronouns referring to such antecedents are not

always in the masculine singular form. (See "IF SOMEONE COULD MAKE YOUR CHILD A GENIUS, WOULD YOU LET THEM?")

anyplace or *any place?*

In informal speech or writing, *anyplace* sometimes serves as a substitute for *anywhere,* especially in the sense of "in, at, or to any place" and in the idiom meaning "to have any success." (The adverb that *anyplace* may stand in for has its own informal uses. See *ANYWHERE.*)

I looked but couldn't find the report anyplace.

Recent graduates are finding it hard to get anyplace in some law firms.

Any place is a straightforward combination of the adjective *any* plus the noun *place.*

Take the seedlings to any place you think they'll grow.

Take the seedlings to any moist place.

anyway, any way, or *anyways?*

In the sense of "no matter what manner" or "haphazardly," *anyway* and *any way* are usually interchangeable.

Anyway (or any way) you look at it, the problem is enormous.

The paint was drizzled anyway (or any way) on the canvas.

Read the poem anyway (or any way) that pleases you.

However, the two-word form is used if a preposition comes first (and, of course, if another word intervenes).

Read the poem in any way that pleases you.

Read the poem any original way.

In the sense of "at least," "nevertheless," or "in any case," *anyway* (like another solid adverb, *anyhow*) is used.

They may not understand, but tell them anyway.

Anyway, it's a useful exercise.

In the sense of "no matter which course or direction," the adjective-plus-noun combination *any way* is used.

Any way he moves his rook will lessen his chance of winning.

Anyways sometimes replaces *anyway* in informal speech or writing, especially in certain regions, communities, or social groups.

anywhere or *anywheres?*

In formal as well as informal contexts, the adverb *anywhere* generally means "in, at, or to any place."

I looked but couldn't find the report anywhere.

Informally, *anywhere* is used in the sense of "at all; to any extent."

Her voice isn't anywhere near top form today.

It is also used in the following informal idioms. (For more on accepted expressions whose meanings are not the same as the literal meanings of the words that make them up, see How come the clock isn't going?)

> *anywhere from* (meaning "any amount, rate, time, and the like, between stated limits")

> A room in that hotel costs anywhere from $60 to $250.

> *get anywhere* (meaning "to have any success")

> Recent graduates are finding it hard to get anywhere in some law firms.

Only in very casual speech or writing does *anywheres* take the place of *anywhere*.

Apologize, sí; *finalize,* no.

From the vehement condemnation of *finalize*, one would think it was the first English verb formed by adding *-ize* to an adjective or noun. *Apologize*, for instance, combining *apology* and *-ize*, appears in *The Oxford English Dictionary* with a 1597 citation from Samuel Daniel:

> "Enforced to apologize With foreign states for two enormous things."

Here, with dates—though not necessarily the earliest ones—are some other *-ize* verbs given in the *OED:*

criticize (1649)   John Milton: "To let goe his Criticizing about the sound of Prayers."

dramatize (1810)   Sir Walter Scott: "They are busy dramatizing the Lady of the Lake here and in Dublin."

economize (1820)   Washington Irving: "He is calculating how he shall economize time."

formalize (1597)   Richard Hooker: "The same Spirit . . . doth . . . formalize, unite, and actuate his whole race."

galvanize (1853)   Charlotte Brontë: "Her approach always galvanized him to new and spasmodic life."

idealize (1795)   William Taylor: "Italy is here idealized into a terrestrial paradise."

Jesuitize (1644)   Richard Harwood: "Either the Jesuite doth Platonize, or Plato did Jesuitize, when he first sent abroad his *Deos intermedios.*"

modernize (1860)   William Makepeace Thackery: "Gunpowder and printing tended to modernise the world."

regularize (1833) John Stuart Mill: "Philosophy . . . rarely sets aside the old [classifications], content with correcting and regularizing them."

theorize (1638) Thomas Herbert: "Let us theorize a little upon the Mathematiques."

vandalize (1845) Richard Ford: "The noblest monuments of art and piety have been vandalized."

zoologize (1861) Archibald Geikie: "He had botanized and zoologized . . . from the Shetlands to the Channel Isles."

By the time the *OED* got around to including *finalize* (in its 1972 *Supplement*), it simply gave its origin as the adjective *final* + *-ize* and defined it as a transitive verb ("to complete, bring to an end, put in final form; to approve the final form of") and occasionally an intransitive verb ("to bring something to completion, to conclude"). It cites as the first occurrence a private letter dated May 4, 1922, in the files of the G. & C. Merriam Co.: "Our Mr. S. Jaboor writing from New Zealand . . . says that you are still finalizing matters with Mr. Forbes."

Several American dictionaries include similar dispassionate entries for *finalize*. *Webster's New World Dictionary,* for example, defines the verb as "to make final; bring to completion." The *Oxford American Dictionary* gives as the meaning "to bring to an end" and "to put into its final form," but in a usage note it warns the reader: "Careful writers do not use *finalization* or *finalize*."

Leading the chorus of critics, *The American Heritage Dictionary of the English Language,* Second College Edition, adds this usage note to its straightforward definition ("to put into final form; complete"):

"*Finalize* is frequently associated with the language of bureaucracy and so is objected to by many writers. The sentence *we will finalize plans for a class reunion* was unacceptable to the vast majority of the Usage Panel. While *finalize* has no single exact synonym, a substitute can always be found from among *complete, conclude, make final,* and *put in final form*."

Not surprisingly, the *Harper Dictionary of Contemporary Usage,* whose co-author, William Morris, was editor in chief of the 1969 edition of *The American Heritage Dictionary,* also condemns *finalize:* 86 percent of its panel of consultants said no to the use of the word in writing; 74 percent, in casual speech. One of those voting no, the feature writer John O. Barbour, said, "Not unless we can tentativize a date for tomorrow."

Many others object to *finalize.* Strunk and White (*The Elements of Style*) call it "a pompous, ambiguous verb." Rudolf Flesch (*The ABC of Style*) calls it "jargon." Frederick T. Wood (*Current English Usage*) calls it "an ugly word, un-English, and quite unnecessary." Eric Partridge (*Usage and Abusage*) calls it "superfluous and ugly."

But is *finalize* simply gobbledygook, jargon, and a pompous, ambiguous, ugly, and unnecessary coinage intended to replace established words like *complete, finish, stop,* and *conclude*? Does it have no special connotation that makes it as popular as it is? Of all the verbs that have to do with bringing something to a close, does it not alone convey the sense of putting that something in final

form by handling all details connected with it, sometimes even by obtaining final approval? And might trying to describe that entire process without using *finalize* sometimes lead to wordiness?

We constantly choose among near-synonyms to express the particular shade of meaning we have in mind. The verbs *collaborate, collude, connive, conspire,* and *scheme,* for example, have similar meanings, but if we want to convey the notion of planning and acting together secretly in order to commit a crime, we use *conspire,* not *scheme,* for *scheme* has to do with planning in a deceitful way, though not necessarily an illegal act. So, too, when we talk about making known or communicating information by signals, we use the verb *signal;* but when we talk about making something remarkable or noteworthy or drawing attention to it, we use *signalize.*

Finalize is, of course, more appropriate in technical or specialized contexts than in conversation, informal writing, or literary works. Negotiations, treaties, contracts, and processes are sometimes finalized.

> "Once an article is accepted for publication a committee of board members is selected to work with the author to finalize the piece for publication." (Letter from the *Harvard Educational Review*)

> "Elisabeth Aslin, his predecessor's deputy, had finalised long awaited plans for a complete overhaul of the major galleries, roof, plumbing and wiring—work which would have spared the museum much expense in later years." ("Sir Roy Strong," London *Sunday Times*)

> "The Giants are finalizing plans to televise at least 40 of their home games this season to Northern California cable-TV subscribers on a pay-per-view basis." (Tom Gilmore, *San Francisco Chronicle*)

As the sun sinks in the west the day is not finalized. Yet what word ought not to be used at the right time and in the right place? Elizabeth Barrett Browning wrote, "How do I love thee? Let me count the ways." She did not write, "Let me itemize the ways."

As for the charge of ugliness, *finalize* may not fall trippingly from one's lips, but does *distinguish* or *sympathize*? Is *finalize* any uglier in print than, say, *financial* or *authorize*?

The strongest defense of *finalize,* as of any other word or construction, is usage itself. If the word continues to be spoken and written by many people, in time it will settle comfortably into the language alongside *bowdlerize, familiarize, industrialize, legalize, macamadize, neutralize, plagiarize, recognize, subsidize, tantalize,* and the hundreds of similar verbs we accept without question. Forming verbs from nouns and adjectives by adding *-ize* is simply one of the ways English changes and grows. (Except in a few words regularly spelled with an *s,* like *advertise, advise, apprise, chastise,* and *surprise,* the suffix *-ize* is ordinarily used in the United States. In Britain *-ise* appears more often in print, in words like *organise, criticise,* and *specialise;* however, the Oxford family of dictionaries gives the *-ize* forms in the main entries unless the verbs are invariably spelled with an *s.*)

People pained by *finalize* may consider other verbs ending in *-ize* to be objectionable recent coinages as well.

"Our progress was slow as Mother paused to <u>botanize</u> until we got to a wide, flagged circle which is shaded by a muscular fig tree."

" 'I want to see Lady Sylvia wearing white satin and the family lace and diamond, and to <u>sentimentalize</u> over the days when my fox-terrier bit the stuffing out of her doll.' "

"As Nakamura-san struggled to get from day to day, she had no time for <u>attitudinizing</u> about the bomb or anything else."

Botanize, used by V. S. Pritchett in his story "The Fig Tree" (1979), came into the language in 1767. *Sentimentalize,* used by Dorothy Sayers in the Lord Peter Wimsey story "The Entertaining Episode of the Article in Question" (1928), dates from 1812. And *attitudinize,* used by John Hersey in a *New Yorker* piece on Hiroshima (1985), has been around since 1784.

In the process of gaining acceptance, new *-ize* verbs do not immediately drive out older verbs with the same or similar meanings. For centuries *jeopard* and *jeopardize,* for example, existed side by side, meaning "to put in jeopardy; to expose to loss, injury, or death." Eventually *jeopard* fell by the way, so that today a sentence like "Let us not allow small-minded judges to jeopard freedom of the press" would strike us as quaint. Yet even in the early twentieth century *jeopardize* was condemned as being unnecessary, because the verb *jeopard* already existed, or as being improperly derived either from *jeopard* or—like *jeopard* itself—from *jeopardy.*

Moisturize also had to fight for acceptance. The verb has been used since the 1940s, especially in connection with cosmetics applied to the skin. The one it took its place beside, *moisten,* is a relative newcomer too, dating from the late sixteenth century. That was about the time when *moisture* was becoming obsolete as a verb (it is still around as a noun) and two hundred years after *moist* had made its appearance as a verb. (*Moist* is still used as an adjective but, according to the *OED,* its use as a verb is limited to dialect.)

Sometimes nonce *-ize* words, that is, those coined and used for a particular occasion, catch on and remain in the language. The *OED* notes that *concertize,* meaning "to sing or play in a concert," first appeared in the April 1883 issue of *Harper's Magazine;* whatever the cries of outrage that may have ensued, musicians have been concertizing ever since (whether performing as soloists in concerts or, in keeping with the prevailing sense of *concertize,* making concert tours). *Litanize* is not generally recognized as a verb, but a nonce use like this one, in Richard Mitchell's *Less Than Words Can Say,* may have started it on its way, with the meaning "to engage in a repetitive, litanylike recital or account":

"The one [the professor of education] litanizes about carefully unspecified developments in philosophy, psychology, and communications theory, and the other [the neighborhood lout looking for a score] sticks up the candy store."

On the other hand, like countless other single-use words, *litanize* may disappear from the language.

apt, likely, or *liable?*   See *likely, apt,* or *liable?*

around **or** *about*?   See *about* or *around*?

around **or** *round*?

One of the ways American English differs from British English is in its prefer-ence for *around* over *round* in most of the prepositional and adverbial senses of these words. In each of the following sentences, for example, the *around* that seems natural in the States would ordinarily be replaced by *round* in Britain.

Saturn's rings revolve around the planet in the plane of its equator.

The fall television season seems to come around every month.

Hearing the shot, the police officer looked around.

We used to sit around the kitchen table, drinking coffee and talking.

Please have the garage send the car around.

The library is around the corner.

I'm afraid I'm in debt the year around.

As they opened the door, they drew their capes around them.

There's plenty of cake to go around.

The distinction between *around and round* is not as sharply drawn as it used to be, however. More and more, Americans are using the words interchange-ably, especially in compound modifiers.

the year *around* (or *round*)

an *all-around* (or *all-round*) athlete

around-the-clock (or *round-the-clock*) coverage

Round is not a contraction of *around,* so it is not written with an apostrophe (*'round*).

as, as if **or** *like*?   See *like* or *as, as if*?

as, **in comparisons.**   See *as . . as* or *so . . . as*?; **Is it me you like better than her?; Kilimanjaro is taller than any mountain in Africa.**

as . . . as **or** *so . . . as*?

The correlative construction *as . . . as* indicates the equality or sameness of two persons, things, qualities, or actions.

Tax reform was *as* good *as* dead that year.

The waiter moved *as* gracefully *as* a ballet dancer.

Sometimes the comparison is ironic.

My partner is *as* loyal *as* my bathroom scale.

You shop *as* frugally *as* a Defense Department purchasing agent.

In the past it was considered incorrect to use *as . . . as* in negative comparisons: only *so . . . as* would do. But nowadays that requirement no longer holds, so the choice is left to the speaker or writer.

Car insurance is not so (or as) expensive in small towns as in large cities.

The ozone layer had never been so (or as) carefully monitored as it was in the late 1980s.

Meticulous people used to—indeed, some may still—make an even subtler distinction between the two forms. This is their reasoning: If, in the speaker's or writer's mind, both elements being compared seem more or less equal, *as . . . as* is appropriate. However, if one element in the comparison seems to possess a notable degree of whatever is being considered, *so . . . as* should be used. For example:

Rice is not as fattening as pasta.

does not imply that the speaker or writer regards either rice or pasta as particularly fattening. He or she is making a simple comparison of their caloric values. However:

Rice is not so fattening as pasta.

suggests that, in the opinion of the speaker or writer, pasta is unusually rich in calories in comparison to rice.

In deciding whether to use *as . . . as* or *so . . . as*, English-speakers may unconsciously weigh all those shades of meaning. The fact is, the *so . . . as* construction is not obsolete; its uses are just no longer rigidly prescribed.

The structure and meaning of a sentence are sometimes lost if the pair *as . . . as* or *so . . . as* is not held together. For example:

The temperature in London can be as high if not higher than in Nairobi.

needs another *as:*

The temperature in London can be as high as, if not higher than, in Nairobi.

To avoid the stilted break in the sentence, some people usually complete the first comparison before going on to the second.

The temperature in London can be as high as in Nairobi, if not higher.

The first *as* or *so* is sometimes omitted in a correlative construction. The novelist Walker Percy, for example, wrote:

"I have been aloof and correct as a Nazi officer in occupied Paris."

Critics of this usage would say that the winner of the National Book Award for Fiction should have inserted *as* before *aloof.*

For the way adjectives and adverbs are modified to show their positive, comparative, and superlative degrees, see EXCITINGER TIMES LIE AHEAD.

WHETHER THE PRONOUN following the second *as* should be in the subjective or objective form is widely debated. The choice often depends on the meaning. For instance:

Jeremy dreams of skiing as much as *she.*

implies "as much as she does." But:

Jeremy dreams of skiing as much as *her.*

implies "as much as he dreams of her."

The form, or case, of pronouns is discussed more fully in THE BALL DROPPED BETWEEN HE AND THE LEFT-FIELDER; IS IT ME YOU LIKE BETTER THAN HER?; US TV WATCHERS HAVE STRONG CONVICTIONS; and WHO WOULD YOU TURN TO FOR HELP?

as far as

In both formal and informal speech and writing, *as far as* is commonly used as a conjunction meaning "to the extent or point that."

As far as immigration policy is concerned, the Senate is sharply divided.

She's still in New Delhi and, as far as her family knows, plans to stay there.

Your report on the meeting is all right, as far as it goes.

Ignoring that established usage, some people occasionally omit the words which follow *as far as* and which are generally considered necessary for complete grammatical construction.

As far as immigration policy, the Senate is sharply divided.

She's still in New Delhi and, as far as her family, plans to stay there.

This truncated, informal construction may have come about by analogy with the stand-alone prepositional phrase *as for,* meaning "with reference to" or "concerning."

As for immigration policy, the Senate is sharply divided.

Yet even those who treat *as far as* elliptically are selective in their omissions. Few would expect their listeners or readers to supply the missing words in a sentence like this:

Your report on the meeting is all right, as far as.

as follows

Whether one thing or a hundred, what will next be told or explained is often introduced by *as follows.* The verb in this idiomatic phrase is always singular, regardless of whether the main subject and verb in the sentence are singular or plural.

The procedure for entering a number in the memory of a Touch-Tone telephone is as *follows:* First you touch the "record" key. Then you touch the keys for the number you wish to record. Finally, you touch the location on the directory card where you wish to store the number.

The three <u>elements</u> required in all photographic typesetting <u>are</u> as *follows*: a master <u>character</u> image, a light source, and a photo- or <u>light</u>-sensitive material.

as if or *as though*?

As if and *as though* can be used interchangeably to mean "as it, or one, would if."

The train rolled along *as if* (or *as though*) it were on air.

Ralph looked *as if* (or *as though*) he had seen a ghost.

Even H. W. Fowler, the British arbiter of usage, says so. Even the *Harper Dictionary of Contemporary Usage,* with its generally stern "panel of 166 distinguished consultants on usage," says so. And *The Oxford English Dictionary* says so, giving citations for the two expressions from as far back as the year 1300. So there is no point in looking for subtle distinctions between *as if* and *as though.*

What is far from settled, however, is whether *like* can be used in place of either *as if* or *as though* (as in "Ralph looked *like* he had seen a ghost"). On this point, see LIKE OR AS, AS IF?

Nor is there agreement on whether a subordinate clause introduced by *as if* or *as though* requires a verb in the subjunctive mood. That is, should we say "I felt as though I *were* floating though space" or "I felt as though I *was* floating though space"? For a discussion on the use and overuse of the subjunctive, see THE HEADWAITER ASKED IF I WERE ALONE.

as if or *like*?   See *like* or *as, as if*?

as well as or *and*?

Like *and, as well as* sometimes means "in addition to." Yet many people are apprehensive about saying or writing *as well as* because their English teachers told them, years ago, that the term ought not to be used lightly. According to the rule, which was generally stated with more feeling than clarity, *and* joins elements of equal grammatical value.

The singers and the dancers drew large crowds.

But *as well as* gives more weight to the second element. So much more, in fact, that the term comes closer to meaning "and not only" than "in addition to." Thus:

The singers as well as the dancers drew large crowds.

singles out the dancers for attention, giving the singers secondary importance.

Anyone who wanted to could construe this statement by the *New York Times* writer Daniel Goleman as falling within that rule:

"In the last two decades, psychologists have come to realize that physical attractiveness, in <u>males as well as females</u>, carries with it an impressive array of social and psychological benefits. . . ."

It can be said to suggest that we all expect physical attractiveness to be somehow related to females but might be surprised to learn that it concerns males as well. (As this last sentence shows, the phrase *as well*, when placed after the second element of the pair, need not imply "and not only." It means simply "in addition," and thus does not come under the *as well as* rule.)

But does the rule apply to this statement by another *New York Times* writer, Frank Rich?

"Mike Ockrent's lovingly archaic <u>direction, as well as</u> Stanley Lebowsky's <u>pit band</u>, have been drilled to Broadway's higher standard. . . ."

Is Rich telling us that the pit band's good performance is a given, and that what is newsworthy is the fact that the direction was also good? Surely not. Surely he is either saying that both were good or emphasizing the high quality of the direction, with the remark about the pit band thrown in as an afterthought.

Nowadays most people do not remember the subtle old rule. And those who do, know better than to try imposing it on anyone else.

A REAL DIFFERENCE between *and* and *as well as* has to do with subject-verb agreement. A subject consisting of two nouns or pronouns joined by *and* ordinarily takes a plural verb.

The singer and the dancer *were* a hit.

However, a phrase introduced by *as well as* generally does not affect the number of the subject and verb.

The singer as well as the dancers *was* a hit.

The singers as well as the principal dancer *were* a hit.

According to strict usage, in the above statement by Frank Rich *has*, not *have*, should therefore follow *pit band*. (For more on subject-verb agreement, in number, see FISH AND CHIPS IS ON THE MENU AGAIN.)

assimilation. See **Grampa got his strenth back last Febuary.**

awhile or *a while*?

The noun *while*, in the sense of "a period or space of time," is often preceded by the article *a*.

It's been a while since Paula became a forest ranger.

Our house guests left a while ago.

That article-noun combination can, in turn, be preceded by a preposition.

I promise to return your VCR *in* a while.

Please stay *for* a while instead of rushing off tomorrow.

The adverb _awhile_ means "for a while; for a short time."

Let's sit and talk awhile.

Constructions in which a preposition is placed before _awhile_ have been generally disapproved. Yet the distinction between _awhile_ and _a while_ is gradually breaking down as more and more people write the solid form for both the adverb and the article-noun combination.

We drove our new car around town awhile (or for awhile).

Unless, of course, another word comes between the _a_ and the _while_.

We drove our new car around town for a short while.

B

baby talk. See **Din-din, then beddy-bye.**

back-formation. See **Burglars burgle and peddlers peddle, so why don't janitors janit?**

bad or *badly*?

It's almost impossible to say or write either of these words without having somebody object. One complaint has to do with using *badly* in a sentence like:

I feel badly about canceling our appointment.

True, *badly* is an adverb, adverbs modify verbs, and *feel* is a verb. But here, the critics say, the adjective *bad* (in the sense of "sorry" or "distressed") should modify *feel*, because instead of performing an action *feel* serves as a linking verb; that is, it connects a subject and a predicate adjective (a modifier that refers back to the subject). So, with the subject being *I*, *feel* must be followed by the adjective *bad*.

I feel bad about canceling our appointment.

Many students were taught the *feel bad* rule by being told that *feel badly* can refer only to touching or handling something incorrectly. But not everyone learned that point of grammar, or else a lot of those who did no longer pay any attention to it. Indeed, so many educated English-speakers use *feel badly* nowadays, especially in informal speech and writing, that it is almost a mark of pedantry to hold to *feel bad*.

The second, somewhat milder complaint has to do with using the adverb *badly* in the sense of "very much" or "greatly."

We need a vacation badly.

Even though this meaning was well established in the nineteenth century, particularly in informal usage, some traditionalists would like the adverb to be limited to its earlier senses of "in a bad manner; harmfully, unpleasantly, incorrectly, wickedly," and the like.

Our vacation went badly.

They would be doubly dismayed to see the offending sense conveyed by an adverb that, without its characteristic *-ly* ending, looks like an adjective.

"He'd contemplated that often, thought about how much he wanted one, but always ended up asking himself why, if he wanted it so bad, he didn't go after it."(Margaret Truman, *Murder in Georgetown*)

"Once in his life had he set foot on this unnamed unclaimed untenanted patch of weeds and that was when he saw Ethel Rosenblum and wanted her so bad he fell down."(Walker Percy, *The Second Coming*)

For more on the controversy over predicate adjectives and adverbs, see PEO-PLE WHO WANT TO ARRIVE SAFE DON'T DRIVE DRUNKENLY.

The ball dropped between he and the left-fielder.

The center-fielder was probably charged with an error; the play-by-play announcer should have been. A personal pronoun that is the object of a preposition or a verb is ordinarily in the objective form, or case (*me, him, her, us, them*).

The ball dropped between *him* and the left-fielder.

Dad called to ask about you and *her*.

How about giving Pat and *me* a share of the winnings?

Will you believe Arthur and *them* now?

What about the rest of *us* commuters?

Instead we often hear the subjective forms (*I, he, she, we, they*), even from people who probably know better.

In introducing an installment of "Lillie," a series on Lillie Langtry in PBS's *Masterpiece Theatre*, Alistair Cooke said that Prince Edward's code of behavior was "well understood between <u>he</u> and his mistresses."

Asked about the 1.65 million-dollar mansion she and her husband had just bought, San Francisco Mayor Dianne Feinstein said, according to the reporter Carl Nolte, " 'It is time for Dick and <u>I</u> to have our own house.' "

After missing a program because he had been stuck in an elevator, Willard Scott, the weatherman on the *Today Show*, was quoted by the columnist Leah Garchik as having said that " 'NBC has made Jane Pauley, Bryant Gumbel and <u>I</u> promise never to travel in the same elevator again.' "

The reason why this rule of grammar is violated more often in speech than in print is that editors and proofreaders usually have time to catch and correct errors. But apparently the editorial staff that worked on the book *Growing Up in a London Village* was somewhere in center field, for this is what the reviewer Kathleen Nott wrote in the *Observer:*

"Phyllis Willmott's 'write' is almost always good and her grammar and syntax irreproachable—with one exception. Therefore I reproach her, for, again and again, using 'I' when she means 'me'; e.g. 'between Gran and I'; 'Mum taught Wally and I.' Didn't the proof-reader tell her or wouldn't she listen?"

Perhaps Larry McMurtry's editor or proofreader didn't tell him either, or else he wouldn't listen, because in *All My Friends Are Going to Be Strangers* he says:

"I could imagine Emma and I trying to be together in Flap's company, and I knew neither of us wanted to."

If Earl Wilson had editorial advice, he ignored it the day his newspaper column began, "Dear Diary: A guy like I gets into strange situations. . . ."

And Roger M. Williams, the European editor for *Tennis* magazine, said in an article that he wrote on the French village of Barbizon (presumably edited by someone else):

"But for my wife and I, who live in Paris, as well as for many other Parisians and foreign visitors, it provides a perfect site for a weekend getaway."

Yet it isn't as though editors are always right and authors wrong. Abigail Van Buren's editor, for instance, committed the unforgivable sin in preparing a manuscript for publication: changing right to wrong. This contrite letter appeared in the syndicated advice column:

"Dear Abby: I confess. In a foggy moment I 'fixed' your September 4 sentence to read that in your house company 'had to listen to my sister and I' play violin duets. All those shocked readers should blame 'I' and not you. —Your befogged Editor."

All those shocked readers indeed! Probably no construction is more irritating to those who don't use it than *between you and I*. Why is it so common? Perhaps because *you and I, she and he, we and they,* or a similar phrase is often used as a compound subject, generally at the beginning of a sentence or clause.

You and *she* are very much on Dad's mind.

Arthur and *we* always tell the truth.

My sister and *I* played violin duets.

Both *he* and the left-fielder overran the ball.

Therefore people tend to think of a noun or a pronoun in combination with a pronoun in the subjective form as an inseparable unit, regardless of where it falls in a sentence and whether it is in fact a subject or an object.

Or perhaps it is because schoolteachers and writers of books on grammar and usage insist so fiercely on the correctness of *it is I, it is we,* and so on that those under their influence always use constructions of the *between you and I* type, just to play it safe.

The above rule on the form of a pronoun applies also to a pronoun that is in apposition—that is, one that appears alongside a noun or another pronoun and denotes the same person or thing. This means that a pronoun in apposition to a subject is likely to be in the subjective form:

The joggers, *he* and Betty, came into view.

and a pronoun in apposition to an object, in the objective form:

The rain drove them—*him* and Betty—indoors.

This rule is sometimes ignored, whether through carelessness or for literary effect. Joan Didion, in *A Book of Common Prayer*, for example, has a character say, "We don't have anything in common any more. . . . You and me," even though *you and I* might be expected to be in apposition to the subjective *we*.

Because speakers and writers are most likely to be confused momentarily when a pronoun either is joined to a noun or another pronoun by a conjunction like *and* or *or,* or is in apposition to a noun or another pronoun, there ought to be a simple test for the correct form, or case. There is: drop everything but the pronoun in question and see how the sentence sounds. For example, in "Dad called to ask about you and she," what is left without *you and?* "Dad called to ask about she." Does *she* sound right as the object of the preposition *about?* No, but *her* does. So the sentence should be "Dad called to ask about you and her." Similarly, a grammarian who turned Joan Didion's sentences around would conclude that since "Me don't have anything in common" doesn't sound right, the appositive *you and me* ought to be changed to *you and I.*

Yet testing for grammatical "correctness" does not always work. What editor or proofreader would have reminded T. S. Eliot that an appositive pronoun should have the same grammatical form as the principal one? And then urged him to change *you and I* to *you and me* in these opening verses of "The Love Song of J. Alfred Prufrock," which are among the most memorable in twentieth-century English poetry:

"Let us go then, you and I,
When the evening is spread out against the sky"

THE OTHER HALF of the rule is not always observed either; that is, the objective form of a personal pronoun is often used when the subjective form is called for (see US TV WATCHERS HAVE STRONG CONVICTIONS). As to which form should be used with *be, than,* and *as,* opinion is still sharply divided (see IS IT ME YOU LIKE BETTER THAN HER?).

B.C.; A.D.

B.C., the abbreviation for "before Christ," follows the year or century number. It should always be used to designate the era before Christ.

680 B.C.   fifth century B.C.

A.D., from the Latin *Anno Domini* ("in the year of the Lord"), is now taken to mean "of the Christian era." Traditionally, this abbreviation precedes the year or century number:

A.D. 530   A.D. sixth century

However, by analogy with B.C., it may also follow it.

"One million years ago, back in 1986 A.D., Guayaquil was the chief seaport of the little South American democracy of Ecuador, whose capital was Quito, high in the Andes Mountains." (Kurt Vonnegut, *Galápagos*)

"One hundred fifty of the 160 stations that make up the Association of Independent Television Stations have agreed to air the controversial W. R. Grace & Co. ad, 'Deficit Trials: 2017 A.D.,' which the three networks have refused to run. . . ." (John Carmody, *Washington Post*)

Unlike B.C., A.D. need not be used except to prevent ambiguity (as in references to the early Christian era or when years or centuries before as well as after Christ are given).

in 1066   by the eleventh century A.D. 26

in the first century B.C. and the first two centuries A.D.

Both abbreviations are usually set in small capitals in books and magazines:

680 B.C.   A.D. 530

and in full capitals in newspapers and typescript:

680 B.C.   A.D. 530

because, **after** *reason.*   See **The reason why a chicken crosses a road is because it wants to get to the other side.**

belabor or *labor*?

The history and development of these two verbs have been intertwined for centuries. For a time both meant "to work or toil." *Labor* took on the sense of applying blows, especially to an animal. *The Oxford English Dictionary* gives this citation from 1594:

"The Asse . . . if he be laboured with a cudgell, he setteth not by it."

But the *OED* notes that this sense of *labor* is now virtually obsolete, having been gradually absorbed by *belabor*, in which the prefix *be-* is attached for emphasis. (For more on prefixes and suffixes, see WHO NEEDS A RABBIT'S FOOT MORE: AN UNLUCKY PERSON OR A LUCKLESS ONE?)

Nowadays disagreement over the two verbs centers on whether one *labors* or *belabors* a matter—an argument, a question, a point, or even the obvious—by taking considerable pains with it, indeed, sometimes developing it in too great detail. Traditionally, *labor* alone conveyed this sense.

"There is no need, surely, to labor men's creative dominance in the worlds of art and science." (J. Donald Adams, *The Magic and Mystery of Words*)

More and more, however, *belabor* is being used to convey the notion of adding more details than necessary.

"Everybody knows that, I suppose, and the point hardly seems worth belaboring." (Herbert R. Mayes, *Saturday Review*)

"The book is informative and avowedly 'personal'—not highly analytical, except where Ocampo herself is quoted, and, although refreshingly straightforward, it sometimes belabors its points." (Celia Betsky, *Smithsonian*)

Or is the trend toward *labor* again? In the first (1976) edition of *On Writing Well,* for example, William Zinsser wrote:

"If I may belabor the metaphor of carpentry, it is first necessary to be able to saw wood neatly and to drive nails."

But in the second (1980) and third (1985) editions, Zinsser asks the reader's permission to *labor* the carpentry metaphor.

below.   See *above; below.*

bemuse **or** *amuse*?

When Queen Victoria rebuked someone—or so the story goes—she didn't say, "We are not bemused." She said, "We are not amused." *Amuse* suggests an agreeable occupation of the mind, especially by something that appeals to one's sense of humor, whereas *bemuse* (generally used in the passive voice) conveys two very different meanings: being muddled or stupefied and being plunged in thought or preoccupied.

Not everyone is as clear about that distinction, which is still made in even the least prescriptive dictionaries. So we sometimes see or hear the verbs used interchangeably. Richard Bernstein, chief of the Paris bureau of the *New York Times*, for example, recalled:

> "As a student in Paris some time ago, I found myself late one afternoon in the middle of a bemused crowd of Parisians at the information counter of the big department store B.H.V."

In the next paragraph we learn that the crowd had been entertained, not stupefied or preoccupied, for as Mr. Bernstein continued to struggle with the pronunciation of a French word "the room seemed to grow dark, the snickering crowd to deepen."

That *bemuse* and *amuse* are sometimes confused is not surprising. *Muse*, which implies contemplation or reflection so deep as to absorb one completely, is derived from the Old French word *muser,* meaning either "to ponder" or "to loiter." In *bemuse* the prefix *be-* makes the first sense even more emphatic. In *amuse* the shortened prefix *ad-* intensifies the second sense. (For more on how prefixes and suffixes can alter the meanings of words, see WHO NEEDS A RABBIT'S FOOT MORE: AN UNLUCKY PERSON OR A LUCKLESS ONE?)

beside **or** *besides*?

Although they have several related meanings, the two words are not interchangeable. Both are often used as prepositions, *beside* generally in the sense of "by or at the side of; near" and *besides* in the sense of "over and above; in addition to."

> The house is beside the railroad tracks.

> Besides the cost, consider the delay.

These are some other prepositional uses of *beside:*

> "compared with"

>> Beside your efforts, mine are insignificant.

"apart from; not connected with"

Your explanation is beside the point.

In idiomatic usage, *beside oneself* means "almost out of one's senses from a strong emotion."

The widower was beside himself with grief.

Besides has a second prepositional sense: "other than; except."

There was no one in the store besides the owner and one customer.

As an adverb, it has several meanings:

"moreover; furthermore"

The walk will do you good, and besides you'll get to see the sunset.

"in addition"

Upstairs there is a billiard room and a library besides.

"otherwise; else"

My truck has four tires but very little besides.

between each; between every

The constructions *between* + *each* + a singular noun and *between* + *every* + a singular noun are illogical. They are illogical because the preposition *between* implies "by twos" or "in pairs" but the adjectives *each* and *every* refer to one of two or more persons or things considered separately. So:

I take vitamins between each meal.

The planes are thoroughly checked between every flight.

would make more sense if the prepositional phrase in each sentence were changed, for example, to:

I take vitamins between meals.

I take vitamins after each meal.

The planes are throughly checked between flights.

The planes are thoroughly checked between one flight and the next.

Yet, illogical or not, the *between each* and *between every* constructions have been around for a long time and show no sign of yielding to grammarians' entreaties to go away.

between or *among*?   See *among or between?*

between you and I.   See **The ball dropped between he and the left-fielder.**

bi- or *semi-*?

A section of *Literary Market Place: The Directory of American Book Publishing* deals with magazines published specifically for the book trade industry. Users of *LMP* can tell at a glance how often, say, *Printing News, Small Press Review*, and *Book Arts Review* are issued, for these are labeled "weekly," "monthly," and "quarterly," respectively. Nor are they apt to have trouble with the "semimonthly" *Library Journal,* since the prefix *semi-* has only one time-related sense: "twice in a specified period."

But what about "bimonthlies" like the *Horn Book Magazine:* are they published twice a month or every two months? And "biweeklies" like *IDP Report:* are they issued twice a week or every two weeks? What causes the confusion is the prefix *bi-*, which has two contradictory senses related to time. One sense is "coming, happening, or issued every two."

In deciding to hold *biweekly* meetings, the club chose every other Thursday evening.

Are flowers and seeds produced in the first or second year of a *biennial's* two-year life cycle?

The Hans Christian Andersen awards are presented *biennially* (or *biannually*), in even-numbered years.

The second sense of *bi-*, virtually overlapping that of *semi-*, is "coming, happening, or issued twice during every."

Deposits are made *bimonthly*: on the first and the fifteenth.

Considering yearly checkups insufficient, many dentists recommend *biyearly* ones.

Some newspapers publish cumulative indexes *biannually*: in January and June.

So, to be sure of being understood, many Americans work around the blurred *bi-* distinctions. Instead of *biweekly,* they are likely to say *every two weeks,* on the one hand, and *twice a week* or *semiweekly,* on the other. They often replace *bimonthly* with either *every two months* or with *twice a month, twice-monthly,* or *semimonthly.* And they might change *biannual* (or *biennial*) and *biannually* (or *biennially*) to *every two years* or to *twice a year, twice-yearly, semiannual (semiannually),* or *half-yearly.*

"Judge Judith McConnell of San Diego Superior Court issued the order giving Mr. Batey custody and Mrs. Batey twice-monthly visitation rights in a closed hearing June 18." (Associated Press)

"The twice-yearly journal [*Maledicta*] explains that it specializes in 'uncensored studies and collections of "offensive" words and expressions, in all languages.' " (David P. Garino, *Wall Street Journal*)

Although *Literary Market Place* uses the label "bimonthly" to show the *Horn Book Magazine*'s frequency of publication, the journal itself leaves no room for ambiguity. Its masthead says that it "is published six times a year in January, March, May, July, September, November."

As for *IDP Report, LMP* lists its frequency of publication as "biweekly," as does the newsletter on information and data base publishing itself. But *Ulrich's International Periodicals Directory,* taking advantage of a handy Briticism meaning "at two-week intervals," notes that *IDP Report* is published "fortnightly."

blame for or *blame on?*

By the time some of us were taught never to say or write "The fire was blamed on arson"—but instead "Arson was blamed for the fire"—the battle was already lost. For more than a century, educated speakers and writers of English had been using one construction about as often as the other, so it was futile for schoolteachers to insist on adherence to a rule that hardly anyone knew existed.

Several of the leading American newspapers do not agree on which preposition should follow *blame.* Like most current dictionaries and usage guides, *"The Washington Post" Deskbook on Style* notes:

> "*Blame* as a verb may take either *for* or *on*; John is *blamed for* the defeat; the defeat is *blamed on* John."

The *"Los Angeles Times" Stylebook,* mindful of both the rule and its widespread rejection, says:

> "It is preferable to *blame someone for something* than to *blame something on someone.* But the latter is permissible."

The *New York Times* sides with the few purists who are still holding out. The *blame on* entry in its *Manual of Style and Usage* is unequivocal:

> "This is to be avoided: *The wreck was blamed on carelessness.* Since the wreck is not the target of the blame, it should be: *Carelessness was blamed for the wreck. The wreck was attributed to carelessness.*"

And no wonder. Theodore M. Bernstein, for many years the managing editor of the *Times,* said in *The Careful Writer,* one of his guides to writing:

> "*Blame on* always has been and remains a casualism, no matter how many educated people have used it carelessly. . . . Just as you cannot censure *on,* so you cannot *blame on.* The remedy is to find substitutes—forms of *attribute to* or *lay to*—or to change the construction, making it *blame for* or *put the blame on.*"

What or who might logically be said to be the target of the blame is beside the point. English is full of expressions and constructions that are thoroughly respectable even though their full meanings are not immediately obvious from the meanings of the individual words that make them up. That's what idioms are. (For more on idioms, see How COME THE CLOCK ISN'T GOING? and "Some Troublesome Idiomatic Prepositions," a table at the back of the book.)

blends. See **Oxbridge workaholics never stop for brunch.**

bloopers. See "Kinkering Congs Their Titles Take"; Russian is written in the Acrylic alphabet; "You're a goody-goody gumshoes."

bring, take, or *fetch?*

Bring, in strict usage, has to do with carrying or leading a person or thing to the place thought of as "here" or to a place where the speaker or writer will be.

> Would you mind bringing the letter to me now?

> Please bring the records to my office tomorrow.

> In 1629 five ships brought four hundred settlers from England to America.

Take refers to carrying or leading a person or thing to the place thought of as "there" or to a place, specified or implied, away from where the speaker or writer is or will be.

> Would you mind taking the letter to the post office?

> Remember to take the records with you when you leave.

> In 1629 five ships took four hundred settlers from London to the Massachusetts coast.

Fetch, which is more commonly used in Britain than in the States and which nowadays strikes many Americans as quaint, conveys the notion of going after something, getting it, and bringing it back.

> I want a dog that will cheerfully fetch the newspaper every morning.

Those who do not observe the traditional distinction between *bring* and *take* are more likely to use *bring* where *take* is called for than the other way around. Eugene Kennedy, for instance, began a chapter in his biography of Mayor Richard Daley this way:

> "They brought him to the Nativity of Our Lord Church the next day at noon, when winter was just a few minutes old."

Although *brought* might conjure up a picture of Kennedy addressing the reader from the steps of the Nativity of Our Lord Church in Chicago, what is meant is that Daley's body was carried (*taken*) to that church from another part of the city.

In an article on advertising gaffes spotted by the public, Bernice Kanner noted that someone had complained to General Mills that the copy on a Cheerios box should have read, "Wherever you go, take them along," not "Wherever you go, bring them along."

British English and American English.   See There's no home like Eaton Place.

bulls.   See "You're a goody-goody gumshoes."

Burglars burgle and peddlers peddle, so why don't janitors janit?

New words are usually formed in English by attaching a syllable, a group of syllables, or a word to an existing word or word form. For example:

circle (a noun) + *semi-* (a prefix meaning "half") → *semicircle*

act (a verb) + *-or* (a noun-forming suffix meaning "a person or thing that) → *actor*

health (a noun) + *-y* (an adjective-forming suffix meaning "having, full of, or characterized by") → *healthy*

angle (a noun) + *tri-* (a combining form meaning "having, combining, or involving three") → *triangle*

Sometimes the new word takes on a new spelling and pronunciation in the process.

literate (an adjective) + *in-* (a prefix meaning "no, not, without") → *illiterate*

beauty (a noun) + *-fy* (a verb-forming suffix meaning "to make; cause to be or become") → *beautify*

create (a verb) + *-tion* (a noun-forming suffix meaning "the thing that is") → *creation*

(For more on the way prefixes, suffixes, and combining forms change the meanings of words and create new ones, see WHO NEEDS A RABBIT'S FOOT MORE: AN UNLUCKY PERSON OR A LUCKLESS ONE?)

In back-formation—a reversal of the normal process of word-making—a new word is created from an existing one because of a mistaken notion of derivation. That is, a word thought to be the base of another word is, in fact, the more recent one. For instance, according to *The Oxford English Dictionary,* the adjective *greedy,* in the sense of "too eager for gain, wealth, and the like," goes back to around the beginning of the eleventh century. In the seventeenth century, English-speakers invented the noun *greed,* as if this were the base to which the suffix *-y* had been attached earlier to form *greedy,* not the other way around.

And why not make that assumption? Wasn't *healthy* formed by adding the *-y* suffix to *health*? Indeed, analogy is a forceful process in the development of a language, for whether consciously or unconsciously its speakers tend to make new or less familiar words, constructions, and pronunciations conform to the pattern of older or more familiar ones—even if they are unrelated.

Besides *greed,* many other back-formations entered the language so long ago that most of today's English-speakers are not even aware of their unusual origin. *Edit,* for instance, is an eighteenth-century back-formation from *editor,* which had come into use a century earlier. These are some other well-established verbs derived from nouns:

diagnose (nineteenth century), from *diagnosis* (seventeenth century)

donate (a nineteenth-century Americanism), from *donation* (fifteenth century)

escalate (a twentieth-century Americanism), from *escalator* (coined as a U.S. trademark in 1895)

jell (a nineteenth-century Americanism), from *jelly* (fourteenth century)

manipulate (eighteenth century), from *manipulation* (eighteenth century)

orate (seventeenth century), from *oration* (fourteenth century)

peddle (sixteenth century), from *peddler* or *pedlar* (fourteenth century)

peeve (a twentieth-century Americanism), from *peevish* (sixteenth century)

sculpt (nineteenth century) or *sculp* (eighteenth century), from *sculpture* (fourteenth century)

One back-formation that has met with unfaltering resistance is the verb *enthuse*. This Americanism, formed in the nineteenth century from an eighteenth-century sense of the noun *enthusiasm,* has been so vehemently criticized that it is still generally limited to casual conversation and informal writing. Indeed, in citing what it believed to be the earliest usage of *enthuse* (from 1869), the 1933 edition of the *OED* departed from its usual practice of recording back-formations. Unlike *jell,* for example, which was identified simply as "*U.S. colloq.* [Back-formation from *jelly* . . .]," *enthuse* was given this label:

"U.S. (colloq. or humorous.) [An ignorant back-formation from enthusiasm.]"

However, by 1972, when the *OED* published volume 3 of its *Supplement* —with an earlier (1827) citation for *enthuse*—it had recovered enough scholarly detachment to limit its note to: "For '*U.S.*' read '*orig. U.S.*' "

This doesn't mean, of course, that *enthuse* has won the approval of authors of usage guides who see their mission as protecting the language from usages they themselves find distasteful.

In 1915, *Faulty Diction, As Corrected by the "Funk & Wagnalls New Standard Dictionary of the English Language"* said of *enthuse:*

"An ill-formed word, prevalent in some parts of the United States; now a colloquialism meaning to yield to or display enthusiasm."

In 1964, Rudolf Flesch said, in *The ABC of Style: A Guide to Plain English:*

"Enthuse is a verb formed fairly recently by cutting off the tail end of enthusiasm. To me it seems unnatural and ugly. . . ."

(To Flesch, a usage that was then 137 years old was fairly recent.)

In 1979, Strunk and White said of *enthuse,* in *The Elements of Style:*

"An annoying verb growing out of the noun *enthusiasm*. Not recommended."

In 1980, John B. Bremner said of it, in *Words on Words: A Dictionary for Writers and Others Who Care about Words:*

"The Greeks gave us the noun *enthusiasm*, from which somebody coined the ugly verb *enthuse*, branded colloquial by Webster and disapproved by 76 percent of the American Heritage usage panel, but growing in use."

In 1986, Robert Claiborne said of it, in *Saying What You Mean: A Commonsense Guide to American Usage:*

"Like *emote*, a *back formation*, but one with little or no excuse for existence. 'Enthuse over' says nothing more than 'praise'—and takes three extra syllables to say it."

Yet many writers in both the United States and Britain seem to prefer *enthuse over* to a phrase like *be enthusiastic over* or *express enthusiasm for*, and, in certain contexts, to the verb *praise*. George Orwell clearly did when he said of A. E. Housman, in his essay "Inside the Whale":

"Housman, however, did not enthuse over the rambler rose in the week-ending spirit of [Rupert] Brooke and the others."

The following back-formations are among the others that some English-speakers find either offensive or unnecessary and therefore probably do not use in their own speech and writing:

baby-sit (a twentieth-century Americanism), from *baby-sitter* (another twentieth-century Americanism)

It's been years since I've baby-sat.

burgle (nineteenth century), from *burglar* (sixteenth century)

My apartment was burgled twice last year. [Another verb, the Americanism *burglarize*, was also coined about the same time.]

butle (twentieth century), from *butler* (thirteenth century)

I wish I had someone to butle when friends drop in.

destruct (in the sense of being "automatically destroyed," a twentieth-century Americanism), from *destruction* (fourteenth century); *self-destruct* (also twentieth century, with the same meaning as *destruct*) from *self-destruction* (sixteenth century)

The rocket is programmed to self-destruct in orbit.

emote (a twentieth-century Americanism), from *emotion* (seventeenth century)

From the way they emote, you'd think some TV anchors were Method actors.

laze (sixteenth century), from *lazy* (sixteenth century)

We lazed around the house all weekend.

liaise (twentieth century), from *liaison* (nineteenth century)

The cultural attaché was asked to liaise with the education ministry.

sleaze (twentieth century), from *sleazy* (seventeenth century)

How can you go out with a sleaze like him?

Back-formation is by no means at an end. Whether by accident or intention, those who speak and write the language continue to reverse the normal word-making process by creating new words from existing ones, to fill a need, to get a laugh, or for some other reason. Their newly formed words may of course not last, but others, perhaps just as short-lived, will take their place.

Some offices hire special crews to *janit* [from *janitor*] on the night shift.

The plaintiff and the defendant were just *conversating* [from *conversation*].

Was the 1980 Republican Convention held to nominate Governor Reagan or to *coronate* [from *coronation*] him?

The way some adults act around teenagers really *nauses* me *out* [from *nausea*, even though another verb, *nauseate*, already exists].

Large companies are beginning to *vint* [from *vintner*] out-of-state wines.

Are you one of those people who feel *compulsed* [from *compulsion*] to finish reading the *Sunday Times* by noon?

English has many verbs *back-formed* [from *back-formation*] from nouns.

Nor is back-formation the only word-building process that enriches the language. Over the years English-speakers have, for instance:

created new words and changed the meanings of existing ones through the addition of prefixes, suffixes, and combining forms (see WHO NEEDS A RABBIT'S FOOT MORE: AN UNLUCKY PERSON OR A LUCKLESS ONE?).

borrowed foreign words and phrases (see MODOR, WE'VE GOT COMPANY).

incorporated words derived from or associated with the names of people and places (see JOHN BULL AND JOHN HANCOCK ARE NOT JUST ANY JOHNS).

changed the original meanings of words (see FOR A GIRL HE'S QUITE MATURE).

coined new words or new meanings for established words (see DEAR MR. WEBSTER and JOBBED IN A HUMONGOUS SCAM, THE TWEAKED-OUT MOBSTER EXCLAIMED, "PEACHY-KEEN!")

combined two or more words or parts of words in order to form new words (see NASA'S LOX NEEDS NO BAGELS; OXBRIDGE WORKAHOLICS NEVER STOP FOR BRUNCH; and UPSTART NAME-DROPPERS USUALLY GET THE COLD SHOULDER).

clipped off parts of words to make shorter ones (see A VET RUSHED TO THE ZOO BY CAB TO TREAT A HIPPO WITH THE FLU).

made puzzling unfamiliar words look and sound like familiar ones (see COLD SLAW ON MY NEW CHAISE LOUNGE!).

"Burnett goes dramatic as a gaunt Iowa wife."

This newspaper headline suggests that comedienne Carol Burnett's first serious role centered on a woman's relationship to her husband. But no. The 1979 television film *Friendly Fire,* which was based on C. D. B. Bryan's book of that name, was about an episode in the lives of Gene and Peg Mullen, especially about Peg Mullen's actions.

In his syndicated review, Cecil Smith described Burnett's role as that of "a gaunt, hard-bitten wife of an Iowa farmer (Ned Beatty) whose son has been killed in the Vietnam War and who feels the Army is holding something back, that she can't get the truth of just how her boy died." His article made it clear that Beatty's role as Gene Mullen was secondary to Burnett's as Peg Mullen; yet the headline "Burnett Goes Dramatic As a Gaunt Iowa Wife," which appeared in one of the newspapers carrying Smith's review, suggests the opposite. (Smith's original piece, in the *Los Angeles Times,* was titled "Burnett Sticks Her Neck Out.")

Women are often referred to not as people in their own right but as wives, mothers, sisters, and daughters—that is, in terms of their relationship to others, particularly men. A married couple is a "man and wife," not a "husband and wife" or a "woman and husband." Even in father-child relationships, men remain men, as headlines like "Lightning Kills Man, 2 Sons" show. But radio talk-show hosts ask for the views of "listeners and wives of listeners." And radio commentators deplore a shooting that results in the death of "a four-year-old boy and his ten-year-old sister."

Women can do worse than be identified as reflections of their menfolk: they can become entirely invisible. For example:

> "There's nothing more stimulating than smart men talking well, or involved individuals being confronted by newsmen," William Lord, the first producer of public television's *MacNeil-Lehrer NewsHour*, told *Newsday* reporter Paul D. Colford in 1986.

> In introducing "Adventures of Sherlock Holmes II: The Greek Interpreter," in the PBS *Mystery!* series, Vincent Price said he was pleased that in 1986, almost a hundred years after the publication of Arthur Conan Doyle's first Sherlock Holmes story, young people were still interested in the English detective—just as "their fathers and grandfathers before them" had been.

> Jacques Barzun, in his essay "A Writer's Discipline," gives this advice to other writers: "To be sure, a memorandum listing haphazardly what belongs to a particular project is useful. In fact, if you would be a 'full' man as you undertake a new piece of work, you should have before you a little stack of slips bearing the ideas that have occurred to you since the subject first came to life in your mind." And a few pages later: "The ideal situation perhaps is to awaken with the grand design in mind (it was the last

thing thought of before falling asleep), to shave while a matching throng of ideas lathers up within, and to go straight to the blank sheet without exchanging words with anyone.'' (Presumably *anyone* is the writer's wife.)

"Language,'' says Stuart Robertson in *The Development of Modern English*, "is the agent or medium by which men communicate their thoughts to one another. Passing over for a moment the difficulty presented by the term that is most vague here (agent or medium), let us attempt to see how far the rest of the formula is applicable. . . . Does the word *men*, in the first place, express a necessary and correct limitation? Is language the prerogative of man, to the exclusion of the lower animals?''

"Give a newborn eagle 30 days of growth and,'' according to the columnist L. M. Boyd, "it will see four times as well as a man who has 20/20 vision.''

No matter how old and deeply ingrained in the language, and no matter what grammar books, usage guides, and other authorities proclaim, terms that many English-speakers feel do not truly represent females as well as males may disappear. And if they do, it will not be by fiat; not by the wholesale adoption of an artificial genderless vocabulary; not overnight. It will be in the way language usually changes: slowly and through the rearrangement, addition, and rejection of words, phrases, and constructions, as the attitudes of those who use the language change.

For some years, of course, speakers and writers have felt that a number of English terms and usages exclude or denigrate half the population. Besides trying to make up for the lack of a truly generic third-person pronoun (see HURRICANE DAVID LEFT DEVASTATION IN HER WAKE), they have been looking for new forms of expression that carry no pejorative or condescending connotations. Here are a few of the words and phrases that are often discarded, together with some of their replacements:

Old Term	New Term
mankind	*humankind, humanity, human beings, humans, human race, people*
manpower	*workers, work force*
man-made	*synthetic, artificial, manufactured*
man of letters	*writer, scholar*
chairman	*chairperson, chair*
mailman	*mail carrier, letter carrier*
policeman	*police officer*
fireman	*firefighter*
anchorman	*anchor*
men working (as on highway signs)	*road work*

Old Term	New Term
salesman	salesclerk, salesperson, sales representative
congressman	member of Congress, Representative (BUT Congresswoman Patricia Schroeder; former Congressman Thomas P. O'Neill)

Adult female human beings are now usually called *women*, as in *League of Women Voters* and *National Organization for Women*, that word having been rehabilitated in recent years. *Ladies,* on the other hand, is in decline, being used almost solely in the euphemism *ladies' room* and when men are being referred to as *gentlemen,* as in speeches that begin "Ladies and gentlemen." Nor is *lady* often seen or heard nowadays as a modifier (as in *lady doctor, lady executive, lady golfer*). When relevant, *female* or *woman* is ordinarily used, as in a caption reading "First female Supreme Court Justice of Colorado." (It is interesting to note that in 1980, a year before Sandra Day O'Connor became the first woman member of the U.S. Supreme Court, the nine men then sitting on the Court quietly dropped the official designation "Mr. Justice," which had been in use since the early nineteenth century. According to the *New York Times,* Court employees speculated that the change was made "to accommodate the prospect of a woman joining the Supreme Court and to avoid the awkward appellation 'Madam Justice' when that day arrives.")

Most female-gender words ending in *-ess, -ix,* and *-ette* have been replaced by the common forms, so that *authoress, poetess, Jewess, aviatrix,* and *usherette,* for example, generally become *author, poet, Jew, aviator,* and *usher.* Some people are slower to give up *actress, waitress,* and *hostess,* and *-ienne* words like *comedienne.* (In *Who's Who in America,* Carol Burnett described herself as "actress, comedienne, singer.") Histories of the struggle for women's right to vote still use *suffragette,* but current accounts tend to use either the common form, *suffragist,* or a more general descriptive term.

H. W. Fowler, the English lexicographer and arbiter of usage, would have been distressed by this trend toward eliminating feminine endings. As early as 1926, when he published his *Dictionary of Modern English Usage,* he foresaw that, "with the coming extension of women's vocations, feminines for vocation-words" would be "a special need of the future." After all:

"everyone knows the inconvenience of being uncertain whether a doctor is a man or a woman; hesitation in establishing the word *doctoress* is amazing in a people regarded as nothing if not practical."

Those who regularly say and write *human beings, humans, people, men and women, inhabitants, citizens,* and other inclusive, neutral terms, as appropriate in context, probably do so because they realize that not everyone who sees or hears *man* or *men* automatically assumes that all human beings or people generally are meant. Besides making it plain that women also participate in most of what goes on in the world, those broader yet more specific words clear up the ambiguity over whether only males or both females and males are being referred to.

In 1982, when *Roget's Thesaurus of English Words and Phrases* was 150 years old, the British publisher Longman brought out a new edition that did away with the sexist language in the original reference book. Susan Lloyd, the editor of the revised work, was quoted by the United Press as having said:

> "In Roget's day, if you used the word 'caveman,' people probably had a mental picture of cavewomen and cavechildren as well as cavemen. But research has shown that if you use the word 'caveman' today, people think of men, not women."

In its article on the new *Roget's*, the UP reported that "one of England's chief guardians of the language, The Times, reacted sourly." Under the headline "Roget is zonked by a modern Ms," the *Sunday Times*'s front-page story carried this byline: "Sunday Times Reportpersons."

The London *Times* thus joined other decriers of what the *San Francisco Chronicle* columnist Charles McCabe called the "illiterate effeminization of the English language." The *New York Times,* for example, ended an editorial titled "Manguage" with an apology for an earlier one on stamping out sexist words and with this reminder to the readers who had objected to it: "To err is people."

Resistance to some of the proposed gender-blind terms and usages ought, of course, to be expected. To begin with, coinages like *co, coself,* and *herm,* in place of *he or she, his or her,* and *her and him,* cannot be imposed on the language any more than George Bernard Shaw's facetious proposal to change the spelling of *fish* to *ghoti* could. (Shaw's well-known joke went like this: *gh* as in *laugh, o* as in *women,* and *ti* as in *nation.*) Besides, some of the unmistakably neutral terms like *wait-person* for either *waiter* or *waitress* are awkward indeed, and recasting an entire sentence to eliminate intractable *man-* words is more easily called for than carried out.

On the other hand, some of the objections are wide of their mark. In using *reportpersons* in the byline of its story on the 1982 edition of *Roget's Thesaurus,* for instance, the London *Sunday Times* clearly meant to give a witty exaggeration of a nonsexist word. But what is the sexist word that *reportpersons* is supposed to replace: *reportmen*? Even those who seek to rid the language of terms and usages considered offensive to women accept *reporters* without question. Similarly, in the *New York Times*'s little joke "To err is people," does *people* stand for another wholly inoffensive word, *human*? Or do *New York Times* editors believe that the proverb is "To err is man"?

The temptation to invent words from which all traces of supposed male gender have been expunged seems to be irresistible—*shedonism* for *hedonism, girlcott* for *boycott, personners* for *manners, personuscript* for *manuscript,* and so on. Because of its *son* syllable, even *person* is ferreted out and replaced by *perdaughter* and the like. Yet in their efforts to amuse, most of the sit-down comics pay little or no attention to the origin of the words they toy with. For instance:

> *Hedonism* derives from the Greek word *hedone,* meaning "delight."

> Captain C. C. *Boycott* was a land agent ostracized by his neighbors during the Land League agitation in Ireland in 1880. (For other everyday English words taken from the names of people and places, see JOHN BULL AND JOHN HANCOCK ARE NOT JUST ANY JOHNS.)

The *man* in *manners* and *manuscript* comes from the Latin *manus,* meaning "hand."

Person probably goes back to the Etruscan *phersu,* meaning "a mask." The Latin *persona* meant, literally, "an actor's face mask"; hence "a character or person." This extended meaning was carried into Old French, and from there into Middle English.

No one needs to attach false etymologies to English words or to invent new usages for putting women down. The language has more than enough to do the job.

but, **at the beginning of a sentence.** See **"And so it goes."**

but which, but who; and which, and who. See **Tennis is a sport I enjoy but which I don't play well.**

buzzwords. See **In one year and out the other.**

C

can, may, could, might. See **Can I borrow your lawn mower? Not if you might keep it.**

Can I borrow your lawn mower? Not if you might keep it.

In reply to a question like "Can I borrow your lawn mower?" some people still say, with a mischievous smile, "You may if you can." They want to show that they know the traditional distinction between the two auxiliary verbs: *can* denotes ability and *may* denotes permission.

It is not suprising to find this entry in a 1915 booklet titled *Faulty Diction:*

"Can. Misused for *may. Can* always refers to some form of possibility. An armed guard may say, 'You *can* not pass,' since he has physical power to prevent; hence the question 'Can I pass the guard?' is perfectly natural. But where simple permission is referred to *may* should be used. 'May I (not *can* I) use your ruler?' "

It is, however, surprising to find this entry in the third (1979) edition of Strunk and White's *The Elements of Style:*

"Can. Means 'am (is, are) able.' Not to be used as a substitute for *may.*"

Never? Not even in informal writing? Not even in a request for permission that is stated as a negative question, so as to avoid an awkward construction like "Mayn't I go with you?" or a stilted one like "Why may we not see the show?"

Except in formal written English, *can* is in fact used far more often than *may,* whether ability or permission is meant. (The auxiliary verbs are of course not interchangeable, since *may* does not express ability.)

Can I help you?

I can reconstruct the formula if you need it.

You can keep the book as long as you want.

You can't go now; the party is just beginning.

Because of the overlapping senses of *can* and *may,* speakers and writers sometimes eliminate ambiguity by turning to other constructions.

Skateboarders are *able to* use city sidewalks.

Skateboards are *permitted* (or *allowed*) on city sidewalks.

COULD AND MIGHT, the past-tense forms of *can* and *may,* are divided along the same lines. *Could* indicates ability.

The medical team did what it could in the emergency.

No more comprehensive view of the universe could have been devised.

Those who use *can* to denote permission in all but formal written English generally do the same with *could*. Those who prefer *may* generally use *might* as its past tense.

Jerry asked whether he *could* (*might*) borrow my lawn mower.

No longer only the past-tense forms of *may* and *can*, *might* and *could* are now used as equivalents with present and future senses. In references to permission, *might* and *could* ordinarily suggest more formality and diffidence than *may* and *can*.

Might (*could*) I keep the book over the weekend?

BESIDES DENOTING PERMISSION, the auxiliaries *may*, *might*, and *could* indicate possibility. The notion of likelihood is attached to *can* as well.

Can the rumors be true?

In references to the present or future, *may*, *might*, or *could* is followed by the simple form of the main verb. *Might* and *could* express more of a shade of doubt or a smaller degree of possibility than *may*.

You *may* (*might, could*) be right.

We *may* (*might, could*) catch the early train tomorrow.

In references to the past, *might* or *could* is followed either by the simple form of the principal verb:

At first it seemed as though you *might* (*could*) be right.

or by *have* and the past participle of the principal verb:

You *might* (*could*) have been right, but it doesn't matter anymore.

That is, *might* and *could* function in verb phrases with past, present, or future sense, whereas *may* is ordinarily not used as the auxiliary of a verb in a past tense. It is therefore unusual to find *may* in this past-tense construction:

"[Oppenheimer] . . . keyed that cerebral beam of his squarely on the subject, and allowed it to lead where it <u>may</u>." (Michael Brown, *Saturday Review*)

Nor does *may* ordinarily appear in the independent clause of a conditional sentence. So here we would expect President Carter to have used *might* instead:

"Carter told several hundred members of the White House staff at a closed meeting last week that if he had it to do over, 'I <u>may</u> not have asked for the resignations of the Cabinet and staff.' " (James McCartney, Knight News Service) *cannot help but.*   See **I cannot but love that man of mine.**

care less

When it comes to caring less, some people could and others couldn't. The informal idiom implying that one feels the least possible degree of interest, sympathy, or the like was originally *couldn't care less*.

> Go or stay. I couldn't care less.

> Carla couldn't care less whether she gets the job.

Those who liked that informal expression, with its playful double negative, were dismayed by the corruption *could care less*.

> Go or stay. I could care less.

> Carla could care less whether she gets the job.

Some went so far as to look to an authority who might turn back the clock.

> "Dear Abby: I have a friend who frequently says, 'I could care less.' What he means is that he really doesn't care at all. To convey that idea, shouldn't he say, 'I *couldn't* care less'?
>
>   "Al in Oregon.

> "Dear Al: To say 'I could care less' means one could care even less than he does. When one wants to convey that he cares so little that he could not care less, the proper expression is, 'I couldn't care less.' Your friend is careless about his expressions."

But the efforts of conservative English-speakers are not likely to be successful, for *could care less* seems too well established to be dislodged now.

catchwords and catch phrases.   See **In one year and out the other.**

center around

True, a center is the point around which anything revolves, so it is illogical to say or write that something *centers around* or *centers about* something else. What we should say and write instead, some usage guides and dictionaries insist, is *center on, center upon, center in,* or *center at*.
But do educated English-speakers?

> "They are problems that center around the symbols of government. . . ." (Wendell Johnson, former president of the International Society for General Semantics)

> "Writers as different as Samuel Richardson and Gustave Flaubert got into heavy weather the minute they tried to center their books around bores of the stature of Sir Charles Grandison or Bouvard and Pécuchet." (Larry McMurtry, a Pulitzer Prize–winning novelist)

> "The Greek approach to language centered around a question." (Robert E. Morsberger, *Commonsense Grammar and Style*)

"The chief debate [in the Virginia Legislature of 1830–31] often centered about what to do with the emancipated slave. . . ." (Robert Penn Warren, a poet and Pulitzer Prize–winning novelist)

When it comes to language, rules based on logic often go one way and usage another. For other instances in which purists try to protect English from those who speak and write it, see FOR A GIRL HE'S QUITE MATURE; for more idioms, HOW COME THE CLOCK ISN'T GOING? and "Some Troublesome Idiomatic Prepositions," a table at the back of the book.

Christian names. See **Good night, Anwar. Good night, Menachem.**

circumstances, under the or in the?

Those of us who have been saying and writing *under the circumstances,* as in "Under the circumstances, the mayor decided to resign," may be surprised to learn that we shouldn't. The English word *circumstance,* whose plural form means "conditions surrounding and affecting a person," comes from the Latin *circumstantia,* which, in turn, comes from the Latin *circumstare: circum* ("around") + *stare* ("to stand"). According to some grammarians, it is illogical to suppose that what surrounds a person can be *over* or *under* that person. Therefore, *under the circumstances,* in the sense of "conditions being what they are or were," is incorrect and must be replaced by *in the circumstances.*

We might try to convince those logical grammarians that it is they who are wrong, that the laws of physics allow a surrounding body to be over and under, as well as around, a person. But it is simpler to remind them that *under the circumstances* is an idiom—that is, a phrase that is accepted in the language whether or not its meaning can be taken literally—and a longstanding one at that. *The Oxford English Dictionary* gives this citation from 1665: "Every Hypocrite . . . under the same Circumstances would have infallibly treated Him with the same Barbarity."

Less rigid grammarians recognize *under the circumstances'* right to exist but prefer that it not be confused with *in the circumstances.* Citing the *OED* as his authority, the British lexicographer H. W. Fowler, for example, notes, "Mere situation is expressed by '*in* the circumstances,' action affected is performed '*under* the circumstances.'" The American word watcher Theodore Bernstein says that "*in the circumstances* refers merely to existing conditions, and implies a continuing state of affairs," whereas "*under the circumstances* refers to conditions that impel or inhibit action, and implies a transient situation, long or short." But most speakers and writers of English neither know nor care about those fine distinctions. Indeed, many of them, especially Americans, are unfamiliar with *in the circumstances,* using *under the circumstances* much as they use, say, *under those conditions.*

For other instances in which purists have taken on established usage, see FOR A GIRL HE'S QUITE MATURE; for more idioms, HOW COME THE CLOCK ISN'T GOING? and "Some Troublesome Idiomatic Prepositions," at the back of the book.

clichés. See **Lo and behold, it's man's best friend.**

clipped words.   See **A vet rushed to the zoo by cab to treat a hippo with the flu.**

coinages.   See **Dear Mr. Webster.**

Cold slaw on my new chaise lounge!

On hearing her father say where he was going to stay during a business trip, a five-year-old exclaimed, "I know where *hotel* comes from! *Motel*."

We're all etymologists, whether or not we've studied the branch of linguistics that deals with word origin and development. No sooner do we hear or see a new word than we shelve it in our mind, next to one we already know. We may turn to our dictionary to sort out puzzling derivations and meanings (see FOR A GIRL HE'S QUITE MATURE), but to do that we must first have an idea of what we're not clear about. Just as many of us wouldn't bother to look up, say, *water power*—who doesn't know what *water* and *power* mean?—we think we can handle any other word we come across for the first time.

What happens, though, is that in fitting an unfamiliar word into a familiar pattern, we may change its spelling, pronunciation, or meaning. And if, over a long enough period of time, enough people establish the same apparent but incorrect connection, the change may be long-lasting. The process of transforming the language in this way is known as *folk etymology* or *popular etymology*. (Despite the word *folk* or *popular*, this unconscious desire to make sense out of puzzling aspects of the language leads people of all social groups and levels of education to arrive at unwarranted notions about the origin, derivation, and meaning of words.)

Foreign words incorporated into English are especially subject to mistaken association. *Cole*, for example, derives from the Dutch *kool*, which means "cabbage" and is related to *cole*, a genus of plants of the mustard family; *slaw* comes from *sla*, meaning "salad." Because *coleslaw* (or *cole slaw*) is usually served cold, this popular dish made of shredded raw cabbage mixed with salad dressing and seasoning is—logically though unetymologically—often called *cold slaw*. So far the widespread shift in pronunciation has not affected the spelling of the word, except on some restaurant menus.

But both the spelling and the pronunciation of *chaise lounge* have been altered. In French *chaise longue* (literally a "long chair") is pronounced approximately shez' lông'. Finding this couchlike chair ideal for lounging, in that its seat is long enough to support one's outstretched legs, many English-speakers have changed the French *longue* to *lounge*. So many, in fact, that a number of American dictionaries now give *chaise lounge* (shāz' lounj') as a variant spelling and pronunciation. It's safe to assume that in time all English-language dictionaries that set out to record, rather than prescribe, usage will do the same.

These are some of the many other words that English-speakers have unconsciously altered over time so as to make them look or sound like words they already knew:

A *belfry* originally had no bells, but was a movable tower used in ancient warfare for attacking walled positions. In Old High German the word was *bergfrid,* literally "protector of peace," from *bergen* ("to protect") + *frig* ("peace"). In Old French it eventually became *berfrai,* which was altered to the Middle English *belfrei* so as to incorporate *belle* ("bell"), since the modern belfry is the part of a tower or steeple that holds a bell or bells.

The *fish* part of *crayfish* (or its variant, *crawfish*) is due not to the appearance of this small, lobsterlike crustacean but to an alteration of its Middle English name (*crevise*), derived from the Old French *crevice.*

Four centuries or so ago, when a small, furry-tailed, mostly tree-dwelling rodent of the Gliridae family went into hibernation, inhabitants of England who spoke Old French probably said it was *dormeuse,* meaning "sleepy" or "sluggish" (from *dormir,* "to sleep"). Their English-speaking listeners might have associated that adjective with the familiar word for a small rodent—*mous*—and simply turned it into a compound noun with *dor* as a harmless first element. In any case, some linguists speculate that this is the origin of *dormouse.*

To convey the notion of a helpful companion, specifically a wife though sometimes a husband, *helpmate* seemed to make more sense than the earlier form, *helpmeet.* This, though, is a case of a double misunderstanding. *Helpmeet* was never really a word in its own right but, instead, resulted from people's believing it to be a single word in Genesis 2:18: "And the Lord God said, It is not good that the man should be alone; I will make him an help meet for him." (Words that are created through the misreading of manuscripts, the misunderstanding of grammatical elements, and the like, without ever being really established in a language, are called *ghost words.*)

A *Jerusalem artichoke,* a tall North American sunflower whose potatolike tubers are used as a vegetable, is not an artichoke and it is not from Jerusalem. One of its names is *girasol* (or *girasole*), which came into English from Italian, by way of French, and which is pronounced with a "soft" *g* (jir′ə sôl′, jir′ə säl′, or jir′ə sōl′). This foreign word for "sunflower" sounded enough like *Jerusalem* to become just that, so it was attached to the misnomer *artichoke.*

The Middle English name for a northern sea bird that is black above and white below, with a short neck, ducklike body, and brightly colored triangular beak, was *poffin.* Probably through association with *puff* (the young do have an enormous beak and blown-up appearance), the name was eventually changed to *puffin.*

Someone whose expression shows a feeling of shame is said to be *shamefaced.* A fitting adjective, one would think. Indeed, so many English-speakers thought so that they created this word from the Middle English *schamfast,* which in turn derives from the Old English *scamfæst* (from *scamu,* meaning "shame," + *fæst,* meaning "firm").

As an eighteenth-century joke, a dish of melted cheese, often mixed with ale or beer and served on crackers or toast, was given the name *Welsh rabbit*. Thinking that *rare* (in the sense of "unusually good") plus *bit* ("a morsel") must have been intended—after all, what does *rabbit* have to do with such a dish?—people changed both the spelling and the pronunciation to *Welsh rarebit*. Both forms exist side by side today.

Folk etymology is at work all around us, for English-speakers continue to mold their language by turning unfamiliar words into familiar ones, in both speech and writing. In time the words they create may become fully established, either replacing or coexisting with those that raised doubts in the first place. For instance:

Bombastic, meaning "pompous" or "grandiloquent," usually describes high-sounding but unimportant or meaningless language. This is fitting, because just as *bombast* originally denoted a soft material used for padding, the word now suggests padding in language. Yet, probably by association with *bomb*, it is frequently used in the sense of "noisy" or "explosive."

The recital hall was too small for such bombastic music.

A *memento* (from the imperative form of the Latin verb *meminisse*) is anything that serves as a reminder or warning. Nowadays it is especially thought of as a souvenir. And since a souvenir reminds one of a place, a person, or an occasion—that is, a *moment*—*mementos* are fast becoming *momentos*.

As an adjective *minuscule,* from the Latin *minusculus,* means "very small; tiny; minute."

Minuscule quantities of cinnabar turned up in the paint.

To suggest that something is small or of lesser extent than usual, the combining form *mini-*, as in *miniature*, is more often found in everyday speech and writing.

minicomputer   minibus   miniskirt   mini-crisis

So, more and more, people say and write the newly created word *miniscule* instead of the established *minuscule*.

"efforts to make small talk with her acquired the touching quality of futile activity carried on by some miniscule animal, say the turning of a wheel by a white mouse in a cage." (Rebecca West, *The Thinking Reed*)

"In the past couple of years alone, Nicholas Slonimsky has managed to bring out three new books: the Seventh Edition of Baker's Biographical Dictionary of Musicians (with more than thirteen thousand entries spread across more than twenty-five hundred double-column pages of miniscule type. . . ." (Lawrence Weschler, "Profiles," *New Yorker*)

Noisy is the adjective form of the noun *noise,* which denotes a loud, unmusical, or disagreeable sound. Many people assume that *noisome* is also formed from *noise,* to which the suffix *-some* ("like" or "tending to be") has been added, and that *noisy* and *noisome* are therefore synonymous.

We couldn't stand the noisy (noisome) city any longer.

Not so. *Noisome* does end in the suffix *-some,* but its base is the Old French *anoi* ("annoy") from which the first vowel has been dropped. It means "injurious to health" and "foul-smelling."

We couldn't stand the noisome stench of the open sewers any longer.

Penultimate (pronounced pi nul′tə mit) means "next to the last." It comes from the Latin *paene* ("almost") plus *ultima* ("last").

The penultimate letter of the alphabet is Y.

Yet many people use it in the sense of "the highest point of perfection."

Duke Ellington is the penultimate master of swing.

Why they do so is not entirely clear. Perhaps because the adjective *ultimate* means not only "coming after all the others" but also "the greatest or highest possible; maximum; utmost." No matter that *pen* is not a prefix meaning "greater or better than" or "extra, additional," as *super-* is: it sounds like one. Or it may be that some people vaguely associate *penultimate* with the phrase *ne plus ultra* (nē plus ul′trə), which in Latin means literally "no more beyond" and does indeed convey the sense of "the utmost limit, or the highest point of perfection."

Renown and *renowned* are derived from the Latin *nomen* ("name") plus the prefix *re-,* meaning "again." Therefore "a scientist of renown" or "a renowned scientist" is a person who is named publicly again and again for his or her outstanding achievement in science. Although *known* has an entirely different derivation, it is used in much the same way ("a well-known scientist"). Not surprisingly, then, *reknown* and *reknowned* often appear in print. Yet these hybrid forms are still pronounced as though they were spelled without the *k* (ri noun′, ri nound′; not ri nōn′, ri nōnd′).

Throe, meaning "a spasm or pang of pain," is ordinarily used in the plural ("throes of childbirth," "death throes"). The idiom *in the throes of* suggests that someone is in the act of struggling with a problem, decision, task, or the like. The more familiar *throw* is not only pronounced the same way but, because of a shared ancestry, also conveys the notion of rapid motion. Therefore, seeming to make sense without really doing so, *throws* is gaining ground on *throes.*

"Indeed, soon after his return to Vienna, in the throws of his 'self-analysis,' he was to speak of his own pilgrimage, his own 'via dolorosa' on his route to Rome." (J. N. Isbister, *Freud: An Introduction to His Life and Work*)

Folk etymology is but one of a number of processes that lead to the creation of new words or to changes in the meaning of existing ones. For a few of the others, see—besides FOR A GIRL HE'S QUITE MATURE—BURGLARS BURGLE AND PEDDLERS PEDDLE, SO WHY DON'T JANITORS JANIT?; MODOR, WE'VE GOT COMPANY; and JOHN BULL AND JOHN HANCOCK ARE NOT JUST ANY JOHNS.

combining forms.   See **Who needs a rabbit's foot more: an unlucky person or a luckless one?**

come or *go*?

Come conveys the notion of moving from a place thought of as "there" to or into a place thought of as "here." The construction of a particular sentence, however, often reflects the speaker's or writer's intent.

> A pronoun (expressed or implied) and verb in the second person suggest that the motion of the person addressed is in relation to the speaker or writer.

Please come at once.

Are you planning to come to the picnic tomorrow?

> A pronoun and verb in the first person suggest that the motion of the speaker or writer is in relation to the person addressed.

I hope to come to your party.

> A pronoun and verb in the third person suggest that the motion of the person or thing spoken about is in relation to the person or thing approached.

They came to the theater without tickets.

Between 1800 and 1914 almost 35 million people came to the United States.

Go is a more general word indicating motion away from a place thought of as "here" to or into a place thought of as "there."

I'll go if I'm invited.

Are you going to Florida this winter?

She hopes to go home for the holidays.

They went as far as their savings took them.

Fewer students went to Europe last year than the year before.

"Come up and see me sometime."

Now, who could resist Mae West's invitation to come up and see her sometime? Stuffy grammarians, that's who. According to them, the sexy actress should have said, "Come up *to* see me sometime."

Yet for centuries, in both speech and writing, *and* has been used as well as *to* in joining a verb like *come, go, try,* or *write* to another verb in order to form what is sometimes called an infinitive of purpose.

Even people who accept both usages as standard see slight differences between them. For one thing, especially in the United States, some still consider the *to* construction to be more formal than the *and* construction.

The Senate committee will try *to* win approval of its bill before the Easter recess.

Try *and* stay awake during the lecture, will you?

For another, some think that the two forms have subtly different connotations. They see the *and* construction as implying two acts that do not necessarily require great effort but are likely to have a successful outcome.

I'll go *and* pick up a pair of tickets for tonight's game.

Try *and* get some sleep.

Write *and* tell them how much you miss them.

On the other hand, they see the *to* construction as implying a single act with unmistakable purpose or determination but with less certain result.

Go *to* apply for the job this very afternoon.

Please try *to* stop smoking.

Whether or not we consider the two infinitives of purpose to be interchangeable in meaning, we automatically observe certain differences in the way we use them. That's what idiom is all about (see How COME THE CLOCK ISN'T GOING?). For example, in a negative construction with *try*, we use *to*, not *and*. No native English-speaking person would be likely to say or write:

I try *and* never show up late for an interview.

Try not *and* fall asleep in class.

Besides, to show purpose we use *to* plus an infinitive no matter what the form or tense of the preceding verb, but *and* plus an infinitive only if the preceding verb is in the imperative form or future tense. That is, we might say:

Try *to* do better.	OR	Try *and* do better.
I'll try *to* do better.	OR	I'll try *and* do better.
I try *to* do better.	BUT NOT	I try *and* do better.
I am trying *to* do better.	BUT NOT	I am trying *and* do better.
I tried *to* do better.	BUT NOT	I tried *and* do better.
I have tried *to* do better.	BUT NOT	I have tried *and* do better.

Of course, the *and* construction is appropriate if, instead of expressing an infinitive of purpose, we simply want to show that the action of one verb follows that of another. For example, "I try and do better" might mean that, through effort, I manage to do better. Similarly, "I tried and did better" might mean that I tried and, as a result, did better. The same applies to "I have tried and done better."

That is, at her most seductive, Mae West said, "Come up and see me sometime." Yet, whether matter-of-factly or wistfully, she might have said, "You came up and saw me sometimes" or "You used to come up and see me sometimes."

compare or *contrast?*

Compare is used to point out both similarities and differences between people, things, or events that are on the whole alike. When the emphasis is on similarity, whether literal or figurative, the verb is followed by *to*.

Many historians compare Hitler to Attila the Hun.

That Titian nude has been compared to a poached egg on toast.

On the other hand, when specific resemblances and differences are brought out in a more detailed examination, the verb is followed by *with*.

The essay compares Hitler's treatment of conquered peoples with Attila the Hun's.

To show Titian's use of sharp angles and diagonals as well as curves and verticals, his *Young Englishman* is often compared with his *Man with the Glove*.

At least that is the traditional distinction between the two prepositions following *compare*. But that distinction is disappearing. Even when the stress is on similarity, *with* is often used instead of *to*.

"A soft-spoken brunette whose conversation is laced with quiet humor, [Margaret] Atwood has been compared with Joan Didion as a stylist, although she disagrees with that judgment." (William Hogan, "World of Books")

Yet far more often, even when the stress is on clear difference, *to* replaces *with*.

"According to a survey made in the late 1950's, only about 17 percent of Americans were then reading a book, as compared to 34 percent of the Australians and 55 percent of the British." (Robert E. Morsberger, *Commonsense Grammar and Style*)

"She's [Jacqueline Kennedy Onassis] no great beauty, although it must be admitted that, compared to preceding first ladies of the United States such as Mamie Eisenhower and Bess Truman, she was sensational." (Helen Lawrenson, "Jackie at 50")

If usage were logical, *compare favorably* would be used only if what is being singled out had an edge over another in the same category. In other words, "This year's television programs compare favorably with last year's" would mean that this year's are better than last year's. But because usage is not logical, we often see and hear the phrase when attention is being called to something that does not quite measure up to something else. "Margarine compares favorably to butter'' therefore probably means that the ''low-priced spread'' comes close to tasting as good as butter.

Incomparable means that a person, thing, or event is unequaled or matchless, so there is no basis for comparison with anyone or anything else, as in ''incomparable talent'' or ''incomparable skill.'' In both England and the United States, the adjective is more often pronounced in käm'pər ə b'l than in'kəm par'ə b'l.

CONTRAST IS ALWAYS USED to point out differences. The verb (pronounced kən trast') is ordinarily followed by *with*, though sometimes by *to*.

> The survey contrasts the reading habits of Americans with those of Australians and Britons.

> In the brochure San Diego's weather is contrasted to London's.

The noun (pronounced kän'trast) usually takes *between*.

> The contrast between San Diego's weather and London's is startling.

The phrase *in contrast* is followed by either *to* or *with*.

> Calm prevailed on most American college campuses in the seventies, in contrast to the turbulence of the sixties.

> Zeffirelli's *Swan Lake* was in sharp contrast with the performance of Indian classical ballet.

COMPARE AND CONTRAST are not the only verbs that may be followed by more than one preposition. See HOW COME THE CLOCK ISN'T GOING? and ''Some Troublesome Idiomatic Prepositions,'' a table at the back of the book.

comparisons of adjectives and adverbs.
See **Excitinger times lie ahead; Kilimanjaro is taller than any mountain in Africa.**

compose or *comprise*?
See **comprise or compose?**

compound words.
See **Upstart name-droppers usually get the cold shoulder.**

comprise or *compose*?

''The whole comprises the parts; the parts compose the whole.'' Some people memorize this sentence so they will be sure to use *comprise* in the sense of ''to consist of'' and *compose* in the sense of ''to constitute.'' The trouble is, that mnemonic device is like the one for reminding us to feed a cold and starve a fever—or is starve a cold and feed a fever? We think we've learned it by heart, but before we can make it part of our pattern of thought it slips away from us.

In strict usage, *comprise* is limited to expressing the relation of the larger to the smaller. In other words, it takes as its object the various parts that are included in the whole.

> The United States government comprises three branches: the executive, the legislative, and the judicial.

Comprising horns, trumpets, trombones, and a tuba, the brass section began rehearsing.

Compose, on the other hand, expresses the relation of the smaller to the larger. It takes as its object the whole that is made up of the various parts.

The three branches that compose the United States government are the executive, the legislative, and the judicial.

Horns, trumpets, trombones, and a tuba compose the brass section, which began rehearsing.

More and more, people are abandoning that long-held distinction. It isn't that they are using *comprise* and *compose* interchangeably in the first sense ("to consist of," "to include," "to contain"). Indeed, few English-speakers would say or write "The United States government composes three branches." But in the second sense ("to constitute," "to make up," "to form"), many are just as likely—in fact, more likely—to use *comprise* as *compose*. That is, "Three branches comprise the United States government" is coming to be considered an alternative, not a necessarily incorrect, version of "Three branches compose the United States government."

"Her [the Duchess of Alba's] masterworks by Titian, Rembrandt, Rubens, Velázquez, El Greco and Goya comprise what may be the world's most spectacular private collection." (Barbara Barker, *People Weekly*)

"Since the commonest one hundred words comprise about 48 percent of the vocabulary in use, such a filtering system could be relatively efficient, and true frequencies of the remaining vocabulary items could be calculated." (Sidney I. Landau, *Dictionaries: The Art and Craft of Lexicography*)

"By reviewing certain key aspects of the field, the essays that comprise this report may assist those who work with educational books in their dynamic and challenging task." (John Dessauer, *Publishers Weekly*)

Both *composed of* and *comprised of* are often used in the sense of "made up of," "formed by," or "constituted," but not with everyone's approval. Whereas no one objects to "a government composed of three branches," some still regard "a government comprised of three branches" as a loose usage.

A concept-oriented framework may effectuate a consensus of opinion in terms of the maximization of a meaningful continuum of program factors.

Late-1980s talk, right? No and yes. No, because *concept, -oriented, framework, effectuate, consensus of opinion, in terms of, maximization, meaningful, continuum, program,* and *factor* are among the words, phrases, and usages that Laurence Lafore banned in papers written by students in his history classes at Swarthmore College some thirty years earlier (his list appeared in the August 1957 issue of *Harper's Magazine*). Yes, because such words and phrases continue to pervade not only college papers but almost every other form of writing and speech.

Now, there is nothing wrong with those terms or with words like *norm*, *interrelate,* and *organizational* (also on Professor Lafore's long list). Each has one or more specific meanings of particular interest to those who read or write about history, sociology, anthropology, political science, economics, and the like. Surely a speaker at a meeting of the American Philosophical Association need not talk about "Plato's generalized idea of a republic, based on his knowledge of particular instances of that form of government," simply to avoid saying "Plato's concept of a republic."

For centuries people in the same line of work or way of life have used special words and idioms in talking with one another, both to make communication easier and to keep outsiders from knowing what was said. The following are a few of the many contexts in which *jargon* (or *shoptalk* or *argot*) is not only accepted but virtually required. (This specialized language variety was once called *slang*. For a discussion of slang as we know it today, see JOBBED IN A HUMONGOUS SCAM, THE TWEAKED-OUT MOBSTER EXCLAIMED, "PEACHY-KEEN!")

Law. Instead of having defendants in criminal cases say "I do not wish to contest it," for instance, lawyers enter a plea of *nolo contendere* on their behalf; this means that the defendants declare that, without admitting guilt, they will not make a defense.

Real estate. Prospective house buyers and their real estate agents discuss such things as *earnest money, escrow funds, closing costs,* and *amortization.*

Carnivals or circuses. The few surviving *carnies* probably still talk about *grifters* or *grifts* (petty swindlers), the *midway* (the area where sideshows and other amusements are located), *perch acts* (those performed on high poles), and the like.

Sewing. Anyone familiar with patterns would have no trouble following these instructions, by Sandra Betzina:

"Open the [lapped] zipper up and place face down on extended seam allowance. Line up the zipper teeth with the basted seam. Start stitching one inch above the bottom of the zipper stop."

Bridge. Reading about others' games gives bridge addicts vicarious pleasure. This is how the columnists Goren and Sharif described the end of one game:

"When declarer led his last trump, he could afford to part with a club from dummy. East had no option but to let go a club. Now East was thrown in with a club and he had to break the diamond suit for declarer. By simply playing for split diamond honors, declarer avoided losing a diamond trick and landed his contract."

Music. Donald Francis Tovey said this about Brahms's Quintet in B Minor for Clarinet and Strings, op. 115:

"The third movement is unique in form. It begins with a pair of themes in D major, common time, andantino, which, after a climax, come to a quiet close. Then a transformation of these themes in contrapuntal combination, 2/4 time, 'presto non assai' (the beats hardly faster than those of the andantino), is worked out in B minor into a terse binary movement with a contrasted 'second subject' in syncopated rhythm in F sharp minor."

Literary criticism. In an essay titled "An Outline of Poetic Theory," Elder Olson wrote:

"The integral or likeness-dialectic reaches solutions by combination of like with like; the differential or difference-dialectic, by the separation of dissimilars. Thus a criticism integral in its dialectic resolves its questions by referring poetry, for example, to some analogue of poetry, finding characteristics of poetry which are shared by the analogue; whereas a criticism differential in its dialectic resolves its questions by separating poetry from its analogues, finding characteristics which are peculiar to poetry."

Computers. Readers of Steve Roth's "Hardware Review," in the magazine *Personal Publishing,* were told:

"With the standard IBM graphics display for instance, (at a resolution of 320 by 200 dots), you could take one square inch of a 300dpi page, blow it up to the size of the screen, look at it from across the room, and get some approximation of the final printed resolution. Standard IBM graphics are hardly acceptable for <u>what you see is what you get</u> (wysiwyg) page makeup."

However daunting to the uninitiated, the jargon in the above examples works for those in the know, who see it as a precise, economical way to communicate information. The trouble is, jargon has a way of spilling out of such special contexts, where it is appropriate, into general ones, where it isn't. As Professor Lafore feared his history students might, many English-speakers use pompous language and technical-sounding words (preferably long, Latin-derived ones) either to impress their listeners and readers with their authority or to conceal the fact that they have little to say.

To avoid straightforward statements like "The weather will get worse in the next few days" or "We can expect more storms through Wednesday," TV weatherpeople intone, "The weather situation will be characterized by deterioration through Wednesday."

What else would people who work or live in a "floppy-disk environment" say besides:

I'll be with you in a *nanosecond.*

Could I have your *input* on Saturday's grocery list?

Let's *interface* over lunch.

Taking a vacation without at least a month of *downtime* just doesn't *compute.*

To be sure that these teckies are in a *comprehension mode,* advertisers and manufacturers speak the same language. A "New! Trim Handi-Pak" of Trim emery boards, for instance, advises (with arrows inside a perforated patch): "Pull back to access boards."

A 1987 Christian Child Care fund-raising "speedgram" (an ordinary mailing disguised as a telegram) carried this conspicuous "warning" on the envelope: "Deliverability of the enclosed time sensitive material is being carefully monitored."

In passing along Ralph Nader's 1971 criticism of Volkswagens, the *San Francisco Sunday Examiner & Chronicle* thoughtfully provided a translation from jargon into English:

> " 'The fundamental reason to avoid purchasing or riding in any Volkswagen microbus is the gross lack of front collapse distance'— the space between the front end of the car and the driver."

According to the United Press, a research associate at the Masters & Johnson Institute found that women with careers are less interested in sex than women who are unemployed or have dull jobs. What did Constance Avery-Clark give as a reason? Not enough time for intimacy.

> " 'These couples are often unable to spend much time together because of their demanding schedules, and the career wives frequently report difficulty making an effective mental transition from their professional lives to personal time with their respective husbands,' she said."

Just *husbands*, without *respective*, would of course do for most English-speakers, but not for sex therapists, psychologists, and other social scientists, or for those determined to talk like them. These people believe that no unnecessary word should ever be omitted. If they discover that they've put on weight, for example, they don't *decide* to exercise; they *make* (or *take*) *a decision* to exercise. Then they don't exercise *every day* or even *daily;* they exercise *on a daily basis.* Not *to keep in shape,* but *in order to keep in shape.* How? Not *by* swimming *in a rectangular pool,* but *by means of* swimming *in a rectangular-shaped pool.* Fitness is not, in a word, *important;* it is, in two words, *of importance.*

Nature can usually be counted on to smarten up a sentence; that is, anything which is, say, *confidential* can be made grander by being *of a confidential nature.*

> " 'There was swelling and tenderness in the (injured) areas, but everything appears to be not of a serious nature.' " (The administrator of the New York hospital that treated Dan Rather after the TV anchor had been attacked and beaten, as quoted by the Associated Press)

Extant (meaning "still existing," "not extinct," or "not lost or destroyed") is another useful word that, while not adding anything to most sentences, doesn't take much away either. John B. Anderson, the Independent Presidential candidate in 1980, probably knew this when he denied that racism had played a part in his remark that a group of dancing black children had "nice, natural rhythm."

" 'Such a remark could only be interpreted as racist ... if there was not extant unfortunately a certain amount of racism in our society today,' he said." (Associated Press)

(Redundancy, though, has its uses. See SLOW EROSION COMPLETELY DESTROYED THE OLD COLONIAL TOMBSTONE.)

Besides technical-sounding words and extravagant verbal padding, jargon relies on strings of nouns or noun phrases to modify other nouns—the longer the strings, the better. For instance:

The International Monetary Fund was formed to assist countries in meeting their commitments under this *fixed exchange rate system.*

An ongoing study is focusing on the *third world communication networks explosion.*

"In a few days, the street in front of your residence will be given a surface maintenance treatment." (Letter from the Department of Public Works, City of Palo Alto, California)

"Coronary bypass operations are apparently no more effective than drugs for preventing heart attacks or increasing overall survival for severe chest pain patients—except in the worst cases, according to the largest study of its kind." (Rob Stein, United Press International)

"TIAA-CREF annuity preretirement death benefits are payable under a number of methods to help meet different family and financial circumstances." (*The Participant,* a newsletter of the Teachers Insurance and Annuity Association/College Retirement Equities Fund)

Jargon users like the passive voice, because it gives them a place to hide while making them sound important. "The results of this study *are expected* to be published shortly," for example, is less likely to hold the writer to account than "I *expect* to publish the results of the study shortly." Yet evading responsibility is not the only reason why people use the passive voice. For more on this widely criticized construction, see THE PLANE WAS GOT OUT OF BY TWELVE WEARY PASSENGERS.

GOBBLEDYGOOK (sometimes spelled *gobbledegook*) is a special kind of jargon. Perhaps in imitation of the characteristic throaty sound made by male turkeys, the term was first used in its current sense in the 1940s by the U.S. Representative Maury Maverick. Like ordinary jargon, gobbledygook is pompous, roundabout, involved talk or writing, full of long, Latinized words. What sets it apart is that it is mainly thought of as the work of officialdom—particularly of the Washington world of *IGs* ("interagency groups" made up of assistant Cabinet secretaries); *intercepts* (Justice Department jargon for the results of electronic eavesdropping); and *findings* (secret Presidential intelligence orders).

In the *New York Times,* Charles Mohr quoted from a 1985 "report by the Defense Science Board on military applications of new-generation computers and artificial intelligence":

" 'The Naval Ocean Systems Center's investigations into natural language understanding have included the Naval Oriented Message Analyzer and Disambiguator and Vocabularity Extensibility.' "

By comparison, this passage from a "Top Secret" annual report of the Joint Chiefs of Staff, which Jack Anderson cited in 1980, is a model of clear writing:

" 'The United States continues to enjoy important military strengths vis-a-vis Soviet forces.... The United States maintains a qualitative edge in many weapons systems and equipment....

" 'Finally, while the military advantages which the United States derives from its democratic political system and superior technological base defy easy quantification, there is no question but that they weigh heavily in the military balance.' "

An assistant White House press secretary artfully explained how President and Mrs. Reagan would be able to attend the 1985 Statue of Liberty festivities in New York yet avoid Manhattan. According to Bernard Weinraub's *New York Times* story, that official told reporters:

" 'We're going to have surgical strikes with the press.... We're going to take them from a landing zone in White Plains and helicopter them to the sites.... Insert and remove. That's what we're going to do—without burrowing through the streets of Manhattan.' "

The phrases *surgical strikes* and *insert and remove* call to mind the Pentagon's description of the 1983 invasion of Grenada: a "predawn, vertical insertion." Not suprisingly, because gobbledygook has much in common with *double talk, doublespeak,* or *weasel words.* (For a discussion of these purposely ambiguous and misleading words and phrases, which are related to the *Newspeak* of George Orwell's novel *Nineteen Eighty-four,* see "WAR IS PEACE.")

Without making a real effort to do away with the perverse thinking that distorts or reverses the truth to make it more acceptable, Washington officials from time to time make a show of banishing words and phrases generally identified with gobbledygook. One such official, according to United Press International, was the late Commerce Secretary Malcolm Baldrige, who in 1981 took on the challenge of "getting his staff to use the English language correctly." Besides outlawing "such Washington favorites as *prioritize, finalize, viable, orient, parameter,* and *ongoing,*" he forbade "the art of turning nouns or adjectives into verbs—*to interface, to impact,* and *to optimize.*" Also "such bureaucratic crutches as *bottom line, subject matter, prior to* (use *before,* he advised), *needless to say,* and *it is my intention.*" While they are in fashion, some of these terms resemble the topical metaphors and current expressions known as *vogue words* (see IN ONE YEAR AND OUT THE OTHER).

About the time Baldrige was waging his battle, President Leonid Brezhnev took on bureaucratese in the Soviet Union. In 1980, the United Press reported, he urged officials "to speak plainly and put an end to bureaucratic 'cliches and twaddle' in official Soviet propaganda."

" 'One must make a rule of speaking to people in simple and clear language, openly and in a businesslike manner. It is time to discard high-sounding words, bureaucracy and mechanical repetitions. One must get accustomed to writing in such a way that every phrase should express one's own thinking, one's own feelings.' "

Yet it would be wrong to think of gobbledygook as being limited to Washington (or Moscow). As Eugene J. McCarthy and James J. Kilpatrick observe in their book *A Political Bestiary:*

"It is commonly thought that the Gobbledegook resides only at seats of government, chiefly at the seat of national government, but this is not true. The Gobbledegook is equally at home in academic groves and in corporate mazes. He is often observed on military reservations, in doctors' offices, and in judicial chambers. He feeds on polysyllables, dangling participles, and ambivalent antecedents. He sleeps in subordinate clauses. The Gobbledegook is composed mostly of fatty tissues, watery mucus, and pale yellow blubber. The creature is practically boneless. Owing to cloudy vision, once he has launched into a sentence, he cannot see his way to the end."

Indeed, shortly before the Lake Tahoe Acquisitions Act of 1980 was voted on, the *Hollywood Independent* reported:

"Proponents of the measure point out that allowing the land proposed to be purchased instead of being developed will lead to a deterioration of the lake's notoriety for its clear water by destroying the ecological areas which prevent erosion from entering the lake."

In 1978, California Governor Jerry Brown defended his veto of pay raises by arguing that the money saved would end up helping, rather than hurting, local governments and their workers. According to the *San Francisco Chronicle* reporter Larry Liebert:

" 'The sacrifice must be shared, and the number one priority is minimizing, to the maximum degree, the number of layoffs,' Brown said."

In 1980, in filing the first suit to enforce New York State's Plain English Law, the state attorney general described as "gobbledygook" the language used by a branch of the Lincoln Savings Bank in connection with its safe-deposits. The *New York Times* reported that the attorney general "seemed particularly annoyed by this 121-word sentence":

" 'The liability of the bank is expressly limited to the exercise of ordinary diligence and care to prevent the opening of the within-mentioned safe deposit box during the within-mentioned term, or any extension or renewal thereof, by any person other than the lessee or his duly authorized representative and failure to exercise such diligence or care shall not be inferable from any alleged loss, absence or disappearance of any of its contents, nor shall the bank be liable for permitting a co-lessee or an attorney in fact of the lessee to have access to and remove the contents of said safe deposit box after the lessee's death or disability and before the bank has written knowledge of such death or disability.' "

consist of or *consist in?*

Consist of, which means "to be formed or composed of," introduces materials, parts, or ingredients.

Sorvete de abacate is a Brazilian ice consisting of avocado, lemon, and sugar.

Consist in, which means "to be contained or inherent in something, as a cause, effect, or characteristic," introduces a definition or an identifying statement.

Who said that a liberal education consists in the rediscovery of the obvious by the untrained?

That, at least, is the traditional distinction between the two expressions. More and more, however, *consist of* is applied to inherent qualities as well as to material components.

Wealth consists of more than having money.

For other idiomatic phrases in which a change in the preposition may affect meaning, see How come the clock isn't going? and "Some Troublesome Idiomatic Prepositions," a table at the back of the book.

contact

We never hear an objection to *contact* as a noun that has to do with being in touch, communicating, or associating with someone or something.

Many fourteenth-century Europeans came into contact with Asian civilization through the writings of Marco Polo.

Even its American sense of "an influential acquaintance or a connection with such a person" draws few complaints these days.

I have a contact or two in the governor's office.

It's contacts at the police department I'm interested in.

But many people are still pained to see or hear the word used as a verb in the sense of "to get in touch or communication with someone."

The Soviet defectors first contacted the Detroit police.

The distress of that "dwindling minority of conservatives" is nowhere better expressed than in Wilson Follett's *Modern American Usage.*

"Persons old enough to have been repelled by the verb *contact* when it was still a crude neologism may as well make up their minds that there is no way to arrest or reverse the tide of its popularity. Persons young enough to have picked up the word without knowing that anyone had reservations about it may as well make up their minds that a considerable body of their elders abominate it and would despise themselves if they succumbed to the temptation to use it. In this converted noun we have the perfect example of a coinage that has thirty or forty more years of intolerance to face from a dwindling minority of conservatives while enjoying the full approval—and, more important, the increasing use—of a growing majority that will eventually be unanimous. . . . "

A more moderate view not only of the use of _contact_ as a verb but of linguistic change in general appears in _A Dictionary of Contemporary American Usage,_ by Bergen Evans and Cornelia Evans.

"In the sense of to get in touch with a person (_I'll contact Jones and get his reaction_) _contact_ was once a fighting word. The purists, particularly English purists, made an issue of it. Here was an abomination, an Americanism hideously repugnant. But it was a useful figure (after all, _get in touch with_ is also a metaphor and several times as long) and very few business men even knew that the purists existed. Its fault was not so much its impropriety as that it was for a while grossly overworked. It is certainly accepted in spoken English today and will probably become the usual term in written English as well."

Contact is not the first or only English noun-turned-verb. Nor is it the first or only one whose crossover has met with resistance. For more on words that move freely from one part of speech to another, see "ICE CREAM YOUR KIDS TODAY WITH ROCKY ROAD."

continual or _continuous_?

Over the years usage guides have simply defined these two words, which have to do with repeated actions, processes, and conditions, as though the distinctions they set forth were being made by all speakers and writers of English—and if not, why not? _Continual,_ the definitions usually go, means "frequently repeated at short intervals"; _continuous,_ "extending without interruption in either space or time." Giving an example for each definition is no problem.

Poverty and continual bickering broke up the marriage.

The sky was a continuous expanse of blue.

But speakers and writers of English know, just as most dictionaries do, that those adjectives and their adverbial forms so overlap as to be virtually interchangeable. Does Montreal have a continually changing skyline or a continuously changing one? Does a lawbreaker continuously or continually violate the law? Do we continuously or continually repeat our mistakes? Is the basis that most things are done on nowadays continuous or continual?

Like other English words that refuse to behave as they are told to, _continual_ and _continuous_ must be used either loosely, without concern for precise meaning, or precisely, with no time wasted on loose meaning. Those who can tolerate a certain amount of ambiguity use the word that sounds and looks best on a particular occasion. Those who not only know exactly what both words mean, or once meant, but are certain that their listeners and readers do, too, will settle for nothing less than the "correct" word. And there is a third group, made up of those who know what the words mean, or once meant, but, because they are not certain that anyone else does, use less ambiguous substitutes when they want to be sure to be understood. These realists might sometimes use _periodic, recur-_

rent, repeated, or *intermittent* instead of *continual,* for example, and *constant, persistent, incessant, uninterrupted,* or *unbroken* instead of *continuous.*

contractions. See **Don't she know it'll be dark soon?**

contrast **or** *compare?* See *compare* or *contrast?*

convince **or** *persuade?*

In writing as well as speaking, and on formal as well as informal occasions, many people use these two verbs interchangeably, not knowing that they shouldn't. According to the traditional rule, *convince,* which implies overcoming a person's doubts about the truth of a statement or about the advisability of an action, should not be followed by an infinitive. It is therefore not ''correct'' to write or say:

> President Carter tried to convince the American people to conserve energy.

Instead, we should use either of these alternative constructions:

> President Carter tried to convince the American people that they should conserve energy.

> President Carter tried to convince the American people of the need to conserve energy.

On the other hand, *persuade,* which implies causing a person to do something, especially by reasoning, urging, or inducement, may be followed by an infinitive.

> President Carter tried to persuade the American people to conserve energy.

But this does not mean that *persuade* must be followed by an infinitive. According to the rule, it's ''correct'' to write or say:

> President Carter tried to persuade the American people that they should conserve energy.

> President Carter tried to persuade the American people of the need to conserve energy.

correlative constructions. See *as . . . as* or *so . . . as?*; **Either he or I am right; ''Electric shaver for women with delicate floral design on the handle''; Fish and chips is on the menu again; ''Neither fish nor flesh nor good red herring'';** *whether* or *whether or not?*

could, can, may, might. See **Can I borrow your lawn mower? Not if you might keep it.**

could care less. See *care less.*

couple, several, or *few*?   See *several, few,* or *couple*?

Covered with onions, relish, and ketchup, I ate a hot dog at the ballpark.

A modifier is said to "dangle" when it is not clearly related to another word or word group. Schoolteachers and grammar books generally warn against these two danglers:

1. A past or present participle, that is, a verb form ending in *-ed* or *-ing*. For example: We were *bored*. The play is *boring*.
2. A gerund, or a verb-derived noun ending in *-ing*. For example: *Boring* the audience seems to be the play's only purpose.

Dangling constructions are a problem, not so much because they truly get in the way of understanding but because they are likely to provoke laughter where none is intended. From the sentence "Covered with onions, relish, and ketchup, I ate a hot dog at the ballpark," who wouldn't know that what was covered with onions, relish, and ketchup was a hot dog, not the speaker or writer? Yet the picture conjured up is a comical one in which a hapless baseball fan, hot dog in hand, sits buried under a mound of white, green, and red glop. That's because instead of modifying *hot dog*, the participle phrase *covered with onions, relish, and ketchup* seems to modify *I*. To set the syntactic relationship to rights, the participle phrase must be shifted and several words added.

At the ballpark I ate a hot dog that was covered with onions, relish, and ketchup.

Even when they are not knee-slappers, most sentences with dangling constructions are apt to bring a smile to the lips of their readers or listeners, at least the grammar-conscious ones. Here are some in which a participle phrase dangles:

"Bent over the steering wheel, almost hugging it in his determination to get to the Turners quickly, his eyes were little blue chinks in a set face." (Doris Lessing, *The Grass Is Singing*)

"Wearied by a thousand textbooks and treatises, his [Flaubert's] statements still ring with artistic dedication and integrity." (John Updike, *New Yorker*)

"Watching the girl work the pump, her pulse quietened, her stomach grew quiet again." (Nina Bawden, *Familiar Passions*)

"Driven by blind homesickness that has been the sole, bitter fruit of boarding-school, her homebound train races her to a country-woman's grove." (Lyndall Gordon, *Virginia Woolf: A Writer's Life*)

And some in which a phrase containing a gerund dangles:

"While dutifully mowing the lawn, up-and-down, up-and-down, my vacant mind conjectured about how much fuller the divorce courts and the mental hospitals might be if everyone laid down plastic grass, and denied himself the regular therapy of cutting the domestic pasture at weekly, fortnightly, or where's-that-scythe intervals." (Patrick Ryan, *Smithsonian*)

"Lawyers and reporters had noticed earlier that <u>while speaking from the bench, Rehnquist's words</u> were slurred, a possible symptom of drug dependency." (*Washington Post*)

"<u>They</u> [bacteria] can enter the body through contaminated breaks in the skin or <u>by rubbing the eyes with contaminated fingers</u>." (*Paris Express-Progress*, Arkansas)

Yet many English-speakers believe that although these much-criticized constructions may not be "right," they fit into the language naturally and therefore ought not to be tinkered with. The sentence in Doris Lessing's novel, for instance, would need considerable restructuring to get rid of the dangling participle. To begin with, the initial participle phrase, *bent over the steering wheel*, would have to be given an explicitly stated subject—not the illogical *his eyes* but a noun or pronoun that could serve also as the subject of the principal verb. Other minor changes would have to be made as well.

Bent over the steering wheel, he almost hugged it in his determination to get to the Turners quickly, and his eyes became little blue chinks in a set face.

Another way to make the relationship between the sentence parts both clear and logical would be to turn the participle phrase into a subordinate clause, with *he* as its subject, and to leave *his eyes* as the subject of the principal verb.

As he bent over the steering wheel, almost hugging it in his determination to get to the Turners quickly, his eyes became little blue chinks in a set face.

Yet whatever either of these new versions gained in grammatical "correctness" it might lose in literary style, that is, the way Lessing chose to say what she wanted said.

So-called dangling participles and gerunds are probably as prevalent as they are because of their similarity to the widely accepted idiomatic expressions known as *absolute constructions*. These are also participle or gerund phrases, but they are not bound by the usual relations of syntax. That is, though they modify the rest of the sentence in a general way and are therefore logically connected with it, they are grammatically independent. For instance, "Judging by this month's sales, it's going to be a good year" does not mean that *it* or anything or anyone else is doing the judging; *judging by this month's sales* simply qualifies the main clause in an impersonal, generalized way. Here are some other absolute constructions to which few people would object:

Rents being what they are, more and more students are sharing apartments.

Considering (or *given*) *his qualifications*, it is not surprising that he got the assignment.

Airline maintenance will continue to decline, *all things being equal*.

Based on conversations with her grandfather, she decided to go through the trunk in the attic.

Generally speaking, now is the best time to travel to Indonesia.

Taxes will have to be prepared differently, *beginning next year.*

By doubling the recipe, it is possible to feed the whole group.

In going over the books again, the shortfall was discovered.

ANOTHER KIND OF MODIFIER whose dangling sometimes creates an unintentionally humorous effect is a phrase that contains an infinitive (usually the first-person singular present form of a verb preceded by the marker *to*). The same prescription for correcting a dangling participle or gerund applies to a dangling infinitive phrase as well: either give it an appropriate subject (one that also works for the verb in the main clause) or turn it into a subordinate clause, with a subject of its own. For instance:

To cut costs, lamb chops will no longer be trimmed in most butcher shops.

suggests—at least to strict grammarians—that lamb chops, not butcher shops, are cutting costs. Either of these changes would remove that impression:

To cut costs, most butcher shops will no longer trim lamb chops.

Because most butcher shops must cut costs, they will no longer trim lamb chops.

The following constructions, too, might be criticized as dangling infinitive phrases. Yet many English-speakers consider them acceptable impersonal constructions.

To determine the cause of the persistent pain, the goalie's arm will be X-rayed tomorrow.

The nozzles are inspected annually *to be sure that no toxins escape into the atmosphere.*

STILL ANOTHER KIND of dangling construction is a clause which, because it lacks a subject of its own, seems to modify the wrong part of the sentence. Like a dangling participle, gerund, or infinitive phrase, such an elliptical clause can create momentary confusion or amusement. Every day, for example, travelers must be taken aback by this sign at security checkpoints in American airports:

"Passengers may submit to physical search if desired."

But then, realizing that they are not likely to be the object of the inspectors' sudden desire, they probably simply supply the missing words in the elliptical clause:

Passengers may submit to physical search if *this is desired.* OR Passengers may be asked to submit to a physical search.

The unstated words in many expressions, of course, easily come to mind. For instance, no one has difficulty inferring that *you* is the subject in the sentence "Come here"; that *am* is the second verb in "He is as busy as I"; and that *it is* is the second subject and verb in ''The paint will be ready when needed.'' Yet such well-established constructions demand less mental restructuring on the part of the reader or listener than do dangling elliptical clauses like these:

When magnified more than 20 thousand times, we see single grains of pollen. (When they are magnified more than 20 thousand times, we see single grains of pollen.)

Do not step off the train while in motion. (Do not step off the train while it is in motion.)

Once at work, the Monday-morning stupor soon passes. (Once an employee is at work, the Monday-morning stupor soon passes.)

Sometimes, though, merely supplying a missing subject and another word or two in an elliptical clause is not enough.

If temporarily out of the country, the permanent resident's current address must be sent to the Commissioner of Immigration and Naturalization within ten days after returning. (A permanent resident who is temporarily out of the country must send his or her current address to the Commissioner of Immigration and Naturalization within ten days after returning.)

DANGLING MODIFIERS HAVE A LOT in common with misplaced sentence elements (see ''ELECTRIC SHAVER FOR WOMEN WITH DELICATE FLORAL DESIGN ON THE HANDLE'').

D

Dancing to a samba beat.

A good writer may use sentence fragments for variety and effect, but using sentence fragments does not make a writer good. In fact, most schoolteachers discourage their students from treating single words, phrases, and dependent clauses as if they were complete sentences, with a subject and a principal verb.

This rule on grammatically complete sentences does not ordinarily apply to certain exclamations, greetings, questions, answers, and transitional phrases.

Good grief! High time! Hello. When? Yesterday.

In thirty minutes. Now to the heart of the problem.

Nor to elliptical statements in which the subject or verb is clearly understood.

(You) come in. (Is there) no time?

However, few schoolteachers are likely to include "Dancing to a samba beat" among those exceptions. With its *-ing* ending, *dancing* might be the present participle of the verb *dance*. If so, the whole fragment might be a participial phrase in search of a principal verb or verb phrase and a subject.

Dancing to a samba beat, we watched the sun rise over Rio.

Or, because of the same *-ing* ending, *dancing* might be a gerund, that is, a word that looks like a verb but functions as a noun. In this case the fragment might be a gerund phrase which, together with a predicate, or principal verb, would form a complete sentence.

There is no better way to celebrate Mardi gras than by dancing to a samba beat.

In their staccato effect, sentence fragments suggest haste and even urgency, so they lend themselves to advertisements. This, for instance, is how the *New Yorker* tried to recruit *Fortune*'s advertisers:

"Sitting pretty. Your product, idea, service, nestled among family names, fine products, respected advertisers. What a place to be! Right up there with the best of the best. In The New Yorker. Yes, The New Yorker."

But ads are by no means the only kind of writing that conveys moods and ideas through nonsentences.

"Willie is up there. In the sun, or in the red light of the gasoline flare." (Robert Penn Warren, *All the King's Men*)

"Men, muscles without memory, minds dimmed, plodding, leaving blood-ied footprints in the dirt." (Maya Angelou, "No Longer Out of Africa")

"Operator error. I turn the level down." (Madison Smartt Bell, "Zero DB")

dangling elliptical clauses and gerund, infinitive, and participle phrases.   See **Covered with onions, relish, and ketchup, I ate a hot dog at the ballpark.**

data or *datum*?

The word *datum* comes from the Latin for "what is given." In the general sense of "something known or assumed" or "a fact from which conclusions can be inferred," most people use not that singular form but its plural, *data*. However, in the specialized sense of "a real or assumed thing, used as a basis for calculations or measurements," *datum* and its plural, *datums,* are used in the fields of engineering, geodesy, and geology.

datum line   datum plane   datum point

The surveyors compared the shoreline datums.

Data, not *datum* or *datums,* then, is the word we most often see and hear today. Because it is a plural form, *data* ought, strictly speaking, to be used with a plural verb. And it often is, especially in references to technical subjects.

Data on AC system interconnectors were revised.

Recent data on the nocturnal serenades of toadfish have been sent to a Cornell University laboratory.

Outside the scientific community, *data* is likely to be considered a collective noun—that is, a noun which, like *jury* or *faculty,* is singular in form but denotes a collection of separate people or items. So when the facts or figures from which conclusions can be drawn are thought of as a whole, *data* is likely to take a singular verb.

Reliable data on AIDS cases is hard to come by.

But when the facts or figures in the collection are thought of individually, *data* often takes a plural verb.

The data are, for the most part, unreliable.

Many of the data were supplied by amateur astronomers.

For other loanwords from Latin, and some from Greek, that have more than one plural form in English, see FEW PHENOMENONS ARE MORE EYE-CATCHING THAN STADIA PACKED WITH ALUMNUSES WAVING GLADIOLI.

Dear Mr. Webster.

Americans turn to a dictionary to find out how words are spelled, divided at the ends of lines, and pronounced; what they mean; how they are used; and how they got into the language. Many look upon theirs as a timeless, authoritative

reference work, the product of distant intellectual exertion. Others, however, have an intense personal relationship with theirs, considering it a kind of relative or close friend with whom they go through good periods followed by bad. One day they are elated to discover that *doodlebug* is an Americanism for *ant lion* or that *clown* originally meant "a peasant or farmer." The next day they are disappointed at not finding a word they are looking up or annoyed by the entry they find it in. Then, depending on the seriousness of the irregularity, warm approval becomes either good-natured teasing or a stern lecture.

These lexicographic irregulars are apt to think of the author of their dictionary as "Webster" or "Mr. Webster," even though the work itself lists the staff that compiled it. If they don't use Webster's first name in their monologues, it's probably not because of reticence but because of poor memory: they simply can't recall whether it's Daniel or Noah. (It's Noah, whose *American Dictionary of the English Language* was first published in 1828. Daniel, a statesman, lawyer, and orator who lived about the same time, used words well but didn't spend years trying to help others do so.)

Sometimes they write to Mr. Webster, or at least about him. Richard J. Ferris, the chairman of United Airlines, for instance, said, in an editorial in *United*, the company's magazine:

"The world is rich with entrepreneurs: people—Mr. Webster says—who organize and manage business undertakings, assuming the risks for the sake of profits. As important as entrepreneurs are, however, the world, especially the corporate world, also needs *intrapreneurs*—people not yet recognized in Mr. Webster's dictionary.

"Intrapreneurs are entrepreneurs who work within existing large organizations. . . ."

The sportswriter Ron Thomas began an article on San Francisco's basketball team like this:

"In the next revision of Webster's Dictionary, surely the definition of schizophrenia will be changed to 'The Golden State Warriors.'

"How else can one explain the worst team in the NBA soundly defeating the Philadelphia 76ers and the champion Los Angeles Lakers in back-to-back home games?"

And in a gift carton of "Royal Oranges" from its orchards, the Oregon firm of Harry and David enclosed a flier titled "Good Grief, Mr. Webster! Have You No Soul?" The point, of course, is that such delicious fruit calls for a hymn, not a straightforward definition.

Whether in letters to the publishers of the dictionaries themselves, in letters to the editors of magazines and newspapers, in books and articles, in lectures, or by other means, English-speakers state how they feel about the use of new words or new meanings for established words. This process of word formation is known as *coinage* or *neologism*. (The combining form *neo-* means "new"; *-logy*, a combining form going back to *logos*, the Greek word for *word* itself, means "a specific kind of speaking"; and the noun-forming suffix *-ism* means "the act, practice, or result of"—in this case, of creating a new word.)

Those in favor of the process are apt to describe coinages or neologisms as "worthy and useful additions to the lexicon." Besides *intrapreneur* and *intrapreneurship*, the thousands of candidates brought to Mr. Webster's attention to fill gaps in the language include:

> *hir* (a genderless third-person singular pronoun meaning "his and her" or "his or her," as in "each guest said *hir* goodbyes")

> *three-martini lunch* (a business lunch written off as a tax deduction, from the words *three, martini,* and *lunch*)

> *goo-goo* (a term used in Chicago politics to denote "a good government white liberal")

> *revulate* (a verb meaning "to revolve and rotate at the same time")

> *postjudice* (the opposite of *prejudice*)

On the other hand, those opposed to any change in the language usually qualify a coinage or neologism as *barbarous, bastard, casually conceived, hideous, outrageous,* or the like. Adjectives expressing reproachful contempt, though, are not the only ploy that traditionalists hope will turn away new usages they disapprove of. Another is to deny that the upstart words or senses exist. For example, Laurence Lafore prohibited students in his history classes at Swarthmore College from using certain words, phrases, and usages in their papers. His list, published in *Harper's Magazine* in 1957 under the title "Jargon Control Program," contained this entry:

"meaningful (This word does not exist.)"

But of course *meaningful* exists. *The Oxford English Dictionary* illustrates its definition ("full of meaning or expression; significant") with three nineteenth-century examples, the earliest from 1852.

And, no matter how devoutly many standpatters wish it weren't so:

> *hopefully* now conveys the sense of "it is to be hoped" (as in "Hopefully a cure will be found"), as well as "in a hopeful manner." (See HOPEFULLY.)

> *finalize*, which came into the language in the first quarter of the twentieth century, has taken its place alongside countless other *-ize* verbs, including *humanize* (about 1600), *familiarize* (early 1700s), and *regularize* (about 1830). (See APOLOGIZE, SÍ; FINALIZE, NO.)

> *like* is now, as it was in Shakespeare's time, used as a conjunction meaning "in the way that" or "as" ("Did the ending turn out like you expected?"). (See LIKE OR AS, AS IF?)

This book deals with dozens of other words and usages that have made their way into the language despite efforts to stop them. And, for a general account of the purists' attitude toward changes in the meanings of words, see FOR A GIRL HE'S QUITE MATURE.

Those who demand that dictionaries bar certain coinages seem to believe that English must be protected against the larger body of people who speak and write

it. Even if an American or British dictionary publisher saw its mission as that of a police officer, much as the French and Spanish academies do, it would be powerless to stop the natural development of the language. (For that matter, as critics in France and Spain ruefully point out, neither the French nor the Spanish academy is having much success in warding off change in its own language.)

Dictionary makers may not be infallible, but neither are they capricious. Regardless of the pleading for a new word, sense, or usage—or the fulminating against one—most of them study their citation, or quotation, files very carefully before issuing an update or a revision. First of all, they want to weed out *nonce words,* that is, words coined and used for a single or particular occasion. Let's suppose that an article on real estate said, "The housing market is rapidly becoming empty-nestized" (meaning that couples whose children have grown up and left home are looking for smaller places to live). General English-language dictionaries would not consider this single citation reason enough to include the verb *empty-nestize.* Instead they would ordinarily enter the word only after collecting a number of citations for it, over several years, from different sources, and in the broadest possible geographic area.

The simplest way to add a word or phrase to the language is to invent it, use it, and hope that others will find it worth keeping around. So far the nineteenth-century English writer Lewis Carroll has been quite successful. *White Knight,* the name of Alice's protector in *Through the Looking-Glass,* for instance, has been widely applied to any rescuer; in the 1970s the term *white knight* began to appear frequently in American newspapers with a broader meaning: "a company that prevents a takeover, viewed as unfavorable, of another company by offering better terms for a merger with it." Some coinages, however, relate to specific times. The American writer Tom Wolfe coined *Me Decade,* in 1976, to characterize the decade of the 1970s as one of narcissism, self-indulgence, and a lack of social concern in many people, especially the young.

A number of words and phrases used in English are derived from the names of people or places, whether real-life or fictional. For instance, *georgette* (a thin, durable, slightly crinkled fabric used for women's dresses and blouses) was named after Georgette de la Plante, a Parisian modiste. (For others, see JOHN BULL AND JOHN HANCOCK ARE NOT JUST ANY JOHNS.)

The profusion of prefixes, suffixes, and combining forms, together with the attraction one English word has for another, invites coinage. For instance:

> Any novel or movie can have a *sequel,* that is, a work which is complete in itself but continues a story begun in an earlier work. And the prefix *pre-* means "earlier than" or "prior to." So why not apply *prequel* to a novel or movie that gives the beginning of a story told in a work already released? That's just what a *Los Angeles Times* writer did in 1986, in a column on entertainment sidelights.

> " 'Prizzi's Family,' a 'prequel' to 'Prizzi's Honor,' will hit the bookstores this fall, but author Richard Condon is keeping the screenplay all to himself—for now."

The suffix *-ism* sometimes conveys the notion of devotion to something of one's own, often carried to irrational excess. *Nationalism,* for example,

was coined in the mid-nineteenth century to denote devotion to one's nation, but one of its current connotations is that of narrow or jingoist patriotism. Similarly, words like *racism, sexism,* and *ageism* carry the implication that the devotion to one's race, sex, and age group is accompanied by discrimination against other races, members of the opposite sex, and older people. Any number of coinages, such as *speciesism* (devotion to one's species), are possible. Edward M. Kennedy, Jr., in asking Congress to ban job discrimination against the disabled (he had lost his right leg to cancer), was quoted by the Associated Press as having said, " '*Handicapism* is more profound than racism or sexism.' " Young Kennedy did not, of course, take *handicapism* to mean "devotion to one's handicap," but rather "discrimination against the handicapped."

The noun-forming suffix *-ability* is extremely versatile (as is *-able,* the adjective-forming suffix it corresponds to). Besides producing such words as *durability, wearability,* and *roadability,* we can, for instance, tack the suffix onto the verb set *bounce back* (meaning "to recover strength, spirits, good humor, and so on, quickly"), so as to talk about "the *bounceback-ability* of laid-off workers."

(For more on how prefixes, suffixes, and combining forms can create new words or change the meanings of existing words, see WHO NEEDS A RABBIT'S FOOT MORE: AN UNLUCKY PERSON OR A LUCKLESS ONE?)

Over the centuries slang has provided a steady supply of colorful new words or new senses for established words.

Calaboose, can, clink, cooler, hoosegow, jug, and *slammer* are but a few of the words for *jail* that came into the language as slang.

Headhunter is an established English word denoting a member of any of certain primitive tribes who remove the heads of slain enemies and preserve them as trophies. In twentieth-century slang the word refers to an agent or agency that specializes in recruiting executives or highly skilled personnel (as in "Headhunters are busier than ever at high-tech conventions").

And how are television performers fed the lines they are supposed to speak? By reading a board or placard known in characteristically irreverent slang as an *idiot board* (or *idiot card*).

(For a fuller discussion of slang, see JOBBED IN A HUMONGOUS SCAM, THE TWEAKED-OUT MOBSTER EXCLAIMED, "PEACHY-KEEN!")

Since the middle of the twentieth century, a huge and constantly growing vocabulary has been needed to keep up with the rapid advances in science and technology. True, we still use words like *atom* (from the fifteenth century), *telescope* (from the seventeenth), and *stroboscope* (from the nineteenth), but to them we have added countless new terms and new applications for established ones. Take *particle,* for example. The *OED* gives a citation from 1380 for the sense of "a small part, portion, of division of a whole," and one from 1398 for

the sense of ''a very minute portion or quantity of matter; the smallest sensible, component part of any aggregation of mass.'' But *high-energy particle,* denoting an atomic or subatomic particle with energy greater than a few hundred kilovolts, didn't enter the language until the twentieth century. Nor did *quark, baryon,* or *meson* (a quark is any of three hypothetical particles postulated as forming the building blocks of baryons and mesons and accounting in theory for their properties).

Not long after taking the first step on the moon, in 1969, Neil Armstrong gained a place in American dictionaries, and so did *moonwalk* and *mascon,* the name for a concentration of very dense material beneath the moon's surface. Both of these nouns follow well-established patterns for forming new words in English. *Moonwalk* is made up of two other words: *moon* and *walk.* (For more on compounds, see UPSTART NAME-DROPPERS USUALLY GET THE COLD SHOULDER.) And *mascon* is formed from the first letters in the words <u>*mass*</u> and <u>*concentra-*</u><u>*tion.*</u> (For more on acronyms, see NASA's LOX NEEDS NO BAGELS.)

Although the verb *compute* was used early in the seventeenth century (in connection with calculating, or determining a number, amount, or the like by reckoning), the computer age began in the twentieth century. Not suprisingly, therefore, some of the terms widely used today are entirely new. *Byte* (meaning ''a string of binary units, usually eight, operated on as a basic unit by a digital computer''), for example, is an arbitrary formation, perhaps derived from *bite.* Another word that may have gone into the coinage is *bit* (''a single digit in a binary number system''), which in turn was formed by combining the first and last parts of two other words: *b(inary)* + *(dig)it.* (For more on blends, see OXBRIDGE WORKAHOLICS NEVER STOP FOR BRUNCH.)

Many computer terms, though, are not new words but extensions of established ones. Here are a few, with their newly acquired senses:

> *boot* (a clipped form of *bootstrap,* having to do with loading an entire routine into main memory by loading several instructions that bring that routine in)
>
> *cursor* (a movable, flashing indicator on a computer terminal screen, marking the place for entering or altering a character)
>
> *edit* (to make changes, additions, or deletions in a file containing a program and/or data)
>
> *information* (data processed by a computer and produced as output in a form meaningful to a user)
>
> *load* (to transfer a program and/or data into main memory from an auxiliary storage device, such as a disk)
>
> *memory* (a device that can store data recorded in it and from which the data can be retrieved)
>
> *menu* (a displayed list of the various functions a person can select to perform on a terminal)

mouse (a small, hand-held device that can be moved over the surface of a tablet, causing the cursor to move to a corresponding point on the terminal screen)

read (to sense the data stored on a device)

routine (a set of instructions to solve a specified problem, such as those to find the square root of a number)

Once a word has entered the language, whether by coinage or by any other means, there is of course no way to predict how long it will be around or whether it will take on new meanings before it falls into disuse. In the electronic age, stock-market quotations are no longer recorded on paper tape fed into a telegraphic device known as a *ticker*. Yet well into the 1980s, astronauts back from outer space, Olympic medal winners, and other heroes were still being cheered amid a blizzard of paper as they made their way up Broadway in a *ticker-tape parade*.

differ from or differ with?

Differ from ordinarily has to do with being unlike, with not being the same.

Veneering differs from marquetry.

How can your ideas differ so much from mine?

The phrase also conveys the notion of being of opposite or unlike opinions, of disagreeing.

The secretary of state differed from the secretary of defense on NATO's role in the maneuvers.

But it is *differ with* that usually suggests disagreement.

The secretary of state differed with the secretary of defense on NATO's role in the maneuvers.

I'm sorry to differ with you, but that's not been my experience.

See also How come the clock isn't going? and "Some Troublesome Idiomatic Prepositions," a table at the back of the book.

different from, different than, or different to?

Impatient with argument, many grammar books and usage guides simply tell their readers to say and write *different from*. Strunk and White, for example, quickly dispose of the matter in their *different than* entry:

"Here logic supports established usage: one thing differs *from* another, hence, *different from*. Or other *than*, unlike."

In simple comparisons *different from* and *differently from* indeed have an edge over *different than* and *differently than*, especially in formal speech and writing, but both sets of expressions are established American idioms.

A sphere is different *from* (or *than*) a circle.

Having an idea is far different *from* (or *than*) carrying it out.

Your plan is quite different *from* (or *than*) mine.

Roquefort is ripened differently *from* (or *than*) Limburger.

Many people prefer *than* to *from*, especially in a comparison in which the adjective *different* is part of an adverbial clause, given either in full or with several words missing but understood.

Nowadays children talk to their parents in a different way than they did years ago.

How different small-town life was in the 1920s than [it was] in the 1970s!

In Britain *different from* is the usual form. Though considered incorrect by many, *different to* is also widely used in writing as well as speech.

"When Helen sits sewing, she takes an exemplary posture quite different to heroic statues." (Lyndall Gordon, *Virginia Woolf: A Writer's Life*)

With clear disapproval, the Oxford-educated lexicographer Eric Partridge noted the occurrence of *different than* "more and more frequently in the New York daily and weekly Press." This upstart New Yorkism goes back some three and a half centuries in Britain, *The Oxford English Dictionary* giving this citation from 1644:

"We make use of them in a quite different manner than we did in the beginning."

The *OED* notes that the use of *different than* had been recorded for such well-known British writers as Coleridge, De Quincey, Carlyle, and Thackeray. Yet in recent years the reimportation of this construction has been fought off valiantly on British beaches.

For more on the use of *than* in comparisons, see Kilimanjaro is taller than any mountain in Africa; for a discussion of the form, or case, of pronouns following *than*, Is it me you like better than her?

Din-din, then beddy-bye.

In the first few years of their lives, most children are taught a variety of the language that acquaints them with the grammatical structures, vocabulary, and pronunciation they are expected to forget in the next few. These are the main characteristics of *baby talk:*

Its delivery is slow, singsong, and high-pitched. Most words have lengthened vowels (*b-a-a-d*), and some are given new consonants (*kiss* becoming *tiss*, for example).

Pronouns, auxiliary verbs, prepositions, conjunctions, and articles are dropped. So are inflections that indicate verb tense and possession.

Baby want sleep?

Daddy here, Tweetie.

Now milk.

No, Baby. Mommy beads.

Words and word groups are usually repeated.

Nice doggie, nice doggie.

Say hello, Baby. Say hello.

To express both smallness and tenderness, virtually every word that can take a diminutive gets an *ee*-sounding suffix.

Bobbie mommy duckie kitty birdie

tummy (from *stomach*)

Whenever possible, root syllables or other word elements are doubled to form new words. Sometimes slight changes are made in this reduplication process.

din-din (from *dinner*) *bye-bye dada*

lo-lo (from *pillow*) *night-night nighty-night*

itty-bitty itsy-bitsy

teeny-weeny teensy-weensy

Having been ridiculed out of baby talk by the time they enter school, most children quickly master the variety of English that is spoken by the adults of their community. For years they make do with the limited stock of words that indicate smallness. After exhausting standard adjectives like *small, tiny, minute,* and *minuscule,* and nouns like *soupçon* and *smidgen,* they turn to the few diminutives appropriate to the world of grown-ups. For example:

Those formed with the suffix *-y* or *-ie,* including *Jimmy* (President Carter's official first name, which he preferred to his legal name, *James Earl, Jr.*); *Jerry* (President Ford's nickname); *Ronnie* (President Reagan's nickname); *Teddy* (Senator Edward Kennedy's nickname)

Those formed with the suffixes *-kin* (*lambkin, manikin*); *-let* (*playlet, booklet, piglet*); *-ling* (*princeling, duckling*); and *-ette* (*dinette, statuette*)

Those formed with the prefix *mini-* (*minibus, minicomputer, miniseries, miniskirt*)

And then to words with special diminutive senses, such as *chick, cub, kid, pup,* and *hillock.*

From time to time, however, the pull of their first language becomes so strong that adults lapse into baby talk. With a limitless supply of diminutives and reduplications suddenly at their command, they:

watch *telly* (a Briticism).

sleep in *jams* (or *jam-jams*).

wear *grubbies* around the house.

invite friends over for a *drinkie-poo*.

make as few social *booboos* as possible.

avoid insider stock trading and other *no-nos*.

Indeed, few Americans are surprised to hear a corporate executive end a telephone conversation with *bye-bye*.

disinterested or *uninterested?*

Uninterested means ''not interested'' or ''indifferent.''

> "Let us see what Hitler thought of the masses he moved and how he did the moving. The first principle from which he started was a value judgment: the masses are utterly contemptible. They are incapable of abstract thinking and <u>uninterested</u> in any fact outside the circle of their immediate experience." (Aldous Huxley, *Brave New World Revisited*)

Making *disinterested* synonymous with *uninterested* may seem like an innovation, but it is in fact a revival of an obsolete usage. For many years, while its sense of ''indifferent'' was out of fashion, *disinterested* was used to mean ''not influenced by personal interest or selfish motives; impartial; unbiased.''

> "Great passions may give us this quickened sense of life, ecstasy and sorrow of love, the various forms of enthusiastic activity, <u>disinterested</u> or otherwise, which come naturally to many of us." (Walter Pater, *The Renaissance*)

Now that the earlier meaning of *disinterested* (''indifferent'') has regained currency, *uninterested* has a rival, especially in informal speech and writing. But because the other meaning of *disinterested* (''impartial'') has not yet fallen into disuse, listeners and readers are sometimes left in doubt. For example, does:

The contestants played before three disinterested judges.

mean that the three judges were impartial or indifferent? So, to be sure of being understood, some speakers and writers replace *disinterested* with either *uninterested* or *indifferent* or with *impartial, unbiased,* or a similar word.

One reason for the popularity of *disinterested* may be that two nouns are currently available to indicate ''a lack of interest'': *disinterest* and *disinterestedness*. Just as we say ''Most Americans are remarkably *disinterested* in atonal music,'' we might say ''Most Americans show a remarkable *disinterest* (or *disinterestedness*) in atonal music.''

For *uninterested*, on the other hand, there are only the rarely used *uninterestedness* and the even less common *uninterest*. That is, we might well say ''Most Americans are remarkably *uninterested* in atonal music,'' but are unlikely to say ''Most Americans show a remarkable *uninterestedness* (or *uninter-*

est) in atonal music." Indeed, the noun *uninterest* is virtually limited to understatements in which, for effect, something is expressed by a negation of the contrary. For instance: "The choice of legal counsel is a matter not of *uninterest* to me."

Disinterested and *uninterested*, then, have the same base (*interest*) and their prefixes (*dis-* and *un-*) both mean "not." Yet the two adjectives are not interchangeable at all levels of usage. (For other words with rival prefixes or suffixes, see WHO NEEDS A RABBIT'S FOOT MORE: AN UNLUCKY PERSON OR A LUCKLESS ONE?)

Don't she know it'll be dark soon?

Without contractions, English speech would sound like the reading of a will. Breakfast conversations would go something like this:

Dick: Well, look *who is* here! *You are* up early. *How did* you sleep?

Jane: I *did not. I am* dying for breakfast. *Where is* the coffee? *I would* sell our first child for a cup.

Dick: *It will* be ready in a minute. *It is* perking. *What will* you have with it?

Jane: It *does not* matter. *Anything will* be fine, as long as *it is* quick. The *plumber is* due any minute.

No English-speaker, however determined to be "correct," is likely to get through a day without shortening two or more neighboring words into one. When a spoken contraction is represented in writing, an apostrophe takes the place of the omitted sound or sounds—and therefore the letter or letters that would appear in the standard spelling. Regardless of the number of omissions, a word ordinarily takes only one apostrophe (for instance *shan't*, not *sha'n't*, for *shall not*), though it is possible to imagine two (*couldn't've*, say, for *could not have*). Unlike many abbreviations, contractions are not followed by a period unless they end a sentence. (For a discussion of abbreviations, see AN LL.D. KO'D A BRIG. GEN. AT A BYOB PARTY.)

Some contractions—*o'clock* (from *of the clock*), *ma'am* (from *madam*), and *ne'er-do-well* (from *never-do-well*), for example—are so well established that English-speakers seldom think of the words they stand for. But by far the largest number occur, in mix-and-match fashion, in pronoun-verb combinations and in verb phrases (a main verb plus an auxiliary verb or verbs that help complete the meaning).

Perhaps the most common are constructions in which pronouns accompany present-tense forms of the verb *be* (as in "*I'm* glad *you're* here"). These forms are present also in verb phrases in which *be* is an auxiliary ("*He's leaving* tomorrow"; "*What's going on* here?").

I'm you're he's she's it's we're they're

who's who're what's what're

Have, will, and *would* are among the other auxiliary verbs frequently used in contractions (as in "*You've* given me an idea"; "*It'll* be dark soon"; "*They'd* rather stay another week").

I've you've he's she's it's we've they've who's

I'll you'll he'll she'll it'll we'll they'll who'll

I'd you'd he'd she'd it'd we'd they'd who'd

Conservative grammarians would like to limit the use of some of these contractions. For example, they have no objection to *he's, she's, it's, who's,* and *what's* standing for *he is, she is, it is, who is,* and *what is* (as in "*He's* coming tomorrow"), but they wish the forms were not used for *he has, she has, it has, who has,* and *what has* (as in "*He's* already arrived"). They would also prefer to see *they'll* used for *they will,* not for *they shall.* In the United States at least, such distinctions are now all but ignored. (For more on the *shall-will* controversy, see SHALL YOU RETURN? WE SHOULD LIKE THAT.) One point everyone agrees on, however, is that the contraction *it's,* standing for *it is* or *it has,* ought not to be confused with the possessive pronoun *its* (see ITS OR IT'S?).

In speech, the adverb *not* immediately following a verb is almost always contracted. Otherwise, our conversations would be filled with stilted statements like "I have not a clue," instead of "I haven't a clue"; and "Will you not be there?," instead of "Won't you be there?" These are among the negative contractions we hear and use every day:

isn't aren't hasn't haven't (For another, disputed contraction of *am not, is not, are not, has not,* and *have not,* see AIN'T.)

doesn't don't wasn't weren't didn't hadn't mustn't can't

won't shan't couldn't wouldn't shouldn't

Don't—a shortened form of *do not*—is used today only for the singular and plural of the first and second persons, and for the plural of the third person.

I (or we) don't want to go.

Don't you expect to get the job?

They (or *Betty and Fred* or *The plumbers*) don't plan to come tomorow.

Yet this grammatical rule on subject-verb agreement is often disregarded. Even people who would not think of saying *he go, she go, it go,* for instance, say *he don't, she don't, it don't.* This use of *don't* for the singular of the third person is now considered nonstandard, that is, not conforming to the standards of the language variety of educated speakers. It was standard until the twentieth century, and even today *don't,* like *ain't,* is often used to achieve a desired effect (as in "It don't mean a thing!").

CONTRACTIONS, WE ARE OFTEN TOLD, are appropriate in speech but not in writing—at least not in anything approaching formal writing. Plays and other works of fiction in which dialogue is represented, yes; but not creative writing or expository prose. Not even business letters.

True, writers of textbooks and scholarly works have traditionally avoided contractions, and many novelists and short-story writers have preferred not to use them in narrative passages. Yet, with the fading of the once-sharp distinctions between speech and writing, more and more shortened forms of words and phrases appear in print nowadays. And not only in newspaper and magazine articles, but also in works of fiction and nonfiction—wherever writers choose to address their readers in a relaxed, somewhat informal way.

> "When the president told her she <u>hadn't</u> got the director's job <u>she'd</u> applied for, and offered her the assistant's job, he said he knew <u>she'd</u> be happy that <u>they'd</u> offered the job to a woman, as if he believed <u>she</u> were applying for the job only as a gesture, as a member of a class, interchangeable with any other member, and so it <u>didn't</u> matter that she <u>didn't</u> get the job herself, since it existed for her <u>only</u> symbolically." (Mary Gordon, *Men and Angels*)

> "<u>I've</u> always assumed that one day it suddenly occurred to Napoleon to invade Russia. I grant there are those deliberate types who force themselves to sit down some morning at age thirty-five and decide at what age they will retire, and where they will go on to live and die, but I suspect they <u>aren't</u> numerous; besides, it is just a little un-American, <u>isn't</u> it?" (William F. Buckley, Jr., "The Sporting Scene," *New Yorker*)

> "Corporate raider T. Boone Pickens Jr. said he withdrew a $300 million tender offer for 20 million Diamond Shamrock Corp. shares, but whether the Dallas-based energy concern has permanently foiled Mr. Pickens's takeover attempt <u>isn't</u> clear." (Karen Blumenthal, *Wall Street Journal*)

Instead of being regarded as either-or constructions (always in or always out), contractions, then, are frequently placed where they fall naturally or where the rhythm of a particular sentence or passage calls for them. It is one thing to write:

> This *was*, of course, *not* true of the vast majority of American corporations.

and another:

> This *wasn't* true, of course, of most American corporations.

In Bernard Malamud's novel *The Fixer*, for instance, these two passages appear on the same page:

> "Marfa wept miserably. Ivan Semyonovitch's eyes clouded and he turned away and wiped them on his coat sleeve. Yakov felt like crying but <u>couldn't</u>."

> "The Investigating Magistrate glanced quickly into Marfa's bedroom and stopped at the locked door of the other room as if he were listening, but <u>did not</u> try the knob."

And in a London *Sunday Times* theater review, John Peter said of James Baldwin's *The Amen Corner*, with Carmen Munroe as Sister Margaret:

> "In the theatre, we wonder whether <u>she's</u> sincere, or whether <u>she's</u> settling for love because deep down she knows that <u>it's</u> too late. We <u>do not</u> know, because I suspect Baldwin <u>doesn't</u> know."

Even though contractions are more common in everyday speech than in writing, public speakers—aware of the occasion, the audience, the flow of their sentences—can be as selective as writers in telescoping words. After the 1986 economic summit, in Tokyo, the U.S. secretary of state spoke to reporters about the statement on terrorism that had just been adopted. According to *Time*, an "ebullient" George Shultz said this is what the declaration would mean to Libya's Muammar el-Qaddafi:

> "You've had it, pal. You are isolated. You are recognized as a terrorist."

But, as might have been expected, President Franklin D. Roosevelt used a consistently formal style in his inaugural address of 1933.

> "We do not distrust the future of essential democracy. The people of the United States have not failed. In their need they have registered a mandate that they want direct, vigorous action. They have asked for discipline and direction under leadership. They have made me the present instrument of their wishes. In the spirit of the gift I take it."

double negatives.   See **Not for nothing does Paris claim to be the world's most beautiful city.**

double possessives.   See **Wedding bells are breaking up that old gang of me.**

double talk.   See **"War is peace."**

Drink the water if you dare.

Most people who use a construction like "Drink the water if you dare" probably assume that a listener or reader can easily supply what is missing. Many listeners or readers cheerfully do so, in any of a number of ways. For example:

> Drink the water if you dare (to drink the water).
>
> Drink the water if you dare (to drink it).
>
> Drink the water if you dare (to do so).
>
> Drink the water if you dare (to).

Traditional grammarians, however, are likely to criticize that elliptical construction. To them, it is not enough for a verb to be expressed in one clause and thus to be clearly understood in another: the verb must be repeated in the infinitive form or another infinitive given in its place.

Even if the implied *to* in the last example were expressed, some conservatives would object to its taking the place of an infinitive. That's because they do not accept two generally accepted notions: first, that the preposition *to* signals a following infinitive form of a verb but is not an inseparable part of it; and, second, that both the preposition *to* and the flat, or *to*-less, infinitive can stand alone. They seem not to hear or see elliptical constructions like these, which are used every day at all levels of usage:

They were invited to attend the symposium but do not plan to.

The coach answered only the questions he wanted to.

Please stay longer if you'd like to.

Me join a circus? I'd love to.

(For the other half of the disputed usage—the flat infinitive standing alone—see "SHOP MACY'S AND SAVE.")

Even some people who accept elliptical constructions like "Drink the water if you dare" are uncomfortable with certain other verbs used in that way. They wish they didn't, but they can't help considering sentences of this kind unrefined:

Keep the book if you want.

Please stay longer if you'd like.

Is it too much to ask for *to* at the end? they wonder.

due to

Nobody objects to a sentence like "Double-digit inflation was due to the high cost of imported oil," because it conforms to a traditional rule of grammar. Here an adjective phrase introduced by *due to* modifes the noun *inflation*.

But some people do indeed object to a sentence like "Due to the high cost of imported oil, inflation soared into the double-digit range," because here *due to* introduces an adverbial phrase that modifies the verb *soared*. Yet, over the critics' protests, speakers and writers of English, in both the United States and Britain, frequently use that construction.

"Due to family circumstances, we rarely met, but she wrote often and sent me small gifts." (Truman Capote, *Music for Chameleons*)

"As late as the following morning, small paragraphs would even appear in newspapers having space to fill due to a hiatus in elections, fiendish crimes, and the Korean war . . . ." (Shirley Hazzard, *The Transit of Venus*)

"P.T.A. Representative Ann Kahn said that due to testing, elementary school curriculums are now concentrating on test scores—to the exclusion of basics like good writing." (*Time*)

"Due to the seasonal nature of its business, the Company issues commercial paper or obtains notes to meet short-term interim financing requirements." (Scott, Foresman and Company, *Annual Report*)

"Due to the existence of smear in our perception of sounds, the presence of a certain amount of slur in our pronunciation serves an essential purpose, that of modifying sounds so as to let us know what is coming next or what has gone before." (Robert A. Hall, *Linguistics and Your Language*)

"However, last Sunday, due to an error at the telephone exchange, the tape was not changed." ("What Was On . . .," London *Evening News*)

In each of the examples given above, the critics of the adverbial use of *due to* would substitute *because of* or *owing to*. The latter choice is odd, since *owing* followed exactly the same route as *due:* it started out as a participle that could modify only nouns or pronouns, then became so detached that it can now introduce an adverbial modifier. The only difference between the two phrases is that *owing to* has gained unqualified acceptance in this sense, whereas *due to* still has a way to go. Though it seems a bit formal to many Americans, *owing to* comes easily to Britons—like the schoolboy who, when asked where elephants are found, is said to have replied, "Owing to their large size, elephants are seldom lost."

Those who want to be above criticism in their use of *due to* might apply the "*caused by* or *attributable to* test." Can either of these adjective modifiers replace *due to* without interrupting the flow of the sentence or changing its meaning? For example:

The four-car collision was due to icy streets.

would pass the test. However:

Due to icy streets, four cars collided at Main and Prospect.

would not read smoothly or make sense either as:

Caused by icy streets, four cars collided at Main and Prospect.

or as:

Attributable to icy streets, four cars collided at Main and Prospect.

So the original sentence must be rewritten, either by changing *Due to* to *Because of* or to the now-acceptable *Owing to*, or by introducing a noun to which *due to* can be attached.

E

each other or *one another*?

The compound pronouns *each other* and *one another*, meaning "each one the other," indicate a reciprocal relationship or action. Both are frequently used as the object of a verb or a preposition.

The students photographed each other.

After the trip, members of the tour wrote to one another.

Ordinarily neither phrase is used as the subject of a verb. That is, instead of "The students asked what each other were photographing," we are more likely to say, and especially to write, "Each of the students asked what the other was photographing."

Although the possessive form of *each other* and *one another* is in the singular, a plural noun usually follows.

In time, couples generally come to share each other's views.

The lottery winners asked for one another's autographs.

SOME PEOPLE INSIST that *each other* applies only to two:

Jack and Jill helped each other up the hill.

and *one another* only to three or more:

Flopsy, Mopsy, and Cotton-tail helped one another gather blackberries.

Why they do so is puzzling, because the rule neither fills a need in the language nor reflects usage, past or present.

"The plan is unusual with an introductory recitativo, mainly lyrical, leading to a set of variations, strongly contrasted with each other...." (Edward Greenfield, London *Times*)

"The quality of students' relationships with each other is certainly as important as their relationship with their teacher." (Herb Kohl, *Teacher* magazine)

" 'A restaurant in New York that's their hangout. Where she and Bob go when they want to have an affair with one another.' " (Hortense Calisher, *On Keeping Women*)

"Kate and Evelyn liked one another very much." (Margaret Drabble, *The Middle Ground*)

What is surprising is not that the distinction between *each other* and *one another* is generally ignored but that it has such committed supporters. Eric Partridge's 1973 revision of *Usage and Abusage*, for example, asserts:

"There is a rule—a very simple rule: *each other* applies to two persons, animals, or things; *one another* to three or more. This constitutes, not a mere grammarians' *ex cathedra* but a practical utility; for instance, if the rule is observed, one can be in no doubt that 'They hit each other' refers to two persons, whereas 'They hit one another' refers to three or more. Obviously, to follow the rule is to ensure economy of words."

The style guides of the *New York Times* and the Associated Press also seem to favor economy of words over certain understanding. As though the distinction they make is apparent to everyone, both state:

"Two persons look at *each other;* more than two look at *one another.*"

The AP adds, though not usefully:

"Either phrase may be used when the number is indefinite: We *help each other.* We *help one another.*"

Most other usage guides and dictionaries recognize that the two reciprocal pronouns are interchangeable.

eager or *anxious*?

Some speakers and writers still hold to the traditional distinction between the two most commonly used adjectives that have to do with being moved by a strong and urgent desire or interest—*eager*, which implies enthusiasm, hope, or impatience:

Paula is eager to begin her new job.

I am eager for news about your trip.

and *anxious*, which suggests an uneasiness or concern over the outcome:

Several parents were anxious about their kindergartners' progress in the computer course.

The captain was anxious for the safety of his troops.

Carl was anxious to do well on the bar exam.

But many others ignore the distinction, not so much by using the two words interchangeably as by using *anxious* whether or not there is an element of doubt or concern in the anticipation.

The librarian is always anxious to read to children.

Aren't you anxious to see your family after four months?

e.g. or *i.e.*?

Of the scholarly Latin abbreviations that appear in English printed material, *e.g.* and *i.e.* are among the most common. They are usually found not in ordinary text but in technical writing, and even here they are generally limited to parenthetical references. Yet, because they are often confused, a word about their meanings might be useful.

From *exempli gratia*, *e.g.* means "for the sake of example" or "for example." It introduces an element that adds to what has been stated but is not essential to the meaning.

The experiments dealt with the properties of metallic elements (e.g., lead, potassium, sodium).

From *id est*, *i.e.* means "that is" or "that is to say." It introduces an element that clarifies and bears more directly on the meaning of the statement than does an element introduced by *e.g.*

Lead was shown to have the highest melting point (i.e., 621° F).

Either he or I am right.

When we think about grammatical agreement between verbs and subjects, singular and plural usually come to mind: A verb must agree in number with its subject (see FISH AND CHIPS IS ON THE MENU AGAIN). But a verb is supposed to agree with its subject in person as well as number. That is, the form of the verb depends on whether the subject is speaking (first person), is spoken to (second person), or is spoken of (third person).

The irregular verb *be*, for example, has three forms in the present tense: *am, are, is.*

First person: (I) *am;* (we) *are*

Second person: (you) *are*

Third person: (he, she, it) *is;* (they) *are*

Most verbs, however, have the same form for all but the third-person singular in the present tense. *Come* illustrates this regular irregularity.

First person: (I) *come;* (we) *come*

Second person: (you) *come*

Third person: (he, she, it) <u>*comes;*</u> (they) *come*

This pattern also explains why we give so little thought to the agreement of subjects and verbs in person, at least in the present tense. (For a discussion of the irregularity of English verbs, see THE WALRUS AND THE CARPENTER WEEPED LIKE ANYTHING.)

Yet questions arise from time to time when we try to make verbs agree in person with their subjects. Which, for instance, is "correct":

Either he or I *am* right.

Either he or I *is* right.

Either he or I *are* right.

According to most grammarians, when the subject consists of pronouns of different persons joined by *or* or *nor*, and in *not only . . . but also* constructions, the verb agrees in person with the nearer. So the first sentence—"Either he or I am right"—has considerable authority on its side. And so do these:

Neither they nor she *has* replied.

I suppose that not only I but also she *is* on the mailing list.

Because such sentences usually sound awkward (though no more awkward than suggested improvements like "I suppose that not only I but also she *am* on the mailing list" and "I suppose that not only I but also she *are* on the mailing list"), rewording is often best.

Either he *is* right or I *am*.

They *have* not *replied,* and neither *has* she.

I suppose that not only I *am* on the mailing list but she *is* too.

(For more on *either . . . or* and *neither . . . nor* constructions, see "NEITHER FISH NOR FLESH NOR GOOD RED-HERRING" and "ELECTRIC SHAVER FOR WOMEN WITH DELICATE FLORAL DESIGN ON THE HANDLE.")

Relative pronouns (words like *who* and *which* used to introduce a relative subordinate clause) cause problems as well. Which of these sentences would grammarians approve:

I, who *am* right, will try not to lord it over her.

I, who *is* right, will try not to lord it over her.

The first, and this is why: In a relative clause, the verb agrees in person with the antecedent of the relative pronoun, that is, with the word the pronoun refers to (*I*). But if the antecedent of the relative clause were *her,* this is how the sentence would read:

I will try not to lord it over her, who *is* wrong.

Now, what happens when a relative clause follows a principal clause introduced by *it*? Which would we say or write:

It is they who *cook* supper every night.

It is they who *cooks* supper every night.

The former. *It* does not determine the person of the verb in the relative clause. *It* is the grammatical subject of the principal clause (*It is*), but the actual subject of this clause is the next one, which begins with *they.* According to the rule, the verb in the relative clause agrees in person with the noun or—as in this case— the pronoun that follows the principal verb. So if *they* were changed to *he,* for example, the third-person singular form *cooks* would be right.

It is, of course, useful to know that, as far as verb-subject agreement in person is concerned, "*It is they* who cook supper every night" is correct. Yet many people would say, instead, "*It is them* who cook supper every night," or, even more likely, "*It's them* who cook supper every night." (For more on the dispute over the form, or case, of pronouns after the verb *be,* see IS IT ME YOU LIKE BETTER THAN HER?)

"Electric shaver for women with delicate floral design on the handle."

Few readers of an ad with this opening line would think for a minute that the delicate floral design is anywhere but on the handle of the Lady Sunbeam Rascal. Still, to make it perfectly clear that women are not so decorated, the prepositional phrase used as an adjective (*with delicate floral design on the handle*) ought to be placed immediately after the phrase it modifies (*electric shaver*).

> Women's electric shaver with delicate floral design on the handle. (OR Electric shaver with delicate floral design on the handle, for women. OR For women: electric shaver with delicate floral design on the handle.)

In heavily inflected languages like Old English, Latin, and Modern German, the form of the words themselves indicates to a large extent how they are related in a sentence. But, in Modern English, meaning is conveyed largely through the order in which the words appear. So whether or not misrelated sentence elements actually get in the way of understanding, they can lead the reader or listener to think, at least at first, that the wrong word or word group is being modified.

Modifiers that are misplaced are often lumped together with those that dangle. Indeed, both constructions can cause momentary confusion, both can be awkward, and both can be laughable. The main difference between them is that a misplaced modifier can usually be repositioned within a sentence so that its relationship to what it qualifies becomes both clear and logical, whereas a sentence with a dangling modifier requires rewording. (For more on dangling participle, gerund, and infinitive phrases and dangling elliptical clauses, see COVERED WITH ONIONS, RELISH, AND KETCHUP, I ATE A HOT DOG AT THE BALLPARK.)

In limiting the meaning of other words or word groups in a sentence, modifiers fall into two broad categories: adjectives, which modify mainly nouns or words functioning as nouns; and adverbs, which modify mainly verbs, adjectives, or other adverbs. Although adjectives and adverbs are not assigned fixed positions in a sentence, usage has determined that, by and large, they best convey the meaning if they appear next to the words they modify, or at least where their relationship to these words is unmistakable and logical. In both speech and writing, adjectives and adverbs often find themselves somewhere else.

Adjectives

In English a single adjective or a series of adjectives generally goes immediately before the word or word group it modifies.

> *hot syrup*   *oversize* snow tire   *slow, laid-back* ballads
>
> *green and white* balloons   a *woman's folded* umbrella

Otherwise the effect may be disconcerting. Here, for example:

> There was just enough space in the tote for a *folded woman's* umbrella

Or when the prize-winning novelist Walker Percy says, in *The Second Coming:*

"Her own clothes she had purchased earlier in the day ... <u>a gray Orlon man's work shirt</u> size 14½ neck and 30-inch sleeves. ..."

Yet some phrases with "misplaced" adjectives are widely accepted, especially in informal speech and writing. Who but the most grammar-conscious would think that *a stiff glass of whiskey* can never mean that the whiskey is strong, only that the glass it's in is rigid? Or that *a cheap can of diet soda* can't sometimes mean that the soda is inexpensive, not always that its aluminum container is about to fall apart? (Computers will replace editors the day they are able not only to distinguish between *a cheap can of diet soda* and *a can of cheap diet soda,* but also to see that the word order is in keeping with the writer's style and intent.)

ADJECTIVES CAN BE USED APPOSITIVELY, that is, placed beside other words or word groups by way of further identification or explanation. Whether they precede or follow is usually a matter of preference or emphasis.

The hikers, *tired and cranky,* finally made it back to camp.

Tired and cranky, the hikers finally made it back to camp.

What is important, though, is that the modifier appear next to the noun or pronoun it relates to. Otherwise the sentence—like this one in a *Dallas Times Herald* article by Jim Schutze—is apt to bring the reader up short:

"Those kinds of criticisms are best delivered from comfortable red leather chairs that have been polished by time and ample bottoms, <u>half-shouted, half-mumbled before a crackling fire,</u> in that long moment when the last frail lines of thought flicker across the mind before a long, snoring toasty-toed nap."

If the adjective phrase *half-shouted, half-mumbled before a crackling fire* modifies *criticisms,* Schutze should have placed it after *criticisms,* not after *ample bottoms.* Or, if he felt that such a shift would spoil the cadence, he might have rewritten the sentence.

Clearness and logic usually require, as well, that the noun or pronoun qualified by an appositive adjective be expressed, not merely understood. When it isn't—as in this two-line heading over an article by Caroline Drewes in the *San Francisco Sunday Examiner & Chronicle*—the association is likely to be both incorrect and laughable:

"Writer Edna O'Brien's 'fanatic heart' / <u>Prolific and passionate, her first book</u> was burned in Ireland"

The reader is left to sort out the fact that O'Brien, not her book, was prolific and passionate.

WHEN PREPOSITIONAL PHRASES are used as adjectives, they ordinarily follow the noun or pronoun they modify. As we've already seen, the statement in the Lady Sunbeam Rascal ad would be clearer if *with a delicate floral design on the handle* came after *electric shaver,* not after *women.* Here, too, a misplaced adjective phrase creates an ambiguous, comical effect:

In a *hatbox,* police found a baby anteater *with holes in its lid.*

The remedy is simple: shift the phrase so that it follows the noun it modifies.

In a *hatbox with holes in its lid*, police found a baby anteater.

Police found a baby anteater in a *hatbox with holes in its lid*.

If shifting a prepositional phrase in each of the following sentences is not enough to clarify the relationship between the modifier and the noun or pronoun it relates to, other minor changes might be in order:

As a lawyer, well-crafted prose delights *her*. (Well-crafted prose delights *her, as a lawyer*. OR *As a lawyer, she* is delighted by well-crafted prose.)

Like other twentieth-century composers, Arthur Berger's early music showed the influence of Stravinsky. (*Like that of other twentieth-century composers, Arthur Berger's early music* showed the influence of Stravinsky. OR *Like other twentieth-century composers, Arthur Berger* showed, in his early music, the influence of Stravinsky.)

Custodian: Please dump all *the garbage in the kitchen* tonight. (Custodian: Please dump all the *kitchen garbage* tonight.)

ANOTHER ADJECTIVE CONSTRUCTION that often ends up modifying the wrong word or word group is the relative clause—that is, a subordinate clause introduced by a pronoun like *who, that, which, whom,* and *whose.* Anyone who didn't know better might think that when Penelope Gilliatt said, in her novel *A State of Change:*

"She had seen <u>Marilyn Monroe</u> at the Actor's Studio, <u>who was quite a charming girl</u>."

she meant that the Actor's Studio, not Marilyn Monroe, was quite a charming girl. Not only would Gilliatt not have had such a foolish notion, but to convey it she would surely have changed *who* to *which*, because *who* refers to people and *which* to things (see HEREFORDS, WHO ARE A BREED OF BEEF CATTLE, HAVE WHITE FACES AND RED BODIES). The simplest way to restore clarity and sense would be to shift the adverb phrase to either the beginning or the end of the sentence, leaving the relative clause next to what it properly modifies.

At the Actor's Studio she had seen *Marilyn Monroe, who was quite a charming girl.*

She had seen *Marilyn Monroe, who was quite a charming girl,* at the Actor's Studio.

Each of the following sentences, too, would be less ambiguous if the relative clause were shifted next to the word it modifies, or if minor changes were made in the wording:

The sheriff hit the man on the head with an oar, *which required twelve stitches.* (With an oar, the sheriff hit the man on the *head, which required twelve stitches.*)

There were tuna and meatloaf sandwiches in the *lunchbox, which we ate.* (In the lunchbox there were tuna and meatloaf *sandwiches, which we ate.* OR In the lunchbox were tuna and meatloaf *sandwiches, which we ate.*)

He had a girlfriend who worked in the *county jail that he hoped to marry.* (He had a *girlfriend* who worked in the county jail and *whom he hoped to marry.* OR He hoped to marry his *girlfriend, who worked in the county jail.*)

What are some things she could wear on her *feet that have tough, thick bottoms?* (What are some *things that have tough, thick bottoms and that she could wear on her feet?* OR What *things with tough, thick bottoms* could she wear on her feet?)

(THE OVAL OFFICE WHICH IS IN THE WHITE HOUSE SYMBOLIZES THE PRESIDENCY deals with other aspects of relative clauses, including the use of *that* or *which* to introduce them.)

Adverbs

Most native English-speakers have a sense of where an adverb and the verb it modifies generally belong in a sentence. To emphasize the action of the verb, the adverb goes first (in the case of a verb phrase, before the main verb but after the auxiliary).

The singer *graciously* acknowledged the applause.

The singer *had graciously* acknowledged the applause.

But if the adverb receives special emphasis, it usually goes after the verb.

The singer acknowledged the applause *graciously.*

The singer had acknowledged the applause *graciously.*

When it comes to the position of certain adverbs, like *only, almost, even, ever, merely, just, nearly, scarcely, hardly,* and *quite,* opinions differ. Strict grammarians insist that the meaning of a sentence changes according to where the adverb appears. For example:

Only he likes brewed coffee.

means that others may be satisfied with instant coffee but he likes the real thing. And:

He likes *only* brewed coffee.

means that the unless the coffee is fresh-brewed, not instant, he won't like it. And:

He *only* likes brewed coffee.

means that he likes brewed coffee, all right, but he doesn't, say, take it to the movies.

Yet many good writers believe that clear communication can be achieved without such subtle distinctions in the position of *only, even,* and similar adverbs. (In speech the problem seldom arises, because word stress and intonation can be counted on to clarify the meaning.)

"The students look stricken—I am taking all their wonderful words away. I am only taking their superfluous words away, leaving what is organic and strong." (William Zinsser, *On Writing Well*)

"(And one has one's mean reservations about Zijderveld's dealings with the 'cliché,' 'the home is where the heart is,' which he considers so corny that it could <u>only</u> be found genuinely touching by a foreigner not well versed in the English tongue. Is nothing sacred to him?)" (D. J. Enright, *A Mania for Sentences*)

Also singled out as potential word-order traps are constructions with the adverb *not* and the adjective *all*. Some people maintain that:

All brands of salt do not contain dextrose.

has only one meaning: that there is not a single brand of salt that has dextrose in it. So to convey the idea that some brands of salt contain dextrose but others don't, *not* must be placed immediately before *all*.

Not all brands of salt contain dextrose.

Dissenters may turn, for established usage, to Shakespeare's *The Merchant of Venice*, where one of Morocco's speeches to Portia begins with this famous quotation:

"'All that glisters is not gold—
Often have you heard that told. . . .'"

In fact, the *not all* and the *all . . . not* constructions are now virtually interchangeable.

"All authorities do not sanction this overlapping, but they are waging a losing battle, chiefly because attempting to distinguish the meanings usually requires close study of the context." (Theodore M. Bernstein, *Miss Thistlebottom's Hobgoblins: The Careful Writer's Guide to the Taboos, Bugbears and Outmoded Rules of English Usage*)

"All of Goldwyn's pictures didn't win Oscars, of course—some, in fact, were downright stinkers." (Arthur Marx, *Goldwyn: A Biography of the Man behind the Myth*)

In strict usage, correlative conjunctions (*neither . . . nor; either . . . or; not only . . . but also; not only . . . but;* and similar pairs of connectives) are governed by the rules of parallel construction. That is, a sentence must be so worded that both correlatives are not only logically related but also identical in grammatical structure. For example, in:

The wall *either* was very weak *or* the wind changed direction suddenly.

either is followed by a verb, but *or* is followed by a noun. So, to make the construction parallel, the first correlative (*either*) should be repositioned before the other noun.

Either the wall was very weak *or* the wind changed direction suddenly.

Instead of following those grammatical rules to the letter, many writers of today—like those of past centuries—place pairs of correlatives where they seem to fit naturally in a sentence. Apparently they feel that as long as a nonparallel construction does not confuse the reader, they ought not to be bound by mechanistic formulas.

"They <u>are reported not only by</u> housewives hanging out their clothes and by sportsmen hunting squirrels, <u>but they have been seen by</u> substantial members of the population, such as the vice-president of the bank and the wife of the chief of police." (John Cheever, *Oh What a Paradise It Seems*)

"The girl <u>neither knew what</u> a hero was, <u>nor apparently, that</u> an actor represents a character without being it." (Barbara Tuchman, "Quality and Non-Quality")

"Miss Hellman is <u>not only the leading woman playwright</u> of our time, <u>but of</u> our nation's entire history." (Garry Wills, Introduction to *Scoundrel Time*, by Lillian Hellman)

A PREPOSITIONAL PHRASE used as an adverb can move about more freely than one used as an adjective, as long as its position leaves no doubt about what is being modified and as long as the sentence does not become awkward or unintentionally comical. For example, this statement in *Jacob's Room*, by Virginia Woolf, invites misreading:

"Then the grey Persian cat stretches itself on the window-seat and buffets a moth <u>with soft round paws.</u>"

It wouldn't, though, if the adverb phrase preceded the verb it modifies:

Then the grey Persian cat stretches itself on the window-seat and with soft round paws buffets a moth.

In another sentence an adverb phrase might be entirely clear where Woolf placed it: after a short object following the modified verb.

The teacher *brought out* the difference *by voice inflection.*

But if the object of the verb is either a long clause or has its own modifying phrase, the adverb phrase normally goes before it, sometimes even at the beginning of the sentence.

By voice inflection the teacher *brought out* the difference between big trucks that lumber along and sports cars that dart about.

Otherwise the result is likely to be confusing, laughable, or both.

The teacher *brought out* the difference between big trucks that lumber along and sports cars that dart about *by voice inflection.*

Each of the following sentences, too, would be clearer and more logical if the adverb phrase were shifted to the beginning:

All the participants in the mass were black *at the special request of the archbishop.*

"Israeli Prime Minister Shimon Peres told Egyptian President Hosni Mubarak of the unanimous resolution adopted by the Israeli Cabinet <u>in a telephone conversation.</u>" ("News Summary," *Boston Globe*)

"Average girl is half as tall as she'll ever be <u>by the end of her second year.</u> Average boy is half as tall as he'll ever be <u>by the end of his third year.</u>" (L. M. Boyd, "The Grab Bag")

Adverb phrases are sometimes so ambiguous that shifting them to the initial position doesn't help. Take this statement in a *Chicago Sun-Times* caption on Linda Marchiano, who, as Linda Lovelace, starred in the movie *Deep Throat:*

> "Above, she tells a Senate subcommittee last year that she developed a breast problem from silicone injections she received before making "Deep Throat" <u>against her will</u>."

Did Marchiano resist the silicone injections? If so, *against her will* would more naturally fall immediately after the verb it modifies, *received.* On the other hand, if she objected to acting in the movie that made Linda Lovelace a bedroom word, *against her will* is all right where it is, as part of the prepositional phrase which is introduced by *before* and which also serves as an adverb modifier of *received.*

Or take this *Iberian Daily Sun* account of a London student jailed for having set out to assassinate Margaret Thatcher:

> "Prosecuting counsel Ann Curnow said Eastmond took his mother's stainless steel knife and went to the Prime Minister's residence at 10 Downing Street where Mrs Thatcher was holding a Cabinet meeting <u>before climbing over a wall at Westminster.</u>"

Now, since Mrs. Thatcher probably didn't climb over a wall after her Cabinet meeting, Eastmond must have done the climbing. But when? Right after he took his mother's stainless steel knife? If so, *before climbing over a wall at Westminster*, set off by commas, should precede *went to the Prime Minister's residence.* After he went to 10 Downing Street? In this case, the phrase should follow *Eastmond.*

"Squinting" Modifiers

A modifier is said to "squint" when it is so placed in a sentence that it might just as well relate to what goes before as to what comes after. For instance:

> What the commencement speaker said *so badly* needs saying.

might mean either that the speaker did a poor job delivering the speech or that what the speaker told the graduating class is worthwhile. If the former, *so badly* should precede *said;* if the latter, it should follow *saying.* (Not everyone believes that this adverb should be used in the sense of "greatly" or "very much." See *BAD OR BADLY*?)

These squinting constructions, too, could be set to rights by a shift of the ambiguous modifier:

> Sherwood Anderson described what life in a Midwestern town was like *in 1919* in his novel *Winesburg, Ohio.* (*In 1919,* in his novel *Winesburg, Ohio,* Sherwood Anderson described what life in a Midwestern town was like. OR In his novel *Winesburg, Ohio,* Sherwood Anderson described what life in a Midwestern town was like *in 1919.*)

> Can someone who invests in the stock market *every now and then* make a killing? (Can someone who *every now and then* invests in the stock market

make a killing? OR Can someone who invests in the stock market make a killing *every now and then?*)

Sometimes a slight rewording would make the sentence clearer. For instance:

Getting out of bed *quickly* causes dizziness.

could be altered in either of these ways:

Quickly getting out of bed causes dizziness.

Getting out of bed causes dizziness *quickly.*

But perhaps these versions would sound more natural:

On getting out of bed *quickly,* one can become dizzy.

On getting out of bed, one can *quickly* become dizzy.

Eliot was born in Missouri, however, he spent most of his life in England.

These two independent clauses tell us two things: first, where Eliot was born; second, where he spent most of his life. Contrast or opposition between them is conveyed by *however,* which, like *therefore, thus, nevertheless, moreover, indeed,* and other "heavy" conjunctive adverbs, is usually preceded by a semicolon. (The "light" conjunctive adverbs *yet* and *so* generally take a comma nowadays.)

Using a comma where a semicolon is expected is widely condemned. Most grammar books and schoolteachers have a name for such carelessness: *run-on sentence, comma fault, comma splice.* So in most edited work the sentence about T. S. Eliot would be punctuated like this:

Eliot was born in Missouri; however, he spent most of his life in England.

Substituting a semicolon for the offending comma is not the only remedy for a run-on sentence. With no change in meaning, the somewhat formal *however* and the comma following it might be replaced by the coordinating conjunction *but,* thus producing an ordinary compound sentence that nobody would object to.

Eliot was born in Missouri, but he spent most of his life in England.

Or the sentence might be changed into a complex one, with a subordinate and a main clause.

Although Eliot was born in Missouri, he spent most of his life in England.

Eliot was born in Missouri, though he spent most of his life in England.

And still another possibility is to turn the independent clauses into two separate sentences, each beginning with a capital letter and ending with a period.

Eliot was born in Missouri. However, he spent most of his life in England.

Eliot was born in Missouri. He spent most of his life in England, however.

To form a run-on sentence, the independent clauses need not be linked by either an adverb or a conjunction. All they need by way of transition is a comma.

Eliot was born in Missouri, he spent most of his life in England.

Punctuated even more carelessly than a run-on sentence, though fortunately less frequent, is a *fused sentence*. Here no mark of punctuation at all separates the clauses that are capitalized and punctuated as a single sentence.

Eliot was born in Missouri he spent most of his life in England.

Despite the complaints of grammarians, teachers, and editors, run-on sentences can be found not only in term papers but also in print. Short statements that qualify or contradict each other are the most likely candidates. In its *good* entry, for instance, *The Random House College Dictionary* (1984 edition) gives this example for the sense of "comparatively new or of relatively fine quality":

"Don't play in the woods, you're wearing good clothes."

Here are a few other published illustrations of the usage:

"The notion [that *since* has an exclusive reference to time] is indeed groundless, otherwise how explain such Shakespearean lines as, 'Since mine own doors refuse to entertain me, I'll knock elsewhere,' or 'Since it is as it is, mend it for your own good'?" (Theodore M. Bernstein, *Miss Thistlebottom's Hobgoblins: The Careful Writer's Guide to the Taboos, Bugbears and Outmoded Rules of English Usage*)

"It was exhausting to use your mind all the time, education was exhausting, particularly when it was administered by one's parents." (E. L. Doctorow, *World's Fair*)

"Its wooden floors are worn by years of earnest audiences, its pillared entrance hall strikes an institutional chill." (Lesley Thornton, "British Grail Guide," London *Observer* magazine)

elliptical clauses, dangling. See **Covered with onions, relish, and ketchup, I ate a hot dog at the ballpark.**

English, American and British. See **There's no home like Eaton Place.**

enormity or *enormousness*?

Anyone who applies the word *enormity* to something that is of enormous size or extent is lucky to get off with a charge of loose usage: the offense is ordinarily classified as illiteracy. *Enormity*, linguistic purists insist, should be limited to "great wickedness" or "a monstrous or outrageous act; a very wicked crime."

"Or maybe it wasn't any one act of brutality but rather the enormity of the collective carnage." (Bill Curry, "Houston's Murderous Dilemma")

Enormousness, on the other hand, should refer only to something which very much exceeds the usual size, number, or degree, that is, something which is huge or vast.

As you flew over the Sahara, weren't you overwhelmed by its enormousness?

With such a clear-cut distinction between the two words, why do many English-speakers persist in using the "incorrect" *enormity* instead of the "correct" *enormousness* when they mean greatness of size? It may be that they sense the common origin of both words in the adjective *enormous* (from the Latin *enormis,* "irregular, immoderate, immense"). In fact, we learn from *The Oxford English Dictionary* that the histories of the two words have long been intertwined. In the sixteenth and seventeenth centuries, both nouns conveyed the notion of falling from a right moral standard and even of extreme wickedness (John Donne so used *enormousness*), but in this sense *enormity* gained currency. Moreover, in the eighteenth and nineteenth centuries, both nouns were accepted as synonyms of "hugeness" or "vastness" (Thomas De Quincey's use of *enormity* is cited in the *OED*), but here *enormousness* outlasted *enormity*.

Nowadays users of the language don't see a need for two closely related nouns. When it comes to making a choice, those who don't like the look or the sound of *enormousness* turn to *enormity,* perhaps because it resembles the familiar word *immensity.* After all, it isn't as if those who don't like *hippopotamus* were to arbitrarily replace it with, say, *hippotamy:* except for the informal *hippo,* there is at hand no other word with a closely related meaning.

The suffixes *-ity* and *-ness,* which appear at the end of many nouns, both mean "state, quality, or instance of being." Some suffixes can change the meaning of words in opposite ways as well, for example, *-ful* and *-less* when attached to the word *thank.* Prefixes, which are attached to the beginning of words, perform the same function. For more on the syllables, groups of syllables, or words that are joined to other words to alter their meaning or to create new words, see WHO NEEDS A RABBIT'S FOOT MORE: AN UNLUCKY PERSON OR A LUCKLESS ONE?

epenthesis. See **With lightening speed the mischievious athalete ate the sherbert.**

equally or *equally as?*

Besides being redundant, the combination of *equally* and *as* strikes some people as a gross violation of accepted usage. If the comparison is expressed, they say, *equally* should be dropped.

Some leopards are as affectionate as house cats.

If the comparison is implied, *as* should go.

On the question of back pay, the personnel director was equally adamant.

Yet the phrase *equally as* is here and likely to stay. The *New York Times* television critic John J. O'Connor, for instance, said, in bidding farewell to

"Upstairs, Downstairs" in 1977, that "the second Mrs. Bellamy, Virginia (Hannah Gordon) is equally as charming."

Even those willing to accept the redundancy of *equally as* would probably be unsettled by this passage on the geological evolution of the earth, in *The Columbia History of the World:*

> "The 4.5-billion-year history of this planet points irresistibly to the conclusion that a living organism is created out of his environment, but it also shows that an organism modifies the total environment of his successors. This applies <u>as equally</u> to bacteria <u>as</u> to man."

Simply doing away with *equally* or with *as* (either or both of them) won't do here. To follow the usual patterns of current English, the sentence might be changed to "This applies *equally to bacteria and* to man"; or, if the authors insist on the correlative construction, to something like "This applies *as surely to bacteria as* to man." (See AS . . . AS OR SO . . . . AS? and AS WELL AS OR AND?)

etc.   See *and etc.*

etymology.   See **Cold slaw on my new chaise lounge!; For a girl he's quite mature.**

euphemisms.   See **"Should the inevitable occur . . ."**

Ever so funny jokes can be quite amusing.

In speaking, we can strengthen or emphasize meaning in a number of ways. We can use stress; that is, we can utter certain words or parts of words more loudly or more softly than others. We can use pitch; that is, by the rise and fall of our voice we can give certain words and word groups a higher or lower quality or tone. And we can use juncture; that is we can pause for a longer or shorter time between certain sequences of words. So besides the sense of the words themselves and the way we put them together in sentences, we can count on intonation, or our way of talking, to get our message across.

In writing, we must of course rely more on the words, phrases, clauses, and sentences we put before the reader. To be sure that our meaning is not overlooked, we sometimes supply special emphasis. One way is by using the superlative forms of adjectives and adverbs, as in "His playing was *most delicate*" and "He played *most delicately*" (see EXCITINGER TIMES LIE AHEAD). Another is by having a compound personal pronoun call attention to the person in question ("She tried the case *herself*," for example). And still another is by using an *intensive,* or an *intensifier*, which, as its name suggests, gives force or emphasis. These devices for strengthening meaning are of course not limited to writing; speakers use them all the time.

Most intensives are either adverbs or adjectives, but some noun phrases and prepositional phrases are also used to increase the force of the words they qualify. These are among the most common intensives:

absolutely
actually
altogether
awful, awfully
certainly
clearly
completely
definitely
entirely
ever so
extremely
for certain
for sure
fully
good (as in "We arrived good and early")
highly
indeed
literally (see LITERAL; LITERALLY)
most
much
of course
perfect, perfectly
plainly
quite
real, really
so
such
sure, surely
terribly
too
utterly
very

Most schoolteachers, grammar books, and usage guides have a number of reservations about intensives. Their first criticism is likely to be that intensives can be weakened through overuse and thus have the opposite effect from the one intended. "The recording was *certainly* a hit," for instance, says less than "The recording was a hit"; "I was *really* famished," less than "I was famished." In student papers *very* is most often circled as an ineffective intensive whose omission would make the word it modifies more emphatic.

A second criticism centers on the use of *so, such,* and *too* as simple intensives, without the second half of the comparison each introduces. For example, "It is *so* damp in the tropics" ought to be changed to "It is *extremely* damp in the tropics." Or else to something like "It is *so* damp in the tropics *that* postage stamps have to be kept in waxed paper." Yet *so, such,* and *too* are widely used not only to introduce the first part of a comparison but, especially in informal speech and writing, as well-established intensives in their own right.

A third criticism notes that *real* and *sure* can't possibly modify adverbs, verbs, or other adjectives; only adverbs can. So in "Nights are *real* (or *sure*) cold on the desert," *real* or *sure* must be changed to *really* or *surely*. Nor can *sure* be used in a sentence like "Amarillo sure is a long way from Corpus Christi" or as the affirmative answer to a question like "Do you want to make the trip?" But the fact is, *real* and *sure* are often used as intensive adverbs, though in less formal contexts than *really* and *surely*. For example, Ron Nessen, President Ford's press secretary, titled his book *It Sure Looks Different from the Inside*.

A fourth criticism—and a strong one it is—concerns the use of *awful* and *awfully* as intensives. The standard definitions of *awful* ("inspiring awe," "causing fear," and "full of awe") are usually presented, as though the adjective has not taken on its two informal senses of "very bad, ugly, unpleasant" (as in "an awful meal") and "great" ("an awful bore"). *Awfully* is then put to a similar test. Even those willing to concede that the adverb now means more than "in a way to inspire awe" hesitate to accept its current informal use as an intensive meaning "very; very much; extremely" (as in "That's awfully thoughtful of you"). Much less to recognize that, for many speakers and writers of English, *awful* serves the same purpose ("That's awful thoughtful of you").

A fifth criticism is that *quite* is too ambiguous to serve as an intensive. The adverb once meant "completely; entirely" ("Are you quite sure?") and "really; truly; positively" ("She's quite a swimmer"). But now that it has taken on the sense of "to some, or a considerable, degree or extent; very or fairly," it can be thought to weaken, rather than strengthen, the force of the word it modifies. So saying that a joke is "quite amusing" might just as easily minimize as stress its amusing quality.

A sixth criticism of intensives is implied in the widespread belief that they are extravagant forms preferred by women. The use of *so, such, too,* or the like as a simple intensifying adverb (without a phrase or clause to complete the comparison) is most often mentioned to illustrate this "schoolgirl" style. If it is a style, it seems to appeal to men as well as women.

> "I will make my case not on the grounds that [William] Trevor is now an important British writer (as he is) but mainly on those that he is so pleasurable to read, despite the wry pessimism of his view of life." (John Fowles, "The Irish Maupassant," *Atlantic*)

> "On my list of time's revenges, the last which I wish to cite is that the nature and history of standard English makes so many discussions of it so very silly." (James Sledd, "Something about Language and Social Class," *Halcyon 1986: A Journal of the Humanities*)

> "Entrepreneurs and small businessmen create two-thirds of the new jobs in the U.S., but not too many people realize it...." (John A. Conway, "Trends," *Forbes*)

> "Mind you, the one area that Rupert Murdoch is probably not too worried or angry about is the nonsensical story about the Queen." (Peter Hillmore, "Grave Crisis at Heart of Empire," London *Observer*)

> "Under the entry *thief* that word is shown to have had a perfect welter of spellings...." (Mitford M. Mathews, "Dictionaries Contain Surprises," in *Essays on Language and Usage*)

everyone or *everybody*?

In the sense of "every person," the pronouns *everyone* and *everybody* are used interchangeably. They are written as one word.

Doesn't everyone (or everybody) know who the villain is by now?

I hope that everybody (or everyone) will be here on time.

The two-word construction *every one* refers to every person or thing of those named.

Tell every one of your friends to come.

I'm afraid that every one of the dishes was broken.

When used as subjects, the pronouns *everyone* and *everybody* are singular and take singular verbs.

Is everyone (or everybody) free for lunch?

However, like the pronouns *anyone, anybody, no one, nobody, someone, somebody,* and others, *everyone* and *everybody* can apply to more than one person, of either sex or both sexes. So the pronouns referring to such singular antecedents are sometimes plural. (See "IF SOMEONE COULD MAKE YOUR CHILD A GENIUS, WOULD YOU LET THEM?")

ex-, former, or *late*?   See *former, ex-,* or *late*?

Excitinger times lie ahead.

Harder, safer, grimmer, livelier, or *better* times perhaps, but not *eleganter, leisurelier, troublesomer, gooder,* or *excitinger.* If English were a perfectly regular language, it would have only one way to show that an adjective is of the comparative degree—in other words, that the adjective does not merely state that a certain quality or attribute exists but indicates that the quality or attribute exists to a greater or lesser degree in relation to that of another person or thing. Instead, English has three ways to form the comparative. The first way is to add the suffix *-er* to the positive, or simple, form, so that, for example, *hard* becomes *harder* and *lively* becomes *livelier.* The second way is to leave the positive form unchanged but to place *more* or *less* in front of it, as in *more* (or *less*) *elegant* and *more* (or *less*) *exciting.* And the third way is to make a radical change in the positive form, turning, say, *good* into *better* and *bad* into *worse.* In general, adjectives of one or two syllables take the suffix *-er.* Longer adjectives are ordinarily preceded by *more* or *less,* as are all adjectives formed from the past or present participles of verbs (*hated* and *enticing,* for instance). Only a few adjectives have irregularly formed comparatives.

The same general rules apply to the superlative form of adjectives, that is, the form that expresses the greatest or least degree of the quality or attribute expressed by the positive degree. First, the suffix *-est* may be added to the positive form, so that *hard* becomes *hardest* and *lively* becomes *liveliest.* Second, *most* or *least* is placed in front of the positive form, as in *most* (or *least*) *elegant* and *most* (or *least*) *exciting*. Third, a radical change is made in the positive form, turning *good* into *best* and *bad* into *worst*.

Even though adjectives usually have one way of forming their comparatives and superlatives, the patterns are not necessarily fixed. Someone might, for instance, use *more wicked* or *most wicked* instead of *wickeder* or *wickedest* if the two-word form sounds better in a particular sentence. Double comparatives or superlatives, such as *more wickedest* and *most wickedest,* are generally frowned on nowadays.

As schoolchildren are taught very early, adding *-er* or *-est* to the positive form of certain adjectives affects the spelling of the base words. In one-syllable adjectives (as in any multisyllable ones stressed on the last syllable), a single final consonant preceded by a single vowel is ordinarily doubled (so *grim* becomes *grimmer* and *grimmest*). If the adjective ends in silent *e,* this letter is usually dropped before the suffix (so *safe* becomes *safer* and *safest*). And if the adjective ends in *y,* this letter is usually changed to *i* before the suffix (so *lively* becomes *livelier* and *liveliest*); however, there are many exceptions to this general rule.

According to conservative grammarians, the comparative degree of an adjective is used for only two people or things.

Is brisket of beef *tenderer* (or *more tender*) than ribs?

The rains are *later* this year than last.

And the superlative degree is used for three or more.

Filet mignon is the *choicest* cut of beef, some say.

This is the *latest* rainy season of the past five years.

In practice, however, the superlative degree is often used when only two persons or things are referred to, especially in informal speech and writing.

The twins always compete to see who is the *least* frightened by their bedtime stories.

Opinion is divided, as well, over whether certain adjectives—including *perfect, complete, essential, round, unique, black,* and *dead*—can have comparative and superlative forms at all. Logically they can't, since they denote qualities or attributes that are absolute, that is, not relative to anything else. Something that is *perfect* is flawless, so how can anything be *more perfect* or *less perfect*? Yet such adjectives are often used not in a literal, absolute sense but more loosely, to convey the notion of approximation. The much-quoted preamble to the United States Constitution begins like this:

"We, the people of the United States, in order to form a <u>more perfect</u> Union, establish justice . . ."

Less literary writing and everyday speech also draw on "incomparable" comparisons.

Each omelette he turns out is *more perfect* than the last.

Of all her innovations, adding skylights to Gothic Revival cottages is the *most unique*.

Truer words were never spoken.

They finally crawled out of the cave, *more dead* than alive.

New generations of weapons are being designed, each *deadlier* than the last.

In the painting, the subject's hands are *whiter* than her blouse.

The committee cut the *least essential* projects out of the draft budget.

MANY, BUT FAR FROM ALL, adverbs have comparative and superlative forms, and for the same reason that adjectives do: to indicate a greater or lesser degree, or the greatest or least degree, of the quality or attribute expressed by the positive degree. Adverbs are compared much the way adjectives are. The first group takes the suffixes *-er* and *-est*. These are likely to be "flat" adverbs, that is, adverbs lacking the characteristic *-ly* ending and therefore having the same form as adjectives.

Dick came *later* than Jane, but he wrote *faster* and stayed *longer*.

Those who work *hardest* are tired *soonest*.

In the second, and larger, group the comparatives and superlatives are indicated by *more* or *less* and *most* or *least*. The adverbs so compared are mainly those that end in *-ly*.

If we start out now, we can bike to the beach *more leisurely*.

Of all the hosts in St. Louis, they entertain *most elegantly*.

Many of the *most highly* acclaimed films are *least fondly* recalled.

Some *-ly* adverbs have a flat, or uninflected, form as well.

Please drive *more slowly* (or *slower*).

I wish the carillon played *more loudly* (or *louder*).

Of all the antacids, which works *most quickly* (or *quickest*)?

Critics of flat adverbs would like to see them limited to informal usage. That is, it's all right to paint "Go *slow*" on a road sign and to shout "Come *quick*!" or "Hold *tight*!" in a moment of panic, but not to say, in polite society, "Did the buzzer ring *loud* enough for the butler to hear?" Even English-speakers who are comfortable with flat adverbs rarely use them in long declarative sentences. Nor, for that matter, are they likely to begin any kind of sentence with one ("*Quick* they took their places on stage," for instance), or to place one between an auxiliary and the main verb ("She has *slow* come to the conclusion that gardening takes work").

The third group of adverbs are those that are compared irregularly, much as adjectives are.

Let's hope that whoever does the job *best* isn't treated *worst*.

Like certain adjectives, certain adverbs are considered by some to be beyond comparison. For example, since *squarely* means "at right angles," can one door be *more squarely* hung than another? Can one computer program be designed *most perfectly*? Many English-speakers say yes—after all, absolutes exist only ideally, not in the real world—just as they say that of course the superlative degree of an adverb can refer to only two people or things.

For more on adjectives and adverbs, see AS . . . AS OR SO . . . AS?; FIRST OR FIRSTLY?; KILIMANJARO IS TALLER THAN ANY MOUNTAIN IN AFRICA; MORE IMPORTANT OR MORE IMPORTANTLY?; and PEOPLE WHO WANT TO ARRIVE SAFE DON'T DRIVE DRUNKENLY.

F

farther or further; farthest or furthest?

Whether used as an adjective or as an adverb, *far* has come to have two comparative forms, *farther* and *further*, and two superlative forms, *farthest* and *furthest*. Traditionally, *farther* and *farthest* have referred to distance, whether in space or time.

Rio de Janeiro is farther east than Newfoundland.

St. Louis is the farthest I've traveled down the Mississippi.

Fossils of birds discovered in Texas in 1986 may go back 75 million years farther than any found before.

Further and *furthest* have been used both in references to physical distance and in the sense of "in addition to" or "to a greater degree or extent."

Do you need further information?

The plan ought to be studied further.

Edel's book goes furthest in capturing the spirit of the Bloomsbury group.

That distinction is observed less and less, but not because the words are used interchangeably. What seems to be happening is that *further* and *furthest* are replacing *farther* and *farthest* in all senses, literal as well as figurative. For example, to indicate a transfer point for another line, a sign in a London Underground station reads not "Farther Back" but "Further Back."

FURTHER, NOT FARTHER, appears in the compound adverb *furthermore*, meaning "besides" or "moreover." It is also a verb meaning "to advance" or "to promote."

Will working as an usher further your acting career?

fetch, bring, or take?   See *bring, take, or fetch?*

few, several, or couple?   See *several, few, or couple?*

Few phenomenons are more eye-catching than stadia packed with alumnuses waving gladioli.

Borrowing Latin and Greek nouns seems to have been easier than settling on their English plurals. Rather than decide whether to adopt the original plural forms or to Anglicize them all, English-speakers have done both.

These are some of the nouns whose plural, as well as singular, forms have been left unchanged:

Singular	Plural
addendum (Latin)	*addenda*
alumna (Latin)	*alumnae* (feminine)
alumnus (Latin)	*alumni* (masculine)
corrigendum (Latin)	*corrigenda*
crisis (Greek)	*crises*
locus (Latin)	*loci*
oasis (Greek)	*oases*
schema (Greek)	*schemata*
thesis (Latin)	*theses*

These are some of the nouns that have been given English plural forms to go along with their original Latin ones. The English plurals are more commonly used, whereas the Latin ones are generally reserved for scientific or other special contexts.

Singular	Original Plural	English Plural
appendix	*appendices*	*appendixes*
cactus	*cacti*	*cactuses*
dictum	*dicta*	*dictums*
eucalyptus	*eucalypti*	*eucalyptuses*
formula	*formulae*	*formulas*
forum	*fora*	*forums*
fulcrum	*fulcra*	*fulcrums*
gladiolus	*gladioli*	*gladioluses*
index	*indices*	*indexes*
memorandum	*memoranda*	*memorandums*
planetarium	*planetaria*	*planetariums*

For a smaller group of loanwords, the original Latin or Greek plurals are more commonly used than the Anglicized ones. For instance:

Singular	Original Plural	English Plural
criterion (Greek)	*criteria*	*criterions*
fungus (Latin)	*fungi*	*funguses*
radius (Latin)	*radii*	*radiuses*
spectrum (Latin)	*spectra*	*spectrums*

In a few cases the original Latin plurals are used in some senses and the English in others.

Persona, for example, becomes *personae* for the characters of a drama, novel, or the like, but *personas* in the psychological sense of the outer personality or façade that a person presents to others.

Stadium becomes either *stadia* (the original form) or *stadiums* in most senses; however, in the sense of large, open structures for football, baseball, and other activities, only the English plural, *stadiums,* is ordinarily used.

For several loanwords, English has gone a step further than inventing a plural form to use with the original Latin one.

In one case the original plural has been appropriated for the singular and a new plural created. A form of the Latin word for "to do" or "to act," *agendum* has long had both the Latin plural, *agenda,* and the Anglicized *agendums.* Nowadays, in both speech and writing, *agenda* is commonly used as the singular and *agendas* as the plural. As a logical development of the original sense, the word now refers not only to a program of things to be done but, specifically, to a list of things to be dealt with at a meeting.

Is this the agenda for today's meeting?

Who draws up agendas for stockholders' meetings in your firm?

Another case presents a slight variation: the original plural has been applied to the singular form and a new plural invented—but only in a special sense of the word. The Latin plural of *medium* is *media;* the English form, *mediums,* has been more widely used (in the sense of "persons through whom communications are supposedly sent to the living from spirits of the dead"). But in the 1920s *media* began to be used as a singular form to designate a means of communication that reaches the general public and carries advertising (as in "A media like television is both art and business"). Even more appalling to conservative English-speakers is the growing popularity of *medias* as the plural of *media* ("The story was given broad coverage in all the medias").

In still another case the original Latin plural has come to be used as both the singular and the plural forms in English. (See DATA OR DATUM?)

For some of the many other Latin and Greek words that English has borrowed, see MODOR, WE'VE GOT COMPANY.

fewer or *less*?

Fewer, according to the traditional rule, applies only to number. It modifies count nouns, that is, nouns that have singular and plural forms and that name objects which are countable as separate units.

fewer hours

fewer than thirty jobs

one candidate fewer than in last fall's election

Less, on the other hand, applies only to quantity. It modifies mass nouns, that is, nouns that are neither counted as separate units nor considered as singular or plural.

less coal

less unemployment than a year ago

less time

less joy

To the dismay of those who like neat distinctions, this one does not always hold. For one thing, what seem like countable units because a number is given and because the noun is in the plural are sometimes viewed as a single quantity or sum, so *less,* not *fewer,* is ordinarily used.

The jeans cost less than forty dollars.

With less than ten minutes to play, the game was called.

Less than two days is not enough time to make the trip.

The speaker pointed out that less than a hundred miles separate Florida and Cuba.

For another, math classes teach students to use the phrase *less than,* as opposed to *greater than,* whether or not countable units are involved.

Are five tangelos plus three tangelos less than ten tangelos?

Less, then, is gaining ground on *fewer,* even though it is not yet universally recognized as a synonym.

finalize. See *Apologize,* sí; *finalize,* **no.**

first **or** *firstly?*

Either of these adverbs can be used to signal the beginning of an enumeration. Those who find the *-ly* form too stilted are free to use the "flat" adverb instead.

First (or firstly), sauté the onion in olive oil until it is tender but not brown.

Whatever the choice, though, it's a good idea to apply it consistently throughout the enumeration.

Second (or secondly), add the ham and shrimp, cooking them until the shrimp turns bright pink. Third (or thirdly), slice ripe tomatoes . . .

Otherwise, the readers or listeners will feel as though they are walking along with one foot on the sidewalk and the other in the street.

See also MORE IMPORTANT OR MORE IMPORTANTLY?

Fish and chips is on the menu again.

Grammar, for many people, comes down to one rule: a verb must agree in number with its subject. It is a good idea to keep the rule in mind, for those who ignore it—saying, for example, "Dogs is friendlier than cats"—are likely to be looked down on by educated users of the language.

The first step is to identify each verb and the grammatical subject (a noun or a pronoun) that governs it, no matter where they appear in a sentence or clause. The next step is to decide how to treat them—sentence by sentence, clause by clause. Even a rule as apparently uncompromising as "singular subject, singular verb; plural subject, plural verb" has some give. Here, then, is a fuller statement of the traditional rule, with some widely recognized exceptions.

Singular Subjects

A singular subject, the rule states flatly, takes a singular verb, regardless of whether one or more words intervene.

> The *cargo*, though listed as computer parts on several customs declarations, *was* handguns.

> A *list* of illustrations *describes* the photographs and other artwork in the book.

Although a singular verb is probably always appropriate following a phrase like *list of illustrations*, a plural verb might sometimes better reflect the meaning of, say, *list of projects* (as in "The entire list of projects were carefully reviewed"). Indeed, with many singular nouns followed by some sort of plural modifier, the choice of a singular or plural verb depends on the sense of the particular sentence. Recognizing that intent often outweighs form, English-speakers do not hesitate to use a plural verb to convey the notion of plurality.

> A *pile* of documents *is* now *being distributed* to each stockholder. A *pile* of documents mysteriously *appear* outside my office every Monday.

> A *majority* of the voters *favors* the measure. A *majority* of the voters *want* things done differently at city hall.

> The *number* of Hispanics in the West *has grown* dramatically. A *number* of Hispanics *were* among the volunteers.

Parenthetical expressions

When a singular subject is followed by a phrase introduced by *in addition to, as well as, plus, with, together with,* or the like, the verb ordinarily remains singular.

> According to most critics, the film's *director,* as well as the leading and supporting actors, *was* a sure bet to win an Oscar.

Occasionally, however, such an expression is felt to be so much a part of a compound subject that a plural verb is used.

> *Judith,* as well as her six nieces and four nephews, I am told, *visit* her parents once a week.

When a singular subject is followed by a parenthetical phrase providing information or commentary; by an appositive, that is, a word or expression placed beside another to identify or explain it; or by a word or phrase expressing opposition or antithesis, the verb usually remains singular.

> One, and sometimes two, *is* all the plane will carry.

> The opposition *party,* the Tories, *was* jubilant.

> The *architect,* not the construction workers, *gets* the credit.

Yet a secondary expression that emphasizes plurality sometimes affects the number of the verb.

Her schedule, her daily *comings and goings, wear* me out.

Other usages related to singular subjects

A sentence with a singular subject can of course have a compound predicate, that is, two or more main verbs, along with auxiliary verbs, complements, and modifiers. If it does, each of the verbs governed by that subject should be singular.

The *founder* of the club often *attends* our meetings *and* then *stays* for a chat about the good old days.

Two or more adjectives modifying a singular subject do not ordinarily affect the number of the verb.

Warm and sunny weather is in store.

However, if two or more adjectives reveal different aspects or meanings of a singular subject, a plural verb may be used, to avoid repetition of the noun.

Freudian and Jungian psychotherapy differ in many ways.

Plural Subjects

A plural subject takes a plural verb.

Most young *children,* if left alone, *find* playing with matches an irresistible temptation.

How, Jeff's mother wanted to know, *were* his new, and very elusive, *roommates.*

Heavy *concentrations* of political power, especially in a democracy, *are* unhealthy.

Compound Subjects

According to the rule, two or more singular subjects joined by *and* take a plural verb.

The *founder and* the first *president* of the club often *attend* our meetings.

He, his *daughter,* and his *partner* now *share* the office.

Sometimes the *and* is understood. If so, a comma appears after each element in the compound subject, including the last.

Their *faith,* their *joy,* their *optimism, are* boundless.

There are a number of exceptions to this rule.

1. When the compound subject refers to only one person or thing, the verb must be singular, for sense.

The *founder and first president* of the club often *attends* our meetings.

This is what can happen if the unity of the subject is overlooked:

"When the singer's [Frank Sinatra's] wife, Barbara, held a surprise party to mark his 65th birthday, December 12, William French Smith, Reagan's personal <u>attorney and</u> the <u>man</u> named the day before as attorney general-designate, <u>were</u> among the 200 or so people who traveled to Rancho Mirage, near Palm Springs, for the affair." (Robert Lindsey, New York Times)

2. When the compound subject is felt to be a single entity—that is, if it is plural in form but singular in the notion it conveys—the verb is likely to be singular.

Fish and chips is on the menu again.

Public *health and safety continues* to concern the voters.

Huffing and puffing means the elevator is not working.

"The <u>decline and fall</u> of Mrs Indira Gandhi <u>is</u> gaining momentum, and her controversial son, Sanjay, is plunging with her." (Peter Niesewand, London *Guardian*)

"The fact that 'critical thinking' appears so regularly on the list of objectionable activities conjures up the danger of a <u>school and</u> a <u>society</u> that <u>is</u> both uncritical and unthinking." (Fred M. Hechinger, *New York Times*)

3. When the verb comes before, not after, the compound subject, especially following an introductory word like *there*, *here*, or *such*, the verb is likely to be singular if the first element in the subject is singular. Yet a plural verb is used if the subject is felt to be unmistakably plural.

There *was rioting, burning, and looting* after Dr. King's assassination.

There *is* a steady *rise and fall* of suspense in the story.

Such *was* the *language and* subject *matter* of prime-time TV.

There *was* (or *were*) one ripe *apple,* one half-ripe *plum, and* one green *mango* in the basket.

Here *come Nora and Nick,* bringing up the rear.

4. When *each* or *every* precedes the compound subject, the verb is singular.

Each star and planet is assigned a number on the chart.

Each question and each answer appears on a separate page.

Every Tom, Dick, and Harry comes to dinner.

Subjects Joined by *Or* or *Nor*

Two or more singular subjects joined by *or* or *nor* take a singular verb.

My *brother,* my *sister,* or my *niece writes* the letters in our family.

Either *spring or fall is* a good time to go.

Neither *Paraguay nor Bolivia has* a seacoast.

If one subject is singular and the other plural, the verb agrees in number with the nearer subject. This rule applies to *not only . . . but also* constructions as well.

Either money *problems or a lack* of time *is* his standard complaint.

Neither a *lack* of time *nor* money *problems are* a complaint you'll hear from him.

Not only *newspapers but also television carries* weather reports.

Not only *television but also newspapers carry* weather reports.

Despite the rule that singular subjects connected by *or* or *nor* must take a singular verb, a plural verb is sometimes used in questions and in negative statements, especially in informal speech and writing.

Are Betty or Ted planning to come?

Neither my uncle nor my cousin *have written.*

For more on *either . . . or* and *neither . . . nor* constructions, see EITHER HE OR I AM RIGHT and ''NEITHER FISH NOR FLESH NOR GOOD RED-HERRING.''

Indefinite Pronouns As Subjects

When used as subjects, indefinite pronouns like *each, everybody, everyone, somebody, someone, neither, either, no one,* and *nobody* take a singular verb.

Everybody knows the real story except me.

No one remembers the first coach.

Has either of the novels *come* out in paperback?

None, meaning either ''no persons or things'' or ''not any,'' usually takes a plural verb.

None of the rivers *are* free from pollution.

None come even close.

But if the noun that follows *none* is singular, or if the sense is singular, a singular verb is used.

None of the new wool *is* as soft as the old.

None seems right for my sweater.

When ''not one'' is meant, it is better to say so than to use *none.*

Not one of my favorite teams *made* the playoffs.

By and large, it is not difficult to make these indefinite pronouns agree in number with the verbs they govern. There is, however, resistance to the use of the masculine, singular form of the pronoun (as in ''Everyone took his lunch and ran''). For more on the agreement of a pronoun with its antecedent in person, see HURRICANE DAVID LEFT DEVASTATION IN HER WAKE.

Collective Nouns and Nouns of Quantity As Subjects

Collective nouns, that is, nouns which denote a collection of individuals or items (*family, committee, jury, orchestra, army, crowd,* and so on) take a singular verb if the collection is thought of as a whole:

Does your *family* approve of your roommate?

but a plural verb if the individual members are thought of as acting individually:

My *family complain* about almost everything I do.

(Among the Latin-derived collective nouns that take either a singular or a plural verb are *data* and *media*. See DATA OR DATUM? and FEW PHENOMENONS ARE MORE EYE-CATCHING THAN STADIA FILLED WITH ALUMNUSES WAVING GLADIOLI.)

Nouns of quantity take a singular verb if they express a single idea, that is, if the amounts they refer to are thought of as a whole. On the other hand, they take a plural verb if the amounts are thought of as separate parts of that whole.

Ten minutes of silence *was* observed in memory of John Lennon. *Ten minutes are* five minutes more than this speech should take.

About *85 percent* of the job market *was* in three areas. Only *10 percent* of the new jobs *were* low-paying.

An estimated *$245,000* in property damage *was* reported. *Two hundred dollars were* scattered around the room.

Subjects Governing Linking Verbs

Linking verbs are verbs like *be, appear,* and *seem,* which serve mainly to connect a subject and a complement (the word or word group that completes the sense of the verb). They agree in number with their subject, not with their complement.

Our greatest *pleasure is* visits to the zoo.

Visits to the zoo *are* our greatest pleasure.

However, if *what,* meaning either "that which" or "those which," is the subject of a linking verb, the verb usually agrees with its complement.

What I have in mind *is* an entirely new marketing strategy.

What the book describes *are* the author's imaginary playmates of the past forty years.

Yet the viewpoint may shift even within the same sentence.

What was on sale *were* Nehru jackets and two-vested suits.

For more on linking verbs, see PEOPLE WHO WANT TO ARRIVE SAFE DON'T DRIVE DRUNKENLY.

Subjects Governing Verbs in Relative Clauses

In a relative clause (a subordinate clause introduced by a relative pronoun such as *who, which,* or *that*), the verb agrees in number with the antecedent of the relative pronoun, that is, with the word the pronoun refers to. So in a sentence like:

Chris is a *newcomer,* who *eats* at Spike's Place every night.

the verb is the singular *eats* because *who* refers to the singular noun *newcomer.* Now, in:

Spike's Place is the only *one* of the local diners which *is* open all night.

the verb is the singular *is* because *which* refers to the singular pronoun *one.* That is, among all the local diners, only one is open all night and that one is Spike's Place. And in:

Spike's Place is one of the few *diners* that *are* open all night.

the verb is the plural *are* because *that* refers to the plural noun *diners.* In other words, a few diners, including Spike's Place, are open all night.

Many writers and speakers have trouble with the last construction: *one of those people who . . . ; one of the things that . . .* ; and so on. Unless they begin by identifying the word that governs the verb in the relative clause, they may fail to bring the subject and verb into what is generally considered correct agreement.

"Frankly, I am not one of those college <u>professors</u> who coyly <u>boasts</u> [instead of *boast*] of enjoying detective stories—they are too badly written for my taste and bore me to death." (Vladimir Nabokov, *Lectures on Literature*)

They may also run into difficulty with the form of related pronouns.

" . . . she was not one of those emancipated <u>women</u> who <u>measures</u> [instead of *measure*] <u>her</u> [instead of *their*] own success by the failures of others of <u>her</u> [*their*] sex." (Diana Trilling, London *Times Literary Supplement*)

For more on relative pronouns and the clauses they introduce, see EITHER HE OR I AM RIGHT; "ELECTRIC SHAVER FOR WOMEN WITH DELICATE FLORAL DESIGN ON THE HANDLE"; HEREFORDS, WHO ARE A BREED OF BEEF CATTLE, HAVE WHITE FACES AND RED BODIES; and THE OVAL OFFICE WHICH IS IN THE WHITE HOUSE SYMBOLIZES THE PRESIDENCY.

Misleading Singular and Plural Subjects

Certain nouns that seem to be plural in form may in fact be singular in meaning.

News has become a major industry.

War and Peace, I hear, *was* made into a movie for the fifth time.

Boni & Liveright is perhaps best remembered as Dreiser's publisher.

Did you know that *rabies is* transmitted by bats as well as dogs?

Grammatical subjects ending in *-ics* usually take a singular verb when they denote an art, a science, or a study (*economics* and *linguistics,* for example), or an arrangement or system (*architectonics*). They usually take a plural verb when they denote activities or practices (*histrionics*), or qualities or properties (*atmospherics*). So the same noun may sometimes take a singular verb and at other times a plural one.

Politics is on everyone's mind these days.

Their *politics are* no concern of their employer.

Nouns such as *trousers, pants,* and *scissors* always take a plural verb. Nowadays *odds* usually does, too.

Odds (The *odds*) *are* that the next TV season will be just as interesting as the last one.

flammable or *inflammable*?

In- is a well-known signal that something is the opposite of something else, that something is lacking in some way, or that something is not likely to happen. This prefix occurs in many words, including *inadvertence, infamous, insignificant,* and *invincible.*

No wonder, then, that *inflammable* was assumed to refer to something which is not easily set on fire or which will not burn readily or quickly. Therefore, to warn the public that they were transporting, say, gasoline, which indeed is easily set on fire and burns readily and quickly, trucks carried conspicuous signs reading "flammable." This is now the preferred term in commerce and industry.

But, in fact, the English word *inflammable* does not come from *flammable* plus the negative prefix *in-*. It is borrowed from the Latin *inflammare*, in which *in-*, attached to a word meaning "flame," is an intensive prefix, not the Latin prefix *in-* which indicates negation. Yet, knowing how users of a language tend to fit unfamiliar words into familiar patterns, we ought not to be surprised if one day a well-informed person with an alert mind is described as *telligent.*

For other words that take unexpected turns because of prefixes and affixes, see WHO NEEDS A RABBIT'S FOOT MORE: AN UNLUCKY PERSON OR A LUCKLESS ONE? And for a general discussion of folk etymology, see COLD SLAW ON MY NEW CHAISE LOUNGE!

flaunt or *flout*?

Although these two verbs have the same initial sound, their origins and meanings are quite different. *Flaunt* means "to make a gaudy, ostentatious, conspicuous, impudent, or defiant display."

The May Day parade flaunted the country's latest military hardware.

Betsy threatened to kill her husband if he flaunted his affairs in front of her.

Flout means "to mock or scoff at; show scorn or contempt for."

Many coal-burning factories continued to flout the Clean Air Act.

Most students no longer object to the school's dress code, but a few still flout it.

Those who confuse the words are more apt to say or write *flaunt* when they mean *flout* than the other way around.

"The Government of Iran must realize that it cannot flaunt with impunity the expressed will and law of the world community." (President Jimmy Carter, in a nationally televised speech, December 21, 1979, announcing that he would ask the UN Security Council to impose economic sanctions on Iran. In its front-page story, the *New York Times* quoted the President verbatim; the *San Francisco Chronicle*, however, changed *flaunt* to *flout*.)

"Armed members of the radical People's Mojahedin Organisation yesterday flaunted heavy security in central Tehran by appearing in several of the most crowded parts of the city centre...." (Terry Povey, *Financial Times*, Frankfurt)

"Compounding the evil in the eyes of elders were the many new roadhouses and speakeasies, where young people flaunted Prohibition by drinking beer or cocktails." (Frank Freidel, *America in the Twentieth Century*)

"Sixth graders find out that adult authority can often be directly flaunted, and they find this both challenging and frightening." (C. W. Hunnicutt and others, *The Great Adventure: Teacher's Manual*)

Occasionally, however, *flout* creeps in where *flaunt* belongs.

"The Ku Klux Klan has been 'born again' and is openly flouting its racial hatred." (*Klanwatch*)

flounder or *founder?* See *founder* or *flounder?*

folk etymology. See Cold slaw on my new chaise lounge!

For a girl he's quite mature.

A patently absurd statement if ever there was one! As everyone knows, the word *girl* means "a female child" or "a young woman," so the masculine pronoun *he* cannot possibly refer to it.

Or does everyone know? As recently as the Middle English period (roughly between 1100 and 1500), *girle* or *gurle* was applied to a youngster of either sex, and for those opposed to precipitate changes in the language, that's recently enough. In looking only at the derivation of a word to determine its "proper" meaning, these etymologues are apt to hold beliefs such as these:

A pesticide can *decimate* trees in an orchard only if it selects every tenth tree by lot and then kills it.

Having no activities outside the house, a *hussy* is not likely to take kindly to remarks about her morals.

Greeting cards may convey wishes for a "happy birthday anniversary" but not for a "happy birthday." After all, *birthday* refers to the day of a person's birth, and *anniversary* to the date on which an event occurred in an earlier year.

It is unfair to assume that a person has been drinking just because there's a smell of *liquor* on her or his breath. Who knows? It might be grapefruit juice.

A *villain* is merely a farm servant, so why associate such a person with crime or wickedness?

We wouldn't say that someone has a piece of orange or an orange peel for life, would we? So why say that he or she has a *zest* for life?

What's this nonsense about the Fourth of July being a *holiday*? Christmas and Easter, though, are truly *holy days*.

Before saying "a *myriad* of gifts," one should count to be sure there are ten thousand.

Only foreigners can behave *outlandishly*.

A *nice* person is not agreeable, pleasant, or considerate, but, instead, stupid or foolish.

Why call a trailblazing settler or an innovator in, say, high-energy physics a *pioneer,* when a pioneer is someone at the bottom of the military hierarchy?

An *auditor* examines accounts all right, but only by listening to them.

Journals, such as the *New England Journal of Medicine,* should change their names—or else come out every day.

Unless a *manuscript* is written by hand, it's not a manuscript.

Etymology is of course instructive—and fun as well. With the help of a good dictionary, we can trace a word or other form back thousands of years, both within English itself and to its sources in contemporary or earlier languages. In but a few words, abbreviations, and symbols *Webster's New World Dictionary,* for example, recounts the history of *girl* as it developed from the Indo-European language family, whose origins are all but lost in the recesses of time, to the beginnings of Modern English.

holes bored into twigs
girl (gurl) *n.* [ME. *girle, gurle,* youngster of either sex < ? OE. **gyrele,* ? akin to Brit. southern dial. *girls,* primrose blooms, & LowG. *gore,* young person (of either sex) < ? IE. base **ĝher-,* small] **1.** a female child **2.** a young, unmarried woman **3.** a female servant or other employee **4.** [Colloq.] a woman of any age, married or single **5.** [Colloq.] a sweetheart
☆**girl·friend** (gurl′frend′) *n.* [Colloq.] **1.** a sweetheart of a

This etymology, which appears inside heavy boldface brackets, begins by placing *girl* in the Middle English period. As the symbols < (for "derived from") and ? (for "uncertain; possibly; perhaps") indicate, the Middle English

A *hound* was once just any dog; now the word refers specifically to any of several breeds of large hunting dogs with long, drooping ears, short hair, and a deep-throated bark. (This is an interesting example of semantic shift, because the word *dog* itself orginally referred to a special breed of dog but, through the process of generalization, it has come to be applied to any of a large group of domesticated canines.)

Another form of specialization is the use of a word or phrase that, though unmodified, conveys its meaning as unmistakably as if it were qualified by an adjective or other limiting word. *Success,* for example, originally referred to any result or outcome; yet who uses the word nowadays for anything but a favorable or satisfactory one? *Predicament* and *plight* have gone the other way: they once described any condition, situation, or state of affairs, but *predicament* is now limited mainly to a difficult, unpleasant, or embarrassing one and *plight* to an awkward, sad, or dangerous one.

In the process of *melioration* (sometimes called *amelioration* or *elevation*), a word takes on a meaning considered to be socially or culturally more favorable than its earlier meaning. For instance:

Nice, which derives from the Latin for "not knowing" or "ignorant," meant "stupid" or "foolish" in Old French. Middle English added the senses of "strange" and "lazy," and over time *nice* took on various other meanings, including "difficult to please" and "finely discriminating." Today it is a generalized form of approval, whose various meanings include "agreeable," "attractive," "respectable," and "excellent."

Pioneer, which can be traced back to *peon,* originally referred to a foot soldier who went ahead of the main body of troops, helping to construct or demolish bridges, roads, trenches, and the like. Nowadays, *pioneer* is a commendatory word applied to someone who goes before and prepares the way for others—for example, an early settler in the United States or an innovative scientist. (This elevated sense first came into use in the United States.)

These are some other words whose meanings have been changed for the better through melioration:

In Latin, an *ambactus* is a vassal or servant; however, an *ambassador,* from the same source, is the highest-ranking diplomatic representative of a country.

A *marshal* was originally a groom or, later, a master of the horse in a medieval royal household; the word now often refers to a military officer of the highest rank.

Quaker was originally a derisive word, said to come from George Fox's admonition to "quake" at the word of the Lord; nowadays it is used even by the members of the Society of Friends themselves.

The Gothic-derived word *queen* once meant simply "a woman"; it now denotes the wife of a king.

In the process of *pejoration* (sometimes called *degradation*), a word takes on a meaning considered socially or culturally less favorable than its earlier meaning. For instance:

The Middle English word *huswife* meant just that: "housewife." The current contracted form, *hussy,* is a contemptuous or playful term for a woman, especially one of low morals.

Villain, derived from the Latin *villa,* once referred to nobody more evil than a farm servant. In time, however, the word came to describe a scoundrel or, at the very least, an unprincipled character in a play, a novel, or the like.

These are some other words whose meanings have been changed for the worse through pejoration:

Boor once referred to a peasant or farm worker; it is now generally applied to a person who is rude, awkward, or ill-mannered.

Crafty originally meant "powerful or skillful"; now it means "subtly deceitful; sly."

From its earlier meaning of "a serving boy or male servant," *knave* has come down in status; it now generally means "a dishonest, deceitful person; tricky rascal; rogue."

Silly originally meant "simple; plain; innocent"; now it usually means "foolish, stupid, absurd, ludicrous, etc."

A number of other processes cause the meanings of words to change—some even lead to the creation of entirely new words. For example:

folk etymology, or the change that occurs in the form of a word over a period of prolonged usage so as to give it an apparent connection with some other well-known word (see COLD SLAW ON MY NEW CHAISE LOUNGE!)

back-formation, or the creation of a new word from an existing word because of a mistaken notion of derivation; that is, the new word is thought to be the base of the existing one (see BURGLARS BURGLE AND PEDDLERS PEDDLE, SO WHY DON'T JANITORS JANIT?)

coinage (or *neologism*), or the invention of a new word or of a new meaning for an established word (see DEAR MR. WEBSTER)

foreign words in English.   See **Few phenomenons are more eye-catching than stadia filled with alumnuses waving gladioli; Modor, we've got company.**

former, ex-, or *late?*

When placed before a person's title or occupation, both *former* and *ex-* mean "previous," "earlier," or "past."

former (or *ex-*) Alabama Governor George C. Wallace

former (or *ex-*) President Gerald R. Ford

the *former* (or *ex-*) child actor Shirley Temple

In print, *former* generally appears in running text and the space-saving *ex-* in titles and headlines. Yet, in 1986, a *New Yorker* article quoted E. B. White as having written, in a 1951 issue of that magazine:

"Old West Fifty-sixth Street is incapable of being minked up in this manner, even by our favorite ex-First Lady [Eleanor Roosevelt]."

Former, not *ex-*, ordinarily follows a person's name.

Eleanor Roosevelt, the former First Lady, lived in New York.

The late is ordinarily used only with the name of a person who has recently died (within, say, the preceding decade) and who is not so well known that everyone presumably knows of the death. On both accounts, then, one would probably not say "the late Eleanor Roosevelt" or "the late Winston Churchill." And because the phrase is not used if the person was alive at the time referred to, one would not say "In the mid-thirties the late David Niven arrived in Hollywood from England."

For other meanings of *former*, see FORMER; LATTER.

former; latter

In the sense of "the first mentioned" and "the last mentioned," *former* and *latter* are used either with the nouns they modify or simply with *the*, the nouns being understood. In strict usage, the adjectives refer only to two people or things.

Sears Tower and the World Trade Center were then the tallest buildings in the United States, the former (building) in Chicago and the latter (building) in New York.

In references to more than two, expressions like *first* or *first-mentioned* and *last* or *last-mentioned* ordinarily replace *former* and *latter*.

Sears Tower, the World Trade Center, and the Empire State Building were then the tallest buildings in the United States; the first two had 110 stories, 8 more than the last.

To spare their readers or listeners the effort of figuring out what is meant by *former* and *latter* or their equivalents, some people reword the sentence or repeat the nouns. For example:

Sears Tower, in Chicago, and the World Trade Center, in New York, were then the tallest buildings in the United States.

Sears Tower, the World Trade Center, and the Empire State Building were then the tallest buildings in the United States; Sears Tower and the World Trade Center each had 110 stories, 8 more than the Empire State Building.

Others allow their preference for one adjective or the other to get them into trouble. For instance, at the news conference at which he announced his intention to seek reelection as a senator from California, S. I. Hayakawa, who had been a professor of general semantics before he entered politics, said that government should:

"separate earned income from unearned income [and] tax the former at a lower rate or not at all."

Under questioning from reporters, he repeated his proposal several times and finally asked his top legislative aide to straighten the matter out. According to the aide, Senator Hayakawa had meant to say that government should:

"separate earned income from unearned income [and] tax the latter at a lower rate or not at all."

Asked why the senator had repeatedly substituted *former* for *latter,* the aide explained:

"Semantically, he doesn't like the word 'latter.' "

BESIDES CONTRASTING the first and last named of two people or things, the adjectives *former* and *latter* are used in much the same way in references to time. *Former* means "preceding in time; earlier; past"; *latter,* "later; more recent."

In former years, until President Reagan appointed Sandra Day O'Connor in 1981, no woman had been a member of the U.S. Supreme Court.

In latter years, minor tranquilizers became the most prescribed drugs in the world.

Latter is used, as well, in the sense of "nearer the end or close."

In the latter part of the nineteenth century, the Philippines, Puerto Rico, and Guam became U.S. territories.

Former, however, is generally replaced by *earlier* when "nearer the beginning or start" is meant.

For the use of *former* before a person's title or occupation, see FORMER, EX-, OR LATE?

founder or *flounder?*

Ships that sink *founder;* people who speak or act awkwardly *flounder.* The confusion is not surprising, for the words are related. *Founder* goes back to the Latin *fundus* ("bottom"), to which the notion of falling in or sinking was added in the Old French word *fondrer.* Besides describing the sinking of a ship that fills with water, the English verb *founder* has several other senses, including "to stumble, fall, or go lame" (as a horse); "to become bogged down, or stuck as if in soft ground"; and "to break down, collapse, or fail."

The verb *flounder,* too, has been around for centuries, perhaps having come into the language as a variation of *founder.* Its original meaning—"to struggle awkwardly to move, as in deep mud or snow; to plunge about in a stumbling manner''—telescopes several of *founder*'s senses that are not related specifically to the sinking of ships. Nowadays *flounder* is generally applied to speaking or acting in an awkward or confused manner, with hesitation and frequent mistakes.

Because of the shared senses of *founder* and *flounder*, then, either verb can sometimes be used, depending on the speaker's or writer's intention or preference. For example, in:

A new president was named to take over the *foundering* (or *floundering*) company.

foundering might suggest that the company is on the brink of failure, or, like *floundering*, it might convey the idea that the company is bogged down and thrashing about in confusion. Even a ship can be said to *flounder*, instead of the expected *founder*, if the emphasis is on its being tossed about wildly by the pounding waves, not on its going to the bottom after taking on water.

fragmentary sentence.   See **Dancing to a samba beat.**

functional shift.   See **"Ice cream your kids today with Rocky Road."**

fused participles.   See **"Me carrying a briefcase is like a hog wearing earrings."**

fused sentences.   See **Eliot was born in Missouri, however, he spent most of his life in England.**

G

gerunds: **dangling**, see **Covered with onions, relish, and ketchup, I ate a hot dog at the ballpark; subjects of,** see **"Me carrying a briefcase is like a hog wearing earrings."**

get

The verb *get* is one of handiest and hardest-working (perhaps overworked) words in the English language. *Webster's New World Dictionary of the American Language* gives twenty-two transitive senses, with subdivisions, and three intransitive senses, followed by thirty-four idioms, from *get about* to *get up*. But not even these entries begin to suggest the range of idiomatic uses of *get*.

Other verbs may be more elegant, expressive, or precise.

"*Do* you *have* a library card?" is smoother than "*Have* you *got* a library card?"

"I *caught* cold" is more economical and no less idiomatic than "I *got* a cold."

"Who will *prepare* (or *fix*) breakfast?" is clearer than "Who will *get* breakfast?," since *get* means "receive" or "be given," as well as "prepare."

Yet in certain contexts *get* is far and away the most appropriate verb, especially in casual conversation.

"*Did* I *get* soaked!" is more forceful than "*Did* I *become* soaked!" and, some think, more apt than "*Was* I *soaked*!"

"I tried to phone but *got* no answer" is less stilted than "I tried to phone but *obtained* no answer" and more to the point than "I tried to phone, but no one *answered*."

"When *did* you *get* married?" is less ambiguous than "When *were* you *married*?," because the reply ought to be a single year, if not a precise date, whereas the second question might be answered by a vague statement like "between 1982 and 1986."

"We *didn't get* to Japan," in suggesting that we wanted to go but were somehow prevented from doing so, is richer in meaning than "We *didn't go* to Japan."

And what could take the place of "I *can't get* started with you"?

THESE ARE THE PRINCIPAL parts of the verb *get:*

Present: *get*

Past: *got*

Present participle: *getting*

Past participle: *got* or *gotten*

American English and British English part company over the past participle, and not in the way some people might expect. Contrary to the usual stereotypes—the Americans being the adventurous folk who change their language as often as they change their clothes and the British being so conservative that, if they had their way, they would be speaking in the decasyllabic couplets of Chaucer's time—it is the Americans who have preserved the older form, *gotten,* while the British use only the newer, clipped form, *got* (except in Biblical references and set phrases like *ill-gotten gains*).

Yet it is not true, as some think, that all Americans prefer *gotten* to *got.* Nor is it true that those who say *gotten* do so all the time. The choice depends largely on the context.

To express simple possession or necessity, for example, most Americans use *got,* not *gotten,* with *have* (or a contraction of *have*).

What *have* you *got* in your hand?

He's *got* his eye on the Presidency.

We've *got* to be home by ten.

Others go even further, using a form of the auxiliary verb *have* without either *got* or *gotten* as the past participle.

What *do* you *have* in your hand?

He *has* his eye on the Presidency.

We *have* to (or *must*) be home by ten.

In the senses of "come to be," "become," "acquired," "arrived at," and the like, many Americans do indeed prefer *gotten* to *got.*

"Has the lawn next door ever <u>gotten</u> so high it looked ready for harvest?" (Bob Secter, *Los Angeles Times*)

"Nor do I have a Robert Oppenheimer to write to me as he did to [his brother] Frank eight years later: 'I take it that Cambridge has been right for you, and that physics has <u>gotten</u> now very much under your skin, physics and the obvious excellences of the life it brings.' " (Jeremy Bernstein, *New Yorker*)

" 'Regrets are a waste of time. I'm just kind of surprised that I've <u>gotten</u> here.' " (Melvyn Douglas, quoted by Guy Flately, *San Francisco Chronicle*)

Some use *got* and *gotten* interchangeably in such constructions (if they use the verb *get* at all), depending mostly on which form sounds better to them. *Gotten* is the likely choice in the sense of "become" when progression is implied.

Candy bars *have gotten* smaller and smaller.

Some Americans invariably use *got,* either because they were taught to or because they want to sound British (see THERE'S NO HOME LIKE EATON PLACE).

Often, especially in casual conversation, *got* is added as an intensifier, which seems particularly appropriate when the unemphatic *have* is contracted. In one part of his unfinished poem "Sweeney Agonistes," T. S. Eliot has two characters say:

"You've got to know what you want to ask them"

"You've got to know what you want to know"

And in the other part he has a character say, even more the way people speak:

"But I've gotta use words when I talk to you."

go or *come*?   See *come* or *go*?

gobbledygook.   See **A concept-oriented framework may effectuate a consensus of opinion in terms of the maximization of a meaningful continuum of program factors.**

Goldwynisms.   See **"You're a goody-goody gumshoes."**

Good night, Anwar. Good night, Menachem.

President Anwar el-Sadat, of Egypt, and Prime Minister Menachem Begin, of Israel, became such good friends during the Middle East peace talks at Camp David in 1979 that, according to an American radio newscast, each was calling the other by his "Christian name." This term is indeed widely used for a person's baptismal or given name, as distinguished from the surname or family name. But because Sadat was a Muslim and Begin a Jew, "first name," "given name," or, especially in Britain, "forename" might have been a better choice.

Grampa got his strenth back last Febuary.

Call it laziness or call it economy of motion: the fact is, as long as the sounds they produce are not so distorted as to get in the way of communication, our organs of speech do as little work as possible. By and large, English-speakers rarely complain about the simplification that has taken place in either pronunciation or spelling over the centuries. There is no wave of popular sentiment in favor of replacing the word *fly* with the Old English *fleogan.* Demonstrators do not picket the offices of dictionary makers who show that *p* is no longer pronounced in the word *raspberry.*

What we cannot bear, though, is other people's failure to enunciate all the sounds in words we haven't yet begun to shorten ourselves. Why, for example, must they say gram'pä instead of grand'pä, strenth instead of streŋkth or streŋth, and feb'yōō wer'ē instead of feb'rə wer'ē? In time, of course, these and many other shortened pronunciations will be even more common, for the elimination of sounds and letters from words is one of the ways language evolves. Some elisions are temporary, occurring only in careless or rapid speech; others are repeated often enough to become adopted as the norm. The various phonetic processes by which sounds in words become diminished or even disappear include *assimilation, dissimilation, syncopation,* and *consonant cluster reduction.*

Assimilation

In assimilation a sound is so influenced by a neighboring sound that it tends to become like it. That is, when two adjacent sounds are produced either by the same speech organ or in the same way, one changes to resemble the other.

In one kind of assimilation, two identical sounds coming one after the other are likely to be reduced to one. For example, even though *eighteen* is made up of *eight* plus *teen,* it is pronounced (and written) as though it had only one *t.*

In another kind of assimilation, sounds may become lost when voiced and voiceless consonants are next to each other in a word. (A voiced consonant is one that causes the vocal cords to vibrate when it is pronounced; a voiceless, or unvoiced, consonant causes no such vibration. We can easily tell the difference by placing our fingers over our Adam's apple, which is next to the vocal cords in the larynx, and saying, for instance, *do* and *think.* We will feel a quiver when we pronounce the voiced *d* in *do,* but not when we pronounce the voiceless *th* in *think.*) So a word like *width* is pronounced wit*th,* instead of the usual wid*th,* if the *d* sound is made voiceless by the voiceless *th* sound that comes immediately after it. Even speakers who are ordinarily careful to sound the *d* may elide it into the *th* in rapid speech. The same may happen with *breadth,* which can be pronounced bret*th* as well as bred*th,* and *eighth,* which can be pronounced āt*th* as well as ātt*th.* It may also happen with *strength* and *length,* in which the voiced *g* is followed by the voiceless *th,* but the pronunciations lent*th* and strent*th* are not considered standard; that is, they are not in accord with the level of usage of educated, cultivated English-speakers.

Still another kind of assimilation has to do with ease of articulation. When two similar consonant sounds are neighbors in a word, one may either disappear entirely or be so changed that it has exactly the same sound as the other. Both processes can be seen in *horseshoe,* in which an *s* sound is followed by a *sh* sound. Although some people may clearly enunciate both words in the compound (hôrs′sh o͞o′), most are apt to say either hôr′sh o͞o′ or hôrsh′sh o͞o′. *Suggest* presents another illustration of this kind of assimilation. Americans have traditionally pronounced both *g*'s, giving the first one a "hard" sound and the second a "soft" sound (səg jest′). In the British pronunciation, which is making inroads on American speech, the "hard" *g* is assimilated to the "soft" *g* (sə jest′).

Because *m* and *n* are articulated in much the same way (both are voiced nasal sounds), they are often assimilated—usually with the *n* taking on the sound of *m.* Though still written in words like *hymn, column, solemn,* and *damn,* the *n* is silent. In other words a change in spelling, as well as pronunciation, takes place. The prefix *in-,* for instance, becomes *im-* before base words beginning with *m* (as in *immigrate* and *immortal*).

6. Take care with idiomatic expressions like *the powers that be, suffice it to say,* and *come what may.* The trouble is not so much that they contain verbs in the subjunctive but that they have become trite through overuse. (For more on clichés, see LO AND BEHOLD, IT'S MAN'S BEST FRIEND.)

healthy or *healthful?*

Attaching either *-y* or *-ful* to a noun is likely to produce an adjective that means "full of," "characterized by," or "having" whatever quality is expressed by the noun. So something that is *healthy* ought to be the same as something that is *healthful.* And it is, at least in the sense of "helping to produce, promote, or maintain health."

> Exercising at home can be as healthy (healthful) as at a gym, and it's less expensive.

But, unlike *healthful, healthy* is also applied to someone who is well or in good health ("You certainly look healthy now that you jog every day") and to something that shows or results from good health ("Where did you get such a healthy color?"). Besides, *healthy* is used in informal speech and writing to describe something that is large, vigorous, or the like ("From a puppy, that's a healthy yelp").

For more on the way suffixes and prefixes can change the meaning of words, see WHO NEEDS A RABBIT'S FOOT MORE: AN UNLUCKY PERSON OR A LUCKLESS ONE?

help but.   See **I cannot but love that man of mine.**

Herefords, who are a breed of beef cattle, have white faces and red bodies.

As we learned in school, an adjective clause modifies a noun, or a word or group of words serving as a noun, in a main clause of the sentence. Although *who* (or *whom*), *which,* and *that* are the relative pronouns most often used to introduce adjective clauses, they are not interchangeable.

Who or *whom* refers to people and to animals that are personified or given personal names.

> Aunt Tillie, whom I met on my cousin's yacht, lives in Portugal.

> King Kong, who appeared in one of the earliest science-fiction talkies, is the world's best-known giant ape.

(For the difference between the subjective and objective forms of this relative pronoun, see WHO WOULD YOU TURN TO FOR HELP?)

Which refers to things, including collections of individuals and most animals.

> Gruel, which is made by cooking meal in water or milk, is frequently fed to invalids.

> The Security Council, which was called back from its recess, approved the resolution.

Mules, which are the offspring of a donkey and a horse, are nearly always sterile.

That refers either to things or to people.

Cats that eat canaries get indigestion.

Everyone that has heard the song has liked it.

Finding it unseemly to apply *that* to people, some speakers and writers use *who* or *whom* instead.

Everyone who has heard the song has liked it.

The man whom I helped across the street reminded me of Uncle Herman.

Far more unusual than *that* in references to people is *who*, instead of *which* or *that*, in references to things.

Attached is a list of companies who have sent their employees to management seminars.

Herefords, who are a breed of beef cattle, have white faces and red bodies.

For the use of *that* and *which* in introducing restrictive and nonrestrictive relative clauses, see THE OVAL OFFICE WHICH IS IN THE WHITE HOUSE SYMBOLIZES THE PRESIDENCY; for the placement, or misplacement, of relative clauses, "ELECTRIC SHAVER FOR WOMEN WITH DELICATE FLORAL DESIGN ON THE HANDLE."

A RELATIVE PRONOUN can often be omitted in casual conversation and informal writing.

Here is the recipe (*which, that*) you said you wanted.

Isn't he the man (*whom*) they told us about?

Sometimes, however, such a pronoun is needed for sense or to prevent misreading.

The receptionist phoned me canceled the appointment. (Without *who* or *that* before it, *phoned* appears to be the principal verb, whose subject is *receptionist*.)

The oil cartels deal with is mainly from the Middle East. (*Oil cartels* is too well known a phrase not to be broken, here, by *that* or *which*.)

She writes about the kind of city people simply can't forget. (*City people*, too, ought to be divided by *that* or *which*.)

The omission of relative pronouns is also dealt with in TENNIS IS A SPORT I ENJOY BUT WHICH I DON'T PLAY WELL.

hopefully

Of the people who say, with vehemence, "There's no such word as *hopefully!*," a few probably think that there isn't. Most know that there is; they just don't like the way it is used nowadays.

That unhappy group does not object to the traditional use of *hopefully* as an adverb modifying a single word or phrase—in the sense of "in a way that shows the hope or expectation of getting what one wants."

The picnickers listened *hopefully* to the weather forecast.

What they condemn is its use as an adverbial clause modifying an entire sentence—in the sense of "it is hoped" or "it is to be hoped."

Hopefully, the rain will end before the picknickers set out.

That sentence, they say, should be changed to:

The rain, *it is hoped* (or *one hopes, we hope*, or the like), will end before the picnickers set out.

One would think that their cause was lost by 1974, when Robert C. Pooley, professor emeritus of English at the University of Wisconsin, wrote, in *The Teaching of English:*

"Every class offers its own challenges which the teacher hopefully will recognize and meet."

But no. It seems that the more prevalent the new usage, the greater—or at least the more vocal—the opposition to it. The first (1975) edition of the *Harper Dictionary of Contemporary Usage,* for example, reported that this question had been put to its 136-member "distinguished panel of language experts":

"The adverb *hopefully* is often heard in the sense of 'we hope' in such sentences as 'Hopefully, the war will soon be ended.' Would you accept this formulation?"

The panel replied this way:

In speech: yes, 42 percent; no, 58 percent

In writing: yes, 24 percent; no, 76 percent

Less than ten years later, the panel, then thirty members stronger, was polled again. First the members were reminded of the earlier vote, in which Jean Stafford had mentioned this sign posted on the back door of her house: "The word *hopefully* must not be misused on these premises. Violators will be humiliated." Then they were asked:

"Do you think that this use of *hopefully* is now so frequently heard in the speech of literate Americans that it should be considered acceptable in conversational speech?"

This was their answer, according to the second (1985) edition of the *Harper Dictionary:*

In speech: yes, 30 percent; no, 70 percent

In writing: yes, 17 percent; no, 83 percent

How, then, can we explain the current popularity of a usage that many regard as not simply loose but abhorrent? The answer is simple: no other adverb conveys the notion of "it is hoped" or "it is to be hoped." *Hopably, hopedly,* and *hopingly* are not established in the language, so not surprisingly a word already in existence had its meaning stretched to fill a need. The main objection to *hopefully* as a sentence modifier is that it lacks a point of view; that is, it does not say who does the hoping.

Yet *hopefully* is not the only English adverb that has been so broadened in meaning as to modify an entire sentence. When we read this statement in a 1979 *Washington Post* article:

"Ironically, Congress killed a program in 1975 that by now might have given the U.S. supersensitive new eavesdropping satellites that could be compensating already for the Iranian bases."

did we think that the author, Robert G. Kaiser, meant that Congress had acted in an ironic manner, perhaps using words humorously or sarcastically to convey the opposite of what those words usually mean? Or did we assume that he was calling attention to a situation in 1979 that was far different from what might have been expected when Congress had acted four years earlier?

Who does the regretting in:

Regrettably, terrorist raids are increasing.

Who acts in a frank way in:

His backhand is frankly terrible.

Who behaves in a manner that is easily perceived in:

Apparently, the merger was nothing more than a tax dodge.

Actually, luckily, thankfully, admittedly, and *unfortunately* are a few other sentence adverbs that we use all the time without wondering whose action or state of mind they denote.

How come the clock isn't going?

On being asked this question, is a native English-speaker likely to wonder what the verb *come* has to do with a clock that isn't working properly? No, because *how come?* is one of the countless expressions that speakers, writers, and readers accept without thinking: it is an idiom. Stopping to analyze an idiom is like puzzling over which shoe to put on first.

How come? belongs to the group of English idioms that go counter to the usual patterns of the language. Nowadays the adverb *how* is seldom followed immediately by a form of the verb *come*. But at one time *how comes it that?* or *how does it come that?* was used in the sense of "How does it happen that?" *How come?,* a shortened form of those questions, is now recognized, mainly in the States, as an idiomatic, if informal, equivalent of *why?*

These are some of the many other widely used idioms that do not conform with the way English words are customarily joined together to express thought:

get (have) the best of

Better, the comparative form of the adjective *good,* ordinarily refers to two persons or things; *best,* the superlative form, to more than two. Yet every day we use constructions like "Must you always get the best of a used-car dealer?," in the sense of "Must you always outwit that person?"

go easy on

We all know that *easy* is an adjective and *easily* an adverb, and that adverbs, not adjectives, modify verbs. Yet the widely used idiom is *go easy on*, not *go easily on*, because in this instance *go* is a linking verb.

> The Highway Patrol seems to be going easier on speeders these days.

(For more on linking verbs, see PEOPLE WHO WANT TO ARRIVE SAFE DON'T DRIVE DRUNKENLY.)

somebody else's

In English, adjectives generally precede the words they modify, and only nouns and certain pronouns take possessive endings.

> It is anybody's guess.

> It is no one's business.

> That is the Great Nobody's opinion.

But in *somebody else's* (*someone else's, nobody else's,* and the like) the adjective *else* not only follows the indefinite pronoun *somebody* but has the possessive signal of an apostrophe and *s* attached to it. That's because *somebody else* is now regarded as a compound pronoun; and compound pronouns, like compound nouns, take the possessive inflection at the end. Just as we wouldn't say "It's my *brother's-in-law* car," we'd feel foolish singing a line in a song that goes, "It's *somebody's else* moon above, not mine."

ago

The adjective *ago,* usually following a noun, indicates the past.

> We moved to Detroit five years ago.

And the adverb *tomorrow,* meaning "on the day after today," refers to the future.

> We will move to Detroit tomorrow.

But in a twist of both time and language we say:

> We moved to Detroit five years ago tomorrow.

cannot help but

Despite the objections of grammarians who see not one but two double negatives in the construction, many English-speakers, especially Americans, persist in using the idiomatic *cannot help but* plus an infinitive.

> I couldn't help but eat the whole pizza.

(For more on this point of disputed usage, see I CANNOT BUT LOVE THAT MAN OF MINE.)

ANOTHER GROUP OF IDIOMS consists of expressions whose meanings are different from the literal meanings of the words that make them up. That is, when put together, the individual parts produce a new and greater whole that those who know the language accept without question. For example:

Someone who *lies down on the job* does not stretch out on a workbench. That person puts forth less than his or her best efforts.

A name that is *on the tip of one's tongue* is not written in indelible ink on the pointy end of the movable organ attached to the floor of one's mouth. It is a name that might be said at any moment because it can almost, though not quite, be recalled.

If we *run into* old friends, we ordinarily do not hurt them. All we do is encounter them by chance. And if we later *drop by* their house, we do not fall from a tree onto their front lawn. Instead, we pay them an unexpected visit.

Children who are *underfoot* are not pressed between the floor and their mother's shoe. They are simply in the way.

A sailor who *keeps* his *eyes peeled* (or *skinned*) does not make a habit of cutting away the outer layers of his eyes. He is on lookout, or doing sentry duty.

A convicted criminal who is sent to the penitentiary *for good* (or *for good and all*) is not likely to be happy about it. He or she faces permanent imprisonment.

A proposal that *goes by the board* is not paraded in front of a piece of wood. It is ignored or rejected.

Idioms, then, may look or sound like other expressions we often put together, but whereas in a built-up construction every word counts toward making up the larger meaning, an idiom has a meaning that must be taken as a whole, not by joining the meanings of its various words. "The mayor will *go to* Akron," for example, is a straightforward, nonidiomatic statement about the mayor's travel plans; "The mayor will *go to any length* to get reelected" contains an idiom meaning that the mayor will do whatever is necessary, will scruple at nothing, to win reelection. Similarly, "Kelly *lost* her *watch*" means just what it says, but "Kelly *lost* her *heart* to Michael Jackson" means that she fell in love with the singer.

Some idioms mean the opposite, or nearly the opposite, of what their words seem to say. A person or thing that is *not far from wrong,* for instance, is really not far from *right*. A person or thing that *turns up missing* does not *turn up,* or make an appearance, at all. And something that would be *cheap at half the price* would really be cheap at *double* the price.

Dictionaries list many idioms, by key word, usually at the end of entries. For example, the entry for *hand* is likely to include *on hand,* meaning "near" or "available; ready" ("He had enough cash on hand to buy the Brooklyn Bridge"). Unlabeled idioms, such as *on hand,* are generally considered standard; that is, they are acceptable at any level of usage.

Some idioms are labeled "colloquial" or "informal"—for instance, *on one's own hook,* meaning "by oneself; without getting help, advice, or the like" ("She got a job in a Broadway musical on her own hook"). Either of those labels indicates that the dictionary considers the idioms to be characteristic of informal speech and writing, not by any means substandard, vulgar, provincial, or illiterate.

And some idioms are labeled "slang"—for example, *keep one's shirt on,* meaning "to remain patient or calm" ("I'll be with you in a minute, so will you keep your shirt on?"). That label indicates that the dictionary found the idioms mainly in very informal contexts. (But if slang expressions stay around long enough, they may work their way up the linguistic ladder until they acquire more formal status. See JOBBED IN A HUMONGOUS SCAM, THE TWEAKED-OUT MOBSTER EXCLAIMED, "PEACHY-KEEN!")

It is unlikely that at any given time all dictionaries will agree on which idioms should be considered slang, colloquial, or the like; indeed, as usage changes over time, so do dictionary labels. Nor do dictionaries make judgments about which idioms are clichés, that is, expressions which were once original and forceful but have lost their freshness through frequent use—like *lose one's heart, out of the blue,* and *tired but happy.* (For more on clichés, see LO AND BEHOLD, IT'S MAN'S BEST FRIEND.)

THOUGH MOST PEOPLE ARE UNAWARE of the many generally accepted idioms they either use themselves or encounter in the speech and writing of others, they are quick to spot one gone awry. A native English-speaker who hears someone say "We've only *tapped the surface* of the problem," for example, probably assumes that English is not that person's first language, for the idiom meaning "to do, consider, or affect something superficially" is *scratch the surface.*

Similarly, a nonnative English-speaker who fails to perceive the subtle differences between "I look forward *to seeing* you soon," "I hope *to see* you soon," and "I hope *to be seeing* you soon" may use an unidiomatic variant such as "I look forward *to see* you soon." Analogy is an invaluable tool in learning a language—for native and nonnative speakers alike; but because idioms, by their very nature, go against the grain of a language, patterning unfamiliar constructions on older, familiar ones has its limitations.

Whether English is their first or second language, people sometimes turn out unidiomatic idioms by using a word that does not ring true or by sliding one idiom into another. For examples of such misapplications of established usage, see "YOU'RE A GOODY-GOODY GUMSHOES."

Idiomatic Prepositions

Far more troublesome than either the *How come?* or the *lie down on the job* kind of idioms are combinations of prepositions and other parts of speech. Native English-speakers learn most of these combinations by using them from childhood on, but even they are sometimes perplexed when it comes to deciding what preposition goes with a particular word or phrase. Few nonnative speakers trying to master the language find English idiomatic prepositions anything but diabolical.

Constructions in which the preposition goes before a noun, a personal pronoun, or a word group that functions as a noun are generally not a problem.

The cabin is *on* a mountaintop.

They were sitting *behind* us.

From everything I've heard, the motorbike is first-rate.

Nor do prepositions that go before the infinitive form of verbs, before certain adjectives, and even before a few adverbs cause much difficulty.

It was time *to* go.

He looked like a knight *of* old. (Here *old* is a noun.)

The shot came *from* above.

Placing a preposition like *with* before an adverb like *askance* requires either ignorance of the way English works or a lot of courage.

"There may have been a time when something appearing in print carried the mark of authority. If so, no longer can one take at face value all of the usage employed by even the better publications. Certain dictionaries must be looked at <u>with askance</u>. To make it through a day without encountering in print (let alone in oral speech) solecisms and lapses in taste or judgment (let alone in simple syntax) would be an achievement...." (Sarah Montoya, "Print Pollution")

In constructions in which the preposition follows a noun, an adjective, or a verb, it sometimes seems that only one preposition will do and that it is simply a matter of learning, by practice, which one to use.

He is working *on* a new version of Aesop's fables.

Teenagers are especially vulnerable *to* peer pressure.

Cities must grapple *with* both social and economic problems.

Actually, it is often the context of the sentence, especially what immediately follows the preposition, that determines the choice.

The singer played *with* the audience.

Spotlights played *over* the crowd.

With many words, more than one preposition can be used with no change in meaning.

This is the first time the teams are competing *with* (or *against*) each other.

The shelf was filled with books *on* (or *about, concerning, regarding*) self-improvement.

Do you hanker *after* (or *for*) the good old days?

Although a few constructions are still debated (see, for example, BLAME FOR OR BLAME ON?; CENTER AROUND; CONSIST OF OR CONSIST IN?; DIFFERENT FROM, DIFFERENT THAN, OR DIFFERENT TO?), for the most part the choice of preposition depends on the speaker's or writer's preference and sense of euphony. Someone who generally uses *on*, for instance, may find that in a given sentence *upon* produces a more agreeable combination of sounds.

With many other words, the preposition can cause at least a shift in emphasis.

Scholars are grateful *to* reference librarians.

Scholars are grateful *for* the help of reference librarians.

And with still other words, the preposition can change the meaning. Let's take the adjective *free*, for example.

> With either *from* or *of*, it indicates release from discomfort and the like, or from the control of some other person or some arbitrary power.
>
> The world is virtually free *from* (*of*) smallpox.
>
> After the operation, Fred was free *from* (*of*) pain.
>
> Both in and out of Orwell's novel, people want to be free *from* (*of*) Big Brother.
>
> If only Rebecca had got free *from* (*of*) Mrs. Danvers earlier!
>
> With *from*, it indicates release from an obligation or debt, or exemption from a certain imposition.
>
> Books are free *from* duty.
>
> With *with*, it indicates generosity or lavishness.
>
> He was as free *with* his praise as he was close with his money.
>
> With *in* and sometimes *of*, it indicates lack of restraint.
>
> Was there ever a dancer more free *in* (*of*) spirit than Isadora Duncan?

Deciding which of several possible prepositions is appropriate in a particular context is by no means automatic, not even for native English-speakers. To avoid an unidiomatic slip, speakers and writers sometimes run a series of questions through their mind, as if trying the prepositions on for fit. For instance:

"Do I grieve *at*, *for*, or *over* your loss?"

"Am I sorry you're angry *at* or *with* me?"

"Does one write *in regard to*, *with regard to*, *regarding*, or *as regards* a job offer?"

"Was your bill sent to me *in* error or *by* error? Or *by* mistake?"

Like other idioms, prepositional idioms are learned through practice—hearing them said and seeing them written. Dictionaries are helpful in showing what prepositions are invariably or generally used with certain words. *Webster's New World Dictionary*, for example, does this in three ways: by working the prepositions into the definitions (where they are either italicized and enclosed in parentheses or included in bracketed examples); by adding parenthetical notes to indicate that the prepositions are so used; and by giving idiomatic prepositions in boldface at the end of the entries. This is how *WNWD* shows uses of prepositions with the verb *run:*

rum-r... (rum... ...n. a ...r, ship, etc. ...to)
in smuggling alcoholic liquor —**rum'run'ning** n.
run (run) vi. **ran** or dial. **run, run, run'ning** [altered (with
vowel prob. infl. by pp.) < ME. *rinnen, rennen* < ON. &
OE.: ON. *rinna,* to flow, run, *renna,* to cause to run
(< Gmc. *rannjan*); OE. *rinnan, iornan:* both < Gmc.
renwo < IE. base *er-,* to set in motion, excite, whence L.
origo, ORIGIN & RAISE] **1.** to go by moving the legs rapidly,
faster than in walking, and (in a two-legged animal) in
such a way that for an instant both feet are off the ground
2. a) to go rapidly; move swiftly [a ship *running* before
the wind] b) to resort (*to*) for aid [always *running* to the
police] **3.** to associate or consort (*with*) **4.** to go, move,
grow, etc. easily and freely, without hindrance or restraint
5. to go away rapidly; flee **6.** to make a quick trip (*up to,
down to, over to,* etc. a specified place) for a brief stay
7. a) to take part in a contest or race ☆b) to be a candidate
in an election **8.** to finish a contest or race in the specified
position [to *run* last] **9.** to swim in migration, as upstream
or inshore for spawning, etc.: said of fish **10.** to go, as on
a schedule; ply between two points [a bus that *runs* between Chicago and Detroit] **11.** to go or pass lightly and
rapidly [his eyes *ran* over the page] **12.** to be current;
circulate [a rumor *running* through the town] **13.** to
climb or creep: said of plants [a vine *running* over the
wall] **14.** to move continuously [his tongue *ran* on and on]
15. to ravel lengthwise in a knitted fabric **16.** to function
or operate with or as with parts that revolve, slide, etc.
[a machine that is *running*] **17.** to recur or return to the
mind **18.** to flow [a *running* stream] **19.** to melt and
flow (the wax *ran*] **20.** a) to spread when put on a surface,
as a liquid b) to spread over or be diffused through cloth,
etc. when moistened, as colors c) to be subject to such
spreading of color, as fabric **21.** to be wet or covered with
a flow [eyes *running* with tears] **22.** to give passage to a
fluid; specif., a) to discharge pus, mucus, etc. b) to leak,
as a faucet **23.** to elapse [the days *ran* into weeks] **24.** a)
to appear in print, as in a newspaper b) to appear or be
presented continuously or in a continuing series [a play
that *ran* for a year] **25.** a) to continue in effect or force
[a law *running* for twenty years] b) to continue to occur;
recur [talent *runs* in the family] **26.** to be characterized
by having, producing, using, etc. (with *to*) [their taste
runs to exotic foods] **27.** a) to extend in or as in a continuous line [a fence *running* through the woods] b) to include
so as to show variety (with *from* and *to*) [a repertoire
running from tragedy to comedy] **28.** to pass into a
specified condition, situation, etc. [to *run* into trouble]
29. to sail or float (aground, etc.): said of a ship **30.** to be
written, expressed, played, etc. in a specified way [the
adage *runs* like this] **31.** to be or continue at a specified
size, price, amount, etc. [apples *running* four to the
pound] —vt. **1.** to run along or follow (a specified course
or route) **2.** to travel over; cover by running, driving, etc.
[horses *ran* the range] **3.** to do or perform by or as by
running [to *run* a race] **4.** to subject oneself to (a risk);
incur ☆**5.** a) to get past or escape by going through [to
run a blockade] b) to go past or through without making
a required stop [to *run* a stop sign or a red light] **6.** to
pursue or hunt (game, etc.) **7.** to compete with in or as
in a race; vie with **8.** a) to enter (a horse, etc.) in a race
☆b) to put up or support as a candidate for election **9.** a)
to make run, move, operate, etc. b) to cause to go between
points, as on a schedule c) to cause (a motor or engine)
to idle for a while d) to make (a stocking) run **10.** to
bring, lead, or force into a specified condition, situation,
etc. by or as by running [to *run* oneself into debt] **11.** a)
to carry or convey, as in a ship or vehicle; transport b) to
carry (taxable or outlawed goods) in or out illegally;
smuggle **12.** to drive, force, or thrust (an object) into,
through, or against (something) **13.** to make go, move,
pass, flow, etc., esp. rapidly, in a specified way, direction,
place, etc. [to *run* water into a glass] **14.** ☆a) to be in
charge of; manage [to *run* a household] ☆b) to keep,
feed, or graze (livestock) c) to perform the steps of (an
experiment, test, etc.) d) to cause to undergo a test,
procedure, process, etc. **15.** to cost (an amount) [boots
that *run* $20] **16.** to mark, draw, or trace (lines, as on a
map) **17.** to extend, pass, or trace in a specified way or
direction [to *run* a story back to its source] **18.** to undergo
or be affected by (a fever, etc.) **19.** to flow with, discharge,
or pour forth [gutters *running* blood] **20.** to melt, fuse,
or smelt (ore) **21.** to cast or mold, as from molten metal;
found ☆**22.** to print; esp., to publish (an advertisement,
story, etc.) in a newspaper or magazine **23.** *Billiards,* etc.
to complete successfully (a specified number of strokes,
shots, etc.) in uninterrupted sequence **24.** *Bridge* to lead
(a suit) taking a series of tricks **25.** *Golf* to cause (a ball)
to roll, esp. on a green —n. **1.** an act or period of running
or moving rapidly **2.** a) a race for runners b) a running
pace; rapid gait c) capacity for running **3.** the distance
covered or time spent in running **4.** a trip; journey; esp.,
a) a single, customary, or regular trip, as of a train, ship,
or plane b) a quick trip, esp. for a brief stay c) same as
ROUTE (sense 2) **5.** a) movement onward, progression,
or trend [the *run* of events] b) a continuous course or
period of a specified condition, action, etc. [a *run* of good
luck] **6.** direction or course, as of the grain of wood, a
vein of ore, etc. **7.** a continuous course of performances,

etc. [a play that had a *run* of a year] **8.** a series of continued, sudden, or urgent requests or demands, as by
customers for certain goods, or by bank depositors for
payment **9.** a period of being in public demand or favor
10. a continuous series or sequence, as of cards in one
suit **11.** a continuous extent of something **12.** a flow or
rush of water, etc., as of the tide **13.** a small, swift stream,
as a brook, rivulet, etc. **14.** a) a period during which some
fluid flows readily b) the amount of flow **15.** a) the point
of operation of a machine b) the output during this period
16. a) a kind, sort, or class, as of goods b) the ordinary,
usual, or average kind or type **17.** something in, on, or
along which something else runs; specif., a) an inclined
pathway or course [a ski *run*] b) a track, channel, trough,
pipe, etc. c) an enclosed area in which domestic animals
or fowl can move about freely or feed [a chicken *run*] d)
in Australia, a large grazing area or ranch e) a well-
defined trail or path made and used by animals [a buffalo
run] **18.** freedom to use all the facilities or move freely
in any part (of a place) [to have the *run* of an estate]
19. a) a number of animals in motion together b) a large
number of fish migrating together, as upstream or inshore
for spawning c) such migration of fish ☆**20.** a ravel
lengthwise in something knitted, as in hosiery ☆**21.**
Baseball a scoring point, made by a successful circuit of
the bases **22.** *Billiards,* etc. an uninterrupted sequence
of successful strokes, shots, etc. **23.** *Cricket* a scoring
point, made by a successful running of both batsmen
from one wicket to the other **24.** *Mil.* the approach to
the target made by an airplane in bombing, strafing, etc.
25. *Music* a rapid succession of tones, as a roulade **26.**
Naut. the extreme after part of a ship's bottom, from where
it starts to curve up and in toward the stern —adj. **1.**
melted; made liquid **2.** poured or molded while in a melted
state [*run* metal] **3.** drained or extracted, as honey **4.**
having migrated and spawned: said of fish —**a run for
one's money 1.** powerful competition **2.** some satisfaction
for what one has expended, as in betting on a near winner
in a race —**in the long run** in the final outcome; ultimately
—**on the run 1.** running **2.** hurrying from place to place
or task to task **3.** running away; in retreat —☆**run across**
to encounter by chance —**run after 1.** to pursue or follow
2. [Colloq.] to seek the company or companionship of
—**run along** to leave or depart —**run away 1.** to flee
2. to desert one's home or family **3.** to escape and run
loose, as a horse —**run away with 1.** to depart and take
with one; esp., to steal **2.** to carry/ out of control [his
enthusiasm *ran away with* him] **3.** a) to outdo greatly
all other contestants or performers in b) to get (a prize,
honors, etc.) in this way —**run back** to carry (a football)
toward the opponent's goal, as after receiving a kickoff
—**run down 1.** to cease to run, or stop operating, as a
mechanical device, through lack of power **2.** to run, ride,
or drive against so as to knock down **3.** to pursue and
capture or kill **4.** to search out the source of **5.** to speak
of slightingly or injuriously; disparage **6.** to lessen or
lower in worth, quality, etc.; make or become run-down
7. to read through rapidly ☆**8.** *Baseball* to catch and tag
(a base runner trapped between two bases) —**run for it**
to run in order to escape or avoid something —**run in
1.** to include or insert, as something additional **2.** [Colloq.]
to make a brief stop or visit at a place ☆**3.** [Slang] to take
into legal custody; arrest **4.** *Printing* to make continuous
without a break or paragraph —**run into 1.** to encounter
by chance **2.** to run, ride, or drive against so as to hit;
collide with **3.** to add up to (a large sum of money): also
run to —**run off** ☆**1.** to print, typewrite, make copies of,
etc. **2.** to cause to be run, performed, played, etc. **3.** to
decide the winner of (a race, etc.) by a runoff **4.** to drive
(animals, trespassers, etc.) off or away **5.** to flow off;
drain **6.** same as RUN AWAY —**run on 1.** to continue or be
continued; specif., *Printing* to continue without a break
or new paragraph **2.** to add (something) at the end **3.** to
talk continuously —**run out 1.** to come to an end; expire
or become used up, exhausted, etc. **2.** to force to leave;
drive out —**run out of** to use up a supply of (something)
—**run out on** [Colloq.] to abandon or desert —☆**run out
the clock** *Basketball, Football,* etc. to maintain control of
the ball in the closing minutes of a game —**run over 1.**
to ride or drive over as with an automobile **2.** to over-
flow **3.** to go beyond a limit **4.** to examine, rehearse, etc.
rapidly or casually —**run scared** [Slang] to base one's
actions upon the possibility or likelihood of failure —**run
through 1.** to use up, spend, etc. quickly or recklessly
2. to pierce **3.** same as RUN OVER (sense 4) —**run up 1.** to
raise, rise, make, or build rapidly **2.** to let (bills, debts, etc.)
accumulate **3.** to sew with a rapid succession of stitches
run·a·bout (run'ə bout') n. **1.** a person who runs about
from place to place **2.** a light, one-seated, open carriage
☆**3.** ...

The customary use of prepositions with certain verbs in certain senses should not be confused with verb sets, or phrasal verbs. As the dictionary example shows, none of the prepositions included in the various definitions of *run* changes the meanings of the verb. However, the boldfaced idiomatic phrases at the end of the entry include the verb sets *run after, run along, run away, run away with, run back, run down, run into, run off, run out, run out of, run out on, run through,* and *run up,* in which the verb does indeed take on special meanings when combined with those adverbs. Sometimes prepositions are piled onto the adverbs in verb sets, as in *run out of.* (For more on verb sets, see WASHING DOWN PILLOWS TAKES A STRONG STOMACH.)

Dictionaries are, of course, not infallible guides to idiomatic prepositions. For one thing, even unabridged American dictionaries cannot list every preposition used with every other part of speech or every shade of meaning for those combinations that do appear. For another, dictionaries reflect ever-changing usage. The Brazilian novelist Érico Veríssimo once said that whenever he looked up a word in a Portuguese dictionary to learn which preposition should be used with it, he found himself being quoted as the authority for that usage.

"Some Troublesome Idiomatic Prepositions," a table at the back of this book, lists, with sample sentences, a number of the prepositional idioms that occasionally perplex even native speakers and writers of English.

however or *how ever?*

When it is used as an emphatic form of *how,* the adverb *however* can ask the question "By what means?" or "How in the world?"

However did you get your car to start?

To place greater stress on *ever,* some writers prefer the two-word form, especially in dialogue.

"How ever did you learn her secret?," he asked.

When the adverb *ever* is used in the sense of "at all" or "in any way," it is ordinarily separated from *how* by some other word or words.

How can I ever repay you for your kindness?

SOME ENGLISH TEACHERS AND AUTHORS of usage guides still advise against starting a sentence with *however* when the meaning is "nevertheless; yet; in spite of that; all the same." But nowadays most writers and speakers recognize that where they place the conjunctive adverb depends on what they want to emphasize.

However is ordinarily followed by a comma, and it is preceded by a semicolon if it introduces a dependent clause within the sentence.

All the birds seemed to have left the island. However, by nightfall we had managed to photograph two piedbilled grebes.

All the birds seemed to have left the island; however, by nightfall we had managed to photograph two piedbilled grebes.

All the birds seemed to have left the island; by nightfall, *however,* we had managed to photograph two piedbilled grebes.

(ELIOT WAS BORN IN MISSOURI, HOWEVER, HE SPENT MOST OF HIS LIFE IN ENGLAND deals with constructions in which a "heavy" conjunctive adverb like *however, therefore,* or *nevertheless* is not preceded by the expected semicolon.)

WHEN *however* means "in whatever manner" or "to whatever degree or extent," it introduces a clause or phrase. In this usage, it is not followed by a comma.

However his parents felt about the move, Jeff went to Paris, Arkansas.

The table talk, *however* insipid, went on till midnight.

human or *human being?*

As a noun meaning "human being," *human* was, according to *The Oxford English Dictionary,* used as early as the 1530s. Until the beginning of the eighteenth century it, like the earlier adjective, was written *humane* (the spelling now reserved for another word). Later on, the use of *human* instead of *human being* was harshly condemned. *Faulty Diction, As Corrected by "The Funk & Wagnalls Dictionary of the English Language,"* for example, found it "either archaic, or colloquial and humorous."

Yet that usage persisted, especially in the United States, until it is now accepted by all but the most refractory. *Humans; Humans and Animals;* and *Humans in Universe* are but three of the scores of book titles in which the one-word noun appears.

Many of those who insist that *human* be used not as a noun but as an adjective—to modify the "real" noun, *being*—probably don't hesistate to talk about:

a *liberal,* without adding *person* or *politician*

a *special,* without adding *TV program*

an *extra,* without adding *movie actor*

a *classic,* without adding *work, author,* or *automobile of the period 1925–1942*

Besides adjectives doing duty as nouns, many other English words move freely from one part of speech to another. (For more on functional shift, see "ICE CREAM YOUR KIDS TODAY WITH ROCKY ROAD.")

hung or *hanged?*

In most senses the verb *hang* takes *hung* as the past-tense or past-participle form. For example:

We hung the paintings one above the other.

After she had hung the wallpaper, Meg went to lunch.

The exception is in references to a person's dying or being put to death by tying a rope about the neck and suddenly suspending the body so as to snap the neck or cause strangulation. Here *hanged* is the generally preferred form.

The prisoner hanged himself in his cell.

As the film ends, the villain is hanged by the outraged townspeople.

More and more, however, *hung* is used in all senses. National Public Radio's *All Things Considered,* for example, reported in 1985 that a number of young members of the Arapaho tribe on the Wind River Reservation of Wyoming had hung themselves in a suicide epidemic.

Hurricane David left devastation in her wake.

Since the fourteenth century, English, unlike German, French, and other inflected languages, has had virtually no grammatical gender, that is, no special masculine, feminine, and neuter forms for all nouns, pronouns, adjectives, and articles. English-speakers therefore need not concern themselves with whether, for example, *pencil* and all the words that replace or modify it take a masculine, a feminine, or a neuter ending.

What Modern English does have is a far simpler natural gender, which classifies some nouns and pronouns as masculine, feminine, and neuter, not in accordance with arbitrary convention but with the sex or sexlessness of what the words actually represent. *Man, buck,* and *he,* then, are masculine; *woman, doe,* and *her,* feminine; and *pencil, house, loyalty,* and *itself,* neuter. In addition, some nouns and pronouns are said to have common gender, that is, either masculine or feminine or, in the plural, both (*student, poet, children, people, you, who, they,* and so on).

A few nouns are considered either masculine or feminine for no apparent reason, perhaps because they are holdovers from the days of grammatical gender. Thus, certain personifications like Justice are traditionally feminine, as are the names of nations and ships.

They called out to Justice, but she turned a blind eye.

Whatever her faults, France has a glorious cultural tradition.

We cheered the QE2 as she sailed into port.

Other personifications are traditionally masculine.

When will (Father) Time lay down his scythe and hourglass?

Hurricanes and tropical storms now alternate between feminine and masculine names. The tradition of bestowing only women's names on them ended in May 1978, when the regional coordinating committee of the World Meteorological Organization agreed to a U.S. proposal. Accordingly, the second tropical storm of the 1978 season in the eastern Pacific was called Hurricane Bud, instead of Hurricane Barbara, and the following year the practice was introduced in the Atlantic as well.

The simplified system of English gender makes it relatively easy to apply this part of the grammatical rule on pronoun-antecedent agreement: if a pronoun has an antecedent (a word or a word group that it refers to), it must agree with that antecedent in *gender*. Most English-speakers automatically say or write:

Paul ate *his* lunch at noon, but Madge didn't eat *hers* until two o'clock.

Did you put *your* pen back in *its* box?

The buck stood guard over *his* (or *its*) family.

Trouble starts when the antecedent is a word such as *everybody, everyone, somebody, someone, no one, neither, either,* or *each*. Because such words are considered singular indefinite pronouns in form, the pronouns that refer to them must, under the rule, also be singular. As for gender, one might assume that whether a singular pronoun is masculine or feminine depends on the sense of the sentence; for instance, whether by *everybody* the speaker or writer means only men or both men and women. Not so. Over the centuries, English usage—like that of other languages—has established the masculine singular pronoun as the form applying to both genders. For example, rule C.6, under "Antecedents," in Luella Clay Carson's *Handbook of English Composition: A Compilation of Standard Rules and Usage* (1911) states:

"When a number of persons, masculine and feminine, are spoken of distributively [with each member of the group regarded individually], the pronouns he and his are proper forms of reference (not *their*, not *his* or *her*).

"Each of the students has his peculiar traits."

That rule is still very much alive. After stating that a singular pronoun, not *they*, is appropriate when the antecedent is a distributive expression, the third (1979) edition of Strunk and White's *The Elements of Style*, for instance, gives these examples of incorrect and correct usage:

"Every one of us knows they are   Every one of us knows he is fallible.
fallible.

"Everyone in the community,   Everyone in the community, whether
whether they are a member of the   he is a member of the Association
Association or not, is invited to   or not, is invited to attend."
attend.

Many writers and speakers find it easy to be "correct." To them using *he* and *him* as pronouns for feminine as well as masculine nouns has nothing to do with the domination of women by men but is merely a convention of Modern English. In *Language and Woman's Place*, Robin Lakoff, an authority on linguistic sexism, agrees that the masculine pronoun is "unmarked" or "neutral"; therefore, she says, "when reference is made individually to members of a sexually mixed group, the normal solution is to resolve the indecision as to pronoun choice in favor of the masculine." Not surprisingly, her book contains sentences like this:

"The problem is that, by so doing, a speaker may also give the impression of not being really sure of himself, of looking to the addressee for confirmation, even of having no views of his own."

Somewhat suprisingly, the questionnaire on which the first volume (1985) of the *Dictionary of American Regional English (DARE)* was based contains entries like this:

"If something a person ate didn't agree with him, he might be sick _____ his stomach. (Gesture)."

The Americans whose usage was being surveyed were apparently asked questions with feminine pronouns only when the context so required. For instance:

"What words and expressions are used around here about a man who is very eager to get married? 'He's _____ .' "

"And what expressions about a woman who is very eager to get married? 'She's _____ .' "

However influenced by grammatical "correctness," *DARE* was not carried away. But former California Senator S. I. Hayakawa apparently was when, according to the columnist Mary Ann Seawell, he insisted:

"Abortion is a matter strictly between a patient and his doctor."

Knowing that many people are offended by the use of *he, him,* and *his* as neuter pronouns, some writers and speakers place a disclaimer between themselves and that usage. Mary-Claire van Leunen, for instance, states in the introduction to her *Handbook for Scholars* that in the *everybody . . . his* construction the *his* is "generic, not gendered," and then makes statements like this in the body of the book:

"There is one last reason for every scholar to cite his sources."

Wilma R. Ebbit and David R. Ebbit ended the "Sexist Language" entry in *Perrin's Index to English* with this statement:

"In this book *he* is used to refer to *student* and *writer* not because of bias or obtuseness but in the interest of economy and style."

And Wyatt Cooper waited until he was a third of the way through his autobiographical *Families*, in the middle of a passage about his mother, before saying:

"I will, throughout this book, use the masculine pronoun very often, just as I will speak of the race of man—man has done this or that; man must prevail; man has genius in his head—and I would like to state loudly and clearly that when I say 'man' or when I use 'he,' I mean 'man and woman' and I mean 'he and she'; I do not so state each time because the use of the masculine form is an ancient and historical one, dating from a time when power, both political and personal, was indeed vested in the male, and it is a literary form with which I am comfortable. But that does not mean that I think men are stronger, brighter, more worthy, more steadfast, or more promising than women. . . ."

Yet with the growing awareness that English speech and writing do indeed reflect sexist attitudes (see "BURNETT GOES DRAMATIC AS A GAUNT IOWA WIFE"), many people are turning to constructions that not only are proclaimed to be but look and sound gender-blind. To compensate for the lack of a truly generic third-person singular pronoun, they are changing *he* to *he or she*, *him* to *him or her*, *his* to *his or her*, and so on—sometimes reversing the order. For instance, Lewis H. Lapham, the editor of *Harper's*, wrote in the July 1981 issue:

> "The truth unfortunately has to be discovered every day, by each individual working with the tools of his own thought, imagination, and patient study."

This is how he began an article in the November 1986 issue:

> "As every schoolchild learns before he or she reaches the age of ten, America is always and forever innocent."

If carried to extremes, however, *he or she* constructions can render the reader or listener insensible. For example:

> In the Synonym Game, *a girl or boy* says a word (*he or she* should know, but not give, a synonym for the word). Then *he or she* points or tosses a beanbag to another child, to show that *he or she* should give a synonym. If the second child knows the synonym, *he or she* supplies it. It is then *his or her* turn to give a new word . . .

Without so many awkward joint-gender pronouns, the above example might begin like this:

> In the Synonym Game, *a girl or boy* says a word (knowing, but not giving, a synonym for it), and then points or tosses a beanbag to another child as a challenge to think of a synonym. If the second child knows one, *she or he* gives it . . .

Some writers use *he* in one chapter and *she* in the next, and so on throughout a book. This device, of course, works only in certain nonfiction works, in teacher's guides accompanying textbooks, and the like. And even here the reader, brought up short by the sudden introduction of a pronoun that did not appear in the previous chapter, is likely to wonder, ''Who she?'' or ''Who he?''

Still others favor assigning pronouns according to the sex of the user. In the introduction to *Dictionaries: The Art and Craft of Lexicography,* Sidney I. Landau makes a case for this separate-but-equal approach.

> "The cumulative effect of the iteration of masculine pronouns obliterates the female from one's consciousness. The problem is what to do about it. Proposals to correct the situation strike me as impractical or ludicrous. My own solution is to recommend that men use masculine pronouns for neutral use, because they naturally identify with the masculine gender, and that women use feminine pronouns for the analogous reason. Accordingly, since I am a man and feel comfortable with the masculine pronoun, I will use it in this book. I trust, however, that the context will make clear whether I mean the pronoun to convey physical or grammatical (neutral) gender."

There are other ways of eliminating the so-called neutral pronouns *he*, *him*, and *his*. The first—repeating the noun so as to avoid a pronoun altogether (as in ''The matter was strictly between the lawyer and the lawyer's client'')—goes against the pattern of the language, for taking the place of a noun is precisely what pronouns do. The second—addressing the reader or listener directly (with *you, we, I,* and the like)—is not appropriate in all contexts. The third—employing the neutral *one* (as in "One took one's lunch and ran")—does not come easily to Americans; besides, using this construction consistently takes effort (see ONE SHOULD NOT TELL SECRETS IF YOU WANT TO BE TOLD ANY). And the fourth—adopting a centuries' old plural construction when the meaning is clearly plural (as in "Everybody took their lunch and ran")—runs afoul of the later, artificial rule that a pronoun must agree with its antecedent not only in gender but also in number (see "IF SOMEONE COULD MAKE YOUR CHILD A GENIUS, WOULD YOU LET THEM?").

Nowadays many speakers and writers of English are conscious of what others perceive as a sexist use of the singular pronoun. Some even find ways to avoid it. Yet it hardly seems necessary to go as far as a Stanford student did in saying in a term paper:

"Nixon could have prevented Watergate by making up his or her mind earlier."

I

I cannot but love that man of mine.

There are so many objections to the various constructions which include some or all of the words *can, not, but,* and *help* that it's a wonder anyone dares to use any of them in talking about being unable to keep from doing something.

1. I can but love that man of mine.
2. I cannot but love that man of mine.
3. I cannot help loving that man of mine.
4. I cannot help but love that man of mine.

Almost everyone considers construction 1 to be too stilted for all but very formal occasions. Construction 2 seems quaintly Victorian to most Americans, though many Britons use it. Critics of constructions 2 and 4 see a mild double negative in *not* and *but.* Some—mainly Britons—point to a double negative elsewhere in construction 4: *help,* they say, has the meaning "keep from" or "avoid," so what is being said is "I cannot keep from not to love that man" and thus do not love him. Others—again, mainly Britons—consider construction 4 to be an inadmissible combination of admissible constructions 2 and 3.

In "Can't help lovin' dat man of mine," the subject, *I,* may be missing and the pronunciation may be dialectal, but the choice of construction 3 by the lyricist Oscar Hammerstein II, in the refrain of the popular *Show Boat* tune, is acceptable to all English-speakers.

Regardless of the condemnation from across the Atlantic, Americans are not giving up construction 4, which, like most idioms, sounds natural and right to them, whether or not its meaning can be taken literally. (For more on idioms, see HOW COME THE CLOCK ISN'T GOING?)

"A young white today <u>cannot help but</u> recoil from the base deeds of his people." (Eldridge Cleaver, *Soul on Ice*)

"The broadened definition of art to include doing anything, as well as making anything, is a triumph of democracy: Everyone can be—indeed, <u>cannot help but</u> be—an artist." (George Will, "When Art Becomes Absurd")

"The upcoming lecturer ... <u>cannot help but</u> look at the writings of his distinguished predecessors...." (August Frugé, "Lectures into Books")

"And however flawed the telling of his story, one <u>cannot help but</u> be moved by a man whose belief in freedom and dignity caused him to turn his back on every benefit his society offered." (Monica Collins, " 'Sakharov': A Tale of Hopeless Heroism")

And Eugene Ehrlich, described by his *Newsday* interviewer Sidney C. Schaer as "top editor" of the *Oxford American Dictionary,* said this about the dictionary's usage notes that begin "The careful writer . . .":

"I <u>couldn't help but</u> use that phrase."

Even in Britain resistance to *cannot help but* seems to be weakening.

"She <u>cannot help but</u> picture this child as he was when she last saw him. . . ." (Margaret Drabble, *The Middle Ground*)

Some people ask, Why not give up all four variations and use the simpler, more direct *I love that man of mine* instead? This form is, of course, not only acceptable but the most appropriate one in some contexts. Yet does it convey the idea that love came not easily and spontaneously but in spite of an effort to keep it from happening?

"Ice cream your kids today with Rocky Road."

Ice cream, we all know, is a noun, because it names or denotes a person, thing, place, action, quality, or the like. It can't be a verb, because a verb expresses action, existence, or occurrence. So why did a California dairy treat *ice cream* like a verb, urging us, on its milk cartons, to do it to our kids with a special chocolate flavor called Rocky Road?

It did so because the parts of speech in English—contrary to what we might have been taught—are not fixed. Words do not come packaged like jellybeans. If they did, there would have to be special mixtures as well as the standard varieties. That is, just as bags of assorted jellybeans can be found in candy stores alongside those labeled "cinnamon," "lemon," "licorice," and so on, bags containing only one of the traditional parts of speech apiece would have to make room on the grammar shelf for others filled with nouns-verbs, adjectives-adverbs, prepositions-conjunctions, and the like.

This does not mean that the notion of distinctive parts of speech performing certain grammatical functions is entirely useless. Because of their form and usual position within sentences, certain words fit into the system of Modern English in the same way as other words. Knowing intuitively how words are typically formed and how those words go together, native English-speakers would recognize in a nonsense sentence like:

The wallapatoonies zairly fronced and biggled in the mishy, insidulous kulask.

that *wallapatoonies* and *kulask* are nouns, that *fronced* and *biggled* are verbs, that *mishy* and *insidulous* are adjectives, and that *zairly* is an adverb.

We can test a word for its part of speech, at least in a general way. Take a noun: *ice cream,* for example. Can we form the plural by adding -*s* (as in *smoother ice creams*) and the possessive by adding -*'s* (as in *ice cream's texture*)? Can we form new words with it by adding certain derivational suffixes (*ice creamness*)? Can we place it after an article or a demonstrative pronoun (*an ice cream; this ice cream);* after a preposition (*over ice cream*); and after a single-word modifier (*pink ice cream*)? Can we place it either before or after a verb (*ice cream is good; I like ice cream*)? These are not the only tests for nouns, and certain nouns elude some of the usual tests. The noun *health,* for instance, doesn't have a plural form. Yet, on the whole, the tests are a good check on our intuitive notions about grammatical function.

Does *ice cream* pass the tests for a verb as well as for a noun? Or in using it as a verb did the dairy say something as foolish as "Nevertheless your kids today with Rocky Road"? Can we, by adding certain inflectional suffixes, show third-person singular present (*she ice creams*); past tense (*they ice creamed*); and past and present participles (*he has ice creamed; they are ice creaming*)? Can we, by adding certain derivational suffixes, form new verbs (*ice creamize*)? Can we place a direct object after it (*I always ice cream my birthday cake*)?

Because verbs fit almost anywhere in a sentence, there is no point in testing *ice cream* for location. What is useful, though, is testing for the meaning of the word in the sentence: Does it tell what the subject does, is, or has? If no subject is given, is *you* understood? Because in imperative sentences (those that express commands or urgent requests) *you* is generally understood, not stated, and because imperative sentences usually contain a verb in the form of a flat, or *to*-less, infinitive, might *ice cream* be such a verb? Indeed, in the sentence "Ice cream your kids today with Rocky Road" *ice cream* functions as a verb—more precisely, as a transitive verb in the imperative mood.

USING WORDS AS DIFFERENT PARTS of speech is not new. Nor is it limited to advertising, although it is true that ad writers make the most of the versatility of English linguistic forms. In the 1960s the American Tobacco Company, for example, was turning out ads like this:

> "See how Pall Mall's famous length of fine, rich-tasting tobacco travels and gentles the smoke—makes it mild—but does not filter out that satisfying flavor!"

That invitation came as a surprise to those accustomed to thinking of *gentle* not as a verb but as an adjective. Yet, according to *The Oxford English Dictionary,* as early as 1651 *gentle* was being used a verb in precisely the same sense: "to render gentle, mild, or pleasant." Even earlier, Shakespeare had used *gentle* as a transitive verb, but to convey the notion of ennobling or dignifying, as when he had Henry V say, in his "we happy few" speech:

> "Be he ne'er so vile, / This day shall gentle his condition."

In fact, by Shakespeare's time English words were freely shifting from one part of speech to another.

For words that serve as several parts of speech, it is the context that determines the grammatical function. *Up,* for example, can be used as a noun, an adverb, an adjective, a verb, and a preposition.

> Even with the *ups* and downs in the economy, I refuse to get worked *up,* knowing that when the inflation rate is *up,* the government *ups* my Social Security payments and I head my skiff *up* the river.

Besides, *up* is part of many compounds, including the nouns *upheaval* and *sunup;* the adjectives *uppity* and *up-and-coming;* the verb, noun, and adjective *upset;* the preposition *upon;* and the adverb, adjective, and verb *upstage.*

Best is another of the many adaptable words in English, shifting easily from adjective to noun to adverb to verb.

With its *best* players doing their *best* at what they do *best*, any team can *best* any other team on any given day.

Nouns As Verbs

We've already seen how nouns can be changed into verbs by adding derivational suffixes so as to form, say, *victimize* from *victim* and *glorify* from *glory*. But over the years so many nouns have been used as verbs without any change that we are ordinarily not aware of the functional shift.

The noun *vacuum*, a clipped form of *vacuum cleaner*, was condemned when it was introduced as a verb in the 1920s; Americans were expected to say, for instance, "Have you cleaned the rug with the vacuum cleaner?" Sixty or so years later *vac* was making inroads on the verb *vacuum*. (The British still prefer the verb *hoover*, from the Hoover vacuum cleaner.) Other nouns reluctantly accepted as verbs in the twentieth century—even though they had been so used at least a hundred years earlier—include *feature* ("The menu features banana squash soup"), *loan, research, implement, contact,* and *impact*. (See, for example, LOAN OR LEND? and CONTACT.) The noun *suspicion* has also long functioned as a verb ("I suspicion that's the last we'll hear of them"); yet, probably because *suspect* is now the prestige verb, the use of *suspicion* is considered nonstandard, that is, it differs from the variety of speech or writing generally held to be correct or preferred.

For the most part, though, almost anything goes with nouns that double as verbs. Talking with our bodies, we:

face odds.

shoulder blame.

head committees.

arm ourselves for battle.

toe the mark.

elbow our way into crowds.

nose out gossip.

eye our opponents.

hand money to cashiers.

knuckle down to work.

jawbone price-raising steel companies.

eyeball the height of a building.

foot the bill for summer camp.

leg it home after work.

muscle in on lucrative deals.

try to avoid being *knee-capped* by terrorists.

Always on the move, we:

bicycle (or *bike*) to the library.

roller-skate (or *skate*) in the park.

sail to Mazatlán.

jet to Tokyo.

helicopter from airports into cities.

weekend in Paris.

winter in Palm Beach.

holiday in London.

raft across the Atlantic.

circle the globe.

paddle our own canoes.

We note that it takes work both to *partner* and to *parent;* that in a diseased heart a cell may *spasm* and begin to wither; and that Alexander Haig *caveatted* his testimony during the Senate hearings on his confirmation as secretary of state. We see more and more unknown comedians *guest-host* late-night TV shows. We wish that prices would *plateau* so we could *gift* more at Christmas. We're glad that few football games are *weathered* out, but wish that in those that are played the wide receivers would *defense* better by not *nonchalancing* the ball. We pity Bill Brown, coauthor of *The Bureau: My Thirty Years in Hoover's FBI,* who said in a radio interview that he had been *persona non grata'ed* by the FBI. When we call a plumber, we want him not to *Mickey Mouse* around but to do the job and get out. We're astonished to see well-known companies *chapter 11 it* (that is, file for bankruptcy under federal law).

Verbs As Nouns

Fewer verbs become nouns without changing form than the other way around. One common verb-to-noun route is to add derivational suffixes, so that *establish* becomes *establishment* and *emerge* becomes *emergence*. Another is to add the inflectional suffix *-ing* to form gerunds. These forms function as nouns without losing such characteristics of verbs as the ability to take objects and adverbial modifiers. For instance:

Eating carrots is said to be good for one's eyesight.

Eating well does not have to cost a lot.

Yet many verbs are indeed used as nouns. For example, we:

go for a *ride,* a *swim,* a *hike,* or a *run* around the block.

make a *dash* for good *buys* before there's a *jump* in prices.

greet someone else's pun with the requisite *groan and dig.*

go to the movies for *kicks, laughs,* or a good *cry.*

curse any *delay* in our *search* for an evening's *read.*

make a *play* for the wealthy *catch* we met on our *walk.*

give the *nod* to whoever makes the right *moves.*

have *doubts* about winning life's *struggle* but give it a *try.*

Some Americans and many Britons call something that serves as a border or edging a *surround,* so they would find Quentin Bell's use of it unremarkable. Telling Mollie Panter-Downes about a mosaic paving that his mother (Vanessa Bell), Duncan Grant, and he had made many years earlier, he said:

"We had all signed it, but one of the workmen repairing the cement surround accidentally chipped the signatures off."

Nor can there be much doubt about the meaning of the verb *inhale* turned noun in John O'Hara's story "Hope of Heaven":

"He scratched a match and held it to the cigarette and cocked his head far over to one side and took a deep inhale."

We often hear that for many people around the world life is on the *improve.* And why not? Pressing the verb *improve* into service as a noun has the support of a number of established idioms, including "on the *go,*" "on the *make,*" "on the *run,*" "on the *fly,*" and "on the *mend.*" Besides, no one objects to a phrase like "at one *remove.*"

Adjectives As Nouns

"The <u>clean</u> in your mouth," in case you wondered, was Colgate. Using an adjective as a noun in precisely the same way, another toothpaste commercial—this one for Pepsodent—claimed, "You'll wonder where the <u>yellow</u> went." But the use of adjectives as nouns is by no means limited to the advertising agencies of toothpaste manufacturers. The mystery writer Nicholas Blake, for example, describes "a downtrodden <u>sensitive</u> at the mercy of a drunken father and a sluttish mother." A parking garage notice is headed: "Attention <u>monthlies.</u>" A review of a book on Victorian interior design says, "It hardly sounds like a description of contemporary <u>sleek.</u>" Here are some of the many other adjectives used as nouns:

A *human* is a person (though *human being* is still preferred by some).

A *conservative* wants to preserve established traditions or institutions.

An *antique* is something made in a former period, generally more than a hundred years ago.

A *primitive* is an artist who lacks formal training.

An *extra* is a movie actor hired by the day to play a minor part.

A *commercial* is a radio or TV advertisement.

fashionable,'' and *out*, meaning the opposite, are two such words, having gained widespread acceptance in the second half of the twentieth century.

"The In thing to bring home from Trinidad this year is a big stuffed alligator. Since these have not yet caught on widely, it's still possible to be the only one on your block with a stuffed alligator." (*Saturday Evening Post*, 1964)

"This bar [C. C. McCohen's, on Second Avenue] is such a definitely In place that you almost inevitably feel Out." (*New York Times*, 1964)

Yet, according to *The Oxford English Dictionary*, both words had those special senses as early as the seventeenth century. Here, for example, is a citation for 1687: " 'Tis not with Sermons, as 'tis with Mackrel, to be In, and Out.'' And in 1660 Samuel Pepys, the English politician, wrote in his *Diary* about changing his ''long black cloake for a short one (long cloakes being now quite out).'' Although both *in* and *out* retained those senses in the eighteenth and nineteenth centuries, it was not until the middle of the twentieth that the words themselves became stylish indicators of what is in fashion and what no longer is. How long will *in* and *out* be in? Perhaps as long as car phones. Or jogging. Or vinyl handbags in the shape of bulldogs.

In his *Dictionary of Modern English Usage* (1926), the British lexicographer H. W. Fowler used the term *vogue-words* to describe expressions that suddenly gain popularity, partly because of some people's ''herd instinct & lack of individuality.'' Words and phrases that are so closely associated with certain groups, movements, and the like that they come to be considered slogans are often called *catchwords;* those that sound impressive but have little or only imprecise meaning to nonmembers of the groups that use them, *buzzwords.*

Fowler said that he included a special entry for ''vogue-words'' because:

"young writers may not even be aware, about some of them, that they are not part of the normal vocabulary, but still repulsive to the old & the well-read. Many, it should be added, are vogue-words in particular senses only, & are unobjectionable, though liable now to ambiguity, in the senses that belonged to them before they attained their vogue."

When Margaret Nicholson adapted Fowler's work for Americans (*A Dictionary of American-English Usage, Based on ''Fowler's Modern English Usage,''* 1957), she kept his categories—''old vogue-words,'' ''words owing their vogue to the ease with which they can be substituted for any of several different & more precise words, saving the trouble of choosing the right,'' ''words owing their vogue to the joy of showing that one has acquired them,'' and the like. She also kept most of his examples of vogue words, including these:

acid test	*intrigue* (verb) for *interest*
feasible	nice
happening for *event*	psychological moment
individual	unthinkable

Some of the vogue words on Nicholson's list were, of course, not on Fowler's. *Inferiority complex*, for example, wasn't coined until 1922, and *atomic era* came into use after the first atomic bombs were dropped on Japan in

1945. Conversely, some of the words on Fowler's list probably did not make it to Nicholson's because by then they had lost their special vogue senses—*annex, hectic,* and *forceful,* for example. And on both lists *happening* is given as the vogue word for *event* in the usual sense of an occurrence, not in reference to a spontaneous or improvised theatrical performance or display, because this meaning was not attached to *happening* until the late fifties and early sixties.

By the time Fowler's *Dictionary of Modern English Usage* was brought out in a second edition, revised by Sir Ernest Gowers (1965), virtually all that remained of the original list were the categories (at least six of the seven). Many of the new terms, or new senses of older terms, originated with bureaucrats, businessmen, doctors, psychologists, sociologists, economists, literary critics, and other professionals, and then filtered down to the general public. Here are some of Gowers's vogue words:

alternative	framework
ambience	global
ambivalent	image
appropriate (adjective)	implement (verb)
archetypal	integrate for combine
blueprint for plan	iron curtain
breakthrough for achievement	level
ceiling for limit	overall
challenging	reaction for opinion
climate (figurative sense)	seminal
coexistence	sensational
fabulous	significant for important
factor	target for objective
fantastic	wind of change

Decades later, many of the words on Gowers's list still give the people who say and write them a feeling of status, but they are by no means the only ones in fashion, and some of them have been updated themselves. *Alternative,* for example, would not do alone, so it became *viable alternative.* Gowers saw *integrate* being used more and more in place of *combine,* yet he might have been taken aback by an advertisement for "integrated pest management." And even though in the sixties *reaction* seemed to be replacing *opinion,* from the seventies on, the stylish word was *input*—and not only among those *into* (the informal vogue word for "involved in or concerned with") computers. Ordinary people began to ask one another for their input on everything from the bond market to Woody Allen's latest movie.

To members of a certain group, however, it was "Woody Allen's latest *film,*" for this vogue word became Fowler's "novel variant on its predecessor." (*Movie* had earlier taken its own place beside the older term *motion picture.*) In the late nineteenth and early twentieth centuries, sophisticated, fashionable people were called the *smart set;* in the vogue slang term of the day, they were *classy.* The *beautiful people* who arrived on the scene—often the international one—in the late sixties were also sophisticated and fashionable, but they were identified mainly with the leisure class. The "*film* group"—whether called *yuppies* (young, urban professionals), *yumpies* (young, upwardly mobile professionals), or *trendies*—was made up of educated, stylish, and relatively wealthy Americans who began leading *upscale lives* in the late seventies. They dressed conservatively and casually, as long as the "right" manufacturers' labels were in their button-down shirts and Shetland sweaters. They worked hard to keep their healthy, athletic look. They observed the passing fashions in food and drink, nimbly switching from cocktails to white wine to Perrier; from quiche to crepes to creole; from gelato to sorbet; from espresso to cappuccino. In speaking, they avoided tradespeople's banalities like *Have a nice day!* but were free with other stock words and phrases.

Basically I went home after the ballet.

The *bottom line* is that they left without saying goodbye.

What's your *scenario* for getting invited to the Cape?

I don't *buy into* her vacation plans.

Let's *do lunch* next week.

Pat asked where I'd been, so I *go,* "To the library." Then he *goes,* "Funny, I didn't see you there."

The linguini with prawns is, *quite simply,* the best dish on the menu.

Now that the health club has been renovated, it's lost all its *charisma.*

We separated because we both needed our own *space.*

Many men come from an *aggressive place* and many women from a *nonassertive place.*

The napkins come in *poppy, lettuce, brown sugar, azalea,* and *lobster bisque.*

Science, technology, and medicine have given us many vogue words that bear little relation to their origins.

When two friends meet for a long talk over lunch, they *interface.*

Employees in an office that uses computers work in a *floppy-disk environment.*

Symphony orchestras on cross-country tours produce considerable *fall-out,* especially in rural areas.

A successful lecture depends on the *critical mass* of the audience. That's because of the need for *synergism*—preferably *ongoing synergism*—between the speaker and the listeners.

Security checks at airports are simply a *parameter* of travel nowadays.

Researchers looking into the *topography* of smoking are likely to hear nonsmokers complain about having to inhale *sidestream smoke.*

Everything was *hemorrhaging* in the 1980s: the budget, the Social Security system, terrorism, violence, crime.

Washington also can be counted on to turn out a steady supply of stock phrases. One of them, from the 1980s, describes what many politicians and public officials want most: *wiggle room,* that is, the freedom to make a statement and later draw back without seeming to have shifted position.

Wiggle room might have been in short supply during Watergate, but a number of the words and phrases that we heard or read in 1972 and 1973 are still around. The slang verb *stonewall,* for example, is now applied to anyone's behaving in an obstructive, uncooperative manner, as by refusing to answer or by withholding information during questioning. In pre-Watergate United States, *forthcoming* generally referred to something that was approaching or about to appear, say, a book or motion picture; but time and again the protagonists in the political drama borrowed the British sense of "open," "frank," or "direct." Instead of deciding between *at that point* and *at that time,* almost everyone telescoped the phrase into *at that point in time.*

Other Watergate legacies include *What did he know and when did he know it?; the smoking gun;* and *Watergate* itself. In 1981, on being attacked for having published a Pulitzer Prize–winning story that turned out to be a fabrication, the *Washington Post* went into what Metro editor Bob Woodward (of Watergate fame) called "our Watergate mode: protect the source and back the reporter." Sometimes the suffix *-gate* is enough to label a scandal or a cover-up anywhere in the world (*Billy-gate,* which involved former President Carter's brother; *Koreagate; Chernobylgate; Contragate*).

What more up-to-date way to designate an activity that takes a long time and requires a lot of effort than to name it after the Greek village where the Athenians defeated the Persians in 490 B.C.: Marathon? All in the cause of raising money, either for the public good or the sponsors' profit, there are phone-a-thons, radiothons, telethons, sell-a-thons, walkathons, cure-a-thons, recyclathons, and trash-bag-a-thons.

Using a word that is in style, like following any other current fashion, is not a punishable offense. Indeed, many of the catchwords, buzzwords, and general vogue words that we hear and see came to be catchwords, buzzwords, and vogue words because of their forcefulness and novelty. How refreshing it must have been, for example, to hear the emphatic *no way!* when that phrase was new. The trouble is that people become addicted to stock expressions, repeating them automatically instead of choosing others that are less commonplace, more precise, and better suited to the occasion. Besides, keeping up with the latest fads—never settling for the next-to-latest—is just as difficult with language as it is with anything else. One would no more want to be heard saying *do lunch* when *do luncheon* is in style than to be seen wearing espadrilles when sneakers are in style.

In their need to be fresh and vigorous, on the one hand, and their tendency to become trite, on the other, vogue words are a lot like clichés (see LO AND BEHOLD, IT'S MAN'S BEST FRIEND). They also have a good deal in common with jargon or gobbledygook (see A CONCEPT-ORIENTED FRAMEWORK MAY EFFECTUATE A CONSENSUS OF OPINION IN TERMS OF THE MAXIMIZATION OF A MEANINGFUL CONTINUUM OF PROGRAM FACTORS).

infer or *imply?*   See *imply* or *infer?*

infinitives: dangling, see **Covered with onions, relish, and ketchup, I ate a hot dog at the ballpark;** in elliptical constructions, see **Drink the water if you dare; "Shop Macy's and save";** of purpose, see **"Come up and see me sometime";** split, see **"To err is human; to really foul things up requires a computer."**

inflammable or *flammable?*   See *flammable* or *inflammable?*

intensives.   See **Ever so funny jokes can be quite amusing.**

irregardless or *regardless?*

Some English-speakers who say or write *irregardless* seem to consider it simply a variant of *regardless.*

"Aquarius: ... Stand by your convictions irregardless of others...." (Jeane Dixon, "Horoscope")

"The problem may be that the van is not large like a school bus, but irregardless, it is deserving of the same attention and is to be regarded with the same caution on the roads as any other school bus." (Editorial, *Star-Progress*, Berryville, Arkansas)

Others, knowing that dictionaries label *irregardless* substandard (that is, below the standards of the language variety of educated speakers), use it out of affected illiteracy or to achieve a special effect—just as they might say *ain't* instead of *is not, don't* instead of *do not,* or *muriel* instead of *mural.* (See AIN'T and DON'T SHE KNOW IT'LL BE DARK SOON?)

Because both the prefix (*ir-*) and the suffix (*-less*) mean "without," *irregardless* is redundant. It originated in the States, perhaps as a blend of *irrespective* and *regardless.*

For the use and nonuse of the preposition *of* after *regardless,* see "SHOP MACY'S AND SAVE."

Is it me you like better than her?

If asked "Who is it?" any right-minded person—that is, someone afraid of being caught in the wrong on a point of grammar—would say "It is I." That's because, according to the rule, a personal pronoun used as a predicate complement of the verb *be* is always in the subjective form, or case (*I, he, she, we, they*). In other words, *be* expresses no action and therefore cannot take an object. These are some grammar-book examples of "correct" usage:

It is *I*.   Were these *they?*   I wonder if the mayor will be *she.*

This is *he.*   The winner has always been *he.*

The busiest people in town were the letter carriers and *we.*

Many good writers and speakers of course follow that rule. Yet, in answer to the question "Who is it?" most English-speakers would say "It is me" or "It's me." In other words, even after the verb *be* they would use a pronoun in the objective form (*me, him, her, us, them*). This construction comes naturally, probably because a pronoun that falls at the end of an English sentence is usually in the objective form.

Give it to *me*.   Don't leave without *her*.   Can't you tell *us*?

If, over the years, the objective form of the pronoun replaces the subjective one after the verb *be*, it won't be the first time this construction has undergone change. In Old English (roughly between the years 400 and 1100), the expression was *I it am* (*Ic hit eom*). In the Middle English period (roughly between 1100 and 1500), when Chaucer wrote *The Canterbury Tales*, the phrase became *it am I*. *It* was gradually taken to be the subject, so the verb was changed to *is*, as in "It is I." By the sixteenth century so many people felt that an objective pronoun belonged after a verb that "It is me" took its place alongside "It is I." In Shakespeare's *Twelfth Night*, for example, the same character uses both forms within three lines:

"*Andrew*. That's me, I warrant you.
"*Malvolio*. 'One Sir Andrew'—
"*Andrew*. I knew 'twas I, for many do call me fool."

Nowadays the *It is me*, or objective, construction is firmly established in English speech and writing, sometimes alternating with the subjective form.

"As if it isn't him who always harangues." (Hortense Calisher, *On Keeping Women*, page 14)

"Why he'll never look me in the face and say merely: This is she." (Hortense Calisher, *On Keeping Women*, page 203)

" 'No, no: much worse than that. It had been simply her and me and Thomas. . . .' " (Elizabeth Bowen, *Death of the Heart*)

"This portrait is thought to be her." (Sir Huw Weldon, referring to Catherine Howard, Henry VIII's fifth wife, on PBS's *Royal Heritage*)

Choosing between the subjective and objective forms is sometimes more a matter of etiquette than of grammar. If in conversation someone uses a construction that we consider either too formal or not formal enough, should we stifle our objection and follow our companion's lead or hold to our own usage and thus seem to correct the other person? Television viewers saw such a scene played out in 1986 when, on *60 Minutes*, James Michener revisited the island he had made famous nearly forty years earlier in his Pulitzer Prize–winning *Tales of the South Pacific*. As he and his interviewer, Diane Sawyer, were driving toward the house of a well-known acquaintance of the writer's, Sawyer exclaimed, "That's her!" Michener agreed. "That's she!," he said.

When the pronoun introduces a relative clause, even the "It is me" camp usually switches to the subjective form.

It is *she* who moved to Albuquerque.

Don't you think it is *they* who deserve the prize?

Yet *me* often sounds more natural in this construction too, especially with the contraction *it's*.

It's *me* who is to blame.

(Strict grammarians would point out that *am,* not *is,* belongs in this sentence, because the subject is *I* and the verb should agree with it in person. But many people feel that *am* sounds too pedantic, especially in casual conversation. See EITHER HE OR I AM RIGHT.)

When the infinitive marker *to* is given along with *be,* the standard rule on the subjective form of the pronoun shifts. Few grammarians, however strict, would object to this headline on the cover of *People,* referring to an article on Jane Fonda:

"Would women like to be her?"

Here the pronoun *her* is in the objective form because it is considered a predicate noun completing the infinitive *be.*

OPINIONS DIFFER SHARPLY over the form, or case, of a pronoun following *as* and *than* in comparisons. According to the traditional rule, the subject of a verb takes the subjective form, even when the verb is not expressed but merely understood. In other words, the pronoun is not the object of *as* or *than* but part of a clause whose missing word or words the reader or listener is expected to supply.

I am taller than *he* (is tall).

You drive faster than *I* (drive).

You seem to approve of us more than *they* (do).

They have as much time as *we* (have).

Are you as sleepy as *she* (is)?

Yet, depending on the sentence, the relation between the pronoun and the rest of the implied clause may require the objective form.

Do you like her better than (you like) *me?*

He seems to approve of us more than (he approves of) *them.*

I wish they would treat him as kindly as (they treat) *her.*

Many people, especially in casual conversation, then go on to use the objective form even where strict grammar calls for the subjective form.

I am taller than *him.*

You drive faster than *me.*

You seem to approve of us more than *them.*

They have as much time as *us*.

Are you as sleepy as *her*?

Other aspects of the comparison of adjectives and adverbs with *as, than,* and the like are dealt with in KILIMANJARO IS TALLER THAN ANY MOUNTAIN IN AFRICA.

HOWEVER LIVELY THE DISCUSSION on "It is me," "He is taller than me," and so on, it is but a small part of the long-standing debate over the form of pronouns in English constructions. For more on the subjective versus the objective form of personal pronouns, see THE BALL DROPPED BETWEEN HE AND THE LEFT-FIELDER and US TV WATCHERS HAVE STRONG CONVICTIONS. For views on the form of a much-used relative or interrogative pronoun, see WHO WOULD YOU TURN TO FOR HELP?

its or *it's*?

Its, like such other possessive pronouns as *his, hers, ours, yours,* and *theirs,* does not take an apostrophe. It means "that or those belonging to it."

Iraq plans to increase its oil production.

It's, a contraction of *it is* or *it has*, does take an apostrophe.

It's a pity you can't stay longer.

It's been a long time since you were here last.

For more on contractions, see DON'T SHE KNOW IT'LL BE DARK SOON?

-ize verbs.   See *Apologize*, **sí**; *finalize*, **no.**

J

jargon. See **A concept-oriented framework may effectuate a consensus of opinion in terms of the maximization of a meaningful continuum of program factors.**

Jobbed in a humongous scam, the tweaked-out mobster exclaimed, "Peachy-keen!"

Slang has never been the kind of usage that schoolchildren get an A for mastering. The word, which came into English in the eighteenth century, was originally applied to the specialized vocabulary and idioms that criminals, tramps, and similar groups used so that outsiders wouldn't understand what was being said. (This form of speech is now usually called *cant.*) Later on, *slang* was extended to the specialized vocabulary and idioms of people in the same line of work, way of life, or the like. (This much-criticized manner of speaking and writing is now usually called *shoptalk, argot,* or *jargon.* See A CONCEPT-ORIENTED FRAMEWORK MAY EFFECTUATE A CONSENSUS OF OPINION IN TERMS OF THE MAXIMIZATION OF A MEANINGFUL CONTINUUM OF PROGRAM FACTORS.) Nowadays *slang* generally refers to an informal variety of language—much too informal, many people think—that, in search of fresh and vigorous, colorful, pungent, or humorous expression, develops outside of conventional or standard usage and consists both of coined words and phrases and of new or extended meanings attached to established terms.

Grammar books may no longer condemn slang as uncouth, illiterate, and vulgar, but most of them still recommend that a slang word or expression be used only when one in the general English vocabulary won't do—and then that it be cordoned off by quotation marks. The problem is, who decides whether at a given moment a word or expression is slang, informal, standard, or something else?

Take the word *mob,* whose prevailing sense today is probably that of "any large crowd." It is a shortened form of the Latin *mobile,* which in turn is a shortened form of the Latin *mobile vulgus* ("movable crowd"). The earliest citation that *The Oxford English Dictionary* gives for "the disorderly and riotous part of the population, the roughs, the rabble" dates from 1688.

"The Mobb carried away the very boards and rafters."

A 1691 citation is the first the *OED* gives to illustrate a second meaning: "the common masses of people; the lower orders; the uncultured or illiterate as a class; the populace, the masses."

"An idle Notion . . . that intoxicated the beliefs of the Mob."

Jonathan Swift, the English satirist who wrote *Gulliver's Travels,* vehemently denounced this usage as a vulgarism. Nevertheless, *mob* has become a standard English word. (Another word that Swift sought to banish is the noun *banter,* which the *OED* says was considered slang in 1688 but which is now accepted at all levels of usage. Swift's inability to hold back the natural development of the language by clapping a hand to his head has not kept a number of twentieth-century writers from trying to do the same.)

The *OED* labels as slang a later (nineteenth-century) meaning of *mob*—"a company or gang or thieves or pickpockets working in collusion." But it wasn't until the first quarter of the twentieth century that the word took on the related sense so often attached to it today. An *OED Supplement* gives a 1927 citation as the earliest one for this new sense (which it labels "U.S."): "a more or less permanent association or gang of violent criminals. *The Mob,* a supposed permanent gang controlling much of organized crime in the U.S. and elsewhere." It gives a 1917 citation for *mobster* ("a member of a group of criminals"), characterizing the word as slang of U.S. origin. A number of other current dictionaries find both the new sense of *mob* and the word *mobster* to be slang; among those that don't, several regard either or both of these usages as informal, and several, by assigning no label, consider both to be standard.

Neither dictionaries nor usage-conscious English-speakers, then, can freeze slang expressions for all time, any more than they can the other words and constructions that make up the language. Most slang words and phrases fall into disuse, either gradually disappearing or dropping out of sight the moment their novelty wears off. Others achieve a more formal status, but usually not before they have passed through an informal, or colloquial, stage. Even slang that seems long forgotten may enjoy a revival.

Throughout most of the twentieth century, *peachy-keen* has been in and out of vogue in the United States. For a while it, like *peachy,* meant "fine," "excellent," or "beautiful," just as the noun *peach* denoted a well-liked person or thing. After fading from sight for a number of years, all three words resurfaced, but, through a reversal of meaning, generally in ironic references to that which is not so fine, excellent, or beautiful. In 1980 an article by Donald K. White appeared in the financial section of the *San Francisco Chronicle* under the headline "Everything Is 'Peachy-Keen.' " It began with this reference to a 1939 play-turned-into-movie, by George S. Kaufman and Moss Hart:

> "As Sheridan Whiteside, the acerbic lead character in 'The Man Who Came to Dinner,' would put it in discussing the economy, 'Everything is peachy-keen.' 'Peachy-keen' was always delivered with sarcasm."

In a London *Times* article on the dating of panel paintings, also published in 1980, Geraldine Norman wrote:

> "However, Dr John Fletcher, who is in charge of the work at Oxford, has just come up with a peach of a finding that is destined to stir controversy."

Nowadays most adult Americans who say *peachy-keen, peachy,* or *peach* are apt to stress the word in such a way as to make it clear they are resurrecting Old Slang. In fact, they generally use the same exaggerated enunciation for all slang terms they call up from the past, including such other generalized words of approval as *swell, copacetic, crackerjack, nifty,* and *slick.*

English is filled with slang expressions having to do with deception. One of them is *job,* whose verb senses include "to deceive, trick, or cheat." Another is the Americanism *scam* (probably an altered form of *scheme*), which when used both as a noun and as a verb suggests a *confidence game* (a swindle carried out by gaining the victim's confidence). Other words or senses that came into the language as slang related to fraud and imposture include *bamboozle, chisel, con, flimflam, gyp, hoodwink, snooker, sting,* and *sucker.* Some of these expressions are no longer used very often; some are likely to be regarded as slang for quite a while; some have moved far enough up the usage ladder to be considered informal; and some have made their way into standard English. But, language being far from fixed for all time, the current status of each one of them might very well change.

So might that of *humongous.* Probably a blend of *huge, monstrous,* and *tremendous* (with a *g* added), this slang Americanism means "of enormous size or extent." It has been very popular since its appearance, probably in the late 1960s or early 1970s, but this doesn't mean that in time it won't go the way of *fap,* a slang word meaning "drunk" in Shakespeare's day.

In their search for novelty, color, and humor, more and more English-speakers turn to slang, particularly in everyday conversation. Not surprisingly, when such words and phrases appear in print, it is more likely to be in newspapers and magazines than in books. One reason is that the literary style, or tone, of most dailies, weeklies, and monthlies is less formal than that of most works of nonfiction (and even of fiction, in which slang is limited mainly to dialogue). Another reason is that periodicals are less concerned about the ephemeral quality of slang. No matter that a word or expression may not be around much longer than it takes to recycle the newspaper or magazine it appeared in. Some old, some new, these are examples of the slang published in periodicals of the 1980s:

"But pols [politicians] from both parties played along, hoping that even if the bill didn't end the farm crisis, it might at least keep agricultural interests placated until the 1986 elections." ("Stuffing Farmers, Stiffing Peasants [treating peasants unfairly]," a *New Republic* editorial)

"Few managers seem to realize how important it is to manage the boss or, worse, believe that it can be done at all. They bellyache [complain] about the boss but do not even try to manage him (or her)." (Peter F. Drucker, *Wall Street Journal*)

"Many of us like to talk about our wartime injuries. I've often told my kids [children] how I wrenched my back when I got stewed [got drunk] and rolled out of an upper bunk." (Mike Royko, *Chicago Tribune*)

"The Veterans Administration, looking for the half million deadbeats [people who try to get out of paying for something] who owe the agency $521 million, consulted the federal government's payroll computers," (Associated Press)

"She's Oprah Winfrey, zaftig [Yiddish-derived slang for "having a full, shapely figure"] gab [chatter] queen, soaking up the bubble bathos of life and threatening to send poor, <u>yakked-out</u> [talked-out] Phil Donahue into video menopause." (Stephanie Mansfield, *Washington Post*)

"The Royal Wedding <u>Pig-out</u> [gorging] began promptly at 5:30 A.M. with the traditional opening of the bag of Peanut M & M's." (Anna Quindlen, in a *New York Times* article on Prince Andrew and Sarah Ferguson's wedding)

Slang appeals to public figures speaking in public—even to some old enough to have been taught that such expressions are wanting in refinement.

> From time to time, President Ronald Reagan complained, "I've had it up to my <u>keister</u> [rump]," whether with White House leaks to the media or something else. ("Keister II," *Washington Post*)

> Of Senator Edward Kennedy's disagreement with him on the deregulation of oil prices, President Jimmy Carter said, "That's a lot of <u>baloney</u> [nonsense]."

> Told by Senator Harrison Schmitt that the Carter administration had "<u>screwed up</u> [bungled]" in its inflation forecasting, Secretary of the Treasury W. Michael Blumenthal replied, at a Senate Appropriations Subcommittee meeting, "Yes, but we <u>screwed up</u> in good company." (Associated Press)

> Thomas Aquinas Murphy, chairman of General Motors Corporation, noted, "We haven't been sitting quiet on our <u>ass</u> [rump] and we don't intend to sit quiet on our ass either." (James Flanigan, *Los Angeles Times*)

However tasteless such slang expressions may be to some people, they don't approach the pungent language that is more and more often found in speech and print and that is widely regarded as offensive or objectionable. Dashes indicating the omission of part of a word that has to do with sex or excrement are rapidly being replaced by all four letters. Like all other words and phrases, these are most effective if they are limited to the occasions when the speaker or writer, on the one hand, and the listener or reader, on the other, share a sense of their social purpose.

Teenage talk is by far the richest vein of slang, whose discovery can age an adult almost as fast as having a bus driver ask, "Senior?" This language gulf is, of course, intentionally created by young people who, like the criminals and tramps of the eighteenth century, want a body of words and idioms of their own, one which outsiders, especially parents, are at a loss to understand. Truly current teenage slang is, of course, too short-lived to be recorded in dictionaries or in other books that take more than a month to publish. For example, at various places and times in the 1980s, young people might have said that a mobster who was extremely upset, angry, or irritable at having been jobbed in a humongous scam was *tweaked-out, wigged-out, freaked-out,* or *ticked* (from the earlier slang *tick off*). Almost overnight they would have replenished their word stock with vivid new adjectives. But if in doing so they chose *steamed,* they would have been *naused out* or *grossed out* to discover that this is what their parents might have said in the 1950s.

John Bull and John Hancock are not just any johns.

Besides borrowing common nouns and expressions from all parts of the world (see MODOR, WE'VE GOT COMPANY), English enriches its everyday word stock with proper nouns, both native and imported. Transforming the name of a real-life or fictional place or person into a word or phrase that stands on its own is not the same as attaching a suffix to a proper name or using a proper name to modify a word whose meaning is well established. Not surprisingly, the theological system developed by the French Protestant reformer John Calvin is called *Calvinism;* papers, objects, and other material concerning Abraham Lincoln are known collectively as *Lincolniana;* and the special kind of armchair popularized by the English artist and craftsman William Morris goes by the name of *Morris chair.* But calling a drug that arouses sexual desire an *aphrodisiac,* after Aphrodite, the Greek goddess of love; describing a chronic skeptic as a *doubting Thomas,* after the apostle who at first doubted the resurrection of Jesus; referring to an idealistic visionary as *quixotic,* after the fictional character Don Quixote; and giving an inflated life vest the name *Mae West,* after a shapely American actress—this is inventive word-building, for it takes the language in unexpected directions.

Some of the countless English words and phrases that originated in personal and place names are listed below, with their current senses. An open star indicates (as it does in *Webster's New World Dictionary*) that a word or a particular sense entered the language through American English.

From Place Names

☆*buncome, bunkum*

Meaning: Talk that is empty, insincere, or merely for effect; humbug. (Used in informal speech and writing.)

Origin: Buncome County, North Carolina, in the district whose representative to the U.S. Congress (1819–1821) felt bound to "make a speech for Buncome."

cashmere

Meanings: A soft twilled cloth made principally of fine carded wool obtained from goats of Kashmir and Tibet; a sweater, coat, scarf, or other garment made of such cloth.

Origin: Cashmere, the former spelling of Kashmir, which is a part of the Indian state of Jammu and Kashmir.

china

Meanings: Dishes, ornaments, and the like, made of porcelain; any earthenware dishes or crockery.

Origin: Porcelain originally imported from China.

majolica

Meanings: Enameled, glazed, and richly colored and decorated Italian pottery; similar pottery.

Origin: The Italian word *maiolica* (Majorca), the largest of the Balearic Islands.

paisley, Paisley

Meanings: Characterized by an elaborate, colorful pattern of intricate figures; cloth having such a pattern.

Origin: Paisley, a city in Scotland, where a wool shawl in that pattern was originally made.

Panama, panama (hat)

Meanings: A fine, hand-plaited hat made from select leaves of the jipijapa plant; any similar straw hat.

Origin: Panama, once a main distribution center for those fine hats.

☆*parkerhouse roll*

Meaning: A yeast roll shaped by folding over a flat, round piece of buttered dough.

Origin: Parker House, a hotel in Boston where the roll was first served.

plaster of Paris

Meaning: A heavy white powder, calcined gypsum, which, when mixed with water, forms a thick paste that sets quickly: used for casts, moldings, statuary, and so on.

Origin: Paris, France, whose Montmartre district was the source of the gypsum used in the manufacture.

shanghai

Meanings: ☆To kidnap, usually by drugging, for service aboard ship; (slang) to induce another to do something through force or underhanded methods.

Origin: Said of sailors thus kidnapped for crew duty on the China run.

☆*Watergate*

Meaning: A scandal involving officials who violate public trust through subterfuge, bribery, burglary, and other abuses of power in order to maintain their positions of authority.

Origin: Watergate, a building complex in Washington, D.C., housing the Democratic Party headquarters, burglarized in June 1972 under the direction of government officials.

Waterloo

Meaning: A disastrous or decisive defeat.

Origin: Waterloo, a town in Belgium, where Napoleon was finally defeated (June 18, 1815) by the Allies under the Duke of Wellington, of England, and Field Marshal Gebhard Leberecht von Blücher, of Prussia.

From Classical Mythology

Achilles' heel

Meaning: One's vulnerable or susceptible spot.

Origin: Achilles, a Greek warrior and leader in the Trojan War, who, after killing Hector, was killed by Paris with an arrow that struck his only vulnerable spot: his heel. (His mother is said to have held him by the heel when she dipped him in the River Styx to make him invulnerable.)

Achilles' tendon

Meaning: The tendon connecting the back of the heel to the muscles of the calf of the leg.

Origin: Achilles (see above).

Adonis

Meaning: A very handsome young man.

Origin: Adonis, a youth of extraordinary beauty who was loved by Aphrodite, the Greek goddess of love.

aphrodisiac

Meaning: A drug or other agent that arouses or increases sexual desire.

Origin: Aphrodite, the Greek goddess of love.

Apollo

Meaning: A handsome young man.

Origin: Apollo, the Greek and Roman god of music, poetry, prophecy, and medicine, exemplifying manly youth and beauty.

Cassandra

Meaning: A person whose warnings of misfortune are disregarded.

Origin: Cassandra, to whom Apollo (see above) gave prophetic power to show his love. Later, when thwarted, he decreed that no one should believe her prophecies.

Cupid

Meaning: The god of love, pictured as a naked, winged cherub, as on a valentine.

Origin: Cupid, the Roman god of love, usually represented as a winged boy with bow and arrow (in Greek mythology, Eros).

cupidity

Meanings: Strong desire, especially for wealth; avarice; greed.

Origin: Cupid (see above).

cupid's-bow

Meaning: In the shape of the bow that Cupid is usually pictured as carrying (as in "She is famous for her cupid's-bow mouth").

Origin: Cupid (see above).

eros

Meanings: Sexual love or desire. Also, in psychoanalysis, libido or the psychic energy associated with it.

Origin: Eros, the Greek god of love (in Roman mythology, Cupid).

erotic, erotica, eroticism, erotism, erotogenic, erotomania

Meanings: Having to do with sexual love, instincts, and desires. (*Erotica* denotes erotic books, pictures, and the like.)

Origin: Eros (see above).

herculean

Meanings: Having great size, strength, or courage, or being very powerful or courageous; very difficult (as in "a herculean task").

Origin: Hercules, who, in Greek and Roman mythology, was renowned for feats of strength.

hercules

Meaning: A very large, strong man.

Origin: Hercules (see above).

narcissism, narcism

Meanings: Self-love; excessive interest in one's own appearance, comfort, importance, abilities, and so on. Also, in psychoanalysis, arrest at or regression to the first stage of libidinal development, in which the self is an object of erotic pleasure.

Origin: Narcissus, who, in Greek mythology, was a beautiful youth made to pine away for love of his own reflection in a spring and later changed into a narcissus (see below).

narcissus

Meaning: Any of a genus of bulb plants of the amaryllis family, having narcotic properties.

Origin: Narcissus (see above), whose Greek name, Narkissos, is related to *narcotic*.

Pandora's box

Meaning: A collection of all human ills.

Origin: Pandora, who, in Greek mythology, was the first mortal woman and who, on opening a box out of curiosity, let all human ills into the world.

tantalize

Meaning: To tease or disappoint by promising or showing something desirable and then withholding it.

Origin: Tantalus, son of the Greek god Zeus, who was doomed in the lower world to stand in water that always receded when he tried to drink it and under branches of fruit he could never reach.

Trojan horse

Meaning: A person, group, or thing that seeks to subvert a nation, organization, or the like, from within.

Origin: A huge, hollow wooden horse filled with Greek soldiers and, during the Trojan War, left at the gates of Troy; once it was inside the city, the soldiers came out at night and opened the gates to the Greek army, which destroyed the city.

From the Bible

doubting Thomas

Meaning: A person who habitually doubts; a chronic skeptic.

Origin: Thomas, one of the twelve apostles, who at first doubted the resurrection of Jesus (John 20:24–29).

jeremiad

Meaning: A lamentation or tale of woe.

Origin: The Lamentations of Jeremiah, a book in the Old Testament.

Jeremiah

Meaning: A person who is pessimistic about the future.

Origin: A Hebrew prophet of the seventh and sixth centuries B.C., whose Lamentations appear as a book in the Old Testament.

Jeroboam, jeroboam

Meaning: A large wine bottle, especially for champagne, usually holding about .8 gallon.

Origin: Jeroboam, first king of Israel (I Kings 11:26–14:20).

Jezebel, jezebel

Meaning: A woman regarded as shameless, wicked, or the like.

Origin: Jezebel, the wicked woman who married Ahab, king of Israel (I Kings, II Kings).

Job's comforter

Meaning: A person who aggravates one's misery while attempting or pretending to comfort.

Origin: The remarks that the long-suffering Job made to his "miserable comforters" (Job 16:1–5).

Judas

Meaning: A traitor or betrayer.

Origin: Judas Iscariot, the disciple who betrayed Jesus (Matthew 26:14–16, 48).

Judas tree

Meaning: A popular name for Cercis, a genus of shrubs and small trees of the legume family.

Origin: Judas Iscariot, who, according to legend, hanged himself on such a tree.

Methuselah, methuselah

Meaning: A large wine bottle, especially for champagne, holding 6.5 quarts.

Origin: Methuselah, one of the patriarchs, who lived 969 years (Genesis 5:27).

From Scientists, Inventors, Political Figures, Military Officers, Artists, and Others

bowdlerize

Meaning: To remove passages considered offensive from a book or other material; expurgate.

Origin: Thomas Bowdler (1754–1825), an English editor who published an expurgated edition of Shakespeare.

☆*burnsides* or *sideburns*

Meaning: A style of beard with full side whiskers and mustache, but with the chin cleanshaven.

Origin: Ambrose Everett Burnside (1824–1881), a Union general in the Civil War, who wore his beard that way.

Caesarean section, caesarean section, Cesarean section, Cesarian section

Meaning: A surgical operation for delivering a baby by cutting through the mother's abdominal and uterine walls.

Origin: Julius Caesar, a Roman general and statesman who lived in the first century B.C. and who, some say, was born in that manner.

curie

Meaning: The unit used in measuring radioactivity.

Origin: Marie Curie (1867–1934), a Polish-born chemist and physicist who lived and worked in France and who, in collaboration with her husband, discovered polonium and radium.

diesel, Diesel

Meanings: A type of internal-combustion engine that burns fuel; a locomotive, truck, or car powered by such an engine.

Origin: Rudolf Diesel (1858–1913), the German inventor of the engine.

Fahrenheit

Meaning: Designating or of a thermometer on which, under laboratory conditions, 32° is the freezing point and 212° is the boiling point.

Origin: Gabriel Daniel Fahrenheit (1686–1736), a German physicist who devised the scale.

☆*Ferris wheel*

Meaning: A large, upright wheel revolving on a fixed axle and having seats that hang from the frame: used as an amusement ride.

Origin: George W. G. Ferris (1859–1896), an American engineer who constructed the first one for the 1893 World's Fair in Chicago.

Frankenstein

Meanings: A person destroyed by his or her own creation. Also, popularly, Frankenstein's monster; anything that becomes dangerous to its creator.

Origin: Frankenstein, the title character who creates a monster in a novel by the English writer Mary Wollstonecraft Shelley (1797–1851).

Freudian slip

Meaning: A mistake made in speaking by which, it is thought, the speaker inadvertently reveals his or her true motives, desires, or the like.

Origin: Sigmund Freud (1856–1939), an Austrian physician and neurologist who founded psychoanalysis.

☆*gerrymander*

Meanings: To divide a voting area so as to give one political party a majority in as many districts as possible; to manipulate unfairly so as to gain advantage.

Origin: A satirical coinage from Elbridge *Gerry* (1744–1814), the governor of Massachusetts when the method was employed, plus *salamander,* from the shape of the redistricted Essex County, Massachusetts.

John Hancock

Meaning: ☆One's signature. (Used informally.)

Origin: John Hancock (1737–1793), whose bold and legible signature is the first to appear on the U.S. Declaration of Independence.

☆*lynch law*

Meaning: The lawless practice of killing by lynching.

Origin: Captain William Lynch (1742–1820), a member of a vigilance committee in Pittsylvania, Virginia, in 1780.

macadam

Meanings: Small broken stones used in making roads, especially those combined with a binder such as tar or asphalt; a road made with layers of such stones.

Origin: John L. McAdam (1756–1836), a Scottish engineer who invented the process.

Machiavellian

Meanings: Characterized by the political principles and methods of expediency, craftiness, and duplicity; a follower of such principles and methods.

Origin: Niccolò Machiavelli (1469–1527), a Florentine statesman whose book *The Prince* advocates those principles and methods.

mackintosh or macintosh

Meanings: A waterproof outer coat, or raincoat; the fabric used for this, originally made by cementing layers of cloth with rubber.

Origin: Charles Macintosh (1766–1843), the Scottish inventor of the process.

☆Mae West

Meaning: An inflated life vest used by aviators downed at sea.

Origin: Mae West (1892–1980), a shapely American actress.

martinet

Meaning: A very strict disciplinarian or stickler for rigid regulation.

Origin: General Jean Martinet, a seventeenth-century French drillmaster.

Parkinson's Law

Meaning: Any of several satirical statements expressed as economic laws, including one to the effect that work expands to fill the time allotted to it.

Origin: C. Parkinson (1909–), a British economist, who propounded them.

☆Peter Principle

Meaning: The facetious proposition that employees in an organization tend to be promoted until they reach their level of incompetence.

Origin: L. J. Peter, an American writer who, with R. Hull, wrote *The Peter Principle* (1968).

sandwich

Meaning: Two or more slices of bread with a filling of meat, fish, cheese, jam, or the like, between them.

Origin: John Montagu, 4th Earl of Sandwich (1718–1792), said to have eaten them in order not to leave the gambling table for meals.

Victorian

Meaning: Showing the middle-class respectability, prudery, bigotry, and other characteristics generally attributed to Victorian England.

Origin: Victoria, who set the moral tone of England during her reign as queen (1837–1901).

From Fiction and Legend

Don Juan

Meaning: A libertine or philanderer; a rake.

Origin: Don Juan, who, in Spanish legend, was a dissolute nobleman and seducer of women.

John Bull

Meaning: A personification of England or an Englishman.

Origin: The title character in the satire *The History of John Bull*, by the Scottish writer John Arbuthnot (1667–1735).

malapropism

Meanings: A ludicrous misuse of words, especially through confusion caused by resemblance in sound; a word so misused.

Origin: Mrs. Malaprop, a character in the play *The Rivals*, by the British dramatist Richard Brinsley Sheridan (1751–1816).

(For a discussion of malapropisms, see RUSSIAN IS WRITTEN IN THE ACRYLIC ALPHABET.)

peeping Tom

Meaning: A person who gets pleasure, mainly sexual pleasure, from watching others furtively.

Origin: A tailor named Tom, who, in English legend, was struck blind after peeping at Lady Godiva as she rode naked through the streets of Coventry.

quixotic, Quixotic

Meanings: Extravagantly chivalrous or romantically idealistic; visionary; impractical or impracticable.

Origin: The title character in the novel *Don Quixote*, by the Spanish writer Miguel de Cervantes (1547–1616).

scrooge

Meaning: A hard, miserly misanthrope.

Origin: Ebenezer Scrooge, a character in *A Christmas Carol*, by the English novelist Charles Dickens (1812–1870).

Shangri-La

Meaning: An imaginary idyllic utopia or hidden paradise.

Origin: The scene of *Lost Horizon*, by the English novelist James Hilton (1900–1954).

Shylock

Meaning: A person without sentiment in business matters; an exacting creditor.

Origin: The relentless moneylender in the play *The Merchant of Venice*, by the English writer William Shakespeare (1564–1616).

tam-o'-shanter

Meaning: A Scottish cap with a wide, round, flat top and, often, a center pompom.

Origin: The main character in "Tam o'Shanter," a poem by the Scottish writer Robert Burns (1759–1796).

☆*Uncle Tom*

Meaning: A black whose behavior toward whites is regarded as fawning or servile. (A contemptuous term.)

Origin: The main character, an elderly black slave, in the antislavery novel *Uncle Tom's Cabin*, by the American writer Harriet Beecher Stowe (1811–1896).

K

Kilimanjaro is taller than any mountain in Africa.

This statement is ambiguous. Does it mean that no mountain in Africa is taller than Kilimanjaro? Or does it mean that Kilimanjaro, located outside of Africa, is taller than any mountain on that continent? The confusion arises over the use of *any* and *any other* in comparisons in which a comparative adjective is followed by *than*. (Comparative adjectives usually end in *-er* or take *more* before the positive form: *harder* and *more beautiful,* for example. They are ordinarily used when only two things or people are compared.)

Any indicates that what is being compared does not belong to the group it is compared with. So "Kilimanjaro is taller than any mountain in Africa" implies that Kilimanjaro is not a mountain in Africa. But it is in fact Africa's tallest mountain, located in Tanzania. *Any* would be appropriate if Kilimanjaro were compared with, say, Europe's tallest mountain (Mont Blanc, in eastern France, near the Italian border). Although Kilimanjaro and Mont Blanc are both mountains, they are on different continents and can therefore be said to belong to different groups. And since Kilimanjaro is the taller of the two, the comparison might read:

Kilimanjaro is taller than any mountain in Europe.

On the other hand, to indicate that no mountain in Africa is taller than Kilimanjaro, *any other* is needed, because when this phrase follows *than* it shows that whatever is being compared does indeed belong to the group it is compared with. So here the comparison would read:

Kilimanjaro is taller than any other mountain in Africa.

Else serves the same purpose as *other* in comparisons with *than*. That is, it makes it clear that the person or thing being compared is part of the larger group with which the comparison is made.

More than anyone else, Henry Ford put America on wheels.

Is chicken soup really better than anything else in curing colds?

A comparison is stated differently when a superlative adjective is used (one which usually ends in *-est* or takes *most* before the positive form: *hardest* and *most beautiful,* for instance). Here it is self-contradictory to use *other* to show that the thing or person qualified by the adjective is included in the group it is compared with (ordinarily three or more). So instead of:

Kilimanjaro is the tallest of all other African mountains.

we would say:

Kilimanjaro is the tallest of all African mountains.

Though criticized by some as illogical, superlative comparisons with *of any* are well established.

Kilimanjaro is the tallest mountain of any in Africa.

These guidelines apply also to adverbs, whose comparative and superlative forms closely resemble those of adjectives.

The Broadway play *Cats* was more lavishly produced than any movie.

Cats was more lavishly produced than any other Broadway play.

Cats was the most lavishly produced of all Broadway plays.

Cats was the most lavishly produced of any play on Broadway.

(For a general discussion on the positive, comparative, and superlative degrees of adjectives and adverbs, see EXCITINGER TIMES LIE AHEAD.)

As ANY SOMETIMES FOLLOWS a positive adjective or adverb, that is, one that is in its simple, uninflected, or unmodified form or degree: *hard; beautiful* (for the adjective), *beautifully* (for the adverb). Here a person or thing is said to be equal to all others in its group.

Wyatt Earp had a gun as fast as any in the Old West.

Battleship Potemkin portrays a naval mutiny as realistically as any on film.

Though generally not approved in formal writing, incomplete comparisons with *as* and *than* are common in speech and informal writing.

U.S. birthrates were *as low or lower than* they had ever been. (Instead of: . . . *as low as or lower than* . . .)

Lines at the checkout counters moved *as slowly if not more slowly than* before. (Instead of *as slowly as if not more slowly than* . . .)

Rather than complete the comparison by inserting *as*, it is often less awkward to reword the sentence.

U.S. birthrates were as low as they had ever been, if not lower.

Lines at the checkout counters moved at least as slowly as before.

Adjectives and adverbs in such correlative constructions are dealt with more fully in AS . . . AS OR SO . . . AS? For a discussion on whether a pronoun following *than* or *as* in a comparison should be in the subjective or objective form, or case, see IS IT ME YOU LIKE BETTER THAN HER?

"Kinkering Congs Their Titles Take."

This is what came out of William Archibald Spooner's mouth instead of "Conquering Kings Their Titles Take," the hymn he had planned to announce in the chapel of New College, Oxford. In fact, during his years as warden of that college (1903–1924), the Reverend Spooner unintentionally transposed the initial sounds in so many words that this lapse of speech is known as a *spoonerism*. For example, he is said to have told a student he had just dismissed:

"You have deliberately tasted two worms [for *wasted two terms*] and you can leave Oxford by the next town drain [*down train*]."

and, on other occasions:

"We all know what it is to have a half-warmed fish [*half-formed wish*] within us."

"Yes, indeed; the Lord is a shoving leopard [*loving shepherd*]."

Besides being blamed for or credited with slips of the tongue that might have been thought up by others, the absent-minded English clergyman and educator had something else in common with the American movie producer Sam Goldwyn. He too made the ludicrously illogical or incongruous statements that many people now call Goldwynisms (see "YOU'RE A GOODY-GOODY GUMSHOES"). It would be difficult to improve on Reverend Spooner's greeting:

"I remember your name perfectly, but I just can't think of your face."

Next to the spoonerisms attributed to Spooner himself, probably the best-known one was said by the American radio announcer Harry Von Zell, who introduced the thirty-first President of the United States as "Hoobert Heever [*Herbert Hoover*]."

Such fluffs are common on live radio and television broadcasts. Anchoring the *Independent News* on network television, for example, Morton Dean reported that a U.S. district judge had blocked the drug testing of U.S. Customs Service employees. The judge, Dean said, had found that the program violated constitutional protections against unreasonable "seize and searcher [*search and seizure*]."

Repetition can easily turn a phrase into a spoonerism. After putting the usual mealtime question to many rows of passengers—"Chicken or steak?"—a Delta airlines flight attendant, her eyes glazed, asked, "Sticken or chake?"

Some other spoonerisms:

Do you study Sheets and Kelly (*Keats and Shelley*) this semester?

I never check my bite flag (*flight bag*).

Why is it that every time I take my car downtown the larking pots (*parking lots*) are full?

This is the final calling board (*boarding call*) for flight 608.

Is this the way to Lady Shane (*Shady Lane*)?

Let's not get the heart before the course (*cart before the horse*).

Spoonerisms are related to the linguistic process known as *metathesis*. However, in a spoonerism the initial sounds in two or more adjacent or nearby words are usually interchanged for a moment, whereas in metathesis the transposition ordinarily occurs within a single word and can lead to lasting changes in both spelling and pronunciation. (For more on metathesis, see WELL, I'LL BE A DRITY BRID!)

L

labor or *belabor?*   See *belabor* or *labor?*

late, former, or *ex-?*   See *former, ex-,* or *late?*

latter; former.   See *former; latter.*

lay or lie?

Only three letters long, *lay* and *lie* are sufficiently troublesome to tie the tongues and still the pens of educated speakers and writers of English. The confusion is by now so great that not taking part in it borders on bad form.

Yet how we handle these verbs is often considered a measure of our fluency in the language, so it might be a good idea to sort them out once and for all. The first step is to note the differences in the principal parts of the two verbs.

	lay	*lie*
Present	(I) *lay*	(I) *lie*
Past	(I) *laid*	(I) *lay*
Perfect	(I have, had) *laid*	(I have, had) *lain*
Progressive	(I am, was) *laying*	(I am, was) *lying*
Future	(I will) *lay*	(I will) *lie*

What is probably most difficult to keep in mind is that, with but one exception, the present tense of *lay* is the same as the past tense of *lie*. The exception occurs in the third-person singular.

	lay (present)	*lie* (past)
First person	(I, we) *lay*	(I, we) *lay*
Second person	(You) *lay*	(You) *lay*
Third person (singular)	(He, she, it) *lays*	(He, she, it) *lay*
Third person (plural)	(They) *lay*	(They) *lay*

It would be hard enough to remember that the present tense of *lay* virtually matches the past tense *lie*, person for person and number for number. Having to make an exception of the third-person singular forms turns out to be an added complication in this two-tense comparison.

Some people are unable to resist patterning the past tense of *lie* after the past—instead of the present—tense of *lay*. So they say and write sentences like:

I *laid* (instead of *lay*) down for an hour after lunch.

Others, treating the irregular *lie* as if it were a regular verb, form the past tense by simply adding *-d* to the infinitive. And then are horrified to hear themselves say:

I *lied* (instead of *lay*) down for an hour after lunch.

The perfect and progressive tenses can also be a problem. Substituting the forms of *lie* for those of *lay,* some people say:

Where *have* you *lain* (instead of *laid*) the hammer?

We *are lying* (instead of *laying*) in enough firewood for the whole winter.

Others do just the opposite, using forms of *lay* where those of *lie* belong.

Grandma *had laid* (instead of *lain*) on the floor for hours before a neighbor came by.

Were you *laying* (instead of *lying*) down when I phoned?

HOWEVER GREAT THE IRREGULARITY between the forms of *lay* and *lie,* and within the forms of each verb, it is probably not enough to account for all the confusion. Perhaps the distinction between *lay* as a transitive verb (that is, a verb that takes a direct object to complete its meaning) and *lie* as an intransitive verb (a verb that requires no object) is again becoming blurred, as it was hundreds of years ago. In the last century or so, using the verbs interchangeably has been considered dialectal (limited to certain regions, communities, or social groups), if not downright illiterate. *Lie* has virtually no standard transitive uses today, and *lay* has one main intransitive use.

The hen lays. (*An egg* or *eggs* is understood.)

Lay does have a number of idiomatic intransitive uses, however, including *lay over* (as in "Will the ship lay over in New Orleans?").

THE LAY-LIE TANGLE may also have to do with people's notions of how the two words ought to be used with animate and inanimate things, regardless of whether these things are the subjects or the objects of verbs. Some seem to believe that *lay* is appropriate with inanimate things, so they say, and sometimes even write, a form of *lay* when a form of *lie* is called for. For example:

The pliers *were laying* (instead of *lying*) under the workbench.

Iran *lays* (instead of *lies*) to the west of Afghanistan.

What *lays* (instead of *lies*) ahead?

The pottery has *laid* (instead of *lain*) under the temple for centuries.

Wordsworth wrote about thoughts that *laid* (instead of *lay*) too deep for tears.

Conversely, those who believe that only *lie* is appropriate with animate things are likely to use that verb even though *lay* is the right one.

Lie (instead of *lay*) the baby down.

A blow to the head *lay* (instead of *laid*) Sugar Ray low.

Why have you always *lain* (instead of *laid*) the blame on the weather?

lend or *loan*?   See *loan* or *lend*?

less or *fewer?*   See *fewer* or *less?*

liable, likely, or *apt?*   See *likely, apt,* or *liable?*

lie or *lay?*   See *lay* or *lie?*

like or *as, as if?*

Countless English words move freely from one part of speech to another (see "ICE CREAM YOUR KIDS TODAY WITH ROCKY ROAD"). *Like* is one of those words—up to a point.

It is used as an adjective.

Ten delegates and a *like* number of alternates were elected.

It is used as a noun.

Courses are given in metalworking, electronics, and the *like*.

Have you ever seen the *like* (or *likes*) of him?

It is used as a preposition, meaning:

"similar to"

Some babies are *like* alarm clocks.

"in a manner characteristic of"

Critics say she sings *like* Leontyne Price.

"in accord with the nature of"

It's just *like* you to share the credit.

"in the mood for"

I feel *like* watching TV.

"indicative or prophetic of"

It looks *like* another foggy day.

"as for example"

I'm looking for Mexican food, *like* guacamole and tacos.

It is used informally as an adverb in the sense of "likely."

Like as not, I'll forget my umbrella.

In certain regions and social groups—never in anything close to a formal context—*like* is used in verb phrases that convey the notion of having been on the verge of doing something.

They *like to tore* (or *like to have torn*) the dance hall apart.

(Its standard use as a verb, as in "I like Ike," has a different origin, so it does not enter into this functional shift.)

And, with the approval of almost no one outside their own group, some speakers use *like* without meaning or syntactical function almost anywhere in a sentence.

He's *like* running a bike shop.

Many people who are comfortable with *like* as an adjective, a noun, a preposition, and even an adverb draw the line at its use as a conjunction, whether to mean ''as; in the way that'' or ''as if; as though.'' They insist that *like* must never introduce a subordinate clause—that is, a group of words containing both a verb and a subject in a complex sentence. So they say yes to:

Act *as* you would want others to.

She looks *as if* (or *as though*) she's going to win.

but no to:

Act *like* you would want others to.

She looks *like* she's going to win.

Those on the other side of the long-standing argument see no point in holding out against widespread usages that fit into the system of the language. In their *Dictionary of Contemporary American Usage* (1957), Bergen and Cornelia Evans note that *like* in the sense of ''as'' has long been used as a conjunction introducing a full clause. After citing Keats (''It is astonishing how they raven down scenery <u>like</u> children do sweet meats''), they say that the construction is found also in the writings of Shakespeare, Dryden, Burns, Coleridge, Shelley, Darwin, Kipling, Shaw, Masefield, Maugham, and others. Tennyson was among the minority who considered it a grammatical mistake to use *like* in this way.

Even some English-speakers who freely use *like* for *as* (''You don't act impulsively like I do'') hesitate to use *like* for *as if* or *as though* (''You look like you've just had a nap'')—although this construction, too, is well established. Indeed, in its 1976 *Supplement, The Oxford English Dictionary* deleted the earlier ''obsolete'' label and gave a number of citations in which *like* introduces a full clause. These include:

''The old fellow drank of the brandy like he was used to it.'' (John R. Bartlett, *Dictionary of Americanisms,* 1860)

''None of them act like they belonged to the hotel.'' (*Harper's Magazine,* 1866)

''When you're alone in the middle of the bed and you wake up like someone hit you on the head.'' (T. S. Eliot, ''Sweeney Agonistes,'' 1932)

''For a while it looked like I was going to get shut of it.'' (William Faulkner, *The Hamlet,* 1940)

Uncertain of the acceptance of *like* as a conjunction before a clause, whether replacing *as* or *as if* (or *as though*), many English-speakers limit the usage to informal writing and casual speech. Not surprisingly, it often turns up in interviews or extemporaneous remarks.

On learning that leading California Republican contributors had failed to keep a pledge to support him for a second term, Senator S. I. Hayakawa, a former professor of general semantics, said, " 'It was like they were engaged to one girl but went around and dated another.' " (John Fogarty, "Sen. Hayakawa Feels Jilted")

Helen Gurley Brown, the editor of *Cosmopolitan,* said in an interview, " 'It's like time doesn't exist.' " (Chris Barnett, "The Movie Mogul and 'That Cosmo Girl' ")

Shortly after the Argentine invasion of the Falkland Islands, an unnamed member of the British prime minister's Conservative Party in Parliament said, " 'It looks like she doesn't intend to mess about.' " (Leonard Downie, Jr., "Thatcher Is Dead Set on a Quick British Victory")

Gay Talese complained that while *Thy Neighbor's Wife* was in preparation, " 'I felt like I was writing a book in Macy's window.' " (Kenneth C. Davis, "*PW* Interviews")

Yet, more and more, the much-criticized constructions appear in print. And not only in ads similar to the R. J. Reynolds Tobacco Company's famous 1954 slogan, "Winston tastes good like a cigarette should."

" 'You can take Hollywood for granted like I did,' Cecilia Bradley tells the reader in *The Last Tycoon,* 'or you can dismiss it with the contempt we reserve for what we don't understand....' " (Joan Didion, *The White Album*)

"Like Dan Rather says: 'Courage.' " (Tom Shales, *Washington Post*)

"Americans Eat like There's No Time for Home" (headline on an Associated Press article)

"Letty felt like she spent half her life sitting in offices talking to people about Helen." (Ellen Gilchrist, *In the Land of Dreamy Dreams*)

"His hair was very short, but it didn't look like it had been cut that way. It looked like that was as long as it would grow." (Larry McMurtry, *All My Friends Are Going to Be Strangers*)

The end of the dispute over *like* as a conjunction is nowhere in sight. Those who find the construction appropriate in relaxed, natural English will probably go on using it, regardless of the condemnation of others. Those who, whether out of conviction, habit, or the fear of being criticized, refuse to use it may never give in to the pressure of usage.

Some people are so fearful of using *like* for *as* that they avoid using *like* for *like*. So:

They spin out a simple "Why don't you drive like Paul?" into "Why don't you drive the way Paul does?" or even "Why don't you drive in a manner similar to Paul's?"

They turn "The British, like the French, hold the fork in the left hand while eating" into "The British, as with the French, hold the fork in the left hand while eating.'' (*As with* is appropriate, however, in constructions where neither *like* nor *as* seems to fit. For example: ''As with most sports cars, getting into the RX7 takes some doing.'')

They simply trade in *like* for *as,* regardless of sense, changing ''I felt like a fool'' into ''I felt as a fool.''

like or *such as*? See *such as* or *like*?

likely, apt, or *liable*?

Having been taught that *likely, apt,* and *liable* convey quite different meanings, many people are uneasy about using the words interchangeably—as everyone else seems to be doing. This is the traditional distinction between the three adjectives when, in describing something becoming true or actual, they are followed by an infinitive:

Likely suggests probability or an eventuality that can reasonably be expected.

The prime lending rate is likely to rise during an inflationary period.

Apt suggests a natural or habitual inclination or tendency.

Children are apt to be shy among stangers.

Liable implies exposure or susceptibility to something undesirable.

If you feed a lion, you are liable to lose an arm.

Nowadays, as most American and British dictionaries recognize, *likely* and *apt* are virtually synonymous in implying probability.

"This Presidential election campaign is likely to break our hearts unless we pick up a few giggles and get a little fun along the way." (James Reston, "Reports")

"He [George Shearing] has long been thought of as a jazz pianist, but he is apt these days to play Kurt Weill's 'Mack the Knife' at a very slow tempo, clothing it with thick Bartók chords." (Whitney Balliett, New Yorker)

Although *liable* has not gained equal status, especially in formal usage, many Americans and more and more Britons use this word when they mean *likely* or *apt,* and not necessarily with a negative connotation. For example, in a review of the film *Yes, Giorgio,* starring Luciano Pavarotti, Janet Maslin said:

"Not even his most ardent fans are liable to love it, but they probably won't find it intolerable, either."

However negative its tone, that comment does not imply risk to the fans. And the British novelist Penelope Gilliatt uses *liable* in an entirely positive sense in *A State of Change:*

"Yet all the same, in practically everyone at the party there was some feeling of jubilance as well, as though the day were liable to be a good one if only because trouble was being taken."

Interestingly enough, *liable* once had the wider, neutral sense in which it is now increasingly used. As *The Oxford English Dictionary* notes, it suggested that something was subject to the operation of any agency or likely to undergo a change of any kind.

BESIDES SUGGESTING PROBABILITY, as described above—that is, as an adjective followed by an infinitive—*likely* conveys a similar sense when used as an adverb accompanying a verb in the future tense. According to traditionalists, it must be preceded by a qualifying word like *very, quite, more,* or *most. The Oxford Paperback Dictionary* says that "the use of *likely* as an adverb without *very, most,* or *more* (e.g. in *the rain will likely die out*) is common in the U.S.A. but is not used in standard English." ("Standard English" is defined in the *OPD* as "widely used and regarded as the usual form.") As if to support that view, the style guide of the *Washington Post* gives *it will likely rain* as an example of the adverbial use of the word. Yet at least one other major American newspaper insists that *likely,* in its adverbial use as a synonym for *probably,* be accompanied by *very.* The style guide of the *Los Angeles Times* says:

> "Do not, for instance, write, He will likely attend the convention.
> But it is acceptable to say, He will very likely attend the convention."

American usage, then, is divided, but there is strong support for qualifying the adverb *likely* with another adverb when it is used in the sense of "probably."

No one, of course, objects to *likely* without a qualifier when the word is used as an adjective.

> The story has a likely ending.

linking verbs.   See **Fish and chips is on the menu again; People who want to arrive safe don't drive drunkenly.**

literal; literally

The adjective *literal* and the adverb *literally* are ordinarily associated with fact and reality.

> Some areas of the United States are literal hotbeds of rabies.

> At the opening of the Met, socialites literally rubbed elbows with first-time opera goers in blue jeans.

Yet some people use both words, but particularly the adverb, merely as intensives. That is, to emphasize a point, they toss *literally* into a sentence, as if it had nothing to do with what does or does not go beyond actual fact.

> At the garden party, my hat literally became a shower cap.

> Most expressways have literally become parking lots.

> I literally died laughing at Jack Benny's jokes.

> Sweden literally annihilated the United States in the 1984 Davis Cup Championship.

Those who don't are likely to regard such usage as loose, superfluous, errone-ous, or exasperating. (For more on intensives, see EVER SO FUNNY JOKES CAN BE QUITE AMUSING.)

An LL.D. KO'd a Brig. Gen. at a BYOB party.

If a doctor of laws knocked out a brigadier general, it must have been quite a bring-your-own-bottle party!

All abbreviations are alike in that they are shortened forms of words or phrases. Yet they differ from one another in the following ways.

In most abbreviations, letters are left out:

elev. ("elevation") *blvd.* ("boulevard")

but in a few, letters are substituted:

lb. ("pound") *oz.* ("ounce") *no.* ("number")

Some abbreviations are capitalized:

Dr. ("Doctor") B.C. ("before Christ," "British Columbia")

R.Q. ("respiratory quotient")

but others are lowercased:

apt. ("apartment") *p.* ("page")

Some are written with periods:

LL.D. ("Doctor of Laws") *A.S.P.C.A.* ("American Association for the Pre-vention of Cruelty to Animals") *Mr.* ("Mister")

but others are not:

AFL-CIO ("American Federation of Labor and Council of Industrial Organizations")

LSAT ("Law School Admission Test")

ICBM ("intercontinental ballistic missile")

Cm ("curium")

Those that stand for the names of organizations, institutions, and the like tend to be written solid, that is, with neither periods nor spaces. In Britain, abbrevia-tions of titles of courtesy ordinarily omit the periods they would have in the States (*Mrs, Dr,* and so on).

And some abbreviations are sometimes written with periods and sometimes not, sometimes with slashes instead of periods, sometimes with space between the letters and sometimes not, sometimes with capital letters and sometimes not, and sometimes even with different letters omitted. (For a general discussion of variant spellings, see SAYING GOODBYE MAY BE HARD.)

KO, K.O., k.o.

BYOB, B.Y.O.B.

A.F.C., AFC ("automatic frequency control")

C/D, CD ("certificate of deposit")

GMT, G.M.T, G.m.t. ("Greenwich mean time")

HQ, H.Q., hq, h.q. ("headquarters")

a k a, a.k.a. ("also known as")

Mt., mt., mtn. ("mountain")

There is ordinarily no space after the periods in an established abbreviation like *Ph.D.* or *N.Mex.* However, each initial in a person's name is usually followed by a space (*J. F. Kennedy*), unless the person is referred to by the initials alone (*J.F.K.*).

If they sound like words when their letters are said aloud, some abbreviations are not only shown in the usual shortened form but occasionally spelled out.

okay (from *OK*)

emcee (from *M.C.,* "master of ceremonies")

deejay (from *D.J.,* "disc jockey")

Veep, veep (from *V.P.,* "vice president")

The plurals of abbreviations that are written with internal as well as final periods are generally shown by an apostrophe and *s.*

LL.D.'s   M.B.A.'s   R.Q.'s

The plurals of most abbreviations that are written with no periods or with only final periods take an *s* without the apostrophe.

ICBMs   RQs   apts.   mts., mtns.   Drs.

However, certain abbreviations, especially for titles of courtesy, have their own plural forms with *s.*

Messrs. (from the French *Messieurs,* now used chiefly as the plural of *Mr.*)

Mmes. (the plural of *Mrs.*)

And a few double the singular form without adding *s.*

pp. ("pages")   *ff.* ("folios," "following"—pages, lines, and so on)
ll., ll ("lines")

Abbreviations are sometimes used to form the past tense and the present or past participles of verbs. Whether these abbreviations are written with or without periods, an apostrophe and *-ing* or *-d* are ordinarily added.

KO'ing, K.O.'ing; KO'd, K.O.'d ("knocking out"; "knocked out")

OK'ing, O.K.'ing; OK'd, O.K.'d (BUT *okayed,* from the spelled-out form of the abbreviation)

Yet certain verbs formed from abbreviations—such as the one meaning "to take an overdose, especially a fatal dose of a narcotic"—have different spellings.

OD'ing, ODing; OD'd, ODed

ABBREVIATIONS MAY NOT BE ELEGANT, but they do save space. That's why many of them—including those that stand for units of measure, country and state names, months of the year, and days of the week—are likely to be found in technical writing, tables, footnotes, bibliographies, and so on.

rpm ("revolutions per minute") *kl* ("kiloliter" or "kiloliters")

Mex. ("Mexico") *USA, U.S.A.* ("United States of America")

N.Dak. ("North Dakota"; *ND* is the Postal Service abbreviation) *Aug.*
Wed.

anon. ("anonymous") *ibid.* ("in the same place")

In ordinary writing, abbreviations are for the most part limited to titles accompanying people's names (*Mrs., Dr.*) and to the names of organizations and institutions mentioned often enough to justify the use of their shortened forms (*AFL-CIO, A.S.P.C.A.*). No matter how well established, abbreviations that stand for other words and phrases seldom appear unless they are pronounced letter by letter, as written. That is, B.C. and P.M. would be acceptable, but not *mtn.* or *etc.* Many writers hesitate to use even some well-established abbreviations that sound the way they look; so they are likely to replace *e.g.* with *for example* or *for instance*.

Abbreviations that appear with people's names, then, are almost always considered appropriate, whatever the kind of writing or the level of usage. These are some generally accepted guidelines for their use:

Titles such as *Mr., Mrs., Dr., Mmes.,* and *Messrs.* are rarely spelled out, whether they accompany a full name (that is, a surname plus given names or initials) or only a surname.

Mr. and Mrs. Carl Bryant Ms. R. W. Stevens

Dr. Anderson Messrs. Victor Robinson and Roger Horne

In both formal and informal writing, abbreviations are generally used for titles of college faculty, clergy, government officials, military personnel, and so on, if the abbreviations are followed by full names. However, if only surnames are given, the titles are usually written out.

Prof. Janet S. Morcom	BUT	*Professor Morcom*
Rev. Paul Quinn	BUT	*the Reverend Mr.* (or *Dr.* or *Father*) *Quinn* (NOT *Rev. Quinn* or *the Rev. Quinn*)
Rep. Norma Waters	BUT	*Representative Waters*
Brig. Gen. P. W. Barnard	BUT	*Brigadier General Barnard*

Abbreviations for academic degrees and similar indications of rank or profession follow full names, with no titles before the names.

Anne Van Fleet, LL.D.   (NOT   *Mrs.* or *Dr. Anne Van Fleet, LL.D.*)

Harold Friedman, M.B.A.   (NOT   *Mr.* or *Dr. Harold Friedman, M.B.A.*)

Katherine Forbes, Ph.D.   *Philip R. Winter, C.P.A.*

The abbreviations following the names can also stand alone, as nouns. (For the use of the indefinite article with them, see *A* OR *AN*?)

Mrs. Van Fleet received a *Ph.D.* from Temple University and an *LL.D.* from the University of Chicago.

Two *C.P.A.'s* attended the seminar on tax laws.

Abbreviations for religious orders also follow full names, but practice varies as to the use of titles before the names as well.

Sister Frances O'Hara, O.S.B.   *Margaret Keilly, B.V.M.*

Father Patrick Sullivan, S.J.   OR   *Fr. Patrick Sullivan, S.J.*
or Patrick Sullivan, S.J.   OR   *Rev. Patrick Sullivan, S.J.*

A NUMBER OF OTHER FORMS look very much like abbreviations and are often confused with them. For acronyms, see NASA'S LOX NEEDS NO BAGELS; for clipped words, A VET RUSHED TO THE ZOO BY CAB TO TREAT A HIPPO WITH THE FLU; and for contractions, DON'T SHE KNOW IT'LL BE DARK SOON?

Lo and behold, it's man's best friend.

Most English-speakers would know from the context that this sentence means "Look, it's a dog" (or "Look, it's the dog"). They would have no trouble understanding the *lo and behold* part, because both *lo* and *behold* have been around for centuries as interjections used for calling attention to something or someone. Now the two words are almost always combined in the phrase *lo and behold,* still meaning "Look!" or "See!" As for *man's best friend,* even some cat lovers would probably agree that ever since the Stone Age, long before recorded history, the domestic dog has been the hardest-working, most affectionate, and most loyal animal member of the family circle.

Since the phrases *lo and behold* and *man's best friend* are so widely used, why would anyone question them? Precisely because they are so widely used. They are *clichés,* that is, expressions which, though once fresh and forceful, have become hackneyed and weak through repetition. Although the word *cliché* is particularly fitting, for it was originally applied to a stereotype printing plate, several others also denote staleness or lack of originality in speech or writing. A *commonplace* is any obvious or conventional remark or idea (for instance, "It isn't the heat, it's the humidity"). A *platitude* is a trite remark or idea, especially one uttered as if it were novel or momentous ("A friend in need is a friend indeed"). A *truism* is a statement whose truth is so widely known that its utterance seems superfluous ("Tomorrow is another day"). And a *bromide* is an informal term for a platitude that is especially dull, tiresome, or annoying ("You can't win 'em all").

To become stale through overuse, an expression or an idea must of course start out so vivid and compelling that many people over many years want to make it theirs. How often, for instance, is revenge represented as ''an eye for an eye and a tooth for a tooth''? Yet those who use the dramatic phrase, like those who hear or see it, may not even know that it comes from a reference to justice in Exodus 21:23–24.

"And if any mischief follow, then thou shalt give life for life, Eye for eye, tooth for tooth, hand for hand, foot for foot."

The Bible has given us hundreds of other expressions that are part of our everyday speech and writing. These are but a few:

"Am I my brother's keeper?" (Genesis 4:9)

"the apple of his eye." (Deuteronomy 32:10)

"Great men are not always wise." (Job 32:9)

"There is no new thing under the sun." (Ecclesiastes 1:9)

"A time to love, and a time to hate; a time of war, and a time of peace." (Ecclesiastes 3:8)

"Beware of false prophets, which come to you in sheep's clothing." (Matthew 7:15)

"Physician, heal thyself." (Luke 4:23)

"Charity shall cover the multitude of sins." (I Peter 4:8)

So have works of well-known writers. We needn't have read Shakespeare's *Romeo and Juliet* (act 2, scene 2) to ask ''What's in a name?,'' or *As You Like It* (act 2, scene 7) to observe that ''All the world's a stage.'' In hinting at shady dealings, we may say ''Something is rotten in the state of Denmark'' without giving a thought to *Hamlet* (act 1, scene 4). And ''Now is the winter of our discontent'' is apt to be any bad period we're going through, not the opening line in *King Richard the Third* (act 1, scene 1).

Charles Dickens, too, has provided strong images that have made their way into everyday speech and writing. ''It was the best of of times, it was the worst of times,'' for instance, is from *A Tale of Two Cities*; ''Let sleeping dogs lie'' and ''There wasn't room to swing a cat there,'' from *David Copperfield*. ''Sing no sad songs for me'' is a verse in Christina Rossetti's poem ''Song.'' ''Not with a bang but a whimper'' (which we sometimes ''correct'' to ''Not with a bang but with a whimper'') is the last verse in T. S. Eliot's ''The Hollow Men.'' Among the book titles that make it easier for us to say what we want said are Sinclair Lewis's *It Can't Happen Here*, Hans Fallada's *Little Man, What Now?*, and Thomas Wolfe's *You Can't Go Home Again*.

We constantly draw on sayings, proverbs, and adages like these:

A penny saved is a penny earned.

Never look a gift horse in the mouth.

Honesty is the best policy.

Haste makes waste.

A friend to everybody is a friend to nobody.

Why struggle for originality when such pithy axioms have been expressing wisdom and truth for years?

We borrow figures of speech wholesale as well. Again, it's easier to say that someone is *as slow as a snail* than to think of another description. So we use, and reuse, similes like:

crazy as a loon

cute as a tick

dead as a doornail

sharp as a tack

snug as a bug in a rug

weak as a kitten

it fits like a glove

And, turning to metaphors, we refer to Heaven as the *Pearly Gates,* death as the *Grim Reaper,* the government as the *ship of state,* Broadway as *the Great White Way,* and so on.

But the expressions that are most likely to lose their forcefulness through repetition are idioms, that is, accepted phrases and constructions whose meanings are different from the literal meanings of the words that make them up (see How COME THE CLOCK ISN'T GOING?). The idiomatic phrase *out of the blue,* for instance, has been used so often in the sense of "without being expected or foreseen" (as in "The invitation came from out of the blue") that it is generally considered a cliché. These are some others:

between the devil and the deep blue sea (meaning "between equally unpleasant alternatives")

bury the hatchet ("to stop fighting; make peace")

high and dry ("alone and helpless; stranded")

not for love or money ("not under any conditions")

in a nutshell ("in brief or concise form; in a few words")

by the same token ("following from this")

make waves ("to disturb the prevailing calm, complacency, or the like")

This doesn't mean, of course, that English-speakers ought to avoid all popular idioms. If they did they would have to reinvent their own language every day. And because many of their newly invented expressions would go against the established patterns of the language, they would end up not delighting their listeners and readers with their originality but puzzling and irritating them. Cliché or not, *dribs and drabs,* for example, may call up a more vivid picture than *small amounts* or *small numbers.* It does in a sentence like "Well into the first quarter, fans were still drifting into the stadium in dribs and drabs."

In the same way, when Edwin Newman wrote an article on Prince Charles's speech at the 350th anniversary of Harvard University, he knew that *a dime a dozen* is an overworked informal idiom meaning "abundant and easily obtained." Yet he chose to play the phrase off against the formal style of the rest of the sentence.

> "Hortatory speeches about the imbalance between the material and the spiritual, or the intellectual and spiritual, are a dime a dozen. They do not have to be imported."

It is doubtful, however, that May Sarton had a particular rhetorical device in mind when she wrote this sentence in her novel *The Bridge of Years.* Almost every metaphor that isn't a cliché collides with another nearby.

> "At first she had taken to her work at the university like a duck to water, swimming through her courses with delight, talking a blue streak when she came home, pouring out her discoveries, her face alight."

Writers and speakers sometimes apologize for or disguise clichés they don't want to give up. One way is to say something like "The debate produced more heat than light, to coin a cliché." Another is to change the wording a bit, that is, to give the expression a slight twist without losing the sense. Instead of "They didn't see the forest for the trees," for instance, "They didn't see the forest for the rain." Instead of "We were up against the wall," "We were up against the proverbial wall." Desmond Shawe-Taylor used this ploy effectively in a *New Yorker* book review:

> "These were flashes, however, in a predominantly good-humored pan."

And, by varying a frequently quoted line from *Hamlet,* so did William Scobie in this lead in a London *Observer* article:

> "Something is rotten in the state of Texas."

Anyone who plays a cliché straight, though, ought to get it right. According to an editorial in the *Seattle Post-Intelligencer:*

> "Loyalists and revisionist historians were going at it <u>hammer and tong</u> over the frontiersman's [Davy Crockett's] accomplishments."

Meaning "with all one's might" or "very vigorously," the idiom is *hammer and tongs,* with reference to a blacksmith's work. Similarly, in *Book Publishing: What It Is, What It Does,* John P. Dessauer wrote:

> "To the extent that the emphasis on imagined 'mass' interests neglects these buyers, the industry is <u>cutting its nose to spite its face</u>."

If, in a fit of anger, resentment, or the like, an industry injures its own interests, it *cuts off its nose to spite its face.*

loan or *lend?*

The verb *lend* has to do mainly with letting another use or have a thing temporarily or with letting out money at interest; that is, it is the opposite of *borrow.*

The noun *loan* refers to what is being lent, frequently money. So, everyone agrees, it is all right to say:

> The International Monetary Fund lends money to governments in need of loans.

What is far from all right with some people is that others insist on treating *loan* not only as a noun but also as a verb with exactly the same meaning as *lend*.

> The IMF loans money to governments in need of it.

Dragging a fingernail across a chalkboard does not begin to cause the torment that this usage does. Even well-bred Miss Manners, who disapproves of correcting another's habits, grammatical or otherwise, was driven to tell a Gentle Reader of her newspaper column:

> "Miss Manners . . . cannot . . . stomach the substitution of 'loan' for the verb 'to lend.'"

But this is not a new use of *loan*, whose roots are intertwined with those of *lend*. Indeed, the verb *lend* comes from *lænan*, an Old English verb derived from the noun *læn*, meaning "a loan." The dozen or so citations for the verb *loan* given in *The Oxford English Dictionary* go back to 1200 and include this one from about 1640:

> "In yeares of dearth and Scarcity, [he] loaned to many of them . . . wheat and other corne out of his grayneries."

That is precisely how the word is widely used today, especially in the United States.

> The French government has agreed to loan 150 paintings, sculptures, and other works from Pablo Picasso's personal collection to the Walker Art Center in Minneapolis.

> Would you mind loaning me your bicycle for a few hours?

In its dual role as noun and verb, *loan* has a good deal of company. English is full of words—including *stomach*—that are used as more than one part of speech, and has been for centuries. (For more on this linguistic process known as *functional shift*, see "ICE CREAM YOUR KIDS TODAY WITH ROCKY ROAD.")

loanwords.   See **Few phenomenons are more eye-catching than stadia filled with alumnuses waving gladioli; Modor, we've got company.**

lot; lots

Calling either *lot* or *lots* "a slipshod colloquialism for 'a great many'; as, 'We sold a *lot* of tickets'; 'He has *lots* of friends,'" *Faulty Diction, As Corrected by the "Funk & Wagnalls New Standard Dictionary of the English Language"* said that both are "to be avoided, as are all other vague, ill-assigned expressions, as tending to indistinctness of thought and debasement of language."

But that was 1915, and despite continuing objections to the terms, they are generally accepted as nouns meaning "a great number or amount":

"Both scientific studies proved that there are a lot of raccoons in the suburbs." (A. B. C. Whipple, *Smithsonian*)

Lots of jazz records turned up in the basement.

and as adverbs meaning "a great deal" or "very much":

I hear the company is doing a lot (or lots) better these days.

Love from Buddy and myself.

There is no question about the pronoun forms *myself, yourself, himself, herself, itself, ourselves, yourselves,* and *themselves* being used in a number of ways.

They are used reflexively, that is, with the subject and direct object referring to the same person or thing.

I always sing myself to sleep.

She sent the insurance policy to herself.

We gave ourselves a good talking-to.

They are used as intensives, indicating emphasis or greater force.

The new managers themselves drove the company into bankruptcy.

Hal took over the driving himself.

They are used as quasi nouns referring to a person's true nature or identity.

Ever since their year abroad, they haven't been themselves.

However, many people disapprove of the *-self* forms if either the subjective forms (*I, you, he, she, it, we, they*) or the objective forms (*me, you, him, her, it, us, them*) would do instead. Agatha Christie, for instance, includes this bit of dialogue in her novel *A Caribbean Mystery:*

" 'Right. That cuts out Evelyn Hillingdon, Lucky and Esther Walters. So your murderer, allowing that all this far-fetched nonsense is true, your murderer is Dyson, Hillingdon or my smooth-tongued Jackson.'

" 'Or yourself,' said Miss Marple."

Some Christie fans would have had Miss Marple say, "Or you."

Myself is especially condemned as being either a mark of affected refinement or a cover-up of one's uncertainty whether to use *I* or *me*. These are some of the so-called inappropriate uses of *myself:*

As a substitute for *I* in a compound subject.

My brother and myself will be glad to help.

As a substitute for *me* as the sole object of a verb or preposition.

I am delighted that you will honor myself with a visit.

Everyone left except myself.

As a substitute for *me* as one element of a compound object.

Please join Mother, Roz, and myself for dinner.

Love from Buddy and myself.

In comparisons, after *as* or *than*.

Peg is almost as tall as myself.

My Saint Bernard is only a bit heavier than myself.

Yet those constructions are of long standing; several are widely used today and have the support of dictionaries and linguists. Some people prefer *myself* to *me* as the object of a verb or preposition because they consider it less blunt or emphatic. For example, in the Prefatory Note in the *Concise Pronouncing Dictionary of British and American English*, J. Windsor Lewis wrote:

"These collections have proved useful correctives to the general impressions of myself and colleagues I have consulted."

In *Soul on Ice*, the novelist Eldridge Cleaver wrote:

"In Soledad state prison, I fell in with a group of young blacks who, like myself, were in vociferous rebellion against what we perceived as a continuation of slavery on a higher plane."

And in an article in the London *Times Literary Supplement*, the American writer Diana Trilling wrote:

"women readers, including myself, are more likely to read it as defeat mitigated only by dignity."

Speakers and writers who use *myself* in place of *I* in a compound subject usually do so for the same purpose: to give themselves less prominence, to put themselves at a distance from the situation they are describing. Among the epigraphs that introduce Robert Burchfield's book *The English Language*, for instance, is a fragment of a letter written by Evelyn Waugh:

"Chaucer, Henry James and, very humbly, myself are practising the same art. Miss Stein is not. She is outside the world-order in which words have a precise and ascertainable meaning and sentences a logical structure."

In another published letter, Janet Flanner wrote to a friend:

"Elma, myself, and Herbert Matthews, *The New York Times* correspondent, were the only civilians in uniform on board."

Constructions with pronouns in the *-self* form cannot be considered incorrect. Yet anyone they offend has the right not to use them.

M

mad or angry?

Remembering their teachers' observation that "only insane people and dogs with rabies are mad," some English-speakers hesitate to use what they hear every day: the adjective *mad* in the well-established senses "angry or provoked" and "showing or expressing anger."

Are you still mad at me for not writing?

When a car pulled into the last parking space on the lot, I was so mad I could have chewed the bumper.

Mad is also a noun meaning "an angry or sullen mood or fit," and it occurs in the informal expression *have a mad on*.

Stay away from the coach; he has his Monday-morning mad on.

malapropisms.   See **Russian is written in the Acrylic alphabet.**

manor or manner?

A *manor* was, in feudal England, a district over which a lord exercised authority and which was subject to the jurisdiction of his court; later on it became a landed estate, usually with a main residence, whose owner still holds some feudal rights over the land. In the United States the word usually refers to a mansion or the main residence on an estate or plantation. A *manner* is, among other things, a way in which someone behaves or in which something is done or happens. *Manners* are prevailing social conditions or customs.

Shakespeare used the phrase *to the manner born* to refer to one's familiarity with local customs since birth. In talking to Horatio about the king's customary late-night revelry to the sounds of a trumpet and kettledrum, Hamlet says:

"But to my mind, though I am native here
And to the manner born, it is a custom
More honour'd in the breach than the observance."

Many people, thinking that the expression has to do with good upbringing or ownership by virtue of birthright, write *to the manor born*. *"The Washington Post" Deskbook on Style*, for one, perpetuates this widespread but erroneous notion.

"Manner (behavior); manor (estate). (An aristocrat is to the *manor* born.)"

So does the British Broadcasting Corporation in its television program *To the Manor Born*, but the title is a play on words.

Turning *to the manner born* into *to the manor born* is not the only instance in which English-speakers have adopted a word or phrase because of an incorrect notion about its origin and derivation. For others, see COLD SLAW ON MY NEW CHAISE LOUNGE!

may, might, can, could.   See **Can I borrow your lawn mower? Not if you might keep it.**

"Me carrying a briefcase is like a hog wearing earrings."

When Sparky Anderson, attaché case in hand, made this comment on arriving at the Detroit airport to accept his new job as manager of the baseball team, he might not have realized that he was coming down on one side of a grammatical controversy. According to the opposition, the Tigers skipper should have said:

My carrying a briefcase is like a *hog's* wearing earrings.

The term *fused participle* is often applied to the Sparky Anderson construction, in which a gerund (the *-ing* form of a verb used as a noun) has for its subject a noun or a pronoun that is not in the possessive case. It was coined by the British lexicographer H. W. Fowler, who is regarded by many as the supreme arbiter of English usage. *The King's English*, which he wrote with his brother Frank, was published in 1906; his *Dictionary of Modern English Usage*, in 1926.

In both speech and writing, the possessive form of a noun or pronoun often does seem more natural, especially when the emphasis is on the action of the gerund.

Do you mind *my* (instead of *me*) *keeping* the book overnight?

"She resented <u>their</u> [instead of *them*] <u>catching</u> her with the Raggedy Ann." (Joan Didion, <u>A Book of Common Prayer</u>)

"He was going to sue his own government for millions, he said, because the radiation he had absorbed there had first prevented <u>his</u> [instead of *him*] and <u>Mary's</u> [instead of *Mary*] <u>having</u> children, and now it had caused his brain cancer." (Kurt Vonnegut, <u>Galápagos</u>)

"All she visibly does is to suck in her cheeks like a model and stammer remonstrances about the idea of her <u>husband's</u> [instead of *husband*] <u>moving</u> his job from France to Houston." (Penelope Gilliatt, New Yorker)

But there are times when the possessive form neither sounds nor looks right. The so-called fused participle is more likely to be used if:

the subject, not the action, of the gerund is stressed.

"Weeks or months may pass without <u>Vinnie</u> [instead of *Vinnie's*] <u>feeling</u> any need to add to her hoard of unpurchased objects." (Alison Lurie, *Foreign Affairs*)

the subject of the gerund is a plural noun.

Do you object to political action *committees* (instead of *committees'*) *underwriting* candidates' campaigns?

the subject of the gerund is modified by words coming between it and the gerund itself.

There are doubts about air *pollution* (instead of *pollution's*) in the United States *being* brought under control.

the subject of the gerund is an inanimate object or an abstraction.

A large company has reason to be fearful of its *trademark* (instead of *trademark's*) *becoming* generic.

the subject of the gerund does not logically take a possessive form.

They complained about *everything* (instead of *everything's*) *going* wrong.

metathesis.   See **Well, I'll be a drity brid!**

might, may, can, could.   See **Can I borrow your law mower? Not if you might keep it.**

modifiers: dangling, see **Covered with onions, relish, and ketchup, I ate a hot dog at the ballpark; misplaced,** see **"Electric shaver for women with delicate floral design on the handle"; restrictive and nonrestrictive,** see **The Oval Office which is in the White House symbolizes the Presidency.**

Modor, we've got company.

In the middle of the fifth century, Angles, Saxons, and Jutes swept into England from the lowlands of northern Europe where Denmark and Germany come together. Besides warring among themselves in their conquest of *Englaland* ("land of the Angles"), these Germanic tribes fought the Britons, the Celtic inhabitants who remained after the withdrawal of the Roman legions. Without losing their various Low German dialects entirely, descendants of the invaders began to speak a more or less common language that in time was called *Englisc* ("of the Angles") and is nowadays generally known as Old English. The earliest surviving written documents date from the eighth century.

Most of the words that today's English-speakers use in their daily lives closely resemble those used by speakers of Old English. For example, the Old English word for *mother* was *modor*. Some of the nouns related to the family and to family life that have come down to us from Old English are listed below. The form given for each Old English word is, however, but one of many in use during that period, which lasted roughly from 400 to 1100. *Death*, for example, exists in at least sixteen forms in early manuscripts. (Actually, before the eighteenth century, English spelling was not standardized, so writers spelled words just about as they wanted to.)

brother, from *brothor*	death, from *death*
child, from *cild* (In Old English a *c* followed by *e* or *i* had a *ch* sound.)	father, from *fæder*
daughter, from *dohtor*	home, from *ham*

house, from hus   *son, from sunu*

husband, from husbonda   *wedding, from weddung*

kin, from cynn   *wife, from wif*

life, from lif   *woman, from wifmann, later wim-*
mann
man, from mann

Many of the nouns used nowadays for parts of the body were in the Old English word stock as well. For instance:

arm, from earm   *heart, from heorte*
belly, from belg   *knee, from cneow*
blood, from blod   *mouth, from muth*
body, from bodig   *neck, from hnecca*
ear, from eare   *shoulder, from sculdor*
eye, from eage   *thigh, from theoh*
head, from heafod

So were many nouns related to the world of nature, including these:

day, from dæg   *morning, from morgen*
earth, from eorthe   *rain, from regn*
evening, from æfnung   *star, from steorra*
heaven, from heofon   *tree, from treow*
lake, from lacu   *water, from wæter*
moon, from mona   *wind, from wind*

Virtually all English personal and possessive pronouns came into the language during the Old English period.

I, me, mine, from ic, me, min   *it, from hit (The Old English form of its was his.)*

thou, thee, thine, from thu, the, thin *we, us, our, from we, us (and usic), ure (replacing user)*

ye, you, your, from ge, eow, eower   *their, from hira (Them and they did not come into use until the Middle English period.)*
he, him, his, from he, him (later merged with hine), his

she, her, from seo (replacing heo), hire

Besides, many of the verbs now used day in and day out were around in the Old English period. For example:

bring, from bringan   *learn, from leornian*
come, from cuman   *like, from lician*
drink, from drincan   *love, from lufian*
eat, from etan   *meet, from metan*
go, from gan   *sleep, from slæpan*
hate, from hatian   *start, from styrtan*
have, from habban   *walk, from wealcan*
kiss, from cyssan   *win, from winnan*
know, from cnawan   *work, from wyrcan*
laugh, from hleahhan

And so were most of the current English function words which, though having little or no lexical meaning, are essential in showing syntactical relation or structure. In addition to conjunctions like *and* (from *and* and *ond*) and *but* (from *butan* and *buton*), Old English included prepositions such as these:

at, from æt
by, from be, bi
down, from adune, ofdune
for, from for
in, from in

of, from of, af, æf
to, from to
up, from up, uppe
with, from with

For a view of what was happening both in England and in other parts of the world during the Old and Middle English periods, see the table on pages 4–6.

ENGLISH WAS INFLUENCED by other languages even during the Old English period. From the Celtic inhabitants they encountered, the Germanic invaders picked up mostly local place names. *Legacaestir,* from the Latin *legionum castra* (meaning "camp of the legions"), for example, was contracted to *Caestre.* Today it is known as *Chester,* the country seat of Cheshire.

The Scandinavians had a greater influence on the early English word stock than the Britons. Not only did their various dialects share a common ancestry with those of the Germanic invaders of Britain, but for several centuries Viking pirate ships ravaged the coast of England. By the middle of the ninth century, the Danes had put down settlements in England; and before their expulsion in 1042, Canute the Great had become the first Danish king of England, as well as king of Denmark and Norway. These are some current English words that made their way into Old English from Old Norse:

call
hit
husband
hustings

root
take
wrong

Many more were adopted from Old Norse in the Middle English period (roughly 1100 to 1500). Here is a sample:

anger
die
egg
get
sister
skill

skin
sky
them
they
ugly
want

TOWARD THE END of the Old English period, in 1066, the Norman French, under William the Conqueror, defeated the English at the Battle of Hastings. Besides drastically changing English government, law, religious life, arts, and customs, the Norman domination couldn't help affecting the language. These are among the words that came into English from Anglo-Norman (or Anglo-French, as the dialect spoken by the Norman settlers after the Conquest is sometimes called):

beg	*cupidity*
carpenter	*jury*
catch	*larceny*
citizen	*treasurer*

A far greater influence on the English word stock—indeed, one that was to change it for all time—came not from Norman French but from Central French, whose literature became the standard for much of Europe. From around 1300 on, but especially during the fourteenth and fifteenth centuries, French words flooded into England. Because French is so closely related to its mother tongue, Latin, it is sometimes impossible to tell whether words taken as French are in fact of Latin origin. These are but a few of the many thousands of French words that English—American as well as British—has adopted and naturalized over the centuries:

army	*navy*
authority	*neutral*
bizarre	*ounce*
boutique	*oxide*
city	*parliament*
coiffeur	*pencil*
deceive	*princess*
essay	*quest*
forge	*rage*
government	*random*
hour	*religion*
illusion	*river*
journey	*sacrament*
justice	*second*
letter	*sergeant*
liberty	*table*
library	*valor*
mayor	*village*

THE CONTRIBUTION THAT LATIN has made to the English vocabulary, as well as its grammar, is beyond calculation. Latin words and word elements are so much a part of our everyday speech and writing that we pay little or no attention to them. Many Latin words are derived from Greek, and, as noted above, a large number have come into English by way of French. These are some of the countless Latin-derived words that have helped make English the luxuriant language it is:

accommodate	*intelligent*
animal	*joke*
candidate	*jugular*
circus	*legislate*
dilemma	*medieval*
editor	*miser*
epoch	*narrative*
fact	*nefarious*
genius	*obnoxious*
horizontal	*onomatopoeia*

postpone	tendency
preposterous	urban
quadrant	urge
quip	vanilla
recur	voracious
redundant	wad
sensual	xenophobia
splendid	zealot
tedium	

For the way some Latin prefixes, suffixes, and combining forms change the meaning of certain English words and build others, see WHO NEEDS A RABBIT'S FOOT MORE: AN UNLUCKY PERSON OR A LUCKLESS ONE? For the plurals of Latin loanwords, see FEW PHENOMENONS ARE MORE EYE-CATCHING THAN STADIA PACKED WITH ALUMNUSES WAVING GLADIOLI.

OVER THE CENTURIES thousands of Greek words and word elements have also found their way into English. For many of them the route has not been direct but, instead, has taken detours through other languages, mainly Latin or Latin and French. For example, the ancient Greek word *elaunein,* drawing on an Indo-European base and meaning "to set in motion," became *elastikos* in Late Greek, *elasticus* in Modern Latin, and *elastic* in English. The Greek word *philosophos* (*philos,* "loving," plus *sophos,* "wise") was changed to *philosophus* in Latin, *philosophe* in Old French, *philosophre* in Middle English, and *philosopher* in Modern English.

Here is a sample of Greek-derived words used in English. Besides politics, philosophy, literature, the arts, medicine, and science, they deal with all aspects of everyday life:

alphabet	myth
archipelago	narcissism
biography	orthodox
crisis	paper
diabetes	rhythm
economy	school
energy	skeptic
grammar	sphere
homonym	technique
idiot	uranography
lexicography	zodiac
marathon	

For the plural forms of Greek, as well as Latin, loanwords, see FEW PHENOMENONS ARE MORE EYE-CATCHING THAN STADIA PACKED WITH ALUMNUSES WAVING GLADIOLI.

AND THEN THERE WAS the American tourist in Berlin who was thoroughly unhappy because nobody spoke English—until a waiter, hearing him sneeze, said, "*Gesundheit!*"

When it comes to appropriating words, any language within the sight or hearing of English-speakers has been fair game—and not only since travel and communication have shrunk the world. Like Latin and Greek borrowings, many others have come into English second-, third-, or even fourth-hand. For example, *maven* ("an expert or connoisseur, often especially a self-proclaimed one") is of Hebrew origin, but American English picked it up from Yiddish. And *orange* came into Middle English from the Old French *orenge*, but that's only the last chapter in a long, involved story: the Sanskrit word *naranga*, probably a cognate of the Tamil *naru* (meaning "fragrant") had become *nārang* in Persian; *nāranj* in Arabic; *naranja* in Spanish; and *auranja* in Provençal (through loss of the initial *n*, owing to faulty separation between the article and the noun; see *A* OR *AN*?).

Even after adopting a foreign word to fill a particular gap in their own language, English-speakers sometimes hesitate to use it. A letter from one such irresolute Briton appeared in the *Times* of London, under the heading "An English Patio."

"Sir, In summer my husband and I often sit, entertain our friends or eat meals on a 15 foot square paved area in an L-shaped sunny and wind-free corner of this house, facing the garden, but we don't know what to call it.

"It is not a 'terrace' which I take to be long with ambulatory connotations. 'Patio' is foreign and, we feel, pretentious in spite of the fact that the OED [*The Oxford English Dictionary*] definition almost exactly describes it. To call it 'the pavement' sounds as though we were taking our meals on the front doorstep; 'the backyard' sounds like inverted snobbery. Roget's Thesaurus has not provided a suitable alternative.

"Can anyone please tell us what English word we can use to describe it adequately?

"Yours faithfully,
"Betty Bevan.
"Freshfields, Milnthorpe, Westmorland, Cumbria.
"May 14."

Patio indeed seems to describe the paved area in the Bevans' house. Their reluctance to use the word may be due to its doubly foreign derivation: not only is it of Spanish origin but its current English senses entered the language in the United States.

To many Americans and Britons, it may seem as though foreign words have to do only with food, but in fact they cover the entire range of human activity. A number of borrowings are listed below, not by their most remote origin but by the language from which English adopted them. The words and phrases that entered the language through American English are preceded by an open star (as in *Webster's New World Dictionary*). Also, in keeping with the practice of some English-language dictionaries, including *WNWD*, foreign words and phrases that are encountered with some frequency in English speech and writing but are not completely naturalized are distinguished from those that are fully assimilated. In most printed material, they would be italicized; but because the entire list is in italics, the still-foreign words are underlined here (as they would be in written material).

Algonquian (American Indian)

chipmunk
☆moccasin
☆moose
☆persimmon
☆raccoon
☆squash (edible plant)
☆woodchuck

German

blitzkrieg
cobalt
☆delicatessen
☆frankfurter, frankforter
Gesundheit
glitch
☆hamburger
Lebensraum
☆noodle
poodle
Sturm und Drang
zinc

Hindi

bangle
cheetah
jungle
loot
seersucker
thug

Italian

antipasto
cappuccino
cupola
falsetto
imbroglio
miniature
piccolo
terra cotta
trio
umbrella

Russian

balalaika
cosmonaut
gulag

mammoth
vodka

Spanish

☆*adios*
alligator
☆*bonanza*
filibuster
guerrilla
☆*hoosegow, hoosgow*
junta
<u>*macho, machismo*</u>
peccadillo
politico
sierra
tornado
☆*vigilante*

Yiddish

bagel
chutzpah, chutzpa
☆*klutz*
☆*kvetch*
<u>*mensch*</u>
☆*nudnik*
☆*schlep, schlepp*
☆*schmooze*

ADDING FOREIGN WORDS AND PHRASES to the original Anglo-Saxon word stock is by no means the only way in which English constantly enriches its vocabulary. These are some of the other processes that lead to the creation of new words and to changes in the meanings of existing ones:

Proper nouns are constantly incorporated into the everyday vocabulary of English-speakers. These names of people and places may be native or they may be imported; they may be drawn from real life or they may be the stuff of fiction, myths, and the like. (For more on words derived from or associated with proper names, see JOHN BULL AND JOHN HANCOCK ARE NOT JUST ANY JOHNS.)

During the historical evolution of a language, words are not forever bound by their derivations but may slowly develop new senses or change their meanings. (For more on etymology and semantic shift, see FOR A GIRL HE'S QUITE MATURE.)

To fill gaps that occur in the language, entirely new words are coined or new meanings assigned to established words. (For a discussion of coinages, see DEAR MR. WEBSTER; of slang, JOBBED IN A HUMONGOUS SCAM, THE TWEAKED-OUT MOBSTER EXCLAIMED, "PEACHY-KEEN!"; of compounds, UP-START NAME-DROPPERS USUALLY GET THE COLD SHOULDER.)

Word elements are added to existing words or word forms both to create new words and to change the meanings of words already in use. (For more on prefixes, suffixes, and combining forms, see WHO NEEDS A RABBIT'S FOOT MORE: AN UNLUCKY PERSON OR A LUCKLESS ONE?) Sometimes this usual process is reversed, and so a word thought to be the long-standing base of another word is in fact a newly formed one. (For more on back-formation, see BURGLARS BURGLE AND PEDDLERS PEDDLE, SO WHY DON'T JANITORS JANIT?)

When confronted with puzzling new words, people tend to fit them into familiar patterns by making them look and sound like words they already know. (For more on folk etymology, see COLD SLAW ON MY NEW CHAISE LOUNGE!)

momentarily

Whether because of their early schooling or an acute attack of Anglophilia, some Americans apologize if they catch themselves using *momentarily* to mean anything but "for a moment or short time." They needn't. This is but one of the senses that most American dictionaries give for the adverb.

I momentarily forgot what I was saying.

"In an instant" and "from moment to moment; at any moment" are also given, without a suggestion that they are less than acceptable.

The dispatcher said the rescue team would arrive momentarily.

You may expect to hear from us momentarily.

more important or *more importantly*?

Both of these constructions are widely used in speech and writing:

Not only do buses let you see where you're going but, more important, they are a cheap way to travel.

Not only do buses let you see where you're going but, more importantly, they are a cheap way to travel.

In the first one, the adjective phrase *more important* is a short way of saying *what is more important*. In the second one, the adverb phrase *more importantly* qualifies the clause *they are a cheap way to travel*.

By and large, those who prefer *more importantly* show a greater tolerance for those who use *more important* than the other way around.

See also FIRST OR FIRSTLY?

more than or *over*?　　See *over* or *more than*?

most or *almost*?

Besides expressing the superlative degree of *much, many*, and *more, most* is sometimes used as a shortened form of the adverb *almost*. Some dictionaries and grammar books still criticize this usage, but it is gaining acceptance, particularly in informal speech and writing.

Most, of course, does not freely replace *almost* in the sense of ''nearly,'' and it does not modify verbs. Few English-speakers would think of saying or writing, for example:

The cookie jar is most empty.

I most finished my work.

Most the only time I watch television is on weekends.

The words that *most* does modify are, first, adjectives like *all, any,* and *every.*

Most all of my relatives are in New Mexico.

The pandas can be seen most any day.

We have tea most every afternoon.

Second, pronouns like *all, anybody, everyone,* and *everything.*

Most all came.

Most everyone wanted another ride.

I'll accept most everything you can lend me.

And, third, adverbs like *always, anywhere,* and *everywhere.*

You can buy videocassettes most anywhere.

The train is most always on time.

N

names: given, see **Good night, Anwar. Good night, Menachem; personal and place,** see **John Bull and John Hancock are not just any johns.**

NASA's lox needs no bagels.

NASA, which stands for *National Aeronautics and Space Administration,* looks like an abbreviation (see AN LL.D. KO'D A BRIG. GEN. AT A BYOB PARTY). *Lox* looks like the word for a variety of salty smoked salmon that some people wouldn't think of eating without a bagel, that is, a hard, doughnut-shaped roll. But unlike an abbreviation such as *NRC,* in which each letter is sounded separately, *NASA* is pronounced as an ordinary word formed by its letters (nas'ə). And the kind of *lox* that NASA would have on hand—oxygen in a liquid state, used in a fuel mixture for rockets—is represented by the first letter in *liquid* and the first two letters in *oxygen.*

NASA and *lox* in these senses, then, are *acronyms*—words formed from the first, or first few, letters of a series of words. English has an enormous supply of acronyms, to which government agencies; international organizations; medical, scientific, and technological institutions; and other users of the language are constantly adding. Here are but a few acronymic morsels fished out of the "alphabet soup."

Acronyms in Everyday Use

Amtrak (from *American travel track:* a nationwide system of passenger railroad service)

Fannie Mae, Fannie May (from *Federal National Mortgage Association,* loosely construed as a woman's name)

WASP, Wasp (from *white Anglo-Saxon Protestant*)

WATS (from *wide area telecommunications service:* a telephone service that ties a customer into the long-distance network at a special rate)

yuppie (from *young urban professionnal* + *-p-* + *-ie:* a young professional of the 1980s variously regarded as upscale, ambitious, materialistic, faddish, and the like)

ZIP code (from *zoning improvement plan:* a system devised to speed mail deliveries by means of code numbers assigned by the post office to individual areas and places)

Government Agencies, International Organizations, and the Military

Anzac (from *Australian and New Zealand Army Corps:* a soldier in that corps)

AWACS, Awacs (from *Airborne Warning and Control System:* a system employing high-flying reconnaissance aircraft equipped with a special radar system that can detect and track approaching aircraft, missiles, and the like)

AWOL, awol (from *absent without leave*)

Benelux (from *Belgium, Netherlands, Luxembourg:* an economic union of these three political entities)

HUD (from the Department of *Housing and Urban Development*)

NATO (from *North Atlantic Treaty Organization*)

UNESCO (from *United Nations Educational, Scientific, and Cultural Organization*)

VISTA (from *Volunteers in Service to America:* a U.S. government program for providing volunteers to help improve living conditions in impoverished areas of the country)

Medicine, Science, and Technology

AIDS (from *Acquired Immune Deficiency Syndrome:* a condition characterized by a deficiency in certain leucocytes)

BASIC (from *Beginner's All-purpose Symbolic Instruction Code:* a simplified digital computer language that utilizes common English words and algebra)

CAT scan (from *computerized axial tomography:* a method for diagnosing disorders of the soft tissues of the body, especially of the brain)

GIGO (from *garbage in, garbage out:* a reference to the fact that garbled input to a computer results in garbled output)

laser (from *light amplification by stimulated emission of radiation:* a device in which atoms, when stimulated by focused light waves, amplify and concentrate these waves, then emit them in a narrow, very intense beam)

quasar (from *quasi-stellar radio source:* any of a number of starlike, celestial objects that emit immense quantities of light or of powerful radio waves, or both, and that appear to be extremely distant from the earth)

sonar (from *sound navigation and ranging:* an apparatus that transmits high-frequency sound waves through water and registers the vibrations reflected from an object; used in finding submarines, depths, and so on)

Private Organizations and Institutions

ASCAP (from *American Society of Composers, Authors, and Publishers*)

CARE (from *Cooperative for American Relief Everywhere, Inc.*)

CORE (from *Congress of Racial Equality*)

MADD (from *Mothers against Drunk Drivers*)

NOW (from *National Organization for Women*)

Because acronyms are like ordinary words, those that form plurals and possessives do so in the usual way.

Quasars are fascinating to study.

ASCAP's membership rose last year.

For the use of the indefinite article with acronyms, see *A OR AN*?

nauseated, nauseous, or *nauseating*?

Perhaps some people like to think that there is a clear-cut difference between *nauseated,* on the one hand, and *nauseous* and *nauseating,* on the other. *Nauseated,* they say, applies to someone who feels nausea, that is, someone who is sick at the stomach, with an impulse to vomit.

During the first tour of the chemical plant, two visitors became so *nauseated* that they were taken to the infirmary.

And that *nauseous* and *nauseating* describe only the cause of nausea, that is, something which is sickening or disgusting.

Health officials will investigate the *nauseous* (or *nauseating*) gases coming from the plant.

The group denounced the statement as "nothing but a *nauseating* (or *nauseous*) pack of lies."

Often, however, in a revival of a seventeenth-century usage, *nauseous* replaces *nauseated* in describing a person who feels nausea or becomes sick. This switch occurs especially in informal speech and writing.

During the first tour of the chemical plant, two visitors became so *nauseous* that they were taken to the infirmary.

"It started on the freeway when Frank Malloy broke into a cold sweat. Then, driving into his garage, he became <u>nauseous</u>." (Cleveland *Plain Dealer*)

negatives, double.   See **Not for nothing does Paris claim to be the world's most beautiful city.**

"Neither fish nor flesh nor good red-herring."

This old English saying needs editing. According to the grammatical rule, *neither* and *either* should be used in references to one of two, not three or more.

Either, we are taught, means "one or the other (of two)" or "each of two; the one and the other."

Close either eye.

The baby had a cookie in either hand.

And that *neither* means, "not one nor the other (of two); not either."

Neither twin went swimming.

Yet the adjectives *either* and *neither* have long been used with more than two. *The Oxford English Dictionary* gives, among its citations for *either,* this statement by John Stuart Mill (1848):

"The alternatives seemed to be either death, or to be permanently supported by other people, or a radical change in the economical arrangements."

It is not unusual to find the more-than-two construction in current speech and writing.

Take your choice: either a movie, a play, or a trip to the zoo.

"Outcast and pariah, he has neither friend, wife, mistress, nor sweetheart...." (William Faulkner, *Sartoris*)

"'Neither Mr. Geraldine, nor Ryle, nor Protheroe is tall.'" (Nicholas Blake, *End of Chapter*)

" 'Neither weakness, nor anger nor despair will serve us,' she [Prime Minister Margaret Thatcher] observed." (James Reston, "Reports")

WHEN USED AS A PRONOUN, *either* or *neither* is considered a singular subject and therefore takes a singular verb.

Either of them *is* able to do the job.

Neither seems to be in town.

In a correlative construction—in which, say, the pair *either . . . or* or *neither . . . nor* connects words, phrases, clauses, or sentences of equal rank, so as to express mutual relation—the verb is ordinarily singular if the subjects joined by *or* or *nor* are singular.

Either *Dick or Jane promises* to come.

Neither *he nor she breaks* a promise.

If one subject is singular and the other plural, the verb ordinarily agrees in number with the subject that is nearer.

Either *onions or garlic adds* a good flavor.

Neither *garlic nor onions belong* in this dish.

For exceptions to this general rule on subject-verb agreement in correlative constructions, see FISH AND CHIPS IS ON THE MENU AGAIN. And for correlative constructions that are not parallel because *either . . . or* or *neither . . . nor* is misplaced, see "ELECTRIC SHAVER FOR WOMEN WITH DELICATE FLORAL DESIGN ON THE HANDLE."

EITHER . . . OR AND *NEITHER . . . NOR* constructions are included in the grammatical rule which says that a pronoun should agree in number with its antecedent. That is, a pronoun should be singular if the word or word group it refers to is singular:

Neither Sheldon nor George paid much for *his* dog.

and plural if the word or word group it refers to is plural:

Either the Franklins or the Quinns will bring *their* home movies.

The rule also says that a pronoun should be plural if it refers to both a plural and a singular antecedent connected by *or* or *nor*.

Neither the tenants nor the manager were willing to discuss *their* views on the sale of the building.

However, some people believe that meaning, not a strict grammatical rule, determines the shape of such sentences. They may therefore use a plural pronoun even if the antecedent is singular. For example:

Neither Sheldon nor George brought *their* wife.

In correlative constructions, pronouns are supposed to agree with their antecedents not only in number but in person as well (see EITHER HE OR I AM RIGHT). In other constructions, too, agreement between pronouns and their antecedents is called for but not always easy to achieve. For such agreement in number, see "IF SOMEONE COULD MAKE YOUR CHILD A GENIUS, WOULD YOU LET THEM?"; in gender, HURRICANE DAVID LEFT DEVASTATION IN HER WAKE; and in person, ONE SHOULD NOT TELL SECRETS IF YOU WANT TO BE TOLD ANY.

neologisms. See **Dear Mr. Webster.**

no one, none, or *nobody?* See *nobody, no one,* or *none?*

No time to scan the newspaper? Well, then, just scan it.

Like the Roman god Janus, who faced forward and backward at the same time, some words have meanings that are turned in opposite directions. The verb *scan*, for instance, means both "to look at closely; scrutinize" and "to glance at quickly." So someone might scan the newspaper over breakfast, taking a quick look at the front-page headlines, the sport section, and the TV listings, and in the evening scan it from masthead to "Dear Abby," poring over the news stories, editorials, syndicated columns, financial section, comics, and daily horoscope.

Today *scan* generally connotes a hasty consideration—especially in the United States, where this sense first came into the language—and perhaps in time the other, earlier usage will fall by the way. (*Peruse,* too, originally meant "to examine in detail; scrutinize." Later it took on the meaning "to read carefully or thoroughly; study.'' Now, in its pretentious use as a synonym for *read*, it generally suggests a casual or leisurely reading.)

Draw is another verb that can be used in nearly opposite ways. That is, when we ''draw a curtain'' we may either open or close it. There are many other verbs whose meanings, if not exactly opposite, tend to cancel each other out.

When we *string* a violin, we put strings on it; when we *string* beans, we remove the strings.

When we *spot* a shirt, we stain it with one or more spots; when a dry-cleaning shop *spots* the shirt, it removes the spots.

When we *dust* a cake, we put powdered sugar or something similar on it; when we *dust* a shelf, we wipe the dust off.

When we *stone* a path, we place stones on it; when we *stone* a peach, we remove its stone.

When we *seed* a field, we plant seeds in it; when we *seed* raspberries, we remove the seeds.

When we *stem* an artificial flower, we attach a stem to it; when we *stem* cherries, we remove their stems.

When we *call* a meeting, we summon its members; when we *call* a ballgame, we send the players home.

When we *temper* steel, we harden it; when we *temper* criticism, we soften it.

BESIDES VERBS, English has a good many Janus nouns. *Oversight*, for instance, means both ''a superintendence or supervision'':

A special committee was assigned oversight of the aid program.

and ''an unintentional, careless mistake or omission'':

Through an oversight, the paychecks were not mailed.

Sanction implies approval or permission.

The Board gave its sanction to hiring the city manager's sister.

It also refers to a coercive measure, such as a blockade of shipping, as a means of forcing a nation to stop certain practices.

The United Nations voted sanctions against Iran.

The American *pinch hitter* refers, in baseball, to a player called in to replace a batter considered less likely to do as well in that situation.

With two out in the ninth, Reggie Jackson stepped in as a pinch hitter for the pitcher.

Yet it also denotes a substitute called in at the last moment, usually to replace a better-qualified person who could not be present.

The treasurer had to act as a pinch hitter for the chairman, who was ill.

A *trifle* is generally thought of as a small amount or something insignificant, but—especially in England—it is also a lead-heavy dessert consisting of sponge-cake soaked in wine, spread with jam, and covered with custard, whipped cream, and who knows what else.

AMONG THE JANUS ADJECTIVES, *fast* means both "not easily moved; firm; fixed; stuck":

The rowboat was fast on the sand bar.

and "rapid in movement or action":

The fast squad car overtook the suspect's bicycle.

Although the combining form *-bound* means "headed in a specific direction," it also conveys the opposite notion of "not moving." So someone who is *homebound* is either going home or unable to leave home.

SOME WORDS WITH NEARLY OPPOSITE meanings are used as more than one part of speech. As a noun, *harbor* has the positive connotation of a snug place of refuge or safety.

When the storm broke, we headed for the harbor.

As a verb, however, it suggests concealment for an illegal or unworthy purpose.

Libya was accused of harboring international terrorists.

The day after the parade, New York street cleaners harbored thoughts of mass murder.

As a noun, *cavalier* sometimes refers to a gallant or courteous gentleman.

Once upon a time, cavaliers escorted their ladies to masked balls.

As an adjective, it describes someone who is arrogant, supercilious, or indifferent.

Some executives are cavalier about returning phone calls.

The verb *unbend* means "to become free from constraint, stiffness, or severity."

A group of UN diplomats unbend at a disco every Saturday night.

Yet the adjective *unbending* means "rigid; stiff."

On the issue of reapportionment, the legislature was unbending.

For more on English words that move from one part of speech to another, see "ICE CREAM YOUR KIDS TODAY WITH ROCKY ROAD."

SEVERAL WORDS AND PHRASES fall into the Janus category not so much because of a contradiction in their meanings as because of a shift in emphasis. *Feature,* for example, sometimes calls attention to the particularly unusual, important, or attractive part of a larger whole:

Country and Western music featured the tour.

and sometimes—in fact, almost always nowadays—it does just the opposite, giving prominence to the larger part:

The tour featured Country and Western music.

In other words, *feature* may mean either "to *be* a feature" or "to *make* a feature."

Similarly, the phrase *in charge of* is used both in the sense of "having the responsibility, control, or supervision of someone or something":

One guard was left in charge of ten prisoners.

and (usually with *the*) in the sense of "being under the control or supervision, or in the custody, of someone or something":

Ten prisoners were left in the charge of one guard.

Someone who has something to say, says it. A reporter who finds the statement newsworthy quotes it. At least that's the way interviews usually go. But John B. Judis, a senior editor of *In These Times,* found the verb *quote* turned inside-out in Washington. In a *New Republic* article, he noted:

"One prominent conservative admitted that he was disturbed by 'this anti-Semitism' but added, 'You're never going to get me to quote this,' meaning he wouldn't say so publicly."

BY GIVING ESTABLISHED WORDS and phrases new or extended meanings, slang has created a number of Janus expressions. To the usual meaning of *bad* ("not good; not as it should be; defective"), American slang, especially in Black English, starting in the 1970s, added the opposite sense of "good; stylish; effective."

Taking a bath suggests a pleasant way to spend time—Claudette Colbert immersed in a milk-filled tub or, at the very least, someone with a tired body and lots of time to soak in a water-filled tub. But the slang phrase *take a bath,* meaning "to suffer a heavy financial loss," has an unpleasant connotation.

Chrysler took a bath when small cars invaded the American market.

Bellying up to a bar also sounds like an enjoyable, if somewhat inelegant pastime, since it brings to mind one's moving straight to a counter where alcoholic drinks are served. But when a company, say, a large-car manufacturer in a small-car period, goes *belly up,* it fails.

Pack it in has two contradictory slang meanings. One of them is "to take full advantage of a favorable position."

The oil companies packed it in during the gas shortage of the seventies.

The other is "to admit defeat or failure; cease to do something."

After ten years of marriage, Dick and Jane decided to pack it in.

So does *bomb* in its American and British slang senses. In the States a play or an actor that bombs gets unfavorable reviews. In Britain a bomb is a smashing success and an actor who goes like a bomb gets rave reviews. (The American actor was probably not told beforehand to *break a leg*—a Janus good-luck wish in theater talk.)

For more on slang, see JOBBED IN A HUMONGOUS SCAM, THE TWEAKED-OUT MOBSTER EXCLAIMED, "PEACHY-KEEN!" And for more on differences between American English and British English, see THERE'S NO HOME LIKE EATON PLACE.

WITH SO MANY WORDS and phrases that have opposite or nearly opposite meanings—far more than noted here—it is a wonder that we know which meaning is intended in a given sentence. Yet it is precisely the given sentence that furnishes us the clue, for time after time expressions that would be obscure in isolation become clear from the surrounding words. Who, on reading a receipe that calls for dusting nutmeg on an eggnog chiffon pie, would think of going to the broom closet for a dust cloth?

nobody, no one, or *none?*

The pronouns *nobody* and *no one* both mean "not any person; not anybody." When used as subjects, they are singular and take singular verbs.

Nobody (no one) has shown an interest in the rummage sale.

Is nobody (no one) immune to the virus?

The single-word pronoun *none*, which comes from the Old English words for *not + one*, means "no persons or things." When used as a subject, it is sometimes considered singular and therefore takes a singular verb.

I wanted a potpie, but none was ready to eat.

None of the candidates stands much of a change to be reelected.

But more often than not, *none* is construed as plural, with the meaning "not any," and therefore takes a plural verb.

Are none of the potpies out of the oven?

All the candidates are up for reelection, so none are expected to go on a junket this summer.

Like the pronouns *anyone, anybody, everyone, everybody, someone, somebody,* and others, *nobody* and *no one* can apply to more than one person, of either sex or both sexes. And *none* can apply to more than one person or thing. So the pronouns referring to those antecedents are often plural. (See "IF SOMEONE COULD MAKE YOUR CHILD A GENIUS, WOULD YOU LET THEM?")

nonrestrictive and restrictive modifiers.   See **The Oval Office which is in the White House symbolizes the Presidency.**

normalcy or *normality?*

During the Presidential campaign of 1920, the Republican candidate Warren G. Harding said that "America's need is not heroics but healing; not nostrums but normalcy." From the reaction to that statement, one would think that Harding had unwittingly coined a word for *normality* that was as far-fetched as *normalette, normalectomy,* or *normalaciousness.*

Normalcy is not a nonsense word. Both *-ity* and *-cy* are noun-forming suffixes that mean "quality, condition, state, or fact of being." What probably surprised and amused some of Harding's contemporaries was finding *-cy* tacked onto *normal,* because adjectives ending in *-al* or the əl sound are likely to take *-ity* when they are turned into nouns.

mortal → mortality
fatal → fatality
civil → civility
futile → futility

The *-cy* suffix, on the other hand, occurs in many nouns formed from adjectives or other nouns that end in *-t* or the *t* sound (which is dropped in the process).

militant → militancy
transparent → transparency
accurate → accuracy
truant → truancy
occupant → occupancy

(The *-cy* suffix also denotes position, rank, or office, as in *captaincy,* but this meaning does not enter into Harding's supposed and much-criticized coinage.)

Besides, Harding did not coin *normalcy.* *The Oxford English Dictionary* gives several nineteenth-century citations for the word in scientific contexts. *Normality* is older, more general in meaning, and more widely used.

The suffixes *-ity* and *-cy* are not the only ones that change the meanings of words in the same way. Suffixes can also change the meanings of words in opposite ways, for example, *-ful* and *-less* when attached to the noun *mercy.* Prefixes are similar to suffixes, except that they go at the beginning, not the end, of words. For a discussion of these and other kinds of syllables, groups of syllables, or words that are joined to other words to alter their meanings or to create new words, see WHO NEEDS A RABBIT'S FOOT MORE: AN UNLUCKY PERSON OR A LUCKLESS ONE?

Not for nothing does Paris claim to be the world's most beautiful city.

Until about three hundred years ago, double negatives of the "I haven't seen nobody" kind were accepted in statements of emphatic denial, not only in speech but even in formal writing. King Alfred used them in Old English; Chaucer, in Middle English; and Shakespeare, in Early Modern English. But by the end of the clean-up-the-language campaign of the 1700s, they were well on their way to becoming nonstandard. What made them unsuitable as prestige constructions, according to the reform-minded scholars, was their Englishness: if using two negatives to form affirmative statements was good enough for Cicero, Caesar, and other speakers of classical Latin, how dared the English use them to form emphatic negative ones?

Though most grammar books and schoolteachers no longer insist that "two negatives make a positive," they still roundly condemn the construction. As a result, educated English-speakers dread being caught saying, for example, "I can't hardly stand the suspense" or "You don't look well, neither." Besides being embarrassed at having committed a grievous error of grammar, they would be left wondering whether they had, in fact, said, "I can easily stand the suspense" or "You look well, too." Let people who write street graffiti, like this one in Kingston, Jamaica, believe that two negatives make a forcefully negative statement:

"The poor can't take no more."

There are, however, two other kinds of repeated-negative constructions that are acceptable at all levels of usage. The first is a negative statement that remains negative even though a negative phrase is tacked onto it.

He says he won't take the job, not for a hundred thousand a year.

Nobody in the cabin was awake, not even the cat.

The second is an affirmative statement in which two negatives do indeed cancel each other out. The literal meaning of:

Not for nothing does Paris claim to be the world's most beautiful city.

is that it is for something that Paris claims to be the world's most beautiful city. Turned into a straight emphatic affirmative, the sentence might read something like "Paris indeed has a right to claim to be the world's most beautiful city."

In much the same way, Charles Leroux, in a *Chicago Tribune* article, made an emphatically positive statement about Emily Dickinson.

"Her prose was poetry. She could not *not* be a poet."

Deliberately doubled negatives are sometimes used for variety rather than for emphasis. Joan Didion's "a not atypical *norteamericana*" is, of course, simply a typical *norteamericana*. And, as the Washington correspondent Joseph Kraft showed us in 1980, doubled negatives can be amusing.

"That is probably the best that can be expected this year. For at bottom the fight between Reagan and Carter comes down to a competition as to which of the two unlikely prospects is the least unqualified to be president."

The trouble is, this kind of construction can lead to a style of writing that some may find too convoluted for the straightforward message being conveyed. When, in a *New York Times* article on hand kissing, Paul Hofmann wrote, "In Bonn, things are not much dissimilar," all he meant was that in Bonn things are quite similar. The political scientist Meir Serfaty was even less direct when, in *Current History*, he said this about a Spanish seaport in Africa:

"Having visited Melilla recently, the author found a situation potentially not unlike that of Algeria before independence from France, or Northern Ireland today."

The customary way to make frankly negative statements or affirmative statements that at first glance appear to be negative, then, is to use pronouns like *none* and *nobody;* adverbs like *no, not, hardly,* and *scarcely;* conjunctions like *neither* and *nor;* and prefixes like *un-* and *non-.* Some people, though, perhaps in the hope of creating more eloquent positive statements, combine any of the standard negatives with a word or words that convey a mildly negative sense. What they often turn out, instead, are sentences guaranteed to leave their listeners or readers perplexed for life. For instance:

No complaint is too trivial to be ignored.

Now, that's something to write home about.

Most grammar books have stopped insisting that a sentence not end with a preposition. This so-called rule, which has tyrannized schoolchildren for centuries, was nonsense to begin with, having been invented by English writers who considered it elegant to impose Latin sentence structure on their language. The person most responsible for this particular pedantry is said to be the seventeenth-century poet, critic, and playwright John Dryden, who went so far as to expunge end prepositions from some of his own published works.

Yet, even though the ban has been lifted, many English-speakers are still too intimidated to let a preposition fall naturally, either before or after its object. So for the spontaneous question "Is she the one I'm supposed to send it to?" they believe they must substitute the stilted "Is she the one to whom I'm supposed to send it?" Similarly, they feel obliged to turn "Where did the package come from?" into "From where did the package come?" And instead of following custom and idiom by saying "Now, that's something to write home about," they produce a tortured sentence like "Now, that's something about which one could write home."

Many other speakers and writers, however, are comfortable with end prepositions. Willard Espy, for instance, called a rhyming dictionary, one of his many books on language, *Words to Rhyme With.* And in her novel *Men and Angels,* Mary Gordon said, "What it was, finally, she could come in no way close to."

Schoolteachers are of course right in pointing out that a preposition is often superfluous at the end of a sentence. "Where are you going to?" and "Where are you at?" add nothing to "Where are you going?" and "Where are you?" But, superfluous or not, an end preposition frequently follows a contraction in informal speech. To do away with the offending *at,* a sentence like "He's the person who got me where I'm at" would have to be changed to "He's the person who got me where I am."

The preposition *to* may find itself at the end of a sentence if the infinitive verb form it signals is understood but not actually expressed. For example, anyone seeing or hearing "Bring a friend if you want to" is expected to supply the missing words (either "Bring a friend if you want to bring a friend" or "Bring a friend if you want to do so"). Traditional grammarians, however, object to this and similar elliptical constructions (see DRINK THE WATER IF YOU DARE).

What may look like a preposition floating freely at the end of a sentence may in fact be an adverb that is firmly attached to the preceding verb and thus has every right to be where it is. One of the meanings of the verb set *take up*, for example, is "to make tighter or shorter." So there can be no objection to a sentence like:

Are these the jeans you want me to take up?

Indeed, a preposition is sometimes tacked onto a verb-adverb combination. *Take up with*, say, means "to become a friend or companion of." And if such a verb set falls naturally at the end of a sentence, there is no reason not to place it there.

Who are the jazz buffs you're taking up with?

For more on verb sets, see WASHING DOWN PILLOWS TAKES A STRONG STOMACH.

nowhere or *nowheres?*

The adverb *nowhere* is accepted without question in any kind of speech or writing.

We searched the grounds, but the dog was nowhere to be found.

Nowhere is sprung rhythm better exemplified than in Gerard Manley Hopkins's poetry.

Nowheres, however, is still generally considered a dialectal or an informal usage.

O

of which or *whose*? See *whose* or *of which*?

Once children retire, they spend more time with their parents.

Every language, so the theory goes, has enough words and ways of putting them together to say whatever its speakers want said. English certainly has an enormous stock of words for describing both specific facts and general concepts.

With the word *pride* at hand, why would anyone use the generic term *group* for a company of lions? Indeed, English has at least one special collective word for almost every kind of animal. These are some of them:

Collective Term	Animals
bed	oysters, clams
bevy	quails
brood	birds or fowl (chickens, etc.)
cloud	locusts
clutch	chicks
covey	partridges, quails
cry	hounds
drove	cattle, hogs, sheep
flock	goats, sheep, birds
gaggle	geese
gam	whales
herd	cattle, sheep, elephants, buffaloes
pack	hounds, wolves
pod	seals, whales
pride	lions
school	fish, porpoises, whales
skein	wild fowl

Glasgowite? Glasgowese? Glasgowian? There is no need to invent a name for someone who lives in Glasgow, because there are already special English names for the natives or inhabitants of many cities. Here are some of them:

City	Resident	City	Resident
Athens	*Athenian*	*Liverpool*	*Liverpudian*
Berlin	*Berliner*	*London*	*Londoner*
Boston	*Bostonian*	*Miami*	*Miamian*
Cambridge (Eng.)	*Cantabrigian*	*Moscow*	*Muscovite*
Genoa	*Genoese*	*Paris*	*Parisian*
Glasgow	*Glaswegian*	*Tokyo*	*Tokyoite*
		Vienna	*Viennese*

Nor does anyone have to make up names for figures of speech, that is, expressions in which the words are used in a nonliteral or unusual sense to add vividness, strength, beauty, or the like. As every schoolchild learns, *like* or *as* occurs in a simile, not in a metaphor. Anyone having trouble keeping the many Latin- or Greek-derived figures of speech straight can consult a glossary of literary terms. (There are probably as many around as there are usage guides.) These are the commonest figures of speech used by English-speakers:

Figure of Speech	*Meaning of the Term*
epithet	the use of an adjective, noun, or phrase to characterize a person or thing, often disparagingly ("Did you expect an *egghead* like her to act instead of just sit around and think?")
hyperbole (hī pur'bə lē)	an exaggeration for effect ("I'd have stood in line for a month to hear Janis Joplin")
litotes (līt'ə tēz)	an understatement for effect, in which something is expressed by a negation of the contrary ("Not a few tears were shed")
metaphor (met'ə fôr' OR met'ə fər)	implied comparison in which a word or phrase ordinarily used of one thing is applied to another ("At work he's a tiger; at home, a pussycat")
metonymy (mə tän'ə mē)	the use of the name of one thing for that of another associated with or suggested by it ("Word came from the Oval Office [the President]")
oxymoron (äk'si môr'än)	a combination of two contradictory terms ("sweet bile," "frozen fire")
personification	a representation of a thing, quality, or idea as a person ("Chicago spoke to the poet")
simile (sim'ə lē')	a comparison of two unlike things by the use of *like* or *as* ("At work he's like a tiger; at home, like a pussycat")
synecdoche (si nek' də kē)	the use of a part for a whole, an individual for a class, a material for a thing, or the reverse of any of these ("Black tie is optional"; "We invited the navy for dinner")
zeugma (zoog'mə)	the use of a single word (usually a verb or an adjective) that, though syntactically related to two or more words, seems logically connected with only one ("Carlyle was filled with religious doubt and dyspepsia")

Besides an abundance of terms to describe, classify, and differentiate facts, feelings, and ideas, English has more words with the same or nearly the same meanings than its speakers can ever use. *Drunk,* for instance, has hundreds of synonyms.

So why must a seminar to which many people drive in order to get help in dealing with their alcoholic parents be called a "Workshop for Adult Children of Alcoholics"? Why doesn't English have a word for grown-up sons and daughters, to replace the oxymoronic *adult children;* the stilted *offspring, progeny,* and *issue;* the ambiguous *sons and daughters;* and the informal *kids*? Other languages do. In Italian, for instance, young sons and daughters—all children under, say, eight years of age, for that matter—are referred to as *bambini* (the plural of the masculine *bambino* and the feminine *bambina*), a term for which the English *children* is an exact equivalent. Yet the Italian *figli* (the plural of the masculine *figlio* and the feminine *figlia*) denotes sons and daughters collectively, from birth to death. English borrowed the same Latin roots (*filius*, "son"; *filia*, "daughter"; and *filiatio*, "son and daughter") for a word like *filial*, to describe something appropriate to or due from a son or daughter, as in "We were touched to see such filial devotion." But, unfortunately, it did not get around to devising a collective word for adult sons and daughters that most current English-speakers are comfortable with.

A neuter singular pronoun to replace the traditional *he* and *him* is also needed. Many English-speakers object to a statement like "Everybody was asked to give his opinion," because they consider it sexist. Yet they find "Everybody was asked to give his or her opinion" awkward and, if the construction must be repeated, tiresome. And they hesitate to say "Everybody was asked to give their opinion," for this means doing battle with the grammatical rule that calls for a singular pronoun with a singular antecedent (For more on the agreement of pronouns with their antecedents in number, see "IF SOMEONE COULD MAKE YOUR CHILD A GENIUS, WOULD YOU LET THEM?"; in gender, HURRICANE DAVID LEFT DEVASTATION IN HER WAKE; and in person, ONE SHOULD NOT TELL SECRETS IF YOU WANT TO BE TOLD ANY.)

Another badly needed pronoun, especially in writing or telephoning, is a plural form of *you*. In a face-to-face conversation it's easy enough to nod in the direction of the listener or listeners we mean to include. *Both* narrows the audience to two, whether addressed in person, on the phone, or in writing (as in "I wish you both a happy New Year"). But when it comes to writing to a friend or two but wishing their whole family a happy New Year, we must resort to *all of you*, *you all*, or the informal Southernism *you-all* (which, as Southerners are quick to point out, is pronounced yôl).

Unless it's qualified by an adjective like *old* or *fuddy-duddy*, the word *bachelor* ordinarily carries no stigma. Indeed, it suggests a young unmarried man, even one who has been divorced, enjoying his freedom and grand style of living. On the other hand, *spinster* does not call up a vision of a young, sophisticated, uninhibited woman having too much fun to get married. Partly because of the word's earlier sense of "a woman (rarely a man) who spins thread or yarn," what comes to mind is a woman who is on in years and who has never married, that is, an *old maid*. What English needs, then, is a feminine word more nearly paralleling *bachelor*. For most of today's unmarried women who work and are on their own, *bachelor girl* won't do.

Many other English words and expressions do not take women into account. For instance, a man who acts or speaks as warmly and familiarly as if he were an uncle, or such a man's action or speech, is said to be *avuncular* ("When I told my boss I planned to quit, he gave me some avuncular advice"). Is *auntlike* the best the language can do to describe well-meant advice given by a female boss?

Women can't even be cuckolded. In a review of the movie *Heartburn*, Kathleen Fury wrote:

"Maybe he knew that her mother once told her, 'Men are little boys'; or that her father was the sort of man who'd console his grieving cuckolded daughter with Borscht-belt gags: 'You want monogamy? Marry a swan.' "

But in doing so she went against current usage, because, perhaps in an allusion to the female cuckoo bird's habit of changing mates, the noun and verb *cuckold* apply only to a man whose wife commits adultery.

A word whose tone is somewhere between *boss* and *superior* would also come in handy. "I'm going to the sales meeting with my boss," for instance, may sound too informal; "I'm going to the sales meeting with my superior" always sounds stilted. *Employer* usually won't do, because whoever does the hiring and paying does not necessarily exercise authority over the firm's employees and does not ordinarily accompany them to sales meetings. *The person I report to,* like *my manager* or *my supervisor,* is as sparkling as an entry in an organization chart. In conversation one might say "I'm going to the sales meeting with the *guy* (or *gal, man, woman*) *I work for* (or *with*)." Or, if the listener knows the boss's name, one might give it instead. None of these alternatives quite makes up for the lack of the right word.

Over the centuries English-speakers have been unable to settle on a name for a person with whom one is in love and by whom one is loved. The words they have used, discarded, and occasionally returned to include *sweetheart, sweetie, girlfriend, boyfriend, flame, steady,* and *significant other.* When they were in fashion, *swain* and *beau* were applied only to a man. *Fiancée* and *fiancé* have remained the formal names for a woman and a man who are engaged to be married, and *lover* is still used, but always at the risk of implying a sexual relationship where one might not exist. English, then, needs a word which denotes a regular companion and which is appropriate in formal as well as informal speech and writing.

For lack of a better term for the liver, kidneys, heart, brain, tongue, tripe, and other edible parts of an animal, English-speakers use *variety meat.* It may be an improvement over *offal,* to which the notion of refuse or waste stuff clings, but it's far from satisfactory. It sounds like a euphemism for *cold cuts,* which are in fact a variety of sliced cold meats, though usually served with cheeses. How can a tourist be expected to ask a local, "Which restaurant serves good variety meat in this town?" A descriptive but inoffensive term for the liver, kidneys, heart, brain, tongue, tripe, and other edible parts of an animal would therefore be useful.

On most typewriters the # symbol shares a key with the numeral 3. On pushbutton telephones it has its own function key, which, like the "star" key (*), produces a tone that can be used for a special service. In everyday use it stands for *number* and for *pound,* as a unit of weight.

1512 Eastern Parkway (#12)

6 # potatoes, 2 # onions, 1 sack flour

The symbols + and $, for instance, have specific names (*plus sign* and *dollar sign*), which everyone can recognize and use. So why doesn't #?

one another **or** *each other?*   See *each other* **or** *one another?*

One should not tell secrets if you want to be told any.

A part of the grammatical rule on pronoun-antecedent agreement says that if a pronoun has an antecedent (a word or word group that it refers to), it must agree with that antecedent in *person*. That means not shifting back and forth among the three sets of pronouns that indicate whether the subject is speaking (first person), is spoken to (second person), or is spoken of (third person).

First person
I (we) hope the check will be sent to *me (us)* soon.

Second person
You seem to be making things difficult for *yourself (yourselves)*.

Third person
The pilot said *she* couldn't hear the tower.

Only *a dog* would be so loyal to *its* owner.

This does not mean, of course, that all pronouns in a sentence must be in the same person. Without violating either grammar or sense we say and write:

I hope the check will be sent to *you*.

The pilot said *they* couldn't hear the tower.

Only *a dog* would be so loyal to *us*.

But here antecedence is not involved: the second pronoun in each sentence has its own grammatical function, which is not directly related to the word or word group mentioned earlier.

In this statement in a *Publishers Weekly* review, a pair of first-person pronouns collide with a third-person antecedent.

"In a provocative thesis, Dally, a psychiatrist, claims that <u>each person</u> possesses a 'morbid streak' which <u>we</u> sometimes use constructively to relieve stress, but often allow to damage or destroy <u>ourselves</u> and others."

INDEFINITE PRONOUNS such as *everybody, nobody, anyone, someone, none, either,* and *both* have no antecedents.

Everybody was there.

Did both come?

When an indefinite pronoun is the antecedent of another pronoun, agreement in person is sometimes troublesome. For instance, in:

Do either of you plan to invite your mother?

the antecedent of *your* is, strictly speaking, *either,* not *you.* Therefore, to be grammatically "correct" while still retaining the notion of one or the other of the persons addressed, the question should be reworded so that both pronouns are in the third person:

Does *either* of you plan to invite *his* mother?

But this leads to two other problems in pronoun-antecedent agreement. The first has to do with number: the singular pronoun *his* is often misleading when the sense clearly calls for the plural *their* (see "IF SOMEONE COULD MAKE YOUR CHILD A GENIUS, WOULD YOU LET THEM?"). The second has to do with gender: though defined as grammatically neutral, the masculine pronouns *he, him,* and *his* are not always viewed that way (see HURRICANE DAVID LEFT DEVASTATION IN HER WAKE). Fortunately, in all but the most formal usage the indefinite pronouns are not limited to the masculine, third-person singular when it comes to agreement.

BECAUSE ENGLISH LACKS A FLEXIBLE indefinite pronoun to refer to people generally (French has *on* and German has *man*), *we, you, one, people,* and the like are often used for this purpose. None of these words is entirely satisfactory, not because it cannot be made to work grammatically but because it is not appropriate at all levels of usage. *One* often seems too formal; *we* and *you,* not formal enough; and *people,* like a bad translation from another language.

As speech and writing become less and less formal, more and more speakers and writers address their listeners and readers directly, using *you* or *we,* or both. Pronoun-antecedent agreement presents few problems.

The best way for you to begin is to tie a knot around your thumb.

We sometimes get ahead of ourselves in pursuing our goals.

The intrepid set out on the *one* course. If they observe the traditional British rule of using *one* in all references to the same person, they are sure of achieving pronoun-antecedent agreement, no matter how awkward or tiresome.

If one is accustomed to driving on the left side of the road and suddenly finds oneself in a country that one has never heard of before, much less visited, one is likely to experience culture shock.

Americans are generally more relaxed about combining *one* with other pronouns.

"What is it we are supposed to pray for, if not the decease of our enemies, barring their conversion—at which point they would cease to be one's enemies?" (William F. Buckley, Jr., *Washington Post*)

"Kalb [former State Department spokesman Bernard Kalb] said: 'Now a controversy has swirled up about credibility. You face a choice ... whether to allow oneself to be absorbed in the ranks of silence or voice a modest dissent.' " (Norman Kempster and Lee May, *Los Angeles Times*)

People are also known to allow pronouns to wander away from their antecedents on occasion (see REMOVE THE STRINGS AND ENDS FROM THE BEANS AND COOK THEM IN BOILING SALTED WATER).

or **or** *and?*   See *and* **or** *or?*

oral **or** *verbal?*   See *verbal* **or** *oral?*

The Oval Office which is in the White House symbolizes the Presidency.

A spirited controversy has been going on for years over the use of *that* and *which* to introduce certain kinds of relative clauses (subordinate clauses serving as adjectives), as well as over the punctuation used with such clauses. With H. W. Fowler's *Modern English Usage* held high, the so-called *which* hunters plead for a distinction they say will not only tidy up the language but ensure clarity.

According to the rule, this is the distinction between the two commonly used relative pronouns: if the clause is nonrestrictive—that is, if it describes a quality or a condition of the noun in the main clause but could be omitted without drastically affecting the meaning of the sentence—it should be introduced by *which* and set off by commas in writing (just as it is set off by slight pauses in speech). For example, in:

The Oval Office, which is in the White House, symbolizes the Presidency.

the clause *which is in the White House* tells us something about the Oval Office, but it is not essential. ''The Oval Office symbolizes the Presidency'' is a perfectly sound sentence, from the point of view not only of grammar but also of meaning. Most of us know where American Presidents conduct their business, so it's not a matter of having to distinguish between this Oval Office and all other Oval Offices in the world. The nonrestrictive adjective clause, then, is properly introduced by *which* and set off by commas.

On the other hand, if the adjective clause is restrictive—that is, if it defines or limits the noun in the main clause in such a way as to affect the meaning of the sentence—it should be introduced by *that* and not be set off by commas. In:

The oval office that I built in my barn has an ellipsoid desk.

the clause *that I built in my barn* gives us essential information about this particular office. ''The oval office has an ellipsoid desk'' is a grammatically complete sentence all right, but unless we already know which oval office is meant, we can't make much sense out of the sentence. The adjective clause, then, is properly introduced by *that* and not set off by commas.

Those who have learned this rule on restrictive and nonrestrictive clauses, who are able to keep it in mind, and who see its purpose in preventing ambiguity generally apply it. Indeed, in going through manuscripts, some copyeditors automatically change every restrictive *which* they come across to *that*. And when the 166 members of the panel of the *Harper Dictionary of Contemporary Usage* (1985 edition) were asked whether they regarded the *that / which* distinctions as worth preserving, 62 percent said yes; 55 percent said they observed those distinctions in their own speech, and 68 percent said they did in their own writing.

Some people who know the rule would like to apply it always, but can't manage to. *Harper Dictionary* panel member Edwin Newman, a writer and television correspondent who deplores the decline of American English, said, ''I try to. I try to.'' Not good enough, Mr. Newman, for another guardian of the language, John Simon, caught you writing "'a bookstore which' for 'a bookstore that'" in your book *A Civil Tongue* and, in his own *Paradigms Lost: Reflections on Literacy and Its Decline,* told the world about your peccancy.

Newman is by no means the only language expert to admit to falling from paradigm. Of the thirty panel members whose replies are quoted in the *Harper Dictionary,* only ten seem to say categorically that they apply the rule on using *which* to introduce nonrestrictive clauses and *that* to introduce restrictive clauses.

Yet many good writers believe that a rigid distinction between *that* and *which* at the beginning of restrictive clauses is not necessary either to ensure clarity or to comply with the rules of grammar. What is important, they say, is setting off nonrestrictive *which* clauses with a comma, or commas. Philip Roth, for example, uses commas this way in "Goodbye, Columbus."

"Brenda was quiet and her dress circled her legs, which were tucked back beneath her."

Where Brenda's legs were tucked is an interesting detail, but this information is not essential to the meaning or structure of the sentence.

For restrictive clauses, Roth, like many other writers, uses *which* and *that* interchangeably—with no commas. In the same novella he writes:

"After dinner my bag was carried—by me—up to the guest room which was across from Ron's room and right down the hall from Brenda."

The omission of the comma before *which* shows that there were several guest rooms in the house, the particular one assigned to the protagonist being distinguished from the others. Then, on the next page:

"I unpacked my bag and dropped my clothes into a drawer that was empty except for a packet of dress shields and a high school yearbook."

Without the restrictive *that* clause, the sentence would be grammatically complete ("I unpacked my bag and dropped my clothes into a drawer"), but not especially enlightening. Any old drawer? No, a drawer set apart from all others by its two commonplace but evocative items.

The choice between the relative pronouns *which* and *that* to introduce a restrictive clause often depends on the rest of the sentence. *Which* is sometimes used if *that* appears elsewhere in the sentence as an adjective or as a demonstrative pronoun. So:

That is the hotel *that* was written up in last Sunday's travel section.

might become:

That is the hotel *which* was written up in last Sunday's travel section.

Occasionally, of course, the demonstrative pronoun *that* and the relative pronoun *which* come together, as in:

I want only *that which* I have earned.

Anyone who dislikes this construction can usually change *that which* to *what* ("I want only *what* I have earned").

Another construction where, to some people, *which* sounds more natural than the prescribed *that* is a series of restrictive adjective clauses. For example:

The instrument *that* is the highest-pitched of the string choir, *that* is capable of subtle nuances, and *that* comes closest to the human voice is the violin.

might be less awkward if each *that* were replaced by *which*. Going further, some writers and speakers would omit all but the first relative pronoun, whether *that* or *which*. In fact, unless a relative pronoun is needed for sense or to prevent misreading, it is often dropped entirely, especially in conversation or informal writing. Thus:

Here is the record you said you wanted.

instead of:

Here is the record *that* (or *which*) you said you wanted.

(For more on the omission of relative pronouns, see HEREFORDS, WHO ARE A BREED OF BEEF CATTLE, HAVE WHITE FACES AND RED BODIES and TENNIS IS A SPORT I ENJOY BUT WHICH I DON'T PLAY WELL.)

Not everyone who uses *that* and *which* interchangeably to introduce a restrictive relative clause does so consciously. Many people probably never learned the rules or, if they did, have forgotten them, are confused by them, or see no purpose in them. Few writers, however, are likely to revive the long-abandoned practice of using *that* to introduce a nonrestrictive relative clause set off by a comma.

I lived for ten years in Hong Kong, that I long to see again.

It is therefore surprising to come across this question in Robert A. Hall's book *Linguistics and Your Language:*

"Aren't English, French, and other civilized languages better than savage tongues like Eskimo or Hottentot, that don't even have any written language or literature?"

But perhaps Hall either didn't want the comma after *Hottentot* or else wanted one before *like* as well.

ENGLISH-SPEAKERS WHO OBSERVE the *that / which* rule are ordinarily careful to apply it to other relative pronouns as well. That is, they set off all nonrestrictive relative clauses with commas, but not restrictive ones.

Tax consultants, *who* prepare about 40 percent of all returns in the United States, are busiest between February 1 and April 15. (Nonrestrictive)

Tax consultants *who* sign returns are usually at their clients' side during an IRS audit. (Restrictive)

To your right is the Loop, *where* Chicago's famous shopping center is located. (Nonrestrictive)

The area *where* Chicago's famous shopping center is located is called the Loop. (Restrictive)

For literary effect, some writers intentionally disregard the distinction between restrictive and nonrestrictive relative clauses. For example, early in his novel *The Second Coming*, Walker Percy shows that he knows the rule.

"His partner, Dr. Vance Battle, who sat in the cart at the outside of the dogleg waiting for his third shot, was watching."

Yet later on he has a character whisper:

"Why is it that Americans who are the best dearest most generous people on earth are so unhappy?"

If Percy had wanted to make it clear that the character was saying that Americans taken as a whole are unhappy, not just those who are the best, dearest, and most generous people on earth, he would have placed a comma before *who* and another after *earth*. That is, he would have made the clause nonrestrictive. But such preciseness is not what he intended in this passage. (Nor is showing, with the usual commas, that *best, dearest,* and *most generous* all modify *people*.)

THOSE WHO FAVOR COMMAS with nonrestrictive modifiers but not with restrictive ones don't stop at relative clauses. Whether a word or phrase is set off by commas, they insist, is sometimes the only clue to the meaning of a sentence.

A word or expression that is placed next to another so that the second explains the first is known as an *appositive,* or is said to be *in apposition* with its principal. The appositive is restrictive if it defines its principal, distinguishing it from other persons or things of the same name, group, or class. The appositive is nonrestrictive if it describes or qualifies, but does not limit, its principal and therefore can be omitted without making the sentence incoherent. Restrictive appositives are ordinarily not set off by commas; nonrestrictive appositives are.

For instance, in:

The tenor, Luciano Pavarotti, gained worldwide renown.

the commas around *Luciano Pavarotti* suggest that this name could be omitted without affecting the meaning of the sentence. But could it? Was Pavarotti identified earlier, so as to leave no doubt who is meant? If he wasn't, might the reader not think of another tenor, say, Roland Hayes or Plácido Domingo, who gained worldwide renown? Even if *Italian* were inserted before *tenor,* would the sentence make sense without Pavorotti's name? Didn't other Italian tenors, including Enrico Caruso, gain worldwide renown? In this particular context, then, *Luciano Pavarotti* is so essential in defining *the tenor* that it could not be omitted without robbing the sentence of meaning. It is a restrictive appositive, and therefore should not be set off by commas.

The tenor Luciano Pavarotti gained worldwide renown.

Yet, in another context, it might be appropriate to use *Luciano Pavarotti* as a nonrestrictive appositive, set off by commas.

The Italian tenor who starred in Yes, Giorgio, Luciano Pavarotti, gained worldwide renown.

Only one Italian tenor starred in this film. So naming him, though not out of place, is unessential.

over or *more than?*

Many people become uneasy when they see or hear *over* in expressions of degree, amount, or number, because their English teachers told them that only *more than* will do. *Over*, they were admonished, should be limited to showing location, as in "The moon came over the mountain."

A good many journalists must have had the same English teachers. The style guide of the *Washington Post*, for example, urges its users to:

> "Write *more than* 60 attended, not *over* 60; *over* refers to physical location."

Making a distinction between amounts and age, the style guide of the *Los Angeles Times* says:

> "When referring to amounts it is preferable to use *more than* rather than *over*, which refers primarily to physical position. *Over* may, however, be used to refer to age: *The company has more than 200 employees, most of them over 21; many of them work in a shop over the sales rooms.*"

The Associated Press offers a broader choice, giving this as its style guide entry for *over:*

> "It generally refers to spatial relationships: *The plane flew over the city.*
>
> "*Over* can, at times, be used with numbers: *She is over 30. I paid over $200 for this suit.* But *more than* may be better:
>
> *Their salaries went up more than $20 a week.* Let your ear be your guide."

The notion of using either *over* or *more than*, depending not on a hard-and-fast rule but on the particular sentence, may seem novel, but it isn't. *Faulty Diction, As Corrected by the "Funk & Wagnalls New Standard Dictionary of the English Language*," which was published in 1915, had this to say about *over, not over:*

> "Equivalent to *more than, not more than;* objected to by some critics, but supported by literary usage, and further defensible as having a tinge of metaphor suggestive of overflowing quantity or overtopping height."

The use of *over* to convey the notion of being above, or more than, a stated amount indeed has time on its side. The citations for it in *The Oxford English Dictionary* go back to around 1330.

Most of today's dictionaries show *over* and *more than* as being synonymous, just as they do *under* and *less than*. *In excess of* and *upward of* or *upwards of* also mean "more than" or "over," but they are generally found in jargon-ridden talk or writing (see A CONCEPT-ORIENTED FRAMEWORK MAY EFFECTUATE A CONSENSUS OF OPINION IN TERMS OF THE MAXIMIZATION OF A MEANINGFUL CONTINUUM OF PROGRAM FACTORS).

Oxbridge workaholics never stop for brunch.

English constantly enlarges its vocabulary by creating new words that combine the form and meaning of two existing words. Though usually called *blends*, these coinages are also known as *portmanteau words,* from the French word for a stiff leather suitcase that opens like a book into two compartments.

Attributing to Lewis Carroll the first use of *portmanteau* in the sense of "a factitious word made up of the blended sounds of two distinct words and combining the meanings of both," *The Oxford English Dictionary* cites Carroll's *Through the Looking-Glass* (1872):

> "Well, 'slithy' means 'lithe and slimy' . . . You see it's like a portmanteau— there are two meanings packed up into one word. . . . 'Mimsy' is 'flimsy and miserable' (there's another portmanteau for you)."

Slithy and *mimsy* may not be on everyone's tongue, but several other of Lewis Carroll's blends, also from *Through the Looking-Glass,* have become part of the current English word stock. For example, *chortle,* meaning "to make, or utter with, a gleeful chuckling or snorting sound," may be a combination of *chuckle* and *snort;* and *galumph,* meaning "to march or bound along in a a self-satisfied manner," tacks the front part of *gallop* onto the end of *triumph.*

Carroll may have given blends a fanciful name and invented a few of his own, but such words existed long before Alice stepped into Looking-Glass House. Indeed, many blends are so much a part of the language that few English-speakers give a thought to their origin. Here are a few, some well established at all levels of usage and some generally limited to informal speech and writing or to slang:

br(eakfast) + *(l)unch* = *brunch*

docu(mentary) + *drama* = *docudrama*

fac(t) + *(fic)tion* = *faction* (a kind of fiction based on or incorporating recognizable events, people, and the like)

fan + *(maga)zine* = *fanzine*

flexi(ble) + *time* = *flexitime*

flex(ible) + *time* = *flextime*

gas(oline) + *(alc)ohol* = *gasohol*

Medic(al) + *aid* = *Medicaid*

mo(torist) + *(ho)tel* = *motel*

Ox(ford) + *(Cam)bridge* = *Oxbridge*

pal + *(al)imony* = *palimony*

sit(uation) + *com(edy)* = *sitcom*

sm(oke) + *(h)aze* = *smaze*

sm(oke) + *(f)og* = *smog*

squ(int) + *(p)inch* = *squinch*

sl(um) + *(sub)urb* = *slurb*

stag(nation) + *(in)flation* = *stagflation*

syn(thetic) + *fuel* = *synfuel*

work + *-a-* + *(alco)holic* = *workaholic*

Some blends are far from established in the language, either lasting about as long as it takes to hear or read them or else continuing to have only a small circle of users, aside from their inventors. For example:

Bo(ston) + *(Red S)ox* = *Bosox*

ch(icken) + *(t)urkey* = *churkey*

fl(oating) + *(h)otel* = *flotel* (an oil-drilling platform, with accommodations for the crew)

infan(t) + *(an)ticipate* = *infanticipate*

suppos(edly) + *(prob)ably* = *supposably*

ship(shape) + *(slip)shod* = *shipshod*

A special kind of blend is an *acronym,* which is formed from the first, or first few, letters of a series of words (see NASA's LOX NEEDS NO BAGELS).

P

participles, dangling. See **Covered with onions, relish, and ketchup, I ate a hot dog at the ballpark.**

parts of speech. See **"Ice cream your kids today with Rocky Road."**

passive voice. See **The plane was got out of by twelve weary passengers.**

people or *persons*?

If he had been given an injection of sodium pentothal, Walter Cronkite would surely have confessed that when he said on the *CBS Evening News,* in 1979, that "Pope John Paul II spoke to an audience of 1 million persons in Philadelphia," he really meant "1 million people."

Instead of talking and writing like those they talk to and write for, many television, radio, and newspaper reporters refer to individuals, particularly a specific number of them, as *persons,* not *people.* They may be influenced by an old grammatical rule that goes something like this: *People* is a collective noun—that is, a noun which is singular in form but denotes a collection of individuals, like *army* or *public*—so saying "three people" is as unthinkable as saying "three army." That view probably led Strunk and White to give this advice in their *Elements of Style:*

> "The word *people* is best not used with words of number, in place of persons. If of 'six people' five went away, how many people would be left? Answer: one people."

Not so. "One person," not "one people," is the right answer. Having one *person* left if five of six *people* go away is no less probable, either grammatically or mathematically, than having one *mouse* left if five of six *mice* go away.

Nowadays the word *people* is widely accepted in the sense of "more than one person." In *The Reader over Your Shoulder: A Handbook for Writers of English Prose,* for example, Robert Graves and Alan Hodge say:

> "Nine intelligent people out of ten will reverse the order of the words in the third line, to change the repetition into an antithesis. . . ."

British newspapers generally prefer *people.* According to the London *Times:*

> "Diabetes is a state of chronic hyperglycaemia (too much sugar in the blood) affecting 500,000 people in the United Kingdom."

And the *Observer:*

> "Three women were killed and four other people were injured in an accident involving two vehicles on the A74 north of Elvanfoot, Lanarkshire."

More and more, even American television, radio, and newpaper reporters use *people* with numbers. On the same television newscast on which Walter Cronkite covered the Pope's visit to Philadelphia, in 1979, Bob Faw observed that there had been "several hundred thousand people" in Chicago.

Straddling the *people / persons* issue, the *New York Times* gives this rule in its stylebook:

"In general, use *people* for round numbers and groups (the larger the group, the better *people* sounds), and *persons* for precise or quite small numbers: *One million people were notified. He notified 1,316 persons. He said 30 people had been asked to volunteer. Only two persons showed up. Seventeen persons were injured. . . .*"

Besides contradicting its "persons" rule in the "30 people" example immediately following, the *New York Times* often uses *people* in its news stories even for precise or quite small numbers. Reporting on a fire-damaged cruise ship, for instance, it said:

"All but 17 people, who required medical treatment, reboarded the ship after several hours."

The *Washington Post* also has difficulty applying its house style to its news stories. This is the rule in its stylebook:

"Use *people* when referring to a segment of humanity; use *persons* when referring to individuals. (The *people* of Paris mourned . . . ; hundreds of *persons* attended; 27 *persons* were arrested.)"

This is what a front-page story on a car bomb in West Beirut said:

"A powerful car bomb ravaged a narrow street crowded with motorists and shoppers today in the Arab University quarter, killing 17 persons and wounding at least 50 others. . . .

"About 80 people have died in a wave of bombings in the last 12 days and about 400 have been maimed. . . ."

But to the *Los Angeles Times* the issue is simple and straightforward: "more than one person" are *people*. It says so in its stylebook:

"In general, use *people*, regardless of whether the number is large or small: *There were four people at the door; five hundred people attended the meeting. Person* should be used to refer to a single individual."

and it follows the rule in its news stories. The Associated Press agrees.

"Use *person* when speaking of an individual: *One person waited for the bus.*

"The word *people* is preferred to *persons* in all plural uses. For example: *Thousands of people attended the fair. Some rich people pay few taxes. What will people say? There were 17 people in the room.*

"*Persons* should be used only when it is in a direct quote or part of a title as in *Bureau of Missing Persons.*"

Some speakers and writers, of course, prefer *persons* to *people,* especially when they have specific individuals in mind and when the number is small and precise.

Four persons were named to the steering committee.

Surgeons at that hospital performed heart transplants on forty persons last year.

Yet, clearly, the trend is toward *people,* which many consider less stilted than *persons.*

WHEN NO NUMBER IS GIVEN, *people* is generally used for a group referred to collectively and indefinitely.

People have a right to their opinions.

Do you believe that people's tastes change?

But *persons* is likely to be used if the members of the group are thought of individually.

Persons with at least one child in school were asked to volunteer.

The club was considered off-limits to certain persons.

In its stylebook, the *New York Times* sums up the no-number aspect of the *people / persons* controversy: "The important thing is to avoid the ridiculous: *As we all know, persons are funny.*"

PEOPLE, IN THE SENSE OF THE MEMBERS of a single race, nation, community, or the like, ordinarily takes a plural verb.

Are the Jewish people celebrating the holiday?

The people of Lebanon continue to be sharply divided.

How do the people of North Dakota feel about the measure?

When all human beings or members of more than one race or nation are meant, the plural noun form, *peoples,* is generally used.

In his message, the pope addressed all the peoples of the world.

The peoples of Africa were urged to band together.

People who want to arrive safe don't drive drunkenly.

One of the first things that schoolchildren learn is that adverbs modify verbs (along with adjectives and other adverbs) and that adjectives modify nouns. *Arrive* is a verb, so why isn't it modified by the adverb *safely,* instead of the adjective *safe*? It can be. "People who want to arrive safely don't drive drunkenly" is a perfectly acceptable sentence, in which *safely* conveys the notion "in such a manner as to escape injury."

But "People who want to arrive safe don't drive drunkenly" is also a perfectly acceptable sentence. It is simply a different kind of sentence, in which the verb (*arrive*) is seen as connecting the ultimate subject (the noun *people*) with a modifier (the adjective *safe,* in the sense of "whole" or "uninjured") that refers back to that subject. Such a verb is sometimes called a *linking verb;* and an adjective that completes the sense of a linking verb by modifying its subject is called, among other things, a *predicate adjective* or a *subject complement.*

The choice between *drunkenly* and *drunk,* in the same sentence, closely parallels that between *safely* and *safe.* The adverb *drunkenly* can of course modify the verb *drive,* for it denotes the way people handle a car while intoxicated. On the other hand, since *drive,* like *arrive,* can function as a linking verb, there is no reason for it not to connect *people* with the predicate adjective *drunk,* meaning "overcome by alcoholic liquor."

Be, become, seem, appear, look, feel, taste, smell, and *sound* are almost always used as linking verbs. Other verbs that often are, at least in certain senses, include (besides *arrive, drive,* and the like) *get, go, grow, prove, turn, stay,* and *remain.* Because of the linking verb in each of the following sentences, a predicate adjective is called for. An adverb, though, might be appropriate in another context.

This crab *is* (*looks, tastes, smells*) *delicious.* BUT You never cooked crab more *deliciously.*

The bus driver *looked* (*seemed, appeared*) *frantic.* BUT The bus driver waved her arms *frantically.*

By the time the show was over, we *felt* (*became*) *happy.* BUT We walked *happily* out of the theater.

Isn't it time for the weather to *become* (*turn, grow, get*) *warmer?* BUT I hope tomorrow will greet us *warmly.*

Forecasters say the rest of the month *will remain* (*stay*) *cool.* BUT If only May doesn't *treat* us *coolly!*

With its new director, the orchestra *sounds good.* BUT The orchestra certainly plays *well* nowadays.

Some people, treating the adjective *good* and the adverb *well* interchangeably, would replace *well* with *good* in the last sentence. Such usage is far from universally accepted, however. In fact, depending on who is doing the judging, it is variously regarded as colloquial (characteristic of informal speech and writing); dialectal (characteristic of the language variety used in certain regions, communities, and social groups); and nonstandard (below the standards of the language variety of educated speakers).

Bad and *badly* are also open to question. Most people agree that—whether in the sense of "not good," "spoiled," or "ill"—*bad* is the predicate adjective to use in sentences like these:

This cheesecake *is* (*looks, tastes, smells*) *bad.*

One turn on the merry-go-round and I *felt bad.*

Not everyone goes along with the trend to use the adverb *badly* as a predicate adjective in the sense of "sorry" or "distressed."

We *felt badly* about being late last night.

(For more on this controversial pair, see BAD OR BADLY? And for a discussion of verb-subject agreement as it relates to linking verbs, see FISH AND CHIPS IS ON THE MENU AGAIN.)

***persuade* or *convince*?**   See *convince* or *persuade*?

phrasal verbs.   See **Washing down pillows takes a strong stomach.**

The plane was got out of by twelve weary passengers.

If this is the kind of sentence they have in mind, schoolteachers and writers of usage books are right in telling their students and readers not to use the passive voice. "Twelve weary passengers got out of the plane" is certainly more direct and more forceful.

Voice refers to any of the forms of a verb that show whether the subject of a sentence or clause performs the action indicated by the verb (active voice) or receives the action of the verb (passive voice). The passive voice is easy to spot, for instead of being a simple verb like *takes,* it is a verb phrase that ordinarily includes a form of the verb *be* (*is taken, was taken, had been taken, should be taken,* and so on).

Like "Twelve weary passengers got out of the plane," many other active sentences are an improvement over passive ones. Why not say "Radiologists must wear aprons and gloves to keep exposures to a minimum" instead of "Aprons and gloves must be worn by radiologists if exposures are to be kept to a minimum"? Why not say "Jane loves Tarzan" instead of "Tarzan is loved by Jane"?

But does this mean that the passive voice has no place in English speech and writing? Surely not. Lionel Trilling began an essay on Huckleberry Finn with this active sentence:

"In 1876 Mark Twain published *The Adventures of Tom Sawyer* and in the same year began what he called 'another boys' book.' "

Yet, later on, he began a paragraph with this passive sentence:

"*Huckleberry Finn* was once barred from certain libraries and schools for its alleged subversion of morality."

Trilling might, of course, have written an active sentence here as well ("Certain libraries and schools once barred *Huckleberry Finn* for its alleged subversion of morality"). He chose a passive construction probably because he wanted to emphasize the object of the action rather than the agent performing the action—and for this the active voice is less effective.

On other occasions, too, the passive voice is more appropriate than the active. For instance, when:

the agent of the action is irrelevant, too obvious to mention, or not known.

"Gregorian sold medical supplies in the Soviet Union for 15 years, but was forced to leave in 1984." (Associated Press, "Russian's Typewriter Seized in Libel Case")

"The names of religious holidays and seasons <u>are capitalized</u>." (_The Chicago Manual of Style_)

"Blindness being the fundamental, hidden, and recurring difficulty, it must <u>be</u> consciously and perpetually <u>guarded against</u>." (Jacques Barzun, _On Writing, Editing, and Publishing_)

the emphatic end-of-sentence position is reserved either for the object of the action or for the agent.

"The exploding star <u>is called</u> a supernova." (Robert Jastrow, _Red Giants and White Dwarfs_)

"The only other woman on death row who <u>was sentenced</u> as a minor is Janice Buttrum." (Isabel Wilkerson, "The Youngest Girl to Face Execution")

"BBC spokesmen said their switchboards <u>were</u> literally <u>overloaded</u> Monday night by callers demanding to know who shot J.R. and when the series would reappear in the fall." (Leonard Downie, Jr., "British Go Crazy over 'Dallas' TV Show")

tact, diffidence, understatement, or even ambiguity is fitting in a particular statement or passage.

"Britain's interference with American vessels carrying supplies to France or French possessions <u>is mentioned</u> by most textbooks as a factor inviting war, and rightly so. Objectivity demands, however, that the story of these confiscations <u>be tempered</u> by information which, while not exonerating England, at least accounts for her actions." (_The Historian's Contribution to Anglo-American Misunderstanding: Report of a Committee on National Bias in Anglo-American History Textbooks_)

"These are some lectures (the Clark lectures) which <u>were delivered</u> under the auspices of Trinity College, Cambridge, in the spring of 1927. They were informal, indeed talkative, in their tone, and it seemed safer when presenting them in book form not to mitigate the talk, in case nothing should be left at all." (E. M. Forster, "Note," _Aspects of the Novel_)

"Violence and destruction must <u>be ended</u>—in the streets of the ghetto and in the lives of people." (National Advisory Commission on Civil Disorders, _Report_)

plurals: of Latin and Greek loanwords, see **Few phenomenons are more eye-catching than stadia filled with alumnuses waving gladioli;** variant spellings of, see **Saying goodbye may be hard.**

plus

As an adjective, _plus_ has several meanings, including these:

"indicating or involving addition"

a plus sign

"positive"

a plus quality

"somewhat higher than"

a grade of B plus

"involving extra gain or advantage"

a plus factor

It is also used informally to mean "and more."

She has personality plus.

As A PREPOSITION meaning "increased by" or "added to," *plus* is not the equivalent of the conjunction *and*. This means that the number of the subject and verb is ordinarily not affected by intervening words introduced by *plus*, any more than it is by expressions introduced by *with, together with, as well as, no less than,* and the like. If the subject of the sentence or clause is singular, the verb is singular.

Experience plus course credits *is* all that is needed.

If the subject is plural, the verb is plural.

Course *credits* plus experience *are* all that is needed.

Numbers are usually construed as singular and therefore take a singular verb.

Sixty-three plus twelve *is* seventy-five.

(For more on the agreement of subjects and verbs in number, see FISH AND CHIPS IS ON THE MENU AGAIN.)

In informal speech and writing, the preposition *plus* is sometimes used in the sense of "with the addition of."

Terry came home from Las Vegas cheerful and plus $2,000.

TO THE EXASPERATION OF MANY, *plus* is now widely used as a conjunctive adverb, in place of *also, besides, moreover, furthermore,* and the like.

He was late, plus he forgot his pocket calculator.

We have the time plus we're willing to travel.

This informal usage is objected to, not so much because it presses a preposition into service as an adverb—after all, functional shift goes on all the time in English (see "ICE CREAM YOUR KIDS TODAY WITH ROCKY ROAD")—but because it leads to untidy sentence structure. In carrying the sense from one independent clause of a compound sentence to another, *plus,* like any of the conjunctive adverbs it replaces, ought to be preceded by a semicolon. Instead it gets no more than a comma and sometimes no mark of punctuation at all. (For more on run-on sentences, see ELIOT WAS BORN IN MISSOURI, HOWEVER, HE SPENT MOST OF HIS LIFE IN ENGLAND.)

The critics are no happier to see *plus* as the first word of a sentence, linking that sentence to the preceding one.

The rates are low. Plus you get free transportation to Disneyland.

Indeed, the ultratraditionalists among them even find *also* unacceptable at the beginning of a sentence. Some would settle for *and also,* yet others want no part of that construction either (see "AND SO IT GOES").

P.M.   See *A.M.; P.M.*

portmanteau words.   See **Oxbridge workaholics never stop for brunch.**

possessives: **as subjects of gerunds, see "Me carrying a briefcase is like a hog wearing earrings"; double, see Wedding bells are breaking up that old gang of me.**

precipitous or *precipitate*?

After the seizure of some twenty American tuna boats near the Queen Charlotte Islands off British Columbia in 1979, the U.S. State Department spokesman Hodding Carter said:

"We regret the precipitous action by Canada in seizing our vessels. . . ."

To most Americans who heard or read that statement, the use of the word *precipitous* to describe a hasty or impulsive action probably seemed natural.

That the adjective is used loosely, if not downright incorrectly, in that sense is a secret shared by some dictionaries and usage guides, which would replace it with *precipitate* (and the adverb *precipitately*). And by a small number of writers.

"Any other precipitate action having been sanctioned and demanded by the social order and—even when carried out single-handed—performed in mighty concert." (Shirley Hazzard, *The Transit of Venus*)

Precipitous and *precipitously*, we are told, have to do only with physical steepness.

The precipitous height made him dizzy.

The cliffs rose precipitously from the sea.

A few dictionaries, however, recognize that, in referring to Canada's *precipitous* action, Hodding Carter was simply using a seventeenth-century variant of the seventeenth-century adjective *precipitate*. And so are others who say and write:

The squad beat a precipitous retreat.

Again, Wall Street acted precipitously.

prefixes.   See **Who needs a rabbit's foot more: an unlucky person or a luckless one?**

prepositions: **at end of sentences, see Now, that's something to write home about; idiomatic, see How come the clock isn't going?; "Some Trouble-**

some Idiomatic Prepositions'' (table at the back of the book); **omission of,** see **Drink the water if you dare; "Shop Macy's and save."**

presently

Some people wish they didn't, but many English-speakers, especially Americans, use *presently* to mean not only "in a little while; soon":

Next year's models will be unveiled presently.

but also "at present; now":

The U.S. marriage rate is presently at its lowest level.

How do a number of critics deal with this contradictory and often redundant second sense? By telling it to go away.

"*Presently*. Has two meanings: 'in a short while' and 'currently.' Because of this ambiguity it is best restricted to its first meaning: 'He'll be here presently' ('soon,' or 'in a short time')." (Strunk and White, *The Elements of Style*)

"The standard dictionary meaning of *presently* is *soon*, but most people use it as a pompous synonym for *now*. Better stick to *now*." (Rudolf Flesch, *The ABC of Style*)

"*Presently* means *soon; at present* means *now*." ("*Los Angeles Times*" Stylebook)

"*presently*. Use it to mean *in a little while* or *shortly*, but not to mean *now*." (*Associated Press Stylebook and Libel Manual*)

These and similar exhortations to avoid *presently* in the sense of "now" will probably not stamp out the usage, which, it might be noted, is not new but a revival of one so old that it was abandoned in the seventeenth century. Perhaps in time it will again fall into disuse, just as a third meaning of *presently* ("at once; instantly") did. Meanwhile, it is up to those who use the adverb to decide whether it is likely to be understood in the sense intended, and up to the readers or listeners to take the meaning from the context. As the first two examples show, the tense of the verb modified by *presently*, as well as another word or word group in the sentence, usually helps make the meaning clear.

pronouns, agreement with antecedent: in gender, see **Hurricane David left devastation in her wake;** in number, see **"If someone could make your child a genius, would you let them?";** in person, see **One should not tell secrets if you want to be told any.**

pronouns, form of. See **The ball dropped between he and the left-fielder; Is it me you like better than her?; "Me carrying a briefcase is like a hog wearing earrings"; Us TV watchers have strong convictions; Wedding bells are breaking up that old gang of me; Who would you turn to for help?**

pronouns, reference to antecedent. See **Remove the strings and ends from the beans and cook them in boiling salted water.**

pronouns, relative.   See **Herefords, who are a breed of beef cattle, have white faces and red bodies; The Oval Office which is in the White House symbolizes the Presidency; Tennis is a sport I enjoy but which I don't play well.**

pronouns ending in -*self*.   See **Love from Buddy and myself.**

pronunciation, variant.   See **Grampa got his strenth back last Febuary; Well, I'll be a drity brid!; With lightening speed the mischievious athalete ate the sherbert.**

proper nouns in everyday words and expressions.   See **John Bull and John Hancock are not just any johns.**

proportion

This noun is used in various ways, some to everyone's satisfaction and some not. There is little quarrel with its use in these senses:

"the comparative relation between parts, things, or elements with respect to size, amount, degree, and the like; ratio"

I'd like to see a better proportion of bills, junk mail, and letters in my mailbox.

"the relationship between parts or things, especially a harmonious, proper, or desirable relationship; balance or symmetry"

The quadrangle in the Escorial and the towers rising from its corners are in perfect proportion.

"size, degree, or extent relative to a standard"

According to the city code, the flag outside the cookie factory is not in proportion to the pole.

Nor is there disagreement over the use of *proportion* to mean "a part, share, or portion, especially in its relation to the whole; quota," as long as the relation to other parts or to the whole is expressed.

The proportion of the poor who are women rose sharply during the 1960s.

Some people, though, disapprove of *proportion* if *number* would do instead.

A proportion of women are poor.

Most of the opposition has to do with the use of the plural form of *proportion* in the sense of "dimensions." For a time it was led by Theodore M. Bernstein, who said, in *The Careful Writer: A Modern Guide to English Usage* (1965):

" 'A building of huge proportions'; '. . . super-tankers whose proportions exceed the present facilities of the canal.' Strictly speaking, *proportions* expresses a relationship of one part to another, or of parts to the whole. Except in informal usage it has nothing to do with size. A better word in the examples cited would be *dimensions* or *size*."

Bernstein's followers on this point of usage include John B. Bremner, whose *Words on Words: A Dictionary for Writers and Others Who Care about Words* (1980) is described on the book itself as ''a dictionary for professional writers and others who share'' the author's ''commitment to stemming the onslaught of literary barbarism.'' Lamenting the thinning of the anti-*proportions* ranks, Bremner said:

> "Though 65 percent of the American Heritage panelists consider *proportions* acceptable in such phrases as 'condominiums of huge proportions,' 'floods of huge proportions,' 'taxation of huge proportions,' *dimensions* or *extent* or *size* seems more appropriate, according to the context. *Proportion* strictly refers to the relationship of part to whole. *Epidemic proportions* is a cliché."

Nonetheless, *proportions* is so widely accepted as a synonym for *dimensions*—and has been for centuries—that most English-speakers would find this comment about T. S. Eliot, in William Rose Benét's *Reader's Encyclopedia,* unremarkable:

> "Eliot's reputation grew to almost mythic proportions during his own lifetime."

Most dictionaries enter this sense without comment, and few usage guides still inveigh against it.

provided or *providing*?

For years we were told to use *provided*—never *providing*—as a conjunction meaning ''on the condition or understanding.'' A few dictionaries, grammars, and usage books continue to stand firm, but on the whole the ban against *providing* has been relaxed. So has the insistence on *that* following either word. This means that it is now all right to say and write:

> The house will be theirs next month *provided* (or *providing*) the loan goes through.

> Gloria will start teaching in the fall *provided* (or *providing*) the school district does not lose its bilingual program.

That is still used, of course, especially in formal contexts. It is also helpful in preventing either conjunction from being mistaken for a participle of the verb *provide*. For example, the meanings of these sentences might be easier to grasp if *that* were inserted after *provided* and *providing:*

> You are welcome to join the club provided [that] the member's fee is paid.

> Ronald will become the head of the group providing [that] legal advice is available.

Either conjunction is most appropriate when a requirement or condition is explicitly stated. Both can often be replaced by the less stilted *if*.

> I will open the door if I find the key.

puns.   See **Quit nagging me for a horse.**

Q

Quit nagging me for a horse.

As youngsters we are taught to scorn puns and punsters—to purse our lips, shake our head, and say, "How could you!" or "That's awful!" And this whether the pun is really bad (like "West not, want not," for "Waste not, want not"); moderately inventive ("A pun? My word!," for "Upon my word"); or ingenious (like George S. Kaufman's "One man's Mede is another man's Persian," a twist on the cliché "One man's meat is another man's poison," using words for an inhabitant of Media and of Persia).

Expressing two very different senses of a word at the same moment is considered an offense partly because the punster, it is assumed, wants to be laughed at. As "the lowest form of humor," puns don't deserve a smile, much less a laugh.

However straight-faced the listener is supposed to be, the person who makes the pun is bound by custom to be even more restrained. "No pun intended" is the standard defense against the requisite disdainful look or derisive comment. Perhaps as we become freer from the traditional restrictions on our behavior, a punster and the listener will be permitted to laugh openly and loudly at a play on words, especially if it is a good one that takes both of them by surprise.

Because of its many homonyms, English is an ideal language for punning. (A *homonym*, or *homophone*, is a word with the same pronunciation as another but with a different meaning, origin, and, usually, spelling.) The words played against each other in a pun need not match exactly, only come close in sound or form. In calling their musical fund-raisers *Going for Baroque,* for instance, some public television stations count on the public's familiarity not only with the style of music exemplified by Johann Sebastian Bach, but also with the slang expression *go for broke,* meaning "to risk everything."

Similarly, the *New York Times* gave this headline to a story on the continuing decline in the teaching of foreign languages: "The United States Is Losing the Power of Babble." Here the *Power of Babble* is the ability to speak effortlessly, as proficient foreign-language students might; the *Tower of Babel* alluded to is the one that Noah's descendants tried to build but were prevented from completing by a confusion of tongues (Genesis 11:1–9). No matter that the Biblical tower is sometimes pronounced bā'b'l instead of bab''l: the pun works.

Marshall McLuhan was a master of puns. Here are two from *The Medium Is the Massage,* the first a photo caption:

"The Fairmunt Water Works in Philadelphia, Penna. We impose the form of the old on the content of the new. The malady [melody] lingers on."

"The viewer of Renaissance art is systematically placed outside the frame of experience. A piazza [place] for everything and everything in its piazza [place]."

Copywriters and merchants are, of course, quick to realize that similarity of sound can lead to a humorous word association, which in turn can produce a catchy slogan. For example:

A needlework shop is called Crewel World (*cruel world* being a commonly heard expression; *crewel,* a special yarn used in embroidery and other fancy needlework).

An ad for a brand of expensive whiskey says that it "makes a rich man *pour*" (a *poor* man presumably being unable to afford it).

In a London Underground ad, the Duty Free Shops at Heathrow Airport proclaim, "Don't leave without a good *buy.*"

Another London ad, this one for Perrier, a French sparkling water, reads: "H₂Eau / N'eau calories." (*Eau* being the French word for *water,* the bilingual pun means "H₂O, or water / No calories.")

Unlike deliberate punning, which is an open in-joke, unconscious punning can be disconcerting. Even if an accidental pun doesn't get in the way of understanding, it can easily lead to a double take. That is, the listener or reader at first unthinkingly accepts the message, then, in startled surprise, takes in the second meaning, and finally has to decide whether the statement was meant to be humorous or not. For example:

He nagged his parents for a horse.

Winslow Homer's oil paintings on Civil War subjects included *Prisoners from the Front,* executed in 1866.

"Talk about sex with your wife fully and openly, but without boring the pants off her." (Host of a London radio talk show)

"Cocaine Arrests Shoot Up 271% in Los Angeles" (Associated Press)

"The desert sperm storage bank will be elaborately secure. 'It will be outside the earthquake zone and will have Class A security,' said Quinlan. 'In essence it will be impregnable.'" (Don Branning, "Plans Pushed for City's First Frozen Sperm Bank")

R

rack or *wrack*?

These words can be troublesome because they are sometimes—but not always—interchangeable. As nouns meaning "ruin or destruction," both are used in the phrase *to go to wrack* (or *rack*) *and ruin.*

While we were away, the garden went to *wrack* (or *rack*) and ruin.

Here *rack* is a variant of the older word *wrack,* which originally referred to a damaged, or wrecked, ship.

Both words are also used as verbs meaning "to trouble, torment, or afflict":

He lay in his tent, *racked* (or *wracked*) by fever.

Political turmoil *racked* (or *wracked*) the colonies.

and in the adjective compound meaning "very trying to one's patience or equanimity; causing irritation or exasperation":

Have you ever had the nerve-*racking* (or nerve-*wracking*) experience of waiting in an airport as a standby?

But here *wrack* is derived from *rack,* which originally had to do with stretching and later with a framework for holding something.

On its own, *wrack* now mainly denotes wreckage or a fragment of something that has been destroyed. Either alone or in the compound *sea wrack,* it also refers to seaweed or other marine plant life cast upon the shore.

Rack has many more uses today, particularly in connection with a framework, stand, and the like, for holding or displaying various things:

clothes rack   hatrack   dish rack   pipe rack

and with a device for lifting a car from below.

While you've got the car on the *rack* for the oil change, would you mind checking the muffler?

It also refers to a framelike instrument of torture on which victims are bound and stretched until their limbs are pulled out of place.

Two of the prisoners on the *rack* finally confessed.

As extensions of those various meanings, a number of current expressions include the word *rack.* For instance, *off the rack* applies to ready-made clothing.

The trick is to buy your clothes off the rack but make people think they're tailor-made.

On the rack means "in a very difficult or painful situation."

The selection committee had the applicants on the rack for a month.

Rack one's brains (or *memory* or the like) means "to try very hard to remember or think of something."

All summer the marketing experts have been racking their brains for a new TV commercial.

The slang expression *rack up* means "to gain, score, or achieve"; "to be the victor over or beat decisively"; and "to knock down, as with a punch."

The stock market racked up another fifty points yesterday.

Odds are that Clemson will rack up Missouri in the Gator Bowl.

In frustration, Joe racked up the salesclerk.

The reason why a chicken crosses a road is because it wants to get to the other side.

In the phrase *reason why*, one word or the other can often be dropped without being missed. Either "The reason a chicken crosses a road is no longer a mystery" or "Why a chicken crosses a road is no longer a mystery" is a tighter construction than "The reason why a chicken crosses a road is no longer a mystery."

But redundant or not, *reason why* has become firmly established through centuries of use. Thomas Brown is said to have written this much-quoted quatrain of protest against Dr. John Fell, dean of Christ Church at Oxford, in the seventeenth century:

"I do not like thee, Doctor Fell,
The reason why I cannot tell;
But this I know, and know full well,
I do not like thee, Dr. Fell."

The expression *reason why* can be found in all kinds of speech and writing and at all levels of usage. For example:

"There are three good reasons why we should fight for our language. . . ." (Henry Strauss, "You Americans Are Murdering the Language")

" 'You knew, didn't you? I'm part of you? Close, close, close! I'm the reason why it's no go? Why things are what they are?' " (William Golding, *Lord of the Flies*)

"A second reason why we recognize words as separate entities is that the thought expressed by the sentence varies with the form." (E. H. Sturtevant, *Linguistic Change*)

"One reason why Jacob Rothschild, chairman of the National Gallery trustees, encouraged him to apply was that it now has the money to conduct a comparable programme." ("Profile," London *Observer*)

Not only is the phrase *reason why* firmly established, but some constructions actually require both words. When a modifier comes after *reason,* for instance, *why* is needed to introduce the following clause.

> Charlie always gives a reason, though far from a convincing one, why he won't buckle the seat belt in his car.

Negative constructions, too, sound unnatural without both words.

> In denying the motion, the judge ruled that there was no reason why the defendant's position as president of her company distinguished this case from that of other officials sued in prior actions.

OUR CHICKEN IS NOT going to make it across the road without running into another redundancy: *reason . . . because.* True, using *reason* as the subject of a sentence or clause and *because* in the sense of "for the reason that" can lead to a circular construction. Therefore:

> The reason a chicken crosses a road is because it wants to get to the other side.

means, strictly speaking:

> The reason a chicken crosses a road is for the reason that it wants to get to the other side.

Those who object to this usage—and there are many who do, loudly and persistently—say that *reason* must be balanced by a noun or noun phrase:

> The *reason* a chicken crosses a road is its *determination* to get to the other side.

or by a noun clause introduced by *that:*

> The *reason* a chicken crosses a road is *that* it wants to get to the other side.

Or else *because* can be kept and both *the reason* and the following verb (in this case *is*) dropped.

> A chicken crosses a road because it wants to get to the other side.

All those proposed remedies are indeed universally accepted. But many educated speakers and writers also use the construction *reason . . . because*—and not because they know better but can't resist the temptation to be grammatically incorrect. They simply recognize that *because* has become an established equivalent of *that* in introducing a noun clause.

Both condemned constructions—*reason why* and *reason . . . because*—are sometimes even found in the same sentence. In *Pop Goes America,* for instance, William Zinsser, a well-known writer and teacher of writing, made this comment about the special appeal of the band leader Guy Lombardo:

> "But the main <u>reason why</u> Lombardo became identified as the Ghost of New Years Past, Present and To Come, he says, 'is <u>because</u> "Auld Lange Syne" is our theme song—and was long before anyone ever heard us on the radio.'"

And in *The Gift of Language,* Margaret Schlauch had this to say about the influences of Latin grammar on English:

"Without doubt one of the <u>reasons why</u> logic and grammar have been confused is <u>because</u> both grammarians and logicians have so long been schooled in a classical training."

For more on redundancy, see SLOW EROSION COMPLETELY DESTROYED THE OLD COLONIAL TOMBSTONE.

redundancy. See **Slow erosion completely destroyed the old colonial tombstone.**

regardless or *irregardless?* See *irregardless* or *regardless?*

Remove the ends and strings from the beans and cook them in boiling salted water.

Anyone—not just literal-minded cooks who wish recipes said "Open a can of mushroom soup and add the contents" instead of "Add a can of mushroom soup"—might wonder whether it is the beans or their strings and ends that get boiled. What isn't clearly stated is the antecedent of the pronoun *them;* that is, what does *them* refer to?

There are several ways to clear up the ambiguity. One is to repeat whichever word or word group is meant, saying either:

Remove the ends and strings from the beans and cook the ends and strings in boiling salted water.

or:

Remove the ends and strings from the beans and cook the beans in boiling salted water.

But neither of these sentences expresses its meaning economically, because neither allows a pronoun to do what it does best: replace a noun or refer to the person, thing, or idea designated by the noun. We would not get far in communicating with one another if we never used the relationship or signal words known as pronouns, which make up one of the traditional parts of speech.

Another way to make the cooking instruction clear would be to replace the personal prounoun *them* (the objective form, or case, of *they,* since it is the object of the verb *cook*) with a demonstrative pronoun: *these* if the nearby beans are meant; *those* if the farther-away ends and strings are. Or the sentence might be reworded, omitting the pronoun altogether: "After removing the ends and strings, cook the beans in boiling salted water."

The word *antecedent* (from the Latin *ante,* meaning "before," and *cedere,* meaning "to go") suggests that the word or word group referred to by a pronoun occurs before that pronoun, either in the same sentence or in the previous one. It usually does; indeed, some grammarians insist that no other order is acceptable.

> After *a kindergarten teacher* becomes involved in a plot to overthrow the Laotian government, *she* enlists the aid of an inept detective.

Yet most English-speakers believe that as long as the reader or listener is neither confused nor unduly kept in suspense, there is no reason why a pronoun cannot precede its antecedent.

> After *she* becomes involved in a plot to overthrow the Laotian government, *a kindergarten teacher* enlists the aid of an inept detective.

Although the antecedent of a pronoun is generally described as a noun, it may of course be another pronoun instead. In "They took their box lunches with them," *they* is the antecedent of *their* and *them*. For the sentence to make sense, however, the meaning of *they* must already have been established; quite likely its antecedent was given in the previous sentence ("Margaret and Fernando had to leave early. They took their box lunches with them."). All third-person pronouns, in fact, ordinarily have clearly stated antecedents to identify who or what is being spoken about. On the other hand, first- and second-person pronouns generally do not need them, since there is little doubt about who is speaking or being spoken to. For instance, if a dentist tells a patient "*I*'ll have *your* X-rays in a minute," presumably both know whom the pronouns refer to.

Showing which word or word group a pronoun stands for is less of a problem in conversation than in writing, because the speaker can reword an unclear sentence on the spot if the listener doesn't seem to grasp the meaning. A reader, on the other hand, is often left to figure out the meaning. An Associated Press story, for example, said:

> "Prime Minister Felipe Gonzalez shuffled his cabinet yesterday, and the foreign minister was the first to go—because <u>he</u> felt Spain should pull out of NATO, according to Socialist Party sources."

Did González or the foreign minister feel that Spain should pull out of NATO? Repeating the noun or providing a new one is the simplest way to remove the ambiguity; that is, *he* becomes *González* or *the prime minister* if González is meant; otherwise, *the foreign minister* or *this official.*

The pronouns *it*, *this*, *that*, and *which* are often used to refer not to a particular noun or pronoun but to an entire statement, either expressed or implied.

> "On both sides of what once was called the Iron Curtain, Europe is adrift—with both East and West deeply skeptical of their superpower patrons. Where <u>it</u> comes to rest is critical." (Henry Trewhitt, *U.S. News & World Report*)

> "Despite its title, *Eisenhower: At War* is less a military than a political account. <u>This</u> is a pity, because it means that even his grandson now fosters the <u>myth</u> that General Eisenhower was always the diplomat in uniform, rather than a first-rate military commander—when in fact he was very much the latter." (Russell F. Weigley, *Atlantic*)

> "Under the Senate's proposal, sponsored chiefly by Idaho's Steve Symms, the states would be authorized to fix speed limits up to 65 miles per hour on interstate highways 'located outside of an urbanized area of 50,000

population or more.' <u>That</u> makes sense." (the syndicated columnist James Kilpatrick)

"Warned by his predecessor's fate, DeVoto arranged the manuscript according to subject, <u>which</u> worked out much better." (Dwight Macdonald, *Against the American Grain*)

Many grammarians disapprove of such references as being too general. They would, for example, like to see the *that* in Kilpatrick's article replaced by a word or word group that more clearly sums up what went before.

That proposal (or *the Senate's proposal, that plan, the Senate's plan*) makes sense.

Some references can indeed be so general as to cause confusion. This lead sentence in an article by the reporter Tad Szulc, for instance, surely brought more than a few readers up short:

"U.S. influence in Latin America is eroding steadily on diplomatic, political and economic fronts, and <u>it</u> shows no signs of diminishing."

What is the antecedent of *it*? U.S. influence? If so, can influence be eroding steadily yet show no signs of diminishing? Or does *it* refer to the erosion of that influence, a concept contained in the preceding main clause of the sentence?

When the antecedent of a pronoun is very remote or missing entirely, the reader or listener must make the connection between the pronoun and the concept it refers to.

Will you be able to help me if I need *it?*

At the age of eighty *his* family moved to Missouri.

I never drive a car without power steering. *They* are the easiest to handle.

The attempt to combat nuclear power took on new urgency after the Three Mile Island incident. Grass-roots movements were responsible for *this*.

We finally cleaned the house, *which* it needed very badly.

Anyone asked the question "Will you be able to help me if I need it?" would probably know that *it* stands for the unstated noun *help*. Many speakers and even more writers, however, would supply the missing antecedent by changing *help me* to *give me help*. Or they might change *it* to *help* or *assistance;* but the repetition of *help*, used once as a verb and again as a noun, would be clumsy, and *assistance* would probably be too grand a word in this informal sentence. So style, as well as the need to eliminate ambiguity, plays a part in the reference of pronouns to their antecedents.

A construction heard more and more nowadays indeed stretches the connection between the pronoun *which* and its antecedent. The word is in fact not used as a pronoun at all, but as a conjunction equivalent to *and,* loosely linking a clause with a preceding word, phrase, or other clause.

I went to hear Barbra Streisand in concert, *which* I didn't think she was at her best.

Besides referring unmistakably to their antecedents, pronouns should, according to a long-standing rule of grammar, agree with their antecedents in gender, number, and person (see HURRICANE DAVID LEFT DEVASTATION IN HER WAKE; "IF SOMEONE COULD MAKE YOUR CHILD A GENIUS, WOULD YOU LET THEM?"; and ONE SHOULD NOT TELL SECRETS IF YOU WANT TO BE TOLD ANY).

restrictive and nonrestrictive modifiers.   See **The Oval Office which is in the White House symbolizes the Presidency.**

run-on sentences.   See **Eliot was born in Missouri, however, he spent most of his life in England.**

Russian is written in the Acrylic alphabet.

If it were, a passage in Russian would look something like a wash-and-wear suit, because *acrylic* describes a synthetic fiber used in fabrics. What is meant is *Cyrillic*, the name given to the Slavic alphabet attributed to the ninth-century apostle Saint Cyril and still used, in modified form, in Russia, Bulgaria, and other Slavic countries.

Confusing similar-sounding words of very different meanings is in the tradition of Mrs. Malaprop, a character in an eighteenth-century English comedy. Such a laughable misuse of words is in fact known as a *malapropism* (pronounced mal′ə präp iz′m). Richard Brinsley Sheridan, the author of *The Rivals,* took the name of his character from the French *mal à propos,* meaning "inappropriate." In her best-known blunder (act 3, scene 3), Mrs. Malaprop says that her niece, Lydia, is "as headstrong as an allegory [instead of *alligator*] on the banks of Nile." These are some of the other ludicrous lines that Sheridan put into Mrs. Malaprop's mouth:

"I hope you will represent *her* to the Captain as an object not altogether illegible [for *ineligible*]." (act 1, scene 2)

"Ah! few gentlemen, nowadays, know how to value the ineffectual [for *intellectual*] qualities in a woman!" (act 3, scene 3)

"He is the very pineapple [for *pinnacle*] of politeness!" (act 3, scene 3)

"His physiognomy [for *phraseology*] so grammatical!" (act 4, scene 2)

"but he can tell you the perpendiculars [for *particulars*]." (act 5, scene 1)

Both the malapropian word and the word it sounds like are ordinarily not part of the speaker's everyday vocabulary. That is, we may hear someone—to our horror, even ourselves—say "He's got illusions (instead of *delusions*) of grandeur"; but unless it's simply a slip of the tongue, probably not "I had to borrow floor (instead of *four*) dollars."

The Mrs. and Mr. Malaprops of today make statements like these:

Americans have lost the Protestant work ethnic (for *ethic*).

As always, my broker tried to waylay (for *allay*) my fears.

Television detectives don't take long to pick up a criminal's opus morandi (for *modus operandi*).

She is one of the most enervative (for *innovative*) dress designers in the country.

To many Americans, France is the acne (for *acme*) of sophistication.

A good teacher will illicit (for *elicit*) the answers from the students.

Joan was decimated (for *devastated*) by her husband's death.

Ben is a vociferous (for *voracious*) reader.

The school district is looking for teachers who are affluent (for *fluent*) in Spanish and English.

In that blouse she looked like a powder (for *pouter*) pigeon.

The vagrancies (for *vagaries*) of English spelling cause problems for native speakers and foreigners alike.

His latest novel raises the spectrum (for *specter*) of nuclear war.

That was about the time the South succeeded (for *seceded*) from the Union.

Would you rather have Asti Spumoni (for *Spumante*) or a still wine?

The movie is about a teenager who is tricked into perpetuating (for *perpetrating*) a murder.

Her brother-in-law died of cerebral hemorrhoids (for *a cerebral hemorrhage*).

Because they are usually edited out of published material, malapropisms are more often heard than seen. Some, however, appear in print as direct quotations. In a *Publishers Weekly* article on how publishers decide whether to do a book, Michael Wendroff included this statement by Roger Straus, Jr., president of Farrar, Straus and Giroux:

"It may well be that from time to time a book is outside our normal web [for *warp*] and woof of life. . . . "

According to the *New York Times,* Henry Kissinger told the 1980 Republican National Convention, in Detroit:

"It is not political oratory to assert that another four years like the last four will make disaster irretrievable [for *inevitable*]."

Whether his own or the inventions of jokesters and publicists, Sam Goldwyn's malapropisms have been printed and reprinted for years. After an operation and a difficult recovery, the movie producer supposedly pontificated:

"Well, you just don't realize what life is all about until you have found yourself lying on the brink of a great abscess [for *abyss*]."

These are some of the other malapropisms cited in *Goldwyn: A Biography of the Man behind the Myth,* by Arthur Marx:

"I have been laid up with intentional [for *intestinal*] flu."

"I want to make a picture about the Russian secret police—the GOP [for *KGB*]."

"There is a statue [for *statute*] of limitation."

"Okay, boys, now let's go upstairs and have a little cuddle [for *huddle*]."

Yet Marx makes it clear that, however garbled Goldwyn's thoughts and language, his secretaries were instructed to see that his letters were ''grammatically correct in their final form.''

Richard Daley, the colorful mayor of Chicago, was also known for his malapropisms and, like Goldwyn, was irritated by the jokes about them. Eugene Kennedy cites these slips in *Himself! The Life and Times of Mayor Richard J. Daley:*

"tantrum [for *tandem*] bicycle"

"Alcoholics Unanimous [for *Anonymous*]"

"A man running for a public office to make such a statement without consulting the statue [for *statute*] of Illinois and the laws of Illinois, gentlemen, it's ridiculous." (This malapropism is attributed to Goldwyn as well.)

Shortly after Daley's death in 1976, the *Los Angeles Times* reported that the mayor had once said of his enemies:

" 'They have vilified me, they have crucified me, yes, have even criticized me.... I resent the insinuendoes [for *innuendoes* or *insinuations*]."

Some malapropisms do of course go straight into print.

"At Brooke's request, there were four years of piano lessons, horseback riding, French studies—she speaks fluid [for *fluent*] French—and is now learning Italian." (Phyllis Batelle, "Brooke Shields")

"Even the advertisements in the *New Yorker*, where you'd figure they'd have advertisement grammar police, are ripe [for *rife*] with [sentence] fragments." (Kathleen Donnelly, "Notes & Comments: A Few Thoughts. On Grammar")

"Mornell dislikes America's reliance on an increasingly passive culture, dependent on pills and alcohol, which reaches its nemesis [for *nadir*] in television...." (Christopher Reed, "Why So Many Marriages Are Foundering")

" 'We're very pleased that the committee showed imminent [for *eminent*] good sense and defeated this bill,' said staunch opponent Mayor Dianne Feinstein...." (Reginald Smith, "Assembly Panel Kills Traweek's Condo Bill")

"[California State Librarian Ethel] Crockett was appointed by Gov. Reagan in 1972 and continued to serve with Brown's placid [for *tacit*] approval until recently." (Gale Cook, "The Drive to Get Rid of the State Librarian")

"Accountant/Bookkeeper. . . . This position will run the gambit [for *gamut*] from AR/AP to taxes to financial statements. . . ." (Classified ad, Lowell, Mass., *Sunday Sun*)

"Grampa Turtle lives in the Freeborn Wildlife Preserve. He feels he's approaching middle age—now that he's 433 years old, but he would never think of himself as old, just mature. As such, he likes to dispell [for *dispense*] words of wisdom to all the other animals." (Tag on an "Animal Crackers" stuffed toy)

For the ludicrously illogical or incongruous statements sometimes called Goldwynisms, see "YOU'RE A GOODY-GOODY GUMSHOES"; for the bloopers known as spoonerisms, "KINKERING CONGS THEIR TITLES TAKE."

S

Saying goodbye may be hard.

But writing it is harder. Should the word be spelled *goodbye, good-bye, goodby,* or *good-by*? In standard American usage all four spellings are acceptable, so it is a matter of personal choice.

Different spellings for the same word are very common in English. This is not surprising, because until the eighteenth century, when dictionaries—especially Samuel Johnson's—tried to standardize spelling, English-speakers spelled words just about as they pleased.

Today most English-language dictionaries of any size show several spellings for many words, and treat them in more or less the same way. If a dictionary's research indicates that usage is about evenly divided between variants, the spellings that are close to each other alphabetically usually appear together in the main, boldface entry; in some cases the form found to occur more frequently is listed first. Less common variants that are alphabetically close to the main-entry spelling are generally given at the end of the entry block. *Webster's New World Dictionary,* for example, gives *goodbye, good-bye* as a main entry and *goodby, good-by* as variant spellings, following the definition. For variants that are some distance apart alphabetically, most dictionaries place the definition for the word at the spelling known or judged to be the most common and, through cross-references, direct users who might turn first to other spellings to this entry. Thus, virtually all British and American dictionaries give *inquire* as a main entry, where the word is defined, and show *enquire* as a cross-reference.

Once past the first level of variants—that is, those spellings that are believed to occur with roughly equal frequency—dictionaries disagree somewhat on how other acceptable spellings for the same word should be viewed. In setting down rules for its users to follow, the more prescriptive dictionaries tend to divide these second-level variants into the preferred and the less preferred. On the other hand, dictionaries concerned not with prescribing usage but with reporting the usage of most educated speakers are likely to group all second-level variants into the single category of less frequent occurrence. (In its introductory section, each dictionary describes its system for recording variants.)

Variant spelling is, of course, not simply a matter of which letters appear in what order, as in, say, *upsy-daisy, upsadaisy, whoops-a-daisy*. Compounding plays a major part—that is, whether the word elements have no space, space, or a hyphen between them: for example, *hotshot, hot shot, hot-shot*. Capitalization is involved as well; for instance, a perennial pink with dense, flat clusters of small flowers is called either *sweet william* or *sweet William*. And any special marks, or diacritics, particularly on words borrowed from foreign languages, ought to be taken into account; for instance, *résumé, resume, resumé*. (For a discussion of the large body of words and expressions that English has borrowed from other languages over the centuries, see MODOR, WE'VE GOT COMPANY.)

Words that have different spellings can be found at every level of usage, from the informal to the formal. The variant spellings listed below are, according to *Webster's New World Dictionary*, among those in common use in the United States. The words and phrases that entered the language through American English are preceded by an open star, as they are in that dictionary. Only variants used in the same sense or as the same part of speech are included; therefore, the adjective *mucous* and the noun *mucus*, for example, are not shown. The order in which the variants are listed reflects not a hierarchy of "correctness" but frequency of use at the time the dictionary was being compiled.

aesthetics, esthetics

anymore, any more

ax, axe

☆babbitry, Babbitry

birthrate, birth rate

caliph, calif, kalif, kaliph, khalif

catty-cornered, catty-corner, kitty-corner

chaise longue, chaise lounge

crayfish, crawfish

czar, tsar, tzar

Erlenmeyer flask, erlenmeyer flask

façade, facade

fiord, fjord

goodbye, good-bye, goodby, good-by

guerrilla, guerilla

Halloween, Hallowe'en

hiccup, hiccough

holistic, wholistic

hypotenuse, hypothenuse

jujitsu, jiujitsu, jiujutsu, jujutsu

ketchup, catsup

lady's man, ladies' man

mamma, mama

naiveté, naïveté

☆narc, narco, nark

☆raccoon, racoon

restaurateur, restauranteur

rhyme, rime

☆rock-and-roll, rock 'n' roll

☆smidgen, smidgin, smidgeon

☆Snowbelt, Snow Belt

so-so, so so

sync, synch

taboo, tabu

theater, theatre

though, tho, tho'

tick-tack-toe, tic-tac-toe, tit-tat-toe

☆T-shirt, tee shirt

veranda, verandah

volcanology, vulcanology

whiskey, whisky

whiz, whizz

X-ray, X ray, x-ray, x ray

☆Yellow Pages, yellow pages

yogurt, yoghurt, yoghourt

zombie, zombi

One of the reasons why English has so many variant spellings is the irregular way in which prefixes and suffixes change the form of some, but not all, words to which they are attached. Besides, the affixes themselves are sometimes spelled differently: either *en-* or *in-*, for instance, occurs in a number of words, including *incrust* and *encrust* and *endorse* and *indorse*. (See WHO NEEDS A RABBIT'S FOOT MORE: AN UNLUCKY PERSON OR A LUCKLESS ONE?) British influence can be seen in the preference of some Americans for, say, *speciality* over *specialty*, *traveller* over *traveler*, and *jewellery* over *jewelry*. These are some other frequently used suffixed words that have more than one spelling:

abridgment, abridgement	kiddy, kiddie
acknowledgment, acknowledgement	kidnapped, kidnaped
adviser, advisor	kindergartner, kindergartener
ageism, agism	libelous, libellous
backward, backwards	likable, likeable
bluish, blueish	marvelous, marvellous
catalog, catalogue	nonplused, nonplussed
cigarette, cigaret	programmer, programer
collectible, collectable	programming, programing
cookie, cooky	referable, referrable, referrible
dialogue, dialog	shyest, shiest
discussable, discussible	sliest, slyest
Ecuadorean, Ecuadorian, Ecuadoran	totaling, totalling
employee, employe	toward, towards
eyeing, eying	vendor, vender
flier, flyer	woolly, wooly
geometric, geometrical	worshiper, worshipper

Clearly, no hard-and-fast rules cover the spelling of plurals of nouns. For example:

dwarfs, dwarves	TVs, TV's
trousseaux, trousseaus	wharves, wharfs

Especially those ending in *o*.

archipelagoes, archipelagos	mestizos, mestizoes
fiascoes, fiascos	noes, nos
ghettos, ghettoes	volcanoes, volcanos
halos, haloes	zeros, zeroes
innuendoes, innuendos	

semantic shift.   See **For a girl he's quite mature.**

semi- **or** *bi?*   See *bi-* **or** *semi-?*

sensual **or** *sensuous?*

Many English-speakers are uncomfortable using these adjectives: whichever they choose seems to go too far in suggesting bodily or sexual pleasure. No wonder, for the difference between the two words is not immediately apparent from the parts that make them up. Both have *sense* as their base. And both have adjective-forming suffixes with similar meanings, *-al* conveying the sense of "like" and *-ous* the sense of "characterized by." Yet usage has assigned to *sensual* a connection or preoccupation with the bodily senses, as distinguished from the intellect or spirit, and to *sensuous* the strong appeal of that which is perceived through the five senses. So perfume is advertised as "sensual" and Sarah Vaughan's voice is described as "sensuous."

Efforts to get rid of the connotation of licentiousness, lewdness, or lust that attaches to *sensual* go back hundreds of years. Indeed, according to *The Oxford English Dictonary*, the seventeenth-century poet John Milton apparently invented *sensuous* "to avoid certain associations of the existing word *sensual*."

For more on the way prefixes and suffixes help to determine the meanings of words, see WHO NEEDS A RABBIT'S FOOT MORE: AN UNLUCKY PERSON OR A LUCKLESS ONE?

set or *sit*? See *sit* or *set*?

several, few, or *couple*?

Whether used as adjectives, nouns, or pronouns, *several* and *few* generally refer to a small but indefinite number of things or persons—more than two but not many more. As nouns and pronouns, both take plural verbs.

Adjectives: After several tries, I gave up.

Few houses were still on the market.

Nouns: Several of the shows are in rerun.

Only a few of the shops stay open late.

Pronouns: Several want to be on the waiting list.

Few say they remember the anniversary.

Although the noun *couple* ordinarily refers to two things or persons of the same sort that are somehow associated, from time to time it replaces *several* or *few* in informal speech and writing.

A couple of shows are in rerun.

A couple of the shops stay open late.

When *couple* is used as an adjective—again, informally—the preposition *of* is sometimes omitted.

A couple shows are in rerun.

I saw her a couple days ago.

(For more on the omission of prepositions, see "SHOP MACY'S AND SAVE.")

sexist language. See "Burnett goes dramatic as a gaunt Iowa wife."

Shall you return? We should like that.

Now, let's see . . . I simply expect to be home next weekend, so I say, "I *shall* be home next weekend." If I'm determined to be home next weekend, bus strike or not, I say, "I *will* be home next weekend." If I'm fairly sure that you will be there too, I say, "You *will* be home next weekend." If I'm not sure of your intentions, I ask, "*Shall* you be home next weekend?" And if I'm determined to have you there, I say, "You *shall* be home next weekend."

That is how an American might try to sort out some of the rules on using the auxiliary verbs *shall* and *will* with a flat (*to*-less) infinitive to form the future tense—rules that come so easily and naturally to the English. For example, when asked to promise that he would not forget his friend, even when the friend was a hundred years old, an English toy bear named Pooh replied, apparently without effort, "How old shall *I* be then?"

Authorities on British English have noted that the American and Scottish practice of eliminating *shall* has been making inroads even on Received Standard, or BBC, English. In *Current English Usage,* Frederick T. Wood declares that such a trend "should be firmly resisted, for if the use of *shall* were to drop out of the future we should be deprived of the means of expressing a very material distinction of meaning."

Nor have all American arbiters of usage given up on that distinction. Wilson Follett's *Modern American Usage,* for example, contains a twenty-three page appendix titled "Shall (Should), Will (Would)." It concludes as follows:

> "It is obviously no easy task to survey the essentials of the usage governing *shall* and *will* without either oversimplifying to encourage the inquirer or else disheartening him by exhibiting the full list of complications. It is no service to anyone to represent the difficulties as trifling or nonexistent; or to pretend that there is a clear, cogent, and uniform set of practices; or to deny that certain problems are insoluble and the constructions that breed them are best avoided. Even so, no one should be left with the feeling that, defeated in advance, he may as well give up and leave all discrimination to born hairsplitters. With a little effort anyone can gain a command of the main principles and learn to bypass dilemmas. Neither overconfidence nor defeatism need—or should—rule the mind of those willing to cope with *shall* and *will*."

Yet the fact is, most Americans do not observe the traditional rules on *shall* and *will,* and those who do, do so only in formal speech and writing. Oversimplified, these are the rules: *shall* for the first person and *will* for the second and third persons in references to the simple future; just the opposite to indicate determination, compulsion, obligation, and necessity; and either *shall* or *will* in questions, depending on the degree of intention and on which form the person addressed is likely to use in reply. In legal documents *shall* ordinarily replaces *will* for all persons ("There shall be no partition of the property or any part thereof").

In everyday speech and writing, then, Americans by and large ignore the subtle distinctions between *shall* and *will,* preferring other, less stilted ways to express futurity. The most common device is to use *will* for all persons in references to the simple future.

I will be home next weekend.

Will you be home next weekend?

They will be home next weekend.

For all anyone knows, Americans might be using *shall* more often, but because of their addiction to contractions, especially in speaking but more and more in writing as well, the distinction between *shall* and *will* is blurred: *I'll, you'll, we'll, they'll, she'll, he'll,* and even *it'll* apply to either auxiliary. The contracted form of *will not* is *won't* (from the Middle English *wol not*). However unusual *shall not,* its contraction, *shan't,* is used even less in the States. (For more on contractions, see DON'T SHE KNOW IT'LL BE DARK SOON?)

Another way Americans get around the *shall / will* rules is to substitute the so-called present-tense forms. For example, instead of saying:

I shall leave for Atlanta tomorrow.

they are likely to use any of these forms:

Simple: I leave for Atlanta tomorrow.

Progressive: I am leaving for Atlanta tomorrow.

Emphatic: I do leave for Atlanta tomorrow.

Americans sometimes use *shall* in questions, especially in the first person:

Shall I take out the garbage?

Shall we go?

but here it is usually less a matter of asking whether the person addressed believes that something will happen than of asking whether he or she would like it to. In negative questions, *won't* is almost always used instead of *shan't.*

Won't we run out of money?

And, finally, Americans sometimes use *shall* to express determination.

I shall open the first pizza parlor on the moon.

You shall win the Gold.

However, even in this context *will* ordinarily serves the same purpose: in writing, with *will* italicized or underscored and perhaps with an exclamation mark at the end of a sentence; in speech, with stress on the word *will.*

THOSE WHO FOLLOW the strict rules governing *shall* and *will* ordinarily apply them to their past-tense forms, *should* and *would,* as well. The principal use of *should* and *would* is to express futurity from the standpoint of the past in indirect quotations where *shall* and *will* were used in the direct quotations.

Will is generally changed to *would* for all persons. For example:

"Paula will be home for the weekend," Kit said.

becomes:

> Kit said that Paula would be home for the weekend.

When it comes to changing the first-person *shall* to the past tense, whether *should* or *would* is used depends on the shade of meaning in the direct quotation. If, for instance, *shall* expressed simple futurity, as in:

> "We shall be there too," the twins said.

the indirect quotation becomes:

> The twins said that they would be there too.

If *shall* expressed determination in the direct quotation, *would* is used as well. For example:

> "I shall do no such thing," Michael told the group.

becomes:

> Michael told the group that he would do no such thing.

However, if *shall* expressed a combination of intention and futurity in the direct quotation, either *should* or *would* can be used in the indirect quotation. So:

> "I shall be home by noon," Kit said.

might become either:

> Kit said she should be home by noon.

or:

> Kit said she would be home by noon.

For most Americans most of the time, the choice between *should* and *would* in indirect quotations is as simple as that between *shall* and *will* in direct quotations: *would* for all persons.

> "I think I will be home for the weekend," Kit said.

> Kit said that she thought she would be home for the weekend.

> "Bus strike or not, I will be home for the weekend," Kit said.

> Kit said that, bus strike or not, she would be home for the weekend.

Again, Americans' fondness for contractions simplifies matters.

> Kit said that she thought she'd be home for the weekend.

> Kit said that, bus strike or not, she'd be home for the weekend.

THE AUXILIARIES *SHOULD* AND *WOULD* also have meanings less closely related to *shall* and *will*. Some of these senses are shared, and others are attached to only one of the auxiliaries. When there is a choice, Americans generally prefer *would* for all persons, reserving *should* for the first person in formal speech and writing.

Both express futurity in polite or unemphatic requests.

I *would* (or *should*) be grateful if you would remove my name from your mailing list.

Both are used in statements with implications of uncertainty or doubt.

I *would* (or *should*) think you'd enjoy Key West at this time of year.

One would expect greater enthusiasm for the home team.

And both are used in statements about past conditions, real or unreal.

I *should* (or *would*) have liked to be at Tony's graduation.

They would have remodeled the house, but they ran out of money.

In addition, each auxiliary has its own special senses. Regardless of person, *should* often occurs in the *if* clause of a statement expressing future condition. In this use *would* is considered most appropriate to casual speech and even, by some, to be substandard.

If I (you, he, she, we, they) *should* (not *would*) win the lottery, the IRS will be the first to learn of it.

On the other hand, certain constructions that express condition call for *would*, not *should*.

I (you, he, she, we, they) would go if the company paid.

I (you, he, she, we, they) would be happier if the weather were better.

I (you, he, she, we, they) would be happiest staying at home.

There are two other senses in which *should*, not *would*, is used. One is to convey the notion of obligation, duty, propriety, necessity, and the like.

You should know their address by now.

Children should be read to as often as possible.

The second implies expectation or probability; that is, here *should* is the equivalent of *ought to*.

It should stop raining by early afternoon.

We should have an answer to our letter soon.

The swallows should be back at Capistrano next Tuesday.

(For other auxiliary verbs that express various degrees of probability, see CAN I BORROW YOUR LAWN MOWER? NOT IF YOU MIGHT KEEP IT.)

As an auxiliary, *would* has another sense in which *should* is inappropriate: to express habitual action.

I would go for long walks before supper.

They would phone every night at ten.

The nonauxiliary use of *would* is as a replacement of *I wish*, particularly in literary contexts.

Would that Mozart were still alive!

"Shop Macy's and save."

What's a decent intransitive verb like *shop* doing with a direct object? Why isn't it followed by the preposition *at*? That is what many people asked, some with dismay and others with amusement, when rival stores began turning out ads of the "Shop Macy's and save" kind. Over the years the construction has become part of the language, especially in advertising and in informal speech and writing. So we read in a newspaper column by Herb Caen that "Wendy Link, browsing I. Magnin, overheard a woman complain to a salesgirl. . . ." And we are told, over soothing music in an elevator, "Thank you for stopping Sheraton" or whatever the hotel.

Yet many of today's English-speakers, particularly those with good memories, mourn the loss of every preposition. The trend toward dropping *from* after the verb *graduate* has been especially painful. According to the 1975 edition of the *Harper Dictionary of Contemporary Usage,* 85 percent of the distinguished panel of 136 experts objected to "She *graduated* college" (instead of "She *graduated from* college") in speech; 90 percent, in writing—even "writing of an Informal nature." By the time the panel was polled for the 1985 edition, its members (then 166) felt exactly the same: only 15 percent were willing to hear "She *graduated* college"; only 10 percent, to see the construction in print.

As if the gradual disappearance of *from* after *graduate* were not distressing enough, some people wistfully recall the time when the active form, or voice, of the verb was considered incorrect. That is, only "She *was graduated from* college" would do—not "She *graduated from* college." But whereas the struggle to preserve the preposition *from* goes on, defenders of the passive form of the verb seem to have all but lost their battle. Even in its 1975 edition the *Harper Dictionary* noted, "Today the simpler 'She *graduated from* . . .' is considered entirely acceptable."

Strict grammarians would like to see prepositions restored to elliptical expressions, even though the missing words can easily be supplied by the listener or reader. They object, for example, to what they consider loose usage in certain infinitive constructions.

Though *to* is a sign of the infinitive that follows, most people do not regard it as an inseparable part of the verb. We never expect to find it before the infinitive in constructions like these:

We all hope that you can go.

If you can make the watch *run*, I'll buy it.

You need not *worry*.

I cannot but *wonder* whether telephones will ever work again.

And rarely in constructions like these:

Please *bring* me the phone book.

We hate to eat and *run*.

Yet some traditionalists insist that the flat, or *to*-less, infinitive is inappropriate in constructions like these:

Do you dare *call* off the wedding at this late date?

Help the children *cut* out cardboard animals.

They didn't know whether to go or *stay.*

Some people would not hesitate to lie, *cheat,* or *wheedle* their way up the corporate ladder.

(For the use of *to* in place of the infinitive, or even omitted, see DRINK THE WATER IF YOU DARE; for the replacement of *to* by *and* in infinitives of purpose, "COME UP AND SEE ME SOMETIME".)

Indirect-object constructions also cause some concern. When both a direct object and an indirect object are given, the indirect one ordinarily comes first, as in "Write me a letter." The indirect object can usually be replaced by a prepositional phrase beginning with *to* or *for,* as in "Write a letter to me." When some people omit the direct object, they also drop an unstressed preposition before the remaining indirect object, as in "Write me"; but others want the preposition retained ("Write to me"). What is unusual, at least to most Americans, is a British elliptical construction like this:

"Her screwed-up black glove dropped to the floor. When Jacob gave it her, she started angrily." (Virginia Woolf, *Jacob's Room*)

Omitting prepositions that are customarily used with certain words ought not to be done lightly. For instance, Strunk and White look upon constructions in which *type* immediately precedes another noun as "common vulgarisms." This, they say, is how to correct them:

"that type employee	that kind of employee
I dislike that type publicity.	I dislike that kind of publicity.
small, home-type hotels	small, homelike hotels
a new type plane	a plane of a new design (new kind)"

The Strunk and White criticism has two targets: the failure to include *of* and the use of *type,* instead of *kind,* in vague references to groups that are not explicitly set apart as separate categories.

According to Theodore Bernstein, another authority on usage, the omission of the preposition *of* after *couple* is "substandard': "You cannot say 'a couple horses' and retain the esteem of your cultivated fellows." Yet *couple* is often used with adjectival force immediately before another noun, especially in casual speech and informal writing (see SEVERAL, FEW, OR COUPLE?). So is *plenty,* as in the phrase *plenty time.*

In the sense of "in spite of" or "notwithstanding," *regardless of*—not *regardless* alone—is ordinarily called for.

Buy the yacht regardless of the cost.

We plan to move regardless of whether we sell our house.

However, *regardless* is sometimes used informally to mean "without regard for, or in spite of objections, difficulties, or the like" or "anyway."

Buy the yacht regardless how much it costs.

We plan to move, regardless.

(See also IRREGARDLESS OR REGARDLESS?)

Whether a preposition is included or omitted often depends on the sense. *Inside,* for instance, is ordinarily not followed by *of* unless "in less than a specified time or distance" or "within the space of" is meant.

Let's take the lawn chairs inside the house.

He said he'd be back inside of an hour.

No trees could be seen inside of four acres.

Similarly, *outside* usually stands alone, being followed by *of* only in the informal sense of "other than; except for."

I left my boots outside the door.

Outside of one or two muggings, the trip was fun.

With impunity and no loss of meaning, prepositions are often omitted at the beginning of adverbial phrases.

We left (on) the same day.

Please sing it (in) the way it was written.

Yet failure to include every preposition needed for sense can lead to confusion, or at least compel the reader or listener to sort out the relation between each phrase and the rest of the sentence. Here are some examples of the so-called suspended prepositional construction:

A group of townspeople expressed their admiration and solidarity with the firefighters. (*Admiration* should be followed by *for.*)

The audience was neither enthusiastic nor sympathetic to the performance. (*Enthusiastic* should be followed by *about* or *over.*)

Maud's parents were more distressed than adverse to her going. (*Distressed* should be followed by *at, by,* or *over.*)

Some measurements and related expressions ordinarily take a preposition and others do not.

The panel is six feet *in* diameter.

The panel is six feet square.

Though not necessarily confusing, this statement by *Rolling Stone* writer Fred Schruers would be more in keeping with established usage if *of* were inserted before *average:*

"Randy—call sign Pogo—is average size, or perhaps a tad under...."

On the other hand, unnecessary prepositions can be disconcerting.

The Philadelphia 76ers came *to within* three games of the Conference-leading Boston Celtics. (*To* is superfluous.)

Her paintings are selling *for between* three and five hundred dollars. (The sentence would read better if *between* were omitted and *and* replaced by *to*.)

Mechanics took the engine *off of* the plane. (*Of* is superfluous. However, for sense: The plane took *off from* the roof.)

Because of the way English words are customarily put together, certain prepositions generally go with certain words to convey intended meanings. Dialogue, for example, can be said to be *adapted to* American English, *for* an American audience, *from* a British play. Moreover, prepositions are sometimes expressed and sometimes simply understood. For instance, when we have a favorable opinion about something, we can either *approve* or *approve of* it. (Idiomatic prepositions, which baffle foreigners and sometimes trip up even native speakers, are dealt with more fully in How COME THE CLOCK ISN'T GOING? and "Some Troublesome Idiomatic Prepositions," a table at the back of the book.)

should or *would*?　See **Shall you return? We should like that.**

"Should the inevitable occur . . ."

If it weren't for the name of the mortuary and a picture of a coffin, the Washington, D.C., readers of the ad with this sonorous opening line probably would have missed the allusion to death. Like their superstitious forebears, civilized people at the end of the twentieth century are reluctant to talk about *death* and *dying* (the two words idiomatically given in reverse order), for fear of tempting fate. When faced with the imminent death of a relative or friend, they are likely to say "if anything should happen to her," "if she doesn't pull through," or "if she doesn't make it," instead of "if she dies"—much less "when she dies."

And the relative or friend to whom the inevitable inevitably occurs does not *die*: he or she *passes* (as if declining a chance to bid in a bridge game), *passes away, passes on, departs, expires, succumbs, loses his or her life, is no more, is lost, is taken.* Even lighthearted slang expressions like *go west, check out, kick the bucket, cash in one's chips, shut up shop, buy the farm,* and *push up daisies* are intended to mask the unpleasant fact of death.

Then the dead are not *dead*: they are *no longer living, gone, no more, deceased, departed, late* ("The late Mr. Somebody-or-Other"), *resting in peace.* Newspaper obituaries, however, do use the word *died*; but unless the person is well known, they ordinarily omit the cause of death or use the code words *after a short illness,* for a heart attack, and *after a long illness,* for cancer. The word *cancer* is still neither spoken nor written lightly. In 1985 the London surgeons who operated on Princess Margaret said that the segment of the lung they had removed was *innocent*—not *benign* or *nonmalignant,* and certainly not *noncancerous.* That was about the time when, according to L. M. Boyd, an American hospital began replacing the word *death* with *negative patient care outcome.*

Because speaking about all hitherto unspeakables is in vogue, the taboos against the mention of death are weakening. Colleges offer courses on death and dying, hundreds of books and articles are written on how to do it and how to survive others' doing it, and nurses travel about, lecturing on their care of dying patients. Yet many people, especially those in the business, continue to obscure the reality of death by indirect, genteel references to it. *Charnel, graveyard,* and *cemetery* sounded too much like the burial grounds they are, so *memorial park* and *memory garden* took their place. Similarly, *undertaker* became *mortician* and then *funeral director*. But *funeral* moved on to become *last rites* or *the service,* so as not to call attention to the actual burial or cremation. Other expressions invented to talk around the subject of death are *casket* (which sounds more like a small chest for holding precious jewels than does the blunt word *coffin*), *mortuary chapel, funeral home, funeral parlor,* and *slumber room*.

Not only are *ashes* no longer *ashes* but *remains,* its replacement, are no longer *remains*. Reporting on the 1986 convention of the Cremation Association of North America, whose seminars dealt with such subjects as "Creative Memorialization," Steve Rubenstein quoted the executive director, Jack Springer:

> " 'It's "cremains." . . . Sometimes we go the extra step and say "basic elements." But never ashes.' "

Euphemisms—that is, words or phrases that are considered less distasteful or offensive than the more expressive or direct ones they replace—sometimes stem from a regard for others' feelings, reverence, and a distaste for vulgarity, but more often from fear, prudery, and squeamishness. From the Victorian era we inherited a number of them, not necessarily new words but new uses of old words, to drape a curtain around the human body. *Limb* for *leg,* according to *The Oxford English Dictionary,* is now, and especially in the United States, "in mock-modest or prudish use." But this was not always so: as the *OED* notes, in his *Diary in America* (1839), Frederick Marryat wrote:

> "I am not so particular as some people are, for I know those who always say limb of a table, or limb of a piano-forte."

People may not use *limb* instead of *leg* except as a joke nowadays, but many still say *chest* or *bosom* when they mean *breast*. And how often at Thanksgiving dinner do we hear the *breast* and *thigh* of a turkey referred to as the *light* and *dark meat*?

With exquisite taste, advertising agencies began long ago to advise us how to deal with such problems as *fear of closeness* (read *halitosis* or *bad-smelling breath*), *perspiration* (read *sweat*), and *irregularity* (read *constipation*). Even when some started to talk straight, or at least straighter, they still used euphemisms, mainly *bathroom tissue,* for *toilet paper*. Who but a PR person would have had the delicacy to label a drawer containing nothing but two rolls of toilet paper on a United Airlines plane "amenities"?

Probably no English word has more euphemisms than *toilet,* which once meant "a dressing table" or "the process of dressing or grooming oneself, especially one's hair" but, in its current sense of "a room for defecation or urination," is virtually banned. Over the years it has been replaced by such terms as *lavatory; latrine; water closet* (and its abbreviation, *w.c.*); *restroom* (a sign at the front of an intercity bus in Massachusetts proclaims "This coach is restroom equipped for your convenience''); *washroom; men's room; ladies' room* (despite Marilyn French's book, *women's room* has not caught on); *powder room; comfort station; convenience* (mainly British). The slang words include the British *loo* and the American *throne room, can,* and *john* (a portable toilet on some construction sites is called a Johnny on the Spot).

As they rise to leave a room, people often use other oblique phrases to conceal their destination. Some tell their host that they would like to *wash their hands*—a dangerous ploy in countries where the sink and the toilet are in separate rooms. Some, knowing that everywhere in the world public telephones are usually near public toilets, suddenly remember that they must *make a phone call.* (In *You Might As Well Live: The Life and Times of Dorothy Parker*, John Keats tells us that when one of the members of the Round Table of the Algonquin Hotel asked to be excused to go to the men's room, Parker explained, ''He really needs to telephone, but he's too embarrassed to say so.'') Some Britons, though fewer and fewer, still say they are going to *spend a penny* (a reference to the old-currency, preinflation coin slots on the doors of public toilets). Some Americans say they are going to the *potty* (just before they go *beddy-bye*). Others say that they are answering the *call of nature.* Or that they are going to *make a pit stop,* as though, crash helmet in hand, they had just pulled off the Indianapolis Speedway. But in the United States the most widely used euphemism, with no suggestion of soaking in a tub or taking a shower, is *go to the bathroom.* ''Look, Daddy,'' shouts an American child, pointing out of a car window, ''the cow is going to the bathroom!''

For hundreds of years people have sought to disguise or soften their blasphemy, profanity, swearing, and cursing. The euphemism *gad* was applied to *God* in the early seventeenth century; *gosh* and *golly,* in the eighteenth. Through contraction and alteration, *Jesus* became *gee, gee whiz, jeez,* and *jeepers (gee whiz* and *jeepers* originated in the United States); and *by Jesus* became *bejabbers* (''It scared the bejabbers out of me''). *Cripes* (or *cripe*) and *crikey* (or *crickey*) are euphemisms for *Christ.* *Darn* and *dang* stand for *damn* or *damned; heck,* for *hell*—all mild swearwords by today's standards.

Many recent euphemisms are intended to keep people from seeing themselves as others see them. Census reports notwithstanding, there aren't many *old people* or *old folks* left in the United States; they became *the aged* and *the elderly* on their way to becoming *golden-agers* and *senior citizens (seniors* for short). Sometimes they are called *elders*—as in ''Arthritis strikes infants and elders alike''—but, without a possessive pronoun such as *their* or *our, elders* is too suggestive of dignitaries in the community or the church to fit most occasions. *Exceptional children* once needed special attention because they were gifted; now they need it because they are mentally, physically, or emotionally *disabled* or *disadvantaged* (for a time, *handicapped*).

Despite their reputation for refinement—or perhaps because of it—Britons are less given to euphemisms than Americans. The British Broadcasting Corporation television news, for instance, is captioned for the *hard of hearing,* not the *hearing-impaired.* The British Railway can't seem to make up its mind what to call people who are no longer young, or even middle-aged. ''Be kind to your old folks,'' a BritRail billboard begins, but then it adds, ''Give them a Senior

Citizen Rail Token.'' Yet people over sixty know they are OAPs (Old-Age Pensioners): they carry cards to prove it.

Euphemisms are not the only device for giving something a new name so, the theory goes, it will become something new—and more acceptable. See also ''WAR IS PEACE.''

sit **or** *set?*

Pesky little words, *sit* and *set*. It is not the forms of the verbs that cause the trouble, for *set*'s principal parts are invariable and *sit*'s minor irregularities are learned in childhood.

	set	*sit*
Present	(I) *set*	(I) *sit*
Past	(I) *set*	(I) *sat*
Perfect	(I have, had) *set*	(I have, had) *sat*
Progressive	(I am) *setting*	(I am) *sitting*
Future	(I will) *set*	(I will) *sit*

No, the cause of the trouble is grammar books that have been insisting for years that *sit* is always intransitive (that is, takes no object) and that *set* is always transitive (takes an object). We have become so terrorized by that mischievously strict rule that when it comes time to use one verb or the other, we forget that we know how to speak our own language. True, the distinction generally holds:

Sit by the fire.

Set the pears on the window sill.

but the exceptions are too many and too important to be ignored.

These are some of the ways *sit* is used as a transitive verb:

''to place in a seat; cause to sit; seat'' (often used reflexively)

I sat myself down and gave the matter some thought.

Can you sit the baby up in her highchair?

''Just take the reporter's paper away and sit him down in front of a new kind of computer.'' (William Zinsser, *Writing with a Word Processor*)

''Howard Nielson, a proper contender from Utah who sat next to the heckler, tugged at his coat and tried to sit him down.'' (Mary Mc-Grory, ''Reagan's Show of Teeth'')

''to keep one's seat'' (on a horse, etc.)

Fred's still having trouble sitting the horse.

''to have seats or sitting space for''

Does your car sit four or six?

Besides being used dialectally for all intransitive senses of the verb *sit, set* has its own intransitive senses, which are by no means limited to certain regions, communities, or social groups. Indeed, most speakers and writers of English would agree that:

> When the sun goes below the horizon, it sets. It is a setting sun.
>
> When a hen sits on eggs to hatch them, it sets. It is a setting hen.
>
> When a broken bone grows together, it sets.
>
> When gelatin becomes firm, it sets.
>
> When dye becomes fast or permanent, it sets.
>
> When a hunting dog indicates the position of game by pointing, it sets.

slang.   See **Jobbed in a humongous scam, the tweaked-out mobster exclaimed, "Peachy-keen!"**

Slow erosion completely destroyed the old colonial tombstone.

Erosion is a gradual process of wearing away, as when rain, wind, and chemicals in the air cause stone to deteriorate over the years. Something that is destroyed is done away with; in other words, nothing is left. The colonial period of the United States is generally said to be the time between the landing of the *Mayflower,* in 1620, and the signing of the Declaration of Independence, in 1776. So of the eight words in the sentence "Slow erosion completely destroyed the old colonial tombstone," three—*slow, completely,* and *old*—are redundant; that is, "Erosion destroyed the colonial tombstone" would get the same meaning across.

Because they modify other words, adjectives and adverbs are often found in redundant constructions. (Besides *redundancy,* the use of more words than are needed to express an idea is sometimes called *pleonasm* or *tautology.*) For example, we:

> collect *"authentic* replicas" of paintings, even though a *replica* is an exact reproduction of a work of art (in strict usage, it is one made by the original artist).
>
> marvel at how long it's been since Alexander Graham Bell *"first* invented" the telephone, even though the verb *invent* implies thinking up or producing a device not previously in existence.
>
> accept a *"free gift"* on opening a bank account, even though a *gift* is something turned over without cost.
>
> learn how ingredients in a meat loaf are "combined *together,"* even though *combine* means "to mix together."
>
> ask whether it's still "raining *outside,"* even though, unless the roof is leaking, that's where it always rains.
>
> admire a porcelain bowl that "dates *back"* to the Ming dynasty, even though *date* alone conveys the notion of something having its origin in a definite period in the past.

wonder when the detective in a mystery novel will turn up the "*true* facts," even though a *fact* is a thing that is really true.

are warned about the "*resultant* effects" of sunbathing, even though an *effect* is something brought about by a cause or agent, that is, a result.

apologize for an "*unintentional* oversight," even though an *oversight* is a mistake or omission that is made through carelessness, not on purpose.

English has, as well, many established phrases in which one of two words connected by *and* is essentially a repetition of the other and could thus be omitted without affecting the sense. For instance:

each and every

over and above

hue and cry

ways and means

leaps and bounds

null and void

well and good

Moreover, the same word is often repeated, an unnecessary variation is tacked on, or a superfluous word or phrase is added.

Haven't I asked you *time and time again* not to go?

This year's guests were far *fewer in number*.

The evening courses include, *for example*, financial planning, aerobic dancing, bird watching, *and so on*.

But must the criterion of no more words than are necessary for the expression of an idea be rigidly applied? Do English-speakers always have to be as stingy with their words as if they were sending a telegram? A newspaper headline that reads "Governor Seeks Second Term" may convey its message, but this doesn't mean that the article itself has to omit the *the* and the *a* or retain the simple present-tense verb form. Instead, the lead sentence probably says something like "This morning the Governor announced that he would seek a second term." Dictionaries, too, try to compress the most information in the least space, but this doesn't mean that those who consult them are bound to adopt a terse style of speaking or writing, no matter what the occasion.

Redundancy, then, is not simply a matter of right or wrong. Like other aspects of usage, it ought to be looked at in the light of the speaker's or writer's style and intent, the particular occasion, and the audience. Even though certain words or phrases may not be necessary to the sense, they are sometimes justified by the euphony and rhythm of the sentence. They are also often useful for emphasis or for expressing degrees of some quality (as in *a huge crowd*). Besides, by slowing down the communication a bit, an extra word or two can make it easier for the reader or listener to absorb the message.

Many people will continue to be irritated by redundancies like these:

A high school diploma is a *necessary prerequisite.*

Please be here tomorrow *morning* at 10 A.M.

The *consensus of opinion* seems to favor a shorter workweek.

She *showed* little *apparent* interest in the offer.

Most *successful* programs of natural family planning require hours of instruction to be *successful.*

We reluctantly *decided* to make that *decision.*

" 'I'd be happy if they could keep the status quo just the way it is.' " (Ansel Adams, interviewed on the *CBS Evening News*)

" 'It's the unnecessary regulations we don't need.' " (President Ronald Reagan, interviewed on *Bill Moyers' Journal*)

But it doesn't necessarily follow that they will rail against, say, *Easter Sunday* (even though the annual Christian festival of Easter is always held on a Sunday) or against technically redundant constructions like these:

"Makoniky Head and the old gray house perched on its back got dimmer and dimmer, day after day, until by Thursday morning they had disappeared completely." (Shirley Ann Grau, *The Wind Shifting West*)

"His [Rousseau's] insightfulness remains to haunt his readers two centuries after the book was first written." (Peter Gay, "The Age of Self-Scrutiny: A Reading of the Nineteenth Century," *Halcyon 1986: A Journal of the Humanities*)

"There is, for example, the Rogerian system of ploys where the therapist merely repeats back what the patient says." (Jay Haley, "The Art of Psychoanalysis," in *The Use and Misuse of Language*)

"In the OED Supplement, however, Bob Burchfield and his gang added a few earlier examples without comment, suggesting this particular backformation has a long history behind it that makes it hard to put down." (William Safire, "On Language")

"Alistair Cooke stands alone as the most urbane and scholarly presence on American television." (Terrence O'Flaherty, "Emmy and a Very Deserving Cooke")

"Driving a Budget Rent-A-Car between Sacramento and San Francisco one rainy morning in November of 1968 I kept the radio on very loud." (Joan Didion, *The White Album*)

"If the Government, to get interest rates down, is going to cut, cut and cut again into public expenditure—and ministerial meetings are now about little else—then every other spending department has to give an enormous amount if defence is to be exempted." (Fred Emery, "Putting the Tories on the Defensive")

"Eyewitnesses who saw the escaping killers gave descriptions that were virtually worthless and the local police were amateurish." (Review of Ben Bradlee Jr.'s *The Ambush Murders: The True Account of the Killing of Two California Policemen*, in *Publishers Weekly*)

"It was understood by the Iroquois, who were the greatest of orators, finding the right images and then <u>repeating them again and again</u>, with not less but even more vivid force." (Henry Fairlie, "A Loss for Words")

so . . . as or *as . . . as?*   See *as . . . as* or *so . . . as?*

somehow, someway, or *someways?*

The adverb *somehow* conveys the sense of "in a way or by a method not known, stated, or understood." It is often used in the phrase *somehow or other*.

The understudy somehow learned the lines in half a day.

Somehow or other the sloop made it back to port.

Though disapproved of by a number of people, *someway* is widely used in place of *somehow*.

There isn't time, but I'll get it done someway.

Someways is sometimes heard as well.

someone or *somebody?*

The pronouns *someone* and *somebody* are used interchangeably in the sense of "a person unknown or unnamed; some person." As subjects, they are singular and take singular verbs.

Someone (or *somebody*) is sure to come along and give us directions.

Has *somebody* (or *someone*) picked up the tickets?

However, like the pronouns *anyone, anybody, everyone, everybody, nobody, no one,* and others, *someone* and *somebody* can apply to more than one person, of either sex or both sexes. So the pronouns referring to those antecedents are often plural. (See "IF SOMEONE COULD MAKE YOUR CHILD A GENIUS, WOULD YOU LET THEM?")

someplace or *some place?*

Once considered substandard, the adverb *someplace* is now generally accepted in informal speech and writing as a substitute for *somewhere*.

I'm sure there is a gas station someplace near the next intersection.

The band doesn't care where it goes as long as it goes someplace.

As a noun as well, *someplace* is used informally instead of *somewhere*.

Would you trade your summer home in Vermont for someplace in Arizona?

The two-word combination of adjective + noun is used if another word intervenes.

We're looking for some friendly place to move to.

sometime, some time, or sometimes?

As an adverb, *sometime* means "at some time not known or specified" or "at some unspecified time in the future." It used to mean "sometimes" and "formerly" as well, but these senses are now archaic.

I believe the roof was replaced sometime last year.

His new TV movie will be finished sometime this fall.

As an adjective, *sometime* means "former" or "merely occasional; sporadic."

The sometime football star Joe Namath found a second career in TV commercials.

"A Woman Is a Sometime Thing" (a song in *Porgy and Bess*, by George and Ira Gershwin)

Some time, an adverbial phrase, refers to a period or interval.

It's been some time since postage stamps cost five cents.

Sometimes, an adverb, means "at times; on various occasions; occasionally."

Working lunches sometimes include food.

A sometimes successful actress, Miss Q. recently turned to operettas.

It once meant "formerly," but no longer.

somewhere or somewheres?

Somewhere is used mainly as an adverb.

I believe the cabin is somewhere nearby.

The temperature was somewhere about forty degrees.

It is also used as a noun.

Then they gave up New Orleans for somewhere out West.

I'll find somewhere to put the doghouse.

In certain regions, communities, or social groups in the United States, *somewheres* replaces *somewhere*.

spelling: of words with prefixes and suffixes added, see **Who needs a rabbit's foot more: an unlucky person or a luckless one?**; variant, see **Saying goodbye may be hard.**

split infinitives. See **"To err is human; to really foul things up requires a computer."**

spoonerisms. See "**Kinkering Congs Their Titles Take.**"

subject-verb agreement: in number, see **Fish and chips is on the menu again;** in person, see **Either he or I am right.**

subjunctives.   See **The headwaiter asked if I were alone.**

such as or *like?*

Some people believe there is no difference between *such as* and *like* in the sense of "as for example," so they use the terms interchangeably. Others believe there is a difference but don't know what it is, so they alternate between the terms—uncomfortably. Still others, believing they know the difference, use *such as* in singling out one or more items from a class of indefinite number and *like* in referring to one or more items that, though not belonging to the class under discussion, are similar to those that do. So, according to the confident third group, the sentence:

To impressionist painters *such as* Monet, Renoir, and Degas no theme was insignificant.

means that impressionist painters—among them Monet, Renoir, and Degas—considered every theme significant. However:

To impressionist painters *like* Monet, Renoir, and Degas no theme was insignificant.

means that some impressionist painters—unnamed but similar to Monet, Renoir, and Degas—considered every theme significant.

Because there are more people in the first and second groups than in the third, that subtle distinction is rarely made—and when it is, it usually goes unnoticed. Most dictionaries define each expression in terms of the other.

There is in fact a fourth group. It is smaller than the other two, being made up mostly of those who can't decide between *such as* and *like,* and therefore use *as, as for example,* or *for example* instead.

To impressionist painters, *as* Monet, Renoir, and Degas, no theme was insignificant.

To impressionist painters, *as for example* Monet, Renoir, and Degas, no theme was insignificant.

To impressionist painters—Monet, Renoir, and Degas, *for example*—no theme was insignificant.

IN CONVEYING THE NOTION that not every example that might have been given has been given, *and so on, and so forth, and others,* and similar phrases are redundant in *such as* and *like* constructions. For example, the sentence:

South American ruminants, such as the llama, the vicuña, and so on, make good beasts of burden.

would get its point across in more economical ways, including these:

South American ruminants, such as the llama and the vicuña, make good beasts of burden.

The llama, the vicuña, and other South American ruminants make good beasts of burden.

IF THE PHRASE FOLLOWING *such as* or *like* is nonrestrictive—that is, if it could be omitted without changing the meaning of the sentence—some writers are careful to set it off with a comma or commas.

Courses in modern foreign languages, such as Spanish, French, and Italian, often begin in English and build skills in the new languages.

However, they do not use a comma or commas if the phrase is restrictive—that is, if it qualifies or limits the word it modifies in such a way as to affect the meaning of the sentence.

Foreign language courses such as those designed for American diplomats begin in English and build skills in languages like Spanish, French, and Italian.

For more on restrictive and nonrestrictive modifiers, see THE OVAL OFFICE WHICH IS IN THE WHITE HOUSE SYMBOLIZES THE PRESIDENCY.

SOMETIMES THE *SUCH AS* OR *LIKE* phrase is placed so far from the word it modifies that the sentence can be misread. For example:

A number of nineteenth-century women novelists, such as Jane Austen, Emily Brontë, and Emily Dickinson, wrote about deranged characters.

is not the same as:

A number of nineteenth-century women novelists wrote about deranged characters, such as Jane Austen, Emily Brontë, and Emily Dickinson.

Misplaced sentence elements are discussed more fully in "ELECTRIC SHAVER FOR WOMEN WITH DELICATE FLORAL DESIGN ON THE HANDLE."

suffixes.   See **Who needs a rabbit's foot more: an unlucky person or a luckless one?**

T

take, bring, or *fetch?*   See *bring, take,* or *fetch?*

Tennis is a sport I enjoy but which I don't play well.

Most grammar books and usage guides condemn constructions like these:

> Tennis is a sport I enjoy but which I don't play well.

> Tennis is a sport that I enjoy but which I don't play well.

> Buddy Rich, whom many consider the world's greatest drummer and who formed his own band, was on the program.

The remedy they generally prescribe is parallel construction, with the same pronoun appearing at the beginning of each relative clause. (Relative clauses are subordinate clauses introduced by *who, whom, which, that, what,* and the like.)

> Tennis is a sport *that* (or *which*) I enjoy but *that* (or *which*) I don't play well.

> Buddy Rich, *who* is considered by many to be the world's greatest drummer and *who* formed his own band, was on the program.

Or they recommend rephrasing the sentence, perhaps along these lines:

> Tennis is a sport I enjoy but do not master.

> Though tennis is a sport I enjoy, I do not master it.

> I'm not good at tennis, a sport I enjoy.

> Considered by many to be the world's greatest drummer, Buddy Rich, who formed his own band, was on the program.

But not all writers come up to the standards of most grammar books and usage guides.

> "As we all recognize at once, these are words that have a fairly exact sense, but which also have acquired the ability to fit into a wide variety of everyday contexts...." (Stuart Robertson and Frederic G. Cassidy, "Changing Meanings and Values of Words")

> "The information crossed out is the heading needed to alphabetize and sort the cards, but which will not be repeated in typing the final [index] copy." (Mary Hill and Wendell Cochran, *Into Print*)

For more on the commonest relative pronouns, see HEREFORDS, WHO ARE A BREED OF BEEF CATTLE, HAVE WHITE FACES AND RED BODIES; for the use of *that* and *which* in introducing restrictive and nonrestrictive relative clauses, THE OVAL OFFICE WHICH IS IN THE WHITE HOUSE SYMBOLIZES THE PRESIDENCY; and for misplaced relative clauses, "ELECTRIC SHAVER FOR WOMEN WITH DECORATIVE FLORAL DESIGN ON THE HANDLE."

than, **in comparisons.** See **Is it me you like better than her?; Kilimanjaro is taller than any mountain in Africa.**

than whom. See **Who would you turn to for help?**

that. See **Herefords, who are a breed of beef cattle, have white faces and red bodies; The Oval Office which is in the White House symbolizes the Presidency; Tennis is a sport I enjoy but which I don't play well.**

that; this. See **Remove the strings and ends from the beans and cook them in boiling salted water.**

There's no home like Eaton Place.

On sixty-eight Sunday evenings between January 1974 and May 1979, the upstairs Bellamys and their downstairs servants were invited into some 5 million American homes. Not surprisingly, many of their American hosts feel they should be asked, in return, to call at 165 Eaton Place, in London's Belgravia section. Having sherry in the drawing room of that elegant mansion would be doing what comes naturally to dedicated viewers of public television's "Upstairs, Downstairs," for though they may be Americans on the outside, inside they are English—urbane, witty, and free from nasal twang. Whether they live in Cambridge, Massachusetts, or Oxnard, California, they eat bullock's heart stuffed with veal forcemeat, drink their Scotch whisky neat (that is, without ice, water, or an *e*), and turn to the *OED* (what others call *The Oxford English Dictionary*) to settle Scrabble disputes.

By the time Lord and Lady Bellamy's invitation arrives, the Americans will be well on their way toward mastering BESL (British English as a Second Language). Spelling is the least of their worries. There are of course differences in the way British English and American English words are spelled, but none so great as to get in the way of understanding. Which American used to seeing *center, specialize, flavor, traveler, program, gray, offense,* and the verb *practice* is likely to be confused by *centre, specialise, flavour, traveller, programme, grey, offence,* and *practise*? And which by the hyphens in *co-operate, inter-continental,* and *non-smoker,* even though in the States these words are ordinarily written solid, or by those in *no-one, fox-terrier,* and *rapidly-expanding,* even though in the States these words are usually open? Nowadays if a publishing house in one country buys the rights to a book first issued in the other, it may not bother resetting the type in order to adapt the spellings to local usage.

The senses conveyed by certain words require a bit more attention. Yet, again, the differences are too easily exaggerated. As anyone who reads British and American publications or sees British and American television programs and films knows, most of the enormous word stock is identical, and those words and phrases that are peculiar to one country are becoming less and less alien to the other.

Thanks to their reading, the London-bound Americans have already picked up a number of British-English idioms. Here are some of them, with their American-English equivalents.

British English	*American English*
to stick (slang) " 'People creeping and spying,' said Daphne, utterly tense, 'and then talking vulgarly are two things that I simply cannot <u>stick</u>.' " (Elizabeth Bowen, *The Death of the Heart*)	*to stand, endure*
to cotton on to (slang) " 'He's <u>cottoned on</u> at last <u>to</u> the fact that Pattie and I are separate institutions.' " (Iris Murdoch, *The Time of the Angels*)	*to catch on to*
to be quick on the ball (slang) "He'd slipped up. He'd not been <u>quick</u> enough <u>on the ball</u>." (Agatha Christie, *The Clocks*)	*to be on the ball* + *to be quick at the draw*
to make a loss "The management of the Financial Times yesterday warned that it would be seeking 200 voluntary redundancies [workers liable to dismissal] after disclosing that the paper <u>made a</u> small <u>loss</u> in 1980 for the first time in many years." (London *Times*)	*to take a loss*
to chance one's arm "One only regrets that the editor does not follow the practice of other scholarly dictionaries and <u>chance his arm</u> to the extent of revealing the dates of his earliest recorded references." (Randolph Quirk, *The Linguist and the English Language*)	*to take a chance,* *despite the* *likelihood of* *failure*

(For more on idioms, see How come the clock isn't going?)

So, with a working knowledge of their second language, the Anglophiles cross the Atlantic. They may be insensitive to certain levels of British usage—the ability to distinguish, for example, between an expression best reserved for formal occasions and one that is characteristic of informal speech and writing, between a slang term and one suitable for teatime conversation with the Bellamys—but their enthusiasm more than makes up for that lack.

Directly they arrive at Heathrow from *America* (not *the United States* or *the States,* though these terms are being used more and more), the Americans check their *cases* at the *left-luggage office whilst* they look for a *call-box* from which to phone their hotel. Not because they want to *put on side* (show off), but because they are *on holiday* for only a *fortnight* (two weeks, from "fourteen nights"), they *blue* (squander) a good many *quid* (pounds sterling) to take a taxi from the airport to the hotel *in* Sloane Street. The driver of the boxy black *saloon* (sedan)—high enough, it is said, for a gentleman to wear a top hat—is *too polite by half* (excessively polite); he speaks to the visitors only when they ask him the meaning of this sign on the *motorway* into London: "Football coaches not admitted." (They're buses chartered for soccer games.)

After being *knocked up* (awakened by a knock on the door of their hotel room), the Americans set out to see the town. With the street guide *London AZ* ("a" to "zed") at the ready, they take the *underground* to Piccadilly Circus, knowing better than to expect to see clowns and acrobats, because in Britain a *circus* is likely to be an open space in town where streets converge (not to be confused with a *roundabout,* or traffic circle).

So as not to *queue up* (stand in line) for tickets, they ask the *head porter* at the hotel to *book a stall* (reserve an orchestra seat) at a West End theatre. During the *interval* (intermission) they have a *lager* (beer). They are delighted if the play *bombs,* or *goes like a bomb,* for then it's a smashing success, not the failure it would be in the States.

Soon the Americans are bewildered motorists, driving their *hired* car on the left side of the street; filling it with *petrol;* and seeing that a mechanic wearing a *boiler suit* looks after things under the *bonnet* (hood). They store their maps in the *glove box* and, in case of *thundery* showers, their *wellies* (short for *wellingtons,* waterproof boots named after the Duke of Wellington) in the *boot* (trunk).

Most Britons must have read the observation by Lord Conesford (Henry Strauss) that in the United States "the rule appears never to use one word if you can use three," because they go out of their way to make the visitors feel at home. They do this by:

saying "It's pouring with rain."

labeling a liquid detergent "Washing Up Liquid."

advertising "Fully Filled Sandwiches" on restaurant windows.

displaying "Closing Down Sale" signs on storefronts.

flashing "Walk Now" signs at street corners.

posting "Reduce Speed Now" and "Give Way" signs along highways, and "Picking Up and Setting Down Only" signs in loading zones.

(For other views by Lord Conesford on "American pretentious illiteracy," see WASHING DOWN PILLOWS TAKES A STRONG STOMACH.)

When they are not being helpful to verbose Americans in that way, Britons follow a pretty *rum* (odd) rule of their own: never use one word if you can use none. So, dropping *the* before many nouns that take the definite article in the States, they say:

"Try to behave in future."

"How long were you in hospital?"

"The group will be in U.S.A. a fortnight."

"Stuart left university before the end of the term."

The preface to the *BBC Pronouncing Dictionary of British Names* notes that "in both radio and television, News Division has experimented widely."

WHEN IT COMES TO TALKING as though they were to 165 Eaton Place born, Americans are in trouble, for without any question it is intonation and pronunciation that set British English and American English apart. Of course, not *all* British English or *all* American English. What is generally meant by British English is Received Standard—the dialect spoken by the upper classes of London and nearby southeastern English counties, especially by graduates of the great private schools (which Britons call *public schools*) like Eton and Harrow and of Oxford and Cambridge universities—not the dialects of Britain's many other social groups and regions. And what is generally meant by American English is Northern-Midland, the dialect of educated inhabitants of the Middle Atlantic states, the Middle West, and the Far West, not, for the most part, of New England or the South.

Like all other dialects, Received Standard has been affected by processes that change and shape language over time, but because of its conservatism it has managed to make that time longer rather than shorter. The speech of most of today's British Broadcasting Corporation announcers has more in common with that of Lord and Lady Bellamy, whose household from 1903 to 1930 was chronicled on "Upstairs, Downstairs," than it does with that of today's American Broadcasting Company announcers. And more in common with the speech heard on Boston's Beacon Hill than with Cockney (the dialect of East End Londoners like Ruby, the "Downstairs" scullery maid) or with the speech of Liverpudlians like the Beatles.

If Americans are to be taken for native Belgravians, the first thing they must do is get rid of their nasal twang. (Whether or not they actually have one doesn't matter: Britons insist that Americans talk through their noses.) The second step is to trade in their drawl, or slow speech in which the vowel sounds are especially extended, for what everyone describes as immaculately clipped British speech. Unlike most Northern-Midland Americans, whose deliberate intonation borders on a monotonous drone, speakers of Received Standard talk rapidly and excitedly, with many changes of pitch and rhythm in their sentences—whether they are deploring Britain's entry into the Common Market or commenting on the freshness of the scones they are having with tea. Southern Americans probably come closest to having a Received Standard declarative sentence pattern. That is, they too end a statement such as "I am going out" not with the usual American falling inflection, but with a rising inflection, almost as if it were a question without the interrogatory word ("Are you going out?").

Next, to sound properly British, Americans must place a heavy stress on one syllable in most words, usually the first, and then all but do away with syllables whose vowels are unaccented. Instead of pronouncing *strawberry* as strô'ber'ē and *medicine* as med'ə s'n, they must learn to say strô'bri and med'sin. Once they become proficient at telescoping unaccented syllables, they will be able to pronounce *extraordinary* not as ik strôr'd'n er'ē but as ik strôn'ri. Yet not too proficient, because there are some words whose syllables the British inexplicably do not scant: whether the name of a city or a breed of cattle, *Hereford*, for example, is pronounced her'ə fərd (in the States, the breed of cattle is generally called hʉr'fərd).

Pronouncing individual consonant sounds in the Received Standard manner is not easy either. Americans are well on the way if they can imitate the characteristically British rolled *r* sound between vowels, that is, if they can say *very*, *sorry,* and *America* by tapping the roof of the mouth once with the tip of the tongue, just above the teeth. The *veddy* that American comedians are so fond of is not really a good approximation.

Another British *r* sound that causes Americans difficulty—though less for those who come from eastern New England, the South, and some parts of New York—is the one that falls either before a consonant or at the end of a word not followed by a vowel sound. Instead of stretching out the *r* sound in, say, *third* (thur-r-d) or *never* (nev'ər-r), would-be Belgravians must either drop the *r* entirely or turn it into something like a vowel sound (thud, nev'ə). If, while they're doing so, they remember to telescope unstressed syllables as well (pronouncing *literature,* for example, as lit'rə chə, not lit'ər ə chər), they can feel doubly proud.

On the other hand, they must always be on the lookout for opportunities to insert an *r* between one word ending in a vowel sound (usually the short *a,* the "uh," or the "aw" sound) and another word beginning with a vowel. That is, they should say rush'ər ənd chī'nə for *Russia and China,* and ī sôr ī wuz lāt for *I saw I was late.*

Americans find the British *t* almost as difficult as the *r.* To produce a true *t* sound between vowels, in words like *Patty, later,* and *little,* they must tap the tip of the tongue against the upper gum without vibrating their vocal cords (pa'tē). If they allow their vocal cords to vibrate, they end up with the muddy *d-* like sound they used to make back home (pad'ē). (To tell whether their vocal cords are vibrating, they simply place their fingers over their Adam's apple as they say one of the words; if they feel a quiver, the cords are vibrating.)

However bothersome, the consonant sounds are nothing compared with the vowel sounds. In exchanging their flat *a* for the broad *a* in words like *ask, half, class,* and *aunt*—an essential step on their way to passing as upper-class Britons—Americans must pronounce the sound as if it were somewhere between the "ah" in *calm* and the "aw" in *horn.* To do this they must hold the tongue low and flat in the mouth, a skill that inhabitants of eastern New England and parts of the South are usually better at than most other Americans. But knowing how to pronounce the British broad *a* is only half the battle: knowing when to is just as trying. *Can't* and *castle,* for instance, have the sound, but *can* and *cabin* don't. *Shan't* and *shaft* do, but *shall* and *sham* don't.

As if the broad *a* were not enough, Americans must contend with other *a* sounds. They must, for instance, produce a short *a* (as in *pat*) in comp<u>a</u>triot, <u>pa</u>tronize, exp<u>a</u>triate, and <u>pa</u>tronage. Yet, just as they do in the States, they must use a long *a* (as in *page*) in <u>pa</u>tron and <u>pa</u>triarch.

Americans who have been using a long *e* in words like *economic* (ē'kə näm'ik) should not only continue to do so but extend the practice to <u>e</u>poch, <u>e</u>volution, and pr<u>e</u>decessor. On the other hand, if they have been pronouncing *ego* with a long *e* (ē'gō), they should switch to a short one (eg'ō).

Saying ī'thər for *either* and nī'thər for *neither* is no trick for the many Americans who have been doing so all their lives. Besides using the long *i* in the *-ile* ending of *juvenile, reptile,* and other words in which they might have been doing so all along, they must be sure to do it in all similar words, like *agile* and *mobile.*

Using the wrong *o* sound can give Americans away as being Americans just as switching their fork from one hand to the other while eating can. Guests of the Bellamys must pronounce words like *dog, coffee, cost,* and *loss* not with an "aw" sound, as in *horn,* but with a less rounded "ah" sound, as in *pot.*

They must also remember to use a long *o* in the nouns *process* (prō′ses) and *progress* (prō′gres)—as many of them have been doing in their corporate offices back home—but a short one in the noun *produce* (präd′yo͞os). Southerners and New Englanders generally have less difficulty than most of their compatriots in handling the British "yoo" sound, in words like *duty* (dyo͞ot′ē, to rhyme with *beauty,* not with *snooty*), *stupid* (styo͞o′ pid), and *new* (nyo͞o).

Whether Eaton Place Americans become more Eaton Place and less American depends, ultimately, on their pronunciation of certain words—aside, that is, from their impeccable Received Standard intonation and enunciation. They must pronounce:

suggest as sə jest′ (NOT səg jest′)

schedule as shed′yo͞ol (NOT skej′o͞ol)

privacy as priv′ə sē (NOT prī′və sē)

version as vur′shən (NOT vur′zhən)

They must pronounce *wrath* to rhyme with *moth,* not with *bath; leisure* to rhyme with *pleasure,* not with *seizure.*

What's more, they must know the Received Standard way to deal with British proper names, which seem to have been devised only to bedevil Americans. Besides calling the humorist P. G. *Wodehouse* wood′hous, they must pronounce the last name of Lytton *Strachey,* the Bloomsbury writer, as strā′chē, but that of Geoffrey *Strachan,* the managing director of a London publishing house, as strôn. They must also know that the family name in the seventeenth-century painting *The Cholmondeley Sisters,* in the Tate Gallery, is pronounced chum′lē.

When it comes to geographic and place names, Eaton Place Americans must, of course, pronounce the river *Thames* as temz. They must not sound the *h* in *Birmingham* (bur′miŋ əm), but they must in *Sandhurst* (sand′hurst). And they must sound one *h* but not the other in *Chittlehamholt* (chit′l′əm hōlt). They must resist the temptation to sound the *w* in *Greenwich* (whether they pronounce it grin′ij, grin′ich, or grēn′ich), and the temptation not to sound it in *Gatwick* (gat′wik).

There is one final test that Americans must pass if they are to become 165 Eaton Place regulars. They must stress the first syllable of virtually every word that English has borrowed from the French. So it's brō′shoor′ for *brochure* and vər′mo͞oth for *vermouth.* As for *fillet,* it's fil′it.

though or *although?*

As conjunctions meaning "in spite of the fact that" or "granting that," *though* and *although* are virtually interchangeable, whether the adverbial clause they introduce precedes or follows the main clause.

Though (or *although*) the sun was shining, a sharp breeze came off the lake.

A sharp breeze came off the lake, *although* (or *though*) the sun was shining.

Though, but not *although,* is used as an adverb meaning "however" or "nevertheless." It generally falls at the end of a sentence, with or without a comma to set it off.

A sharp breeze came off the lake, though.

A sharp breeze came off the lake though.

Because *though* is not a shortened form of *although* (indeed, it is the older word from which *although* is derived), it takes no apostrophe. Both words have clipped forms of their own: *though* sometimes appears as *tho* or *tho';* *although,* as *altho.*

till or *until*?

Till is not a contraction of *until.* It therefore requires neither an apostrophe (*'till*) nor an apostrophe and spelling change (*'til*). *Till* is, in fact, the older of the two words, dating from the Old English period. In Middle English, *till* was fused with *un-* (as in *unto*), giving us *untill,* now spelled *until.*

There is no question about *till* and *until* having the same two principal meanings. One is "up to the time of" (a specified time or occurrence):

With only 364 shopping days *till* (or *until*) Christmas, get busy!

The other, in a negative construction, is "before" (a specified time):

The pictures will not be ready *until* (or *till*) next week.

Nor is there much question about both words being accepted at all levels of usage, although some people consider *until* somewhat more formal than *till.* Custom, as well as the writer's or speaker's preference on a given occasion, generally determines the choice of one word over the other. *Until* does seem to be used more at the beginnings of sentences; *till,* within them.

Until I moved to Maine I had never seen snow.

I had never seen snow till I moved to Maine.

"To err is human; to really foul things up requires a computer."

When this sign appeared in banks and shops in the 1980s, two kinds of people read it: those who found it amusing and those who could scarcely resist taking out a pencil to "unsplit the infinitive."

According to the hidebound, no word or words should ever be placed between *to* and what they call the other part of an infinitive. So *to really foul things up* ought to be changed either to *really to foul things up* or *to foul things up really.* Never mind that the clause would read as though a computer had written it: all that matters is not separating the preposition *to* and the simple form of the verb that follows it.

Students of brainwashing techniques would do well to make a case study of the so-called split infinitive. How did nineteenth-century grammarians and the schoolteachers who came afterward manage to indoctrinate so many English-speakers so thoroughly as to turn them away from a construction that is fully established in the language? First, they fostered the illusion that *to* and a verb in the infinitive are an inseparable unit. To do so, of course, they had to ignore what anyone who has ever spoken or written the language knows: that the flat, or *to*-less, infinitive is used all the time. We say and write, for instance, "I hope you can *come*," not "I hope you can *to come*"; and "You needn't *bring* anything," not "You needn't *to bring* anything" (see "SHOP MACY'S AND SAVE"). And, conversely, the marker *to* sometimes takes the place of the infinitive, as in "Don't do any more exercise than you want *to*," instead of "Don't do any more exercise than you want *to do*" (see DRINK THE WATER IF YOU DARE).

The second step was inculcating the notion that only the illiterate and ill-bred "split an infinitive." The younger the converts, the better. In a biting *Dallas Times Herald* article on the children's TV lineup for the fall of 1984, Steven Reddicliffe said of a possible Saturday-morning replacement:

> " 'Conan the Grammarian': A series with a message. As Conan (voice provided by Arnold Stang) slays winged monsters and butts heads with unpleasant beings from distant planets, he lectures his friends Billy and Millie on the proper use of commas and colons. 'Verily,' he says in one episode, 'I say to you, do not split infinitives.' Then he cuts the head off a dragon. Entertaining AND educational."

Those who escape Conan's sword are expected not only to retain a fear of and aversion to the "split infinitive" throughout their lives, but to seize every opportunity to bring miscreants into line. One such dedicated person is the London *Sunday Times* writer who said in an article on President Reagan's 1987 State of the Union address:

> " 'He lost, in those precious 25 minutes, the chance to once and for all regain the high ground,' echoed the conservative and ungrammatical Washington Times."

Next on his or her list of knuckles to be rapped were probably those of the colleague who, in the same issue of the *Sunday Times*, said of Sir Roy Strong, the former director of the Victoria and Albert Museum:

> "It was a calculated act on his part to create that image in the 1960s—he still wears dated double-breasted suits and an assortment of ostentatious headgear—enabling Fleet Street <u>to fondly present</u> him as a character you wouldn't quite dare take home to mother."

Now, this writer understands how the language works. Not an arbitrary rule, but the meaning and flow of a particular sentence determine the position of an adverb—whether the verb it modifies is an infinitive or not. That is, an adverb that receives special emphasis is ordinarily placed after the verb it qualifies.

Fleet Street *presented* him *fondly* as a character.

Fleet Street set out to *present* him *fondly* as a character.

On the other hand, to emphasize the action of a verb it is natural and idiomatic to place an adverb before the verb. (In the case of a verb phrase, the adverb generally goes before the main verb but after the auxiliary.)

Fleet Street *fondly presented* him as a character.

Fleet Street *had fondly presented* him as a character.

Fleet Street set out to *fondly present* him as a character.

In their determination not to "split an infinitive," people sometimes modify the wrong verb. That is, if an adverb is placed before the *to*—as in "Fleet Street set out *fondly to present* him as a character"—it modifies not the infinitive *present* but the principal verb, in this case *set out*.

English-speakers who are at home with the language know where adverb modifiers of verbs go to convey meaning, to show emphasis, and to fit naturally in a sentence. They know that invariably placing an adverb between every *to* and an infinitive is as unidiomatic as never doing so.

"It was not possible to actually 'call' Warren: it was necessary instead to 'place' a call' to Warren. . . ." (Joan Didion, *A Book of Common Prayer*)

"To the degree that [Vincent] Canby and the rest of us bourgeois reviewers have tried to politely introduce our classmates to works not of the Hollywood mainstream I think we have honorably discharged our obligations to our own standards and to the art of film." (Richard Schickel, *Time's* movie reviewer, in a letter to the editors of the *New Republic*)

"It is our business to consciously know about their social utility." (Martin Joos, *The Five Clocks*)

"By the spring of 1979, months before Kennedy is said to even have made up his mind, the Carter campaign had field organizations in Iowa, New Hampshire, and Florida." (Elizabeth Drew, *New Yorker*)

"Now, for the first time in his athletic life, [Sean] Salisbury is wondering what it would be like to be told to 'go see the coach and bring your playbook,' to not even make the team, to 'meet the Turk' (to be cut)." (John Marshall, *Seattle Post-Intelligencer*)

"Instead, White House officials sought to subtly undermine public television by shifting the focus of attack from the Federal Communications Commission, a visible and quasi-independent arena, to the OTP [Office of Telecommunications Policy], which was directly under the president's control." (James Ridgeway, *Village Voice*)

" 'I did not come to Washington to idly observe the squandering of the public's airwaves.' " (Newton Minow, former chairman of the Federal Communications Commission)

to or *and*, in **infinitives of purpose.** See "Come up and see me sometime."

U

uninterested or *disinterested*?   See **disinterested or uninterested?**

until or *till*?   See *till* or *until*?

upon or *on*?

The prepositions *upon* and *on* share various senses, so it is usually up to the speaker or writer to decide which fits in a particular sentence. Those who consider *upon* too literary for most occasions would say or write, for example, *a new movie based on Lincoln's life,* instead of *based upon Lincoln's life; she painted on parchment,* instead of *painted upon parchment.*

Upon originally replaced *on* in conveying the notion of "up and on," as in *the dog jumped upon the table.* But today *on,* or more likely *onto,* is used in this sense.

In their idiomatic uses the prepositions are generally not interchangeable. Native English-speakers ordinarily don't say, for example, *cry upon my shoulder* and practically never *once on a time.*

As an adverb, *on* is used in a number of ways, including, for example, *put your shoes on* and *move on. Upon,* however, has only one use as an adverb, and that is in the sense of "on," for completing a verb.

Is that the kind of canvas that Leonardo painted upon?

Upstart name-droppers usually get the cold shoulder.

Strictly speaking, compound words (or, as they more often called, *compounds*) are words made up of two or more other words that can stand alone in speech or writing. They may be written solid (*upstart, sweetheart*), with a hyphen or hyphens (*name-dropper, brother-in-law*), or as phrases of separate words (*cold shoulder, dining room*).

Compounds differ from the words they consist of in several ways. First, the meaning or meanings that a compound conveys go beyond the established meanings of the individual words. For example, *cold* means, among other things, "very chilly" and "not cordial"; *shoulder* usually refers to the joint connecting the arm with the body, as well as the area extending to the base of the neck. Each word can appear in grammatical constructions and contexts of its own.

When we finally arrived at the dinner, we got a *cold* reception.

Max dislocated his *shoulder* at a Beatles concert.

Yet the separate meanings of these words are both enriched and circumscribed by the compound *cold shoulder,* which, in informal usage, denotes deliberate indifference, a rebuff, a snub, or the like.

Similarly, in describing someone who seeks to impress others by frequently mentioning famous or important people in a familiar way, *name-dropper* means far more than the sum of its parts: *name* and *dropper.* And, as applied to someone who has recently come into wealth, power, or the like, particularly if that person behaves in a presumptuous, aggressive way, *upstart* goes well beyond the meanings of the workaday words *up* and *start.*

Another way in which compounds differ from most phrases has to do with the stress patterns of spoken English. When a compound is solid or hyphenated, and sometimes when it is still open, there is greater stress, or force, on the first element. For instance, in saying this sentence aloud, English-speakers would ordinarily utter both words in the phrase *family dinners* with equal stress or with greater stress on the second element:

Many people find *family' dinners'* enjoyable.

But a compound like *homework* would almost certainly receive greater stress on *home* than on *work.*

Schools seem to be assigning a lot of *home'work'* again.

The verb set *tie in* and the compound adjective and noun *tie-in* also illustrate the falling stress that characterizes compounds.

We hope the ad will *tie' in'* our whole line of office supplies.

Let's do a *tie'-in'* ad for our office supplies.

It is easy to see that the way elements of a compound are said aloud is closely related to the way they appear in print or writing. For instance, when *blackbird* and *trademark* are uttered, both *bird* and *mark* receive less stress than *black* and *trade,* and both compounds are solid. On the other hand, in *black eye* and *trade name* both elements are stressed equally (or perhaps *eye* and *name* somewhat more), and both compounds are open. The stress pattern is generally the same in hyphenated and solid compounds. So in both *tie-in* and *tieback* the second elements, *in* and *back*, receive less stress than *tie,* whereas in *tie clasp* both elements are stressed equally.

The three types of compounds—open, hyphenated, and solid—are by no means fixed in their forms. For one thing, compounds that are open as one part of speech may take a hyphen when they function as another part (so that, say, the noun *state of the art* becomes the adjective *state-of-the-art* and the noun *roller skate* becomes the verb *roller-skate*). For another, open compounds tend to lose the space between their elements.

Following the trend toward eliminating both space and hyphens between short words that are considered a unit, the adverb and adjective phrases *up stage* and *up-stage,* in reference to the back of a stage, became *upstage.* But the process of linguistic change did not stop there. A graphic verb was created to describe the behavior of an actor who draws attention to himself or herself by moving to the back of the stage and thus obliging the other actors to face away from the audience: *upstage.* The verb now applies, as well, to nonactors who draw attention to themselves at the expense of another person or other people in the group.

One reason why some compounds change as slowly as they do—and others not at all—is, as noted above, the usual relationship between the written form of a compound and the stress placed on its elements in speech. *Lame duck* is not likely to be written either as *lame-duck* or as *lameduck* until *duck* receives less stress than *lame,* that is, until English-speakers break their habit of stressing both elements equally and, as they do in *lamebrain,* begin reducing the stress on the second element.

Another reason is that writers and readers find some compounds whose elements are run together both ugly and unreadable. So while *schoolteacher* is acceptable, *schooldistrict* is not, at least so far. Yet, with *stomachache, headache, backache,* and *bellyache* around—looking like the lyrics of a Carmen Miranda samba—it's hard to see why anyone's sensibilities would be offended by *schooldistrict* or, for that matter, by *kellygreen, salestalk, walkingpapers,* or *numberone.*

However slowly, many open compounds do replace the space between their elements with a hyphen. For instance, a spelled-out fraction used as a noun was once written as two words (as in *two thirds of the votes*), but now it is ordinarily hyphenated (*two-thirds of the votes*), just as the adjective form is (*a two-thirds vote*).

The route from hyphenated to solid compounds is smooth and getting faster all the time. A few Americans may even remember that *today* once appeared in print as *to-day; weekend* as *week-end; southeast* as *south-east; carsick* as *carsick; percent* as *per-cent;* and *gatekeeper* as *gate-keeper.*

Yet, in their rush to solid-form status, many open compounds do not pause long enough to take on a hyphen. So *steel worker* became *steelworker, copy editor* became *copyeditor,* and *ball park* became *ballpark.* And the frequently used adverb meaning ''now'' or ''nowadays'' is more likely to appear in print as *anymore* than as *any more.*

Temporary Compounds

A good, up-to-date dictionary can answer most questions about whether an established compound should be written solid, hyphenated, or open. What is more worrisome for writers and editors are the so-called temporary compounds, especially compound adjectives, whose form depends on the grammatical construction of the sentence. Because such phrases are thought of as a unit in a particular sentence, not merely as isolated words, they are sometimes hyphenated to prevent ambiguity. For instance, ''Are you *ready to eat lobsters* tonight?'' is one kind of question; ''Will you bring *ready-to-eat lobsters* tonight?'' another. And ''Are these lobsters *ready to eat*?'' still another (here an idiom meaning ''ready to be eaten'' is at work).

The following guidelines on the treatment of some temporary adjective compounds reflect current American usage, inconsistencies and all:

> A compound adjective that consists of an adjective and a noun is ordinarily hyphenated if it precedes the noun it modifies.

a *small-car* dealer

an *internal-combustion* engine

rapid-fire questioning

a *long-term* loan

the *open-door* policy

The hyphen prevents misreading. Without it, one might think, for instance, that *a small car dealer* is a small person who sells cars, not a person who sells small cars. However, usage sanctions the open style for an adjective compound whose meaning as a unit is so well established that no ambiguity is likely.

a *high school* program

foreign language textbooks

an *open shop* arrangement

a *public television* series

social security benefits

A compound adjective formed by a participle and a noun is usually hyphenated when it precedes the noun it modifies.

nursing-home care

a *frozen-sperm* bank

the *heating-oil* shortage

working-group members

But, again, if a compound is so well established that it is not likely to be misread, the hyphen is often omitted.

cooking school catalogues

a *parking lot* attendant

An adjective compound formed by an adverb and either a participle or an adjective is ordinarily hyphenated when it precedes the noun it modifies. Otherwise the sentence might be confusing. For instance, on first reading, *a fast moving train* might suggest that a fast train, as opposed to a slow one, is in motion, whereas *a fast-moving train* leaves no room for ambiguity.

a *long-standing* controversy

above-mentioned styles

clean-burning fuel

most-pressing problems

still-active members

"TV watchers," that is, if it were changed to "Us have
Clearly not, so in each case the subjective form of the pr

Those who try to follow at least the basic principles of I
it just as disconcerting to see or hear the subjective form o
used when the objective form is required as the other w
"Will you be writing to she and I?" is no improvement ov
be hearing from you?" (see THE BALL DROPPED BETWEEN HE A
The question of which form of the pronoun is appropriate a
in a comparison, after *than* or *as* is still hotly contested (
BETTER THAN HER?).

Some compounds of this kind are hyphenated whether they come before or after the noun they modify.

    high-flying

    ill-suited

    low-priced

    short-tempered

A compound adjective that consists of an adverb ending in *-ly* and either a participle or an adjective is ordinarily open, whether it comes before or after the noun it modifies.

    a *badly administered* program

    an *enormously successful* fund-raiser

    a *wildly enthusiastic* audience

    rapidly occurring events

If the first element of a compound adjective is a flat adverb (one not ending in *-ly*), the compound is ordinarily hyphenated—as long as it precedes the noun it modifies.

    a *well-administered* program   (BUT a program that is *well administered*)

    a *little-known* singer   (BUT a singer who is *little known*)

    the *best-dressed* student   (BUT the student who is *best dressed*)

However, whether it comes before or after the noun, a compound adjective is ordinarily not hyphenated if it is preceded by a modifier of its own.

    a *very well administered* program

    a *distressingly little known* singer

    the *all-time best dressed* student

FEW SOURCES OF ENGLISH WORDS are richer than compounding. Besides drawing on the huge supply of ready-made compounds, speakers and writers are free to put together two or more distinct words to express a single, new idea of their own. Though many of these creations don't outlast the occasions they celebrate, those that other English-speakers find useful will, for a time at least, be part of the common word stock.

Compounding is of course not the only way words are added to the English vocabulary. Among the others is a process by which prefixes, suffixes, and combining forms change the meanings of established words and create entirely new ones. For more on this kind of word building, which is in fact sometimes confused with compounding, see WHO NEEDS A RABBIT'S FOOT MORE: AN UNLUCKY PERSON OR A LUCKLESS ONE?

Us TV watchers have strong convictions.

In the 1960s we were told that "Us Tareyton smokers switch," and by way of proof we were shown photogr… women with blackened eyes. By the end of the 1970s, Tareyton smokers would rather light than fight." The rejection of violence, and perhaps of large amounts o… mendable, but its grammar was as bad as ever. When a subject of a verb, it should be in the subjective form, *they*), not in the objective one (*me, him, her, us, th…* smokers were determined to do instead of something… started out by saying "We Tareyton smokers would ra…

That grammatical rule apparently did not appeal to th… American Presidents, either. Billy Carter said that, o… brother to make a full disclosure about his Libyan con… President:

"'Jimmy, I'm not taking any advice on that. Me and …ing on that and we're going to decide what to do.' …

And after Mrs. Reagan confirmed the rumor that the estranged from the President's son Michael, the United… response:

"'It appears to us that Nancy is attempting to justify…her have not seen their newest grandchild (Ashley, 1…her birth.'"

It is not surprising to hear someone slip up by using… pronoun in a sentence that requires the subjective form,… interview. Yet we sometimes find the same mistake in… and proofreaders are supposed to have gone over the pie… upon the networks to finance public television, *New,*… Kitman wrote:

"They, not us, should pay."

In a question-and-answer column, the *Los Angeles Tim…* began his reply to a television viewer this way:

"You—and now us—have fallen prey to a little adver… to get people to talk about their commercial and pr…

And an article by Dr. James Drane in the *Arkansas Ti…*

"Repent! Who, Us?"

Whether the objective form of a pronoun should be re… form can be easily tested, especially if another elemen… noun in question. Does the sentence sound all right … removed? For instance, would Billy Carter have said … that"? Would Marvin Kitman have written "Us shoul… sentence like "Us TV watchers have strong conviction…

V

verb sets.   See **Washing down pillows takes a strong stomach.**

verbal or *oral*?

Some people discriminate carefully between these two adjectives. They use *verbal* to describe something that is conveyed only in words, whether written or spoken, as distinguished from actions, ideas, or facts.

Besides distributing videocassettes, the engineer gave a verbal description of the project.

And they use *oral* to describe something that is uttered by mouth, or spoken.

The manager gave the employees an oral promise, assuring them that a new contract was being drafted.

However, many people use both *verbal* and *oral* to mean "spoken," resorting to *written* when they want to be certain of being understood. That's why they are so amused by Sam Goldwyn's saying "A verbal contract isn't worth the paper it's written on." (For other Goldwynisms, see "You're a goody-goody gumshoes.")

verbs: active and passive, see **The plane was got out of by twelve weary passengers; irregular,** see **The Walrus and the Carpenter weeped like anything; linking,** see **Fish and chips is on the menu again; People who want to arrive safe don't drive drunkenly; subjunctive mood of,** see **The headwaiter asked if I were alone.**

verb-subject agreement: in number, see **Fish and chips is on the menu again; in person,** see **Either he or I am right.**

A vet rushed to the zoo by cab to treat a hippo with the flu.

Who nowadays doesn't call a *veterinarian* a *vet*, a *zoological garden* a *zoo*, a *taxicab* a *cab*, a *hippopotamus* a *hippo*, and *influenza* the *flu*? The fact is, dropping part of a word or phrase is a natural tendency in English.

The process that turned, say, *veterinarian* (or *veteran*) into *vet* is known as *clipping*, and the words so formed are called *clipped words, clipped forms, clippings,* or *clips*. Many of them start out as slang, and some, like *pen* for *penitentiary,* are not likely to get beyond this highly informal, sometimes humorous, and often picturesque variety of language. (For a discussion of slang, see Jobbed in a humongous scam, the tweaked-out mobster exclaimed,

"PEACHY-KEEN!'') Other clipped forms, like *grad* for the noun *graduate,* eventually find a place in informal speech and writing. And still others, like *piano* for *pianoforte,* do not have to climb the ladder of usage to become accepted as standard.

Like *grad, hippo, pen, piano, vet,* and *zoo,* most clippings retain only the first syllable or syllables of longer words or phrases. For example:

ad (from *advertisement*)
auto (from *automobile*)
champ (from *champion*)
chimp (from *chimpanzee*)
condo (from *condominium*)
co-op (from the noun *cooperative*)
disco (from *discothèque*)
exam (from *examination*)
fan (from *fanatic*)
glad (from *gladiolus*)
hi-fi (from *high fidelity*)
high-tech (from the adjective *high-technology*)
kilo (from *kilogram* or *kilometer*)
lab (from *laboratory*)
limo (from *limousine*)
math (from *mathematics*)
mono (from *mononucleosis*)
Op-Ed, op-ed (from *Opposite Editorial page*)
percent (from *per centum*)
phone (from *telephone*)
photo (from *photograph*)
polio (from *poliomyelitis*) ·
pro (from *professional*)
prof (from *professor*)
pub (from *public house*)
radio (from *radiotelegraphy*)
rhino (from *rhinoceros*)
sci-fi (from *science fiction*)
sleuth (from *sleuthhound*)
stereo (from *stereophonic, stereotype,* or *stereotypic*)
strobe (from *stroboscope*)
typo (from *typographical error*)
van (from *vanguard*)

Cab, too, dropped all but the first syllable of a longer word (the French-derived *cabriolet*), first to denote a horse-drawn hired carriage and later to describe an automobile like a convertible coupe. However, when most people say *cab* nowadays, they think of the shortened form of *taxicab,* which in turn is a shortened form of *taximeter cab.* Similarly, in the formation of *flu,* both the beginning and the end of *influenza* fell by the way. So how a clipped form got that way is not always obvious.

These, though, are clearly words from which the first syllable or syllables have been dropped:

bus (from *omnibus*)
cello (from *violoncello*)
chute (from *parachute*)
coon (from *raccoon*)
copter (from *helicopter*)
pike (from *turnpike*)
possum (from *opossum*)

Some clipped forms undergo spelling changes so as not to lose the pronunciation of the words or phrases they derive from. As noted above, for instance, *high-technology* gives us *high-tech;* yet, to preserve the "hard" *k* sound, a *high-technology* enthusiast is sometimes referred to in print as a *hi-teckie*. Here are some others:

mike (from *microphone*)
nuke (from *nuclear*)
perk (from *perquisite* or *percolate*)
sync, as well as *synch* (from *synchronize* or *synchronization*)

Some words are further altered in the clipping process. *Bicycle* becomes *bike;* *atmospherics* becomes *sferics* (with *spherics* a variant spelling). And although most given names follow the usual patterns (that is, *Vince* from *Vincent; Beth* from *Elizabeth*), others are respelled as well as shortened (*Bill* or *Billy* from *William; Peg* or *Peggy* from *Margaret*).

Clipping is but one of several processes by which words and phrases are shortened. If so many *abbreviations* did not end with a period, they would probably most closely resemble clipped words (see AN LL.D. KO'D A BRIG. GEN. AT A BYOB PARTY). *Acronyms* are not simple shortenings, but words formed from the first, or first few, letters in a series of words (see NASA's LOX NEEDS NO BAGELS). And, unlike clipped words, *contractions* are written with an apostrophe to show where a letter or letters have been omitted (see DON'T SHE KNOW IT'LL BE DARK SOON?). For a general discussion of English-speakers' tendency to drop sounds, letters, and even whole syllables from words and phrases, see GRAMPA GOT HIS STRENTH BACK LAST FEBUARY.

vogue words. See **In one year and out the other.**

voice, active and passive. See **The plane was got out of by twelve weary passengers.**

W

The Walrus and the Carpenter weeped like anything.

No, they didn't. In Lewis Carroll's *Through the Looking-Glass*, "The Walrus and the Carpenter / Were walking close at hand: / They <u>wept</u> like anything to see / Such quantities of sand."

Saying *weeped* instead of *wept* is something that children and nonnative English-speakers are especially likely to do, although adults whose first language is English are sometimes startled to hear themselves make the same kind of mistake. After all, most English verbs form both their past tense and their past participle by adding the suffix *-ed* to the infinitive. So if the infinitive is, say, *paint*, we might say "She *painted* the portrait last year" and "Has he always *painted* still lifes?"

Some infinitives require a spelling change before the *-ed* is added. A single final consonant preceded by a single vowel is ordinarily doubled if the final syllable is stressed, so *slam* becomes *slammed* (but, because the final syllable is not stressed, *total* becomes *totaled*, without a doubling of the *l*). A final *e* is ordinarily dropped, so *smile* becomes *smiled*. And a final *y* is ordinarily changed to *i*, so *satisfy* becomes *satisfied*. (For more on the spelling changes called for when suffixes and prefixes are added, see WHO NEEDS A RABBIT'S FOOT MORE: AN UNLUCKY PERSON OR A LUCKLESS ONE?)

Without thinking about it, we pronounce the regular past-tense and past-participle forms of many verbs as if they ended with the sound of *t* instead of *d* (*laughed*, *talked*, *hoped*, *kissed*, *washed*, *waxed*, for example), even though they are not actually spelled with a final *t*. A few past-tense and past-participle forms, however, do end in *t* (*dealt*, for instance, instead of *dealed*). Some take either the *-ed* or the *-t* ending (so we have, for example, both *leaped* and *leapt* for *leap*, *dreamed* and *dreamt* for *dream*, and *learned* and *learnt* for *learn*). In others, as *-ed* is changed to *-t*, one of the doubled vowels in the infinitive is dropped (so *creep* becomes *crept*, *feel* becomes *felt*, *keep* becomes *kept*, *sleep* becomes *slept*, and *weep* becomes *wept*).

These exceptions to the usual way of forming the past tense and the identical past participle are by no means the whole story of irregular verbs. As most schoolchildren know from hours of drill, scores of other verbs form their past tense and past participle very differently. In several frequently used verbs the infinitive is so changed that the irregular past tense and past participle must simply be learned. For instance:

Infinitive	Past Tense	Past Participle
be	*was*	*been*
buy	*bought*	*bought*
catch	*caught*	*caught*

Infinitive	Past Tense	Past Participle
do	did	done
go	went	gone
have	had	had
leave	left	left
make	made	made
say	said	said
teach	taught	taught
think	thought	thought

In other irregular verbs it is mainly the base, or root, vowel that is changed, sometimes with *-n* or *-en* added to the past participle. Many of these verbs have one irregular form for the past tense and another for the past participle. Here are some:

Infinitive	Past Tense	Past Participle
begin	began	begun
choose	chose	chosen
come	came	come
drive	drove	driven
eat	ate	eaten
fall	fell	fallen
give	gave	given
know	knew	known
lead	led	led
lie	lay	lain (see LAY OR LIE?)
meet	met	met
ride	rode	ridden
run	ran	run
see	saw	seen
sing	sang	sung
sit	sat	sat
speak	spoke	spoken
swim	swam	swum
take	took	taken
wear	wore	worn
write	wrote	written

A number of verbs have more than one generally accepted form for either the past tense or the past participle, or both. In some cases a slightly different meaning is attached to one form or the other. For example, *struck* is the past tense of *strike*. For most senses of the verb, *struck* is also the past participle, but in certain senses, especially "to afflict, as with disease, pain, or death" and "to remove or expunge," as from a list, minutes, records, or the like, *stricken* is more likely to be used. The past tense of *fly* is ordinarily *flew* (as in "The gulls flew straight out to sea"), but when it comes to baseball, it is *flied* ("The batter flied out to the shortstop"). *Hang* has two past-tense and past-participle forms, whose use, many people believe, depends on the meaning to be conveyed (see HUNG OR HANGED?). For the following verbs, though, the choice depends mainly on personal preference.

Infinitive	Past Tense	Past Participle
awake	awoke or awaked	awaked
dive	dived or dove	dived
dream	dreamed or dreamt	dreamed or dreamt
drink	drank	drunk or (informal) drank
dwell	dwelt or dwelled	dwelt or dwelled
fit	fitted or fit	fitted
forbid	forbade or forbad	forbidden
forecast	forecast or forecasted	forecast or forecasted
forget	forgot	forgotten, forgot
get	got	got, gotten
kneel	knelt or kneeled	knelt or kneeled
knit	knitted or knit	knitted or knit
leap	leaped or leapt	leaped or leapt
learn	learned or learnt	learned or learnt
light	lighted or lit	lighted or lit
mow	mowed	mowed or mown
plead	pleaded or (informal or dialectal) pled or plead	pleaded or (informal or dialectal) pled or plead
prove	proved	proved or proven
shred	shredded or shred	shredded or shred
shrink	shrank or shrunk	shrunk or shrunken
sink	sank or sunk	sunk
sneak	sneaked or (informal) snuck	sneaked or (informal) snuck
spring	sprang or sprung	sprung
work	worked or wrought	worked or wrought

The irregularity of still other verbs is no change at all. For example:

Infinitive	Past Tense	Past Participle
beset	beset	beset
cut	cut	cut
hurt	hurt	hurt
let	let	let
put	put	put
read	read	read
set	set	set

PRESENT PARTICIPLES DO NOT CREATE the problems that past participles do. They are all regular in having -ing added to the infinitive ("I am weeping," for example). Certain spelling changes are made, though, in attaching the suffix. That is, *mope* becomes *moping; mop, mopping; infer, inferring;* and so on. These changes, too, are dealt with in WHO NEEDS A RABBIT'S FOOT MORE: AN UNLUCKY PERSON OR A LUCKLESS ONE?

"War is peace."

Nonsense, you say. One cannot hold two contradictory beliefs at the same time, for to do so would be to play tricks with reality. Yet, through just such a process, slogans like "War is peace," "Freedom is slavery," and "Ignorance is strength" are accepted without question in the society brought terrifyingly to life in George Orwell's novel *Nineteen Eighty-four. Newspeak*, the language invented by the authorities in that totalitarian society, has a word for deliberate deception coupled, astonishingly enough, with the firmness of purpose that goes with complete honesty: *doublethink.*

> "To tell deliberate lies while genuinely believing in them, to forget any fact that has become inconvenient, and then, when it becomes necessary again, to draw it back from oblivion for just so long as it is needed, to deny the existence of objective reality and all the while to take account of the reality which one denies—all this is indispensably necessary. Even in using the word *doublethink* it is necessary to exercise *doublethink*. For by using the word one admits that one is tampering with reality; by a fresh act of *doublethink* one erases this knowledge; and so on indefinitely, with the lie always one leap ahead of the truth."

Though *weasel words* (probably so named because of the weasel's habit of sucking out the contents of an egg without destroying the shell), *double talk,* and *doublespeak* are not complete entirely artificial languages, they are similar to *Newspeak* in their intent to distort or reverse the truth. All draw on euphemisms, that is, words or phrases considered less distasteful or offensive than the more expressive or direct ones they replace. Yet, however trying they may be, euphemisms are sometimes used out of kindness, reverence, and a distaste for vulgarity, whereas those other corrupt forms of English invariably seek to mold opinion through deception. (For more on euphemisms, see "SHOULD THE INEVITABLE OCCUR . . .").

Day after day, government agencies, corporations, advertising firms, and individuals turn out purposely ambiguous or misleading words and phrases. (They also use jargon and gobbledygook, which are discussed in A CONCEPT-ORIENTED FRAMEWORK MAY EFFECTUATE A CONSENSUS OF OPINION IN TERMS OF THE MAXIMIZATION OF A MEANINGFUL CONTINUUM OF PROGRAM FACTORS.) Some of the double talk is intended to make the negative seem positive; the sinister, palatable if not downright friendly. For example:

> To many people, *pacification* brings to mind quieting a noisy, fretful baby with a teething ring. During the Vietnam War it meant reducing a village or district to submission through burning and sometimes napalming.

Not everyone approves of nuclear war, but who could object to a *clean bomb,* which produces little immediate fallout as it kills thousands of people?

One could work up an appetite reading about the United States' secret bombing of Cambodia that began early in 1969. These B-52 raids—3,695 of them—were, according to Arnold R. Isaacs's book *Without Honor,* "given the code name Menu; specific target areas, all within a few miles of the Vietnamese border, were called Breakfast, Lunch, Dinner, Supper, Snack, and Dessert."

After a bombing raid in Cambodia, a U.S. Air Force press officer told reporters, "You always write it's bombing, bombing, bombing. It's *not* bombing! It's air support!" For that statement the colonel won the 1974 Doublespeak Award; this prize is given each year by the National Council of Teachers of English (NCTE) to call attention to "misuses of language with pernicious social or political consequences."

President Ronald Reagan gave a new name to the MX intercontinental ballistic missile, which can carry 10 or more warheads: *Peacekeeper.* That inventiveness helped earn him the NCTE Doublespeak Award for 1983.

The U.S. rescue mission that in April 1980 fell apart in the Iranian desert, miles from the hostages in Tehran, was not a failure; it was, in President Jimmy Carter's words, an "incomplete success."

Three American servicemen were killed and 16 injured while unloading a Pershing II missile, not because of an explosion but because of an "unplanned rapid ignition of solid fuel." The U.S. Army major who clarified that point was a contender for the NCTE's 1985 Doublespeak Award. So were the Marine Corps officials who explained that 6 marines had been killed and 11 seriously wounded not in a crash of a helicopter but in its "hard landing."

In its official reports on the status of human rights in countries around the world, the State Department announced, it would refer to killing as the "unlawful or arbitrary deprivation of life." That was half the reason why it won the NCTE's Doublespeak Award for 1984. The other half was its saying that the United States and Caribbean occupation forces were not arresting Grenadians and others suspected of opposing the invasion of Grenada: "We are detaining people. They should be described as detainees." (That was the October 1983 invasion described by the Pentagon as a "predawn, vertical insertion.")

In 1981 the chief economist in the Office of Management and Budget decided that *revenue enhancement* looked better than *tax increase* in a budget fact sheet used by the White House. If that term was not acceptable, he had another one ready: *receipts strengthening.*

When we hear about an *oil spill,* we think of masses of sticky, yellowish-green or black goo despoiling beaches and destroying sea life. But a *pancake*? That's maple syrup time! In 1979 an Associated Press report on oil slicks reaching the Texas coast from a runaway Mexican well included this enticing statement:

> "The first of what are expected to be many large 'pancakes' of oil came ashore Monday evening on Mustang Island about 28 miles south of Arkansas Pass, and two other pancakes were beached in front of hotels in the town of South Padre Island."

Yellowcake sounds delicious too. It is uranium oxide, U_3O_8, processed into fuel for nuclear reactors.

Before, during, and after the near-disaster at the Three Mile Island nuclear plant, in Pennsylvania, the nuclear power industry invented terms like *energetic disassembly* when it meant "explosion"; *rapid oxidation* when it meant "fire"; and *event, incident, abnormal evolution, normal aberration,* and *plant transient* when it meant "reactor accident." To describe *plutonium contamination*, the industry used *infiltration* or said that "plutonium has taken up residence." It won the NCTE Doublespeak Award for 1979.

If funds exchanged or invested in such a way as to conceal their illegal or improper souce were called *dirty money,* we would know what is meant. So, as we learned during the Watergate hearings, they are called *laundered money,* which calls to mind a sunny day with children's pajamas fluttering on a clothesline.

Some cartons of California grapefruit bear the label "Fruit NOT fumigated. Certification based on negative inspection." Whether this means that there is no inspection, that only the grapefruits that need inspection get it, or something else, grapefruit eaters ought to feel reassured.

Advertising gives double-talkers a good opportunity to make the commonplace seem distinguished; the insignificant, momentous.

Page after page of television ads show both a "huge 19″ diagonal" and a "giant 19″ diagonal." But the stores always seem to be out of either a "regular 19″ diagonal" or a "small 19″ diagonal."

Wool that has never been processed has long been known as "virgin wool." Nowadays, notebooks are proclaimed "virgin vinyl."

TV commercials are not commercials on TV; they are "messages"— usually "brief" and "important" ones.

Whatever happened to *singers*? They've become *vocalists*—just as *lawyers* have come *attorneys; mechanics, car maintenance specialists; janitors, engineers* (after a stint as *custodians*); and *stockbrokers, investment bankers.* And for the same reason that *jobs* have become *positions.* When executives lose theirs, they go through a process known as *outplacement;* when workers, some of them *recurrent* (formerly *part-time*) lose theirs, they turn to the *human resources* (once *unemployment*) *office.* Mexican agricultural laborers who enter the United States without working papers used to be called *wetbacks* because many of them crossed the border by swimming or wading the Rio Grande; later they became *illegal aliens* (*illegals* for short) or *undocumented workers;* a new immigration bill sees some as *guest workers.*

When trade in goods, stocks, or a particular commodity slackens, the market goes through a *period of price adjustment.* People in the business hate to use the word *slump.* So do baseball players, whose slumps are simply *periods of adjustment.*

By that same process of discarding a word once its meaning has caught up with it, these are some of the terms double-talked into existence. They can, of course, just as easily be double-talked out of it.

Old Term	New Term
race	*racial status*
ethnic group	*heritage group*
extension course	*continuing education*
classroom desk	*individualized learning station*
riot	*demonstration*
agitator	*activist*
strike	*job action*
scab	*replacement worker*
sex change	*gender reidentification*
mixed marriage	*ecumenical marriage*
alimony	*rehabilitative maintenance*
suicide	*self-termination*
vanity publishing	*self-publishing*
summertime rerun	*encore performance*
heavy rain	*major precipitation event*
secondhand car, used car	*previously owned car*
dashboard (of a car)	*instrument center*
telephone	*voice terminal*
hip flask	*personal-size bottle*
airport waiting room	*boarding lounge*
trailer	*mobile home, RV* (recreational vehicle)
rug, carpet	*floor covering*
picture	*wall hanging*
shoplifting	*inventory shrinkage*
interior decorator	*interior designer*

What used to be a *house* is now a *home.* Foods that have had their nutrients taken out and then put back are *enriched*; those that have had the same thing done to their vitamins are *fortified.* Cartons that have been damaged and later patched are *refreshed.* A mongrel dog isn't even a *mutt* anymore: it's a *random-bred dog.*

Washing down pillows takes a strong stomach.

Anyone reading the headline "How to Wash Down Pillows" would probably be puzzled for a moment, but if the headline were changed to "How to Wash Polyester Pillows," the reader would accept it at once. That's because the verb *wash* ordinarily refers to cleaning something with water or some other liquid. So an article on how to wash polyester-filled pillows would cause no surprise. Yet when *wash* is combined with *down,* it often has to do with eating something and then following it with a drink. So in this case the reader might think that the article gives suggestions not on how to use a liquid to clean down-filled pillows but on how to swallow pillows of any kind and then take a drink to clear the gullet.

Such a double take is less likely in speech. By placing greater stress on *down* as an adjective modifying *pillows* than on *down* as an adverb combined with the verb *wash,* the speaker makes the difference in meaning clear at once.

Adjective: Do you know how to wash *down* pillows?

Adverb: Do you know how to wash down *pillows?*

Countless English verbs, of course, do their job entirely on their own, without being combined with adverbs. *Mince,* for example, has several meanings, including these:

"to cut up or chop up into very small pieces"

Mince the parsley before adding it to the sauce.

"to express or do with affected elegance or daintiness"

Chris minced into the restaurant, waving a gold cigarette holder.

"to lessen the force of; weaken, as by euphemism"

The judge minced no words in sentencing the arsonist.

But none of its meanings is changed by the addition of an adverb. Parsley is minced: it is not minced up, down, about, or out.

Verbs that follow the pattern of *wash* by taking on new meanings when combined with adverbs are called verb sets or phrasal verbs. Because these units add up to more than the sum of the separate meanings of their elements, they are idioms, so shown in most dictionaries. (For more on idioms, see How COME THE CLOCK ISN'T GOING?)

The simple verb *look,* for example, is generally taken to mean "to direct one's eyes in order to see."

Look at the full moon. (Here the preposition *at,* meaning "in the direction of," is not part of a verb set.)

But when adverbs (sometimes with prepositions piled on) are combined with *look,* the verb takes on a dozen or so special meanings. Here are some of them:

Look after means "to take care of; watch over."

Please look after my plants while I'm away.

Look back means "to recall the past; recollect."

Why do so many people over forty look back to the "good old days"?

Look down on (or *upon*) means "to regard as an inferior" or "to regard with contempt; despise."

Many New Englanders look down on Westerners.

It was considered good form to look down on the flower children of the sixties.

Look for means "to search or hunt for" or "to expect; anticipate."

Diogenes went out in broad daylight with a lighted lamp, looking for an honest man.

Don't look for praise when you do a job well.

Look forward to means "to anticipate, especially eagerly."

Are you looking forward to your trip to Cochabamba?

Look in (on) means "to pay a brief visit (to)."

I'll look in on Grandpa between planes.

Look into means "to investigate."

A committee is looking into cost overruns.

Look on means "to be an observer or spectator" or "to consider; regard."

While the driver grabbed the gunman, the passengers merely looked on.

We look on you as a true friend.

Look out means "to be on the watch; be careful." In British idiomatic usage it also means "to select or find by inspection."

Look out! There's a rock in the road.

While you're in America, would you please look out books on the Gold Rush for me.

Look out for means "to be wary about" or "to take care of."

Look out for mudholes on the coastal highway.

Phil always looks out for Número Uno.

Look over means "to examine; inspect."

Two auditors are looking over the company's books.

Look to means "to take care of; give attention to"; "to rely upon; resort to"; or "to look forward to; expect."

Look to your own life style before lecturing to me about mine.

Don't look to Sandra for moral support.

Economists look to a drop in unemployment next year.

Look up means "to search for in a reference book or the like"; "to pay a visit to; call on"; or "to get better; improve."

Do you look up many words in a dictionary?

Be sure to look us up when when you come to town.

Business is looking up.

Look up and down means "to search everywhere" or "to examine with an appraising eye; scrutinize."

After looking up and down for their child, the Joneses called the police.

The personnel director looked the applicant up and down.

Look up to means "to regard with great respect."

Students used to look up to their teachers more than they do nowadays.

Adverbs with opposite, or nearly opposite, meanings usually lead to different, though not necessarily opposite, senses in the verb sets they are part of.

When we *put acquaintances up,* we provide a place for them to stay. When we *put acquaintances down,* we belittle them.

Someone who *dresses up* wears clothes that are more elegant than usual. Someone who is *dressed down* is scolded severely.

A gambler who *settles up* learns what is owed and then either pays or receives the right amount. A gambler who *settles down* probably takes a regular job and stops gambling.

Though slight, there is even a difference between a house that *burns up* and one that *burns down:* the former burns completely and the latter burns to the ground. Yet there is virtually no difference between, say, a bargaining session that *winds up* and one that *winds down:* both come to an end.

THE BRITISH OFTEN CRITICIZE AMERICANS for attaching adverbs to verbs. In an article titled "You Americans Are Murdering the Language," Henry Strauss, the first Baron Conesford, saw a "serious threat" in the "deplorable American habit of destroying the simple, strong transitive verb by pointless additions of adverbial particles." According to that foe of "American pretentious illiteracy," adverbs are added to verbs in the United States not for the legitimate purpose of changing the meanings that certain verbs have when they stand alone (like *take* until *to* is added), but "merely for the sake of verbosity." Hardhitting Lord Conesford confronted his American readers with hard-hitting questions, including these: "Are you sure that 'face up to' is better or stronger than face?" "Is it really better 'to meet up with' a man than to meet him. . . . ?"

"Mrs Thatcher faced up to Labour's legacy last night—a shocking £2,000 million bill." (London *Daily Express*)

"Rupert poured himself out some more sherry." (Iris Murdoch, *A Fairly Honourable Defeat*)

"He [Thomas Murray] had a good mind and his children felt that he would have made a lawyer because of his enjoyment of a discussion in which he would <u>weigh up</u> the pros and cons...." (K. M. Elisabeth Murray, *Caught in the Web of Words: James Murray and the "Oxford English Dictionary"*)

"But predisposition does not inevitably <u>trigger off</u> results, and just because high-schools work to instill habits, it does not follow that the habits get instilled." (Randolph Quirk, *The Linguist and the English Language*)

"And the universe in general was no longer waving and wobbling. It had <u>steadied down</u>." (Agatha Christie, *The Sleeping Murder*)

"The central core is absolutely Post-Impressionism, but we were trying to <u>widen</u> it <u>out</u>." (John House, quoted in a *Smithsonian* article by Bennett Schiff in connection with a Royal Academy exhibition of which House was a curator)

This "scattering of feeble particles," which Lord Conesford could not understand anyone with an eye and an ear for English tolerating, is a bad habit that the British must have picked up from the Americans a long time ago.

"It has been a hopeless labour to <u>glean up</u> words, by courting living information." (Samuel Johnson, in the Preface to his *Dictionary*, 1755—twenty-one years before the American Declaration of Independence was written)

" 'Collar that Dormouse!' the Queen <u>shrieked out</u>." (Lewis Carroll, *Alice's Adventures in Wonderland*, 1865)

weasel words. See **"War is peace."**

Wedding bells are breaking up that old gang of me.

This, our eyes and ears tell us, can't be: the sentence should end with "that old gang of *mine*." But why not *me*, since, according to a long-standing grammatical rule, when a possessive pronoun is replaced by an *of* phrase, the pronoun that follows *of* is ordinarily in the objective form, or case, not the possessive? In other words, if "Whatever happened to their portrait?" becomes "Whatever happened to the portrait of them?," why doesn't "Wedding bells are breaking up my old gang" become "Wedding bells are breaking up that old gang of me"? Because of an English idiom that goes back hundreds of years, and English idioms are not logical (see How COME THE CLOCK ISN'T GOING?). So in constructions indicating possession (whether outright possession or the notion of one among many), most of us accept without question not only the possessive form of a pronoun but also the redundant *of*, which in itself indicates possession.

a friend of his   some shoes of theirs   a cousin of yours

the classmate of hers who jogs to school

Most educated English-speakers use the same odd construction—again, without giving it any thought—in references to people or animals, though usually not to inanimate objects. Even when a possessive noun follows *of*, it ordinarily keeps its possessive form so as to distinguish it as one among others. Thus,

Pamela's friend is apt to become *a friend of Pamela's* (not *a friend of Pamela*); *Fido's companion, a companion of Fido's* (not *a companion of Fido*); and *the prince's classmate, a classmate of the prince's* (not *a classmate of the prince*).

This *double possessive*, or *double genitive*, as it is sometimes called, occurs at all levels of speech and writing. In an article on the Wedtech scandal, the *New York Times* reported:

> "The consultant, E. Robert Wallach, a San Francisco lawyer and a close friend of Meese's, helped defend Meese against charges of misconduct after Meese was nominated as attorney general in 1984."

And in a popular article on early-childhood education the historian Henry Steele Commager wrote:

> "It was there [in Germany] that Friedrich Froebel—himself a disciple of Pestalozzi's—introduced the kindergarten in 1837 and, what's more, provided it, for the first time, with a formal educational philosophy."

Yet, however widespread, the possessive form of the noun is by no means universal. Many people prefer the common, or uninflected, form—that is, the noun without an added *s* (an apostrophe and *s* in writing).

> "A particularly witty cousin of my father, a woman who read English voraciously and favored Jane Austen, declared that 'Woolworth supplies the refugee with all his needs, and whatever Woolworth doesn't have, the refugee has no business wanting.' " (Julia Hirsch, "Why Is There No German Refugee Novel?")

> "[Frank] Harris was a friend of Shaw..." (Brendan Gill, "The Theatre: Happy Liar")

> "On the eve of that marriage, a friend of the duke arrived from London with more blunt, bad news." (Don Cook, "Duchess of Windsor, 89, Dies in Paris")

The double possessive is too awkward in most compound constructions.

> "Deaver, who is a close friend of President Reagan and his wife, Nancy, left the government last May...." ("Deaver Lobbying Case")

Using it with certain qualifying words may go against the grain of the language as well. So, instead of a pronoun in the possessive form, idiom may call for one in the objective form. For instance, in referring to someone whose identity has been established, an English-speaker might say "About that mysterious death of his. . . . ," but not "You'll be the death of mine yet." Or, "This heart of mine is about to break," but not "I felt fear deep in the heart of mine." The television anchorwoman Christine Craft followed idiomatic usage when, after the U.S. Supreme Court refused to consider her lawsuit, she said:

> " 'I am very disappointed by the decision of the court not to take our case ... but deep in the heart of me, I know we've won a moral victory.' "

Sentences in which nouns are kept in their common form seem less cluttered and therefore clearer than those in which the double possessive, with its apostrophe and *s*, appears. But is the common-form construction always clear? Some-

one who didn't know, for example, that Brancusi was a sculptor might think that the phrase *a student of Brancusi* referred to a student who either lived in a place called Brancusi or was learning a martial art called Brancusi, whereas *a student of Brancusi's* leaves no doubt about the relationship. On the other hand, those who use the double possessive in every *of* construction that remotely suggests possession run the risk of misleading their readers or listeners. *A photograph of Ansel Adams's* is not the same as *a photograph of Ansel Adams*. If a photograph taken of the photographer is meant, the second phrase should be left as it is, without an apostrophe and *s*. The first phrase refers to a photograph taken by Adams; to make this meaning unmistakable the preposition might be changed from *of* to *by*.

Well, I'll be a drity brid!

If the American comedian George Gobel had used this line on his television shows of the 1950s, his fans would have been puzzled. What's a *drity brid*? On the other hand, most people living in the British Isles some nine to five centuries earlier would probably have found those two words to be the only understandable part of that self-effacing exclamation, because in Middle English a *brid* was what we now call a *bird* and *drit* was what we now call *dirt*.

The transposition of letters or sounds within words is one of the ways in which English spelling or pronunciation changes over time. This process is known as *metathesis* (mə tath′ə sis), from a Greek word meaning "changed in position or form," "altered," or "transformed." Here are some current words that underwent a spelling or pronunciation change, or both, on their way either from Middle English to Modern English or from Old English to Middle English:

Current Word	Middle or Old English Form
bird	*brid* (ME)
clasp	*clapse; claspe* (ME)
dirt	*drit* (ME)
fresh	*fersc* (OE)
grass	*gærs; græs* (OE)
little	*littel* (ME)
third	*thridde; thirde* (ME); *thridda* (OE)
thirty	*thritti; thirti* (ME); *thritig* (OE)
through	*thurgh; thrugh* (ME); *thurh* (OE)
wright	*wyrhta* (OE)

Iron was hardly changed in spelling (it was *iren* in both Old and Middle English), but it is now pronounced as if the *o* came before, not after, the *r* (ī′ərn).

As is clear from the dozens of "mispronunciations" we hear in everyday speech, the process of metathesis is still going on. President Dwight D. Eisenhower was neither the only nor the last person to shift the *l* sound to the final syllable in *nuclear;* indeed, his much-criticized pronunciation, nōō′kyə lər, is so prevalent today that it virtually exists alongside nōō′klē ər or nyōō′klē ər. The following sentences illustrate other interchanges of sounds in current speech:

A number of D. H. Lawrence's works have been *bowdlerized* (bōl'dər īz'd, instead of boud'lə rīz'd or bōd'lə rīz'd).

It's a summer movie especially for *children* (chil'dərn, instead of chil'drən).

Do you keep track of your cholesterol (klə res'tə rōl', instead of kə les'tə rōl' or kə les'tə rôl') level?

Special monitors in the cardiac care unit record any *fibrillation* (fil'ə brā'shən, instead of fib'rə lā'shən or fī brə lā'shən).

Do you play an *instrument* (in'stər mənt, instead of in'strə mənt)?

Would you like an *introduction* (in'tər duk'shən, instead of in'trə duk'shən)?

Your kindergarten performances are *irrelevant* (i rev' ə lənt, instead of i rel' ə vənt).

I'm in the market for some new *jewelry* (jōōl'ə rē, instead of jōō'əl rē).

The vocal cords are located in the *larynx* (lär'niks, instead of lar'iŋks).

They belong to another *modernistic* (mäd'rə nis'tik, instead of mäd'ər nis'tik) school of painting.

I was drenched in *perspiration* (pres' pə rā'shən, instead of pʉr'spə rā'shən).

You've got yourself into a fine *predicament* (pʉr dik'ə mənt, instead of pri dik'ə mənt)!

Is that a *prescription* (pər skrip'shən, instead of pri skrip'shən) drug?

Yehudi Menuhin was a child *prodigy* (prä'jə dē, instead of präd'ə jē).

Did you buy your house through a *realtor* (rē'lə tər, instead of rē'əl tər)?

Diane may need an operation on her *sacroiliac* (sak'ər il'ē ak, instead of sak'rō il'ē ak or sā'krō il'ē ak).

The above examples of transposed sounds within words are, of course, not the same as the countless variant pronunciations that educated speakers of English choose between—for instance, hə ras' or har'əs for the verb *harass*. When two or more pronunciations are given in *Webster's New World Dictionary*, the order in which they are entered does not necessarily mean that the first is preferred to or is more correct than the one or ones that follow. In most cases, the order indicates that, on the basis of available information, the form given first is the one most frequent in general cultivated use. Where usage is about evenly divided, since one form must be given first, the editors' preference generally prevails. So unless it is qualified by ''now rarely'' or ''occasionally,'' or some such note, any pronunciation that is entered in the dictionary represents a standard use.

Yet a number of standard variants—that is, pronunciations shown in the dictionary as equally acceptable—do involve the interchange of sounds within words. For example, *apron*, though perhaps more frequently pronounced ā'prən, is also pronounced ā'pərn by many educated people, depending partly on where the word falls in the sentence, whether it is stressed, and other considerations. The same is true of *hundred*, which is sometimes pronounced hun′dərd and other times hun′drid. As for *comfortable,* it is more likely to be pronounced kumf′tər b′l, with the *r* and the *t* sounds transposed, than kum′fər tə b′l. (Another standard variant is kumf′tə b′l.)

Metathesis ordinarily affects speech long before it does spelling. In fact, there is no way of knowing whether—or if—a permanent spelling change will follow a shift in sounds within a word. *Cholesterol,* with the first *l* and *o* sounds transposed, seems to be moving from speech to the typesetter, if we can judge by Stanton Delaplane's syndicated column as published in at least one newspaper:

"When you stir the cream in by homogenizing, the fat seeps into you and becomes chloresterol."

Spoonerisms, the unintentional transposition of sounds (usually the initial ones) in two or more words, are sometimes considered a form of metathesis. The difference is that metathesis is a linguistic process which reflects the way a large number of people hear or see sounds and letters in words over a long period of time (or believe they hear or see them that way); spoonerisms, on the other hand, are momentary slips of the tongue which would ordinarily not be repeated except by chance or because they are considered amusing. For more on spoonerisms, see "KINKERING CONGS THEIR TITLES TAKE."

Metathesis is related to two other processes that affect the spelling or pronunciation of words. In one, sounds or letters are added (see WITH LIGHTENING SPEED THE MISCHIEVIOUS ATHALETE ATE THE SHERBERT). In the other, sounds or letters are dropped (see GRAMPA GOT HIS STRENTH BACK LAST FEBUARY).

what or *which?*

When we want to know more about something or someone, we often ask questions that begin with *what* or *which.*

What school? Which class?

These interrogative pronouns (or adjectives, as they are sometimes called) are used in slightly different contexts. *What,* the more general of the two, calls for a selection from an open-ended set of alternatives, whose exact number the speaker does not know. *Which* narrows the range of possibilities, implying that the speaker is familiar enough with the alternatives to ask for a specific choice among them.

In asking "What school did you go to?," for example, the speaker need not know—indeed, is probably not interested in knowing—how many schools of all kinds there are in the world. All that is wanted is one name from among the lot: "Oberlin," "ballet school," "Berlitz," or the like. On learning that the listener went to Oberlin, the speaker might follow up the first question with "Which class?" This implies that both the speaker and the listener know that Oberlin has one graduating class a year and that what is being asked for is the precise year in which the listener was graduated.

Here are a few more *what* and *which* examples:

Unknown Set of Alternatives	Known Set of Alternatives
What gains has organized labor made in the last decade?	Which gains made by organized labor in the last decade are the most significant?
What flag is that ship flying?	Which Scandinavian country has a flag with a yellow cross on a field of blue?
What new TV programs are scheduled for this fall?	Which TV programs do you usually watch?
What colors go with a cerise rug?	Which colors are at the ends of a rainbow?
What rock singers have been composers as well?	Which rock singer composed "Rocky Raccoon"?

whatever or *what ever?*

The one-word form is always used as an adjective meaning "of no matter what type, degree, quality, or the like":

Buy whatever furniture you think the room needs.

"being who it may be":

Whatever gym teacher told you that, it isn't true.

or (following the word it modifies) "of any kind":

The plumber arrived with no tools whatever.

Either alone or preceded by *or*, *whatever* also occurs in the informal idiom meaning "anything else of the sort."

Use a calculator, your fingers, (or) whatever.

Moreover, the one-word form, which goes back to the early fourteenth century, is generally used as an emphatic variant of the pronoun *what*, sometimes to introduce a question expressing perplexity or wonder:

Whatever do you mean by that remark?

sometimes in the sense of "anything that":

You can make the sauce with whatever you have on hand.

and sometimes in the sense of "no matter what":

Whatever you may think, I'm taking a year off.

However, some writers prefer the two-word form to introduce a question, especially in dialogue.

"What ever can you be thinking of?" she asked.

When *ever* is used as an adverb in its own right, to mean "at all" or "in any way," it is ordinarily separated from *what* by some other word or words.

What can I ever do that will please you?

whenever or *when ever*?

Whenever—written as one word—is always used as a conjunction meaning "at whatever time":

Call whenever you find work.

or "on whatever occasion":

I hope you'll stay with us whenever you come to town.

In informal writing, *whenever* is used also as an emphatic form of the adverb *when,* to express surprise or bewilderment.

Whenever did you meet John Lennon?

Whenever will you learn the rules of the game?

However, some writers prefer the two-word form to introduce a question, especially in dialogue.

"When ever will you make up your mind?" Father asked.

As an adverb in its own right, meaning "at all" or "in any way," *ever* is ordinarily separated from *when* by some other word or words.

When will I ever make it to Broadway?

wherever or *where ever*?

As a conjunction meaning "in, at, or to whatever place or situation," *wherever*—written as one word—is always used.

We hope you'll write to us, wherever you are.

In informal writing, the single-word form is used also as an emphatic form of the adverb *where,* to express surprise or bewilderment.

Wherever did you get that idea?

However, some writers prefer the two-word form to introduce a question, especially in dialogue.

"Where ever do you think you're going with the baby?" Bud growled.

As an adverb in its own right, meaning "at all" or "in any way," *ever* is ordinarily separated from *where* by some other word or words.

Where will I ever find another 1936 World's Fair T-shirt?

whether or *if*?   See *if* or *whether*?

whether or *whether or not*?

Sometimes the *or not* is redundant, and sometimes it isn't. When *whether,* in introducing an indirect question, could be replaced by *if,* the *or not* is ordinarily dropped.

Let me know *whether* (or *if*) you need money.

Jill wonders *whether* (or *if*) she'll have time to wash the car.

But the *or not* is needed when alternatives are presented as having equal importance and *if* cannot take the place of *whether*.

Here's some money *whether or not* you need it.

Jill will wash the car *whether* she wants to *or not*.

Whether or no means "in any case," "come what may."

I'm leaving town after graduation whether or no.

However prim and old-fashioned *whether or no* may seem today, it was considered an intruder early in the twentieth century. *Faulty Diction, As Corrected by the "Funk & Wagnalls New Standard Dictionary of the English Language"* (1915) described it as a "phrase that has by usage been legitimated, though *whether or not* is more strictly correct."

which.   See **Herefords, who are a breed of beef cattle, have white faces and red bodies; The Oval Office which is in the White House symbolizes the Presidency; Remove the strings and ends from the beans and cook them in boiling salted water; Tennis is a sport I enjoy but which I don't play well.**

which or *what*?   See *what* or *which*?

who; whom.   See **Herefords, who are a breed of beef cattle, have white faces and red bodies; The Oval Office which is in the White House symbolizes the Presidency; Tennis is a sport I enjoy but which I don't play well; Who would you turn to for help?**

Who needs a rabbit's foot more: an unlucky person or a luckless one?

Neither ought to leave home without a good-luck charm. The prefix *un-*, at the beginning of *unlucky*, and the suffix *-less*, at the end of *luckless*, both suggest that something is lacking. These two linguistic elements, then, are alike in denoting the absence of luck (which is always good unless we say it's bad).

Prefixes and suffixes, which together are known as affixes, give English much of its richness and flexibility. Although they do not convey meaning when standing alone, these syllables or groups of syllables alter the meanings of words they are joined to, and they also create new words. In the words *affix*, *prefix*, and *suffix* themselves, three different prefixes are joined to the word *fix*.

> *Ad-*, meaning "motion toward, addition to, nearness to," occurs in words like *admit* and *adjoin*. In *affix* it becomes *af-* because of the initial sound in *fix*, which is also of Latin origin. (Changes in the pronunciation and spelling of prefixes are discussed below.)

Pre- in *prefix* means "before, in place, in front of." (It also means "before in time," as in *presuppose* or *prewar;* "before in rank, superior, surpassing," as in *preeminent;* and "preliminary to, in preparation for," as in *preschool.*)

Sub-, which is changed to *suf-* in *suffix* for the same reason that *ad-* is changed to *af-* in *affix,* means "under, beneath, or below" here. (Its other meanings include "lower in rank, position, or importance," as in *subhead;* "to a lesser degree than, somewhat, slightly," as in *subhuman;* and "forming a division into smaller or lesser parts," as in *subdivide.*)

English-speakers automatically play mix-and-match with affixes. It's just as well that we don't stop to think how complex the game is, for if we did we would surely become tongue-tied. For instance, many prefixes besides *un-* convey the notion of "not," "without," or "opposite," yet we are no more likely to attach them randomly to words than we do *un-*. One of those prefixes, *a-,* occurs in words like *amoral,* but just as we wouldn't think of saying or writing *unmoral,* we automatically stop short of *alucky.* We find *dis-* in words like *dishonest*—but *dislucky* or *unhonest*? *In-* appears in words like *incorrect*—but *inlucky* or *uncorrect*? And we come across *non-* in words like *nonstop*—but *nonlucky* or *unstop*?

Suffixes, too, can have the same or closely related meanings and still not be considered interchangeable at the end of all words. When Warren G. Harding was campaigning for the Presidency, he caused a furor by saying *normalcy* instead of *normality,* even though *-cy* and *-ity* are both often used in the sense of "quality, condition, state, or fact of being" (see NORMALCY OR NORMALITY?). So are a number of other suffixes, including *-ance* (as in *vigilance*), *-dom* (as in *boredom*), *-ery* (as in *slavery*), *-hood* (as in *falsehood*), and *-or* (as in *candor*).

CERTAIN AFFIXES MAY CONVEY the same notion but have subtle shades of meaning that set them apart. For example, as noted above, *non-, in-,* and *un-* are all used to give negative force to words. *Non-,* however, is sometimes less emphatic than the other two prefixes, which often suggest an opposite or reverse meaning. Thus, both *nonhuman* and *inhuman* mean "not human," but *nonhuman* does not imply the absence of those qualities expected of a civilized human being, such as compassion, mercy, and benevolence, as *inhuman* does. Both *non-American* and *un-American* mean "not American," but *non-American* does not denote opposition or danger to the United States, its institutions, and the like, as *un-American* does.

Besides giving words (especially nouns, adverbs, and adjectives such as *lucky*) an opposite or reverse meaning, *un-* often indicates a reversal of the action of verbs. Thus, a *locked* door can be *unlocked,* a *chained* dog *unchained,* a *tied* shoelace *untied,* and a *buttoned* coat *unbuttoned.* At other times *un-* is used only as an intensifier; that is, though it may place greater emphasis on a word, it does not change the meaning. So a bolt that becomes *unloosened* is neither less nor more likely to fall off than one that becomes *loosened.*

A good many nouns and adjectives are turned into verbs by the prefix *en-,* with the meaning "to make, make into or like, cause to be" (*encircle* and *enfeeble,* for example). Some of these newly formed verbs can be written with *in-* instead, with no change in meaning. By and large, Americans seem to prefer *embitter* to *imbitter, empower* to *impower, endorse* to *indorse, enmesh* to *inmesh,* and *entrench* to *intrench*—but *ingrain* to *engrain, inquire* to *enquire,* and *inquiry* to *enquiry. Ensure* and *insure* are also interchangeable when they mean either ''to make sure or certain; guarantee; secure'':

> The state will take measures to *ensure* (or *insure*) compliance with the safety regulations.

or ''to make safe; protect'':

> Safety devices have been installed to *insure* (or *ensure*) workers against accidents.

But when it comes to contracting to be paid or to pay money in the case of loss of life, property, or the like, *insure,* not *ensure,* is ordinarily used.

The suffixes *-ic* and *-ical* are often interchangeable in the sense of ''like, having the nature of, characteristic of'' (as in *biologic* and *biological, geometric* and *geometrical, sociologic* and *sociological*), yet certain adjectives formed with them have special or differentiated meanings as well. *Classical,* not *classic,* is ordinarily applied to music that conforms to certain established standards of form, complexity, musical literacy, and so on. An event that is famous in history—for example, the establishment of the United Nations—is described as *historic* rather than *historical;* on the other hand, a novel that is based on or suggested by people or events of the past is called a *historical* novel, not a *historic* novel. And someone who avoids any waste in managing his or her money is generally said to be *economical,* not *economic.* (Aside from these instances in which the choice of *-ic* or *-ical* depends on the context, certain adjectives always take either one suffix or the other. Mount Saint Helens, for example, is *volcanic,* not *volcanical;* controlling pollution is *critical,* not *critic.*)

Not suprisingly, *-less* and *-ful* ordinarily give opposite meanings to words: *thankless* and *thankful,* for example. Yet, surprisingly, *shameless* and *shameful* are often used as if they meant precisely the same.

> Their behavior at the party was *shameless* (or *shameful*).

A closer look, though, shows a subtle difference between these two adjectives. *Shameless* ordinarily refers to someone who lacks shame, modesty, or decency; someone who is brazen or impudent. *Shameful* describes someone or something that brings or causes shame or disgrace; that is unjust, immoral, or indecent; that is offensive. So improper behavior at a party is more likely to be called *shameful* than *shameless.*

Some words go in such different directions when they take on different affixes that, over time, the common derivation and shared meanings of the new words become blurred. For example, both *gracefully* and *graciously* have *grace* as the base word; the suffixes *-ful* and *-ious* mean ''characterized by,'' as does the adverb-forming suffix *-ly.* However, something done *gracefully* shows beauty of form, composition, movement, or expression:

> The dancer moved gracefully across the stage.

whereas something done *graciously* suggests personal qualities of kindness, courtesy, charm, politeness, and the like:

The dancer graciously accepted the bouquets tossed to him by the audience.

Judicial and *judicious, transient* and *transitory, restless* and *restive, variance* and *variation, nobleness* and *nobility, luxurious* and *luxuriant, religiousness* and *religiosity,* and *simpleness* and *simplicity* are among the many other pairs of words that share certain senses while allowing each word in the pair to reserve at least one sense for itself. (See also BELABOR OR LABOR?; BEMUSE OR AMUSE?; ENORMITY OR ENORMOUSNESS?; and FLAMMABLE OR INFLAMMABLE?)

WE PAY LITTLE ATTENTION to most of the changes that certain words must undergo so that prefixes and suffixes can be added to them. Indeed, as we speak or write we are scarcely aware of the various parts into which a word is divided, much less how one part is joined to another. For example, we use *a-*, one of the many prefixes that convey the sense of "not" or "without," in words like *amoral, anemia,* and *apolitical;* however, to ease the transition before another vowel, we change the *a-* to *an-*, as in *anesthetic* and *anorexia*.

The pronunciation of a number of prefixes is affected by assimilation—the phonetic process in which a sound is so influenced by a neighboring sound that it tends to become like it (see GRAMPA GOT HIS STRENTH BACK LAST FEBUARY). As noted above, the prefixes in *affix* and *suffix* end in *f* because they are followed by *fix*, which is also of Latin origin. That is, *ad-* retains its spelling and pronunciation in words like *admit* but not in certain other groups of words. It becomes, for example, *ac-* before *c* or *q* (*accurate, acquire*), *ag-* before *g* (*aggravate*), *ar-* before *r* (*arrest*), and *a-* before *sc, sp, st* (*ascendancy, aspersion, astringent*).

Following much the same pattern, *sub-* retains its form in words like *submarine* but not in other groups of Latin-derived words. In its various senses, it is assimilated, for instance, to *suc-* before *c* (*success*), to *sum-* before *m* (*summon*), to *sur-* before *r* (*surreptitious*), and often to *sus-* before *c, p, t* (*susceptible, suspend, sustain*).

Whether used in the sense of "no, not, without" (as in *inactive*) or as an intensive in certain words of Latin origin (as in *instigate*), the prefix *in-* does not always retain its usual pronunciation and spelling. Instead it is assimilated to *il-* before *l* (*illiterate*), to *ir-* before *r* (*irregardless*), and to *im-* before *m, p,* and *b* (*immodest, impossible, imbalance*).

Another of the many prefixes that change because of assimilation is *com-*, whether used in the sense of "with or together" (*combine*) or as an intensive (*command*). It becomes, for example, *col-* before *l* (*collaboration*), *cor-* before *r* (*corroborate*), and *co-* before *h, w,* and all the vowels (*cohabit, co-worker, coauthor, coefficient, coincidence, cooperate, co-understanding*).

However extensive, changes in the spelling and pronunciation of prefixes are by no means the only ways in which words are altered when affixes are attached. As schoolchildren are taught, the final *e* of a word is ordinarily dropped before a suffix beginning with a vowel. In *falsehood*, therefore, *-hood* does not alter the spelling of *false*, but in *falsity* the *-ity* does; the word *sense* remains intact in *senseless,* as it does in *nonsense,* but in *nonsensical* it loses its final *e.* Because *-er, -ed, -ing, -able,* and other vowel suffixes absorb an *e* preceding them, *ramble* becomes *rambl(e)er, rambl(e)ed, rambl(e)ing; village* becomes *villag(e)r;* and *love* becomes *lov(e)able.*

Yet there are two exceptions to this general rule. First, if the final *e* of a word is preceded by another vowel, both vowels are ordinarily retained before the suffix is attached. The entire word *see* therefore appears in *seeable;* however, what would be the third *e* is dropped from *overseer.* Second, the final *e* is retained in words that would otherwise lose their "soft" *s* or *g.* Thus *peace* becomes *peaceable; notice, noticeable; arrange, arrangement;* and *knowledge, knowledgeable.* Yet many English-speakers, Americans as well as Britons, prefer to retain the final *e,* even though it is not necessary to the pronunciation, in words such as *lik(e)able, lov(e)able,* and *acknowledg(e)ment.* (For a discussion of variant spellings, see SAYING GOODBYE MAY BE HARD.)

Certain words ending in a consonant also undergo spelling changes when suffixes are added. If a one-syllable word ends in a single consonant preceded by a single vowel, the final consonant is doubled before a vowel suffix. So *stop* becomes *stopped, stopper, stopping, unstoppable.* But if a one-syllable word ends in a single consonant preceded by two vowels, the final consonant is not doubled before a vowel suffix. So *stoop* becomes *stooped* and so on.

As long as their last syllable is stressed, words of more than one syllable follow the same general pattern as one-syllable words. So *transmit* becomes *transmitted, transmitting, transmitter, transmittance.* But, because the last syllable is not stressed, *travel* becomes *traveled, traveling, traveler* (though most Britons and some Americans prefer the double *l* here as well). If the stress shifts from the last syllable after the suffix is added, the final consonant remains single too. So even though *prefer* becomes *preferred* and *preferring* (because the last syllable of the base word continues to be stressed), it does not add a consonant in *preferable* or *preference* (because here the stress shifts to the first syllable).

In most words ending in *y,* the *y* is changed to *i* before a suffix is added. For example, *happy* becomes *happier, happiest, happiness,* and *merry* becomes *merrier, merriest, merriment.* However, although *dry* becomes *drier* and *driest,* it retains its *y* in *dryness; shy* becomes either *shyer* and *shyest* or *shier* and *shiest,* but in either case *shyness;* and *enjoy* becomes *enjoyment.*

Words to which certain suffixes are joined may change their form in other ways as well. A final *t* is dropped before *-cy,* for instance, as when *delinquent* becomes *delinquency* and *confederate* becomes *confederacy.* An *i* is often inserted between a base word and the adjective-forming suffix *-fic* (meaning "making, creating"), so that *honor* is turned into *honorific.* However, in this process most base words are shortened or otherwise altered: *science,* for example, as it becomes *scientific; beautify* as it becomes *beautific;* and *terror* as it becomes *terrific.*

HYPHENS ARE FAST DISAPPEARING from words formed with prefixes or suffixes, just as they are from many compound words. Some of the new words are easy to read, while others require a closer look. Nobody has trouble picking out *infra-* and *structure* in *infrastructure,* but *infrared* looks like the past participle of a verb called *infrare.* (For a discussion of compounds, see UPSTART NAME-DROPPERS USUALLY GET THE COLD SHOULDER.)

A hyphen is likely to be omitted even if a prefix ends with the same letter as the first letter of the following word, or if a suffix begins with the same letter as the last letter of the preceding word.

intraarterial
preeminent
reelect
cooperate
microorganism
haillike
posttest

There are, however, several exceptions to the general guidelines on the omission of hyphens. First, a hyphen is retained to prevent a serious misreading or a truly unsettling combination of letters.

de-emphasize
semi-independent
anti-intellectual
anti-union
co-op ("a cooperative")
co-worker
wall-less
scroll-like

Second, a hyphen is retained to distinguish between two words with a similar form but different meanings.

pre-pare ("to pare beforehand"); prepare ("to make ready")

re-cover ("to cover again"); recover ("to find or get back something that one has lost")

re-sound ("to sound again"); resound ("to make a loud, echoing, or prolonged sound")

Third, a hyphen is retained to separate duplicated prefixes.

re-repeal
sub-subdivision

Fourth, a hyphen is retained to separate a prefix from a capitalized word or a numeral.

ante-Victorian
Neo-Darwinism
pre-Columbian
post-1945

POLYTETRAFLUOROETHYLENE has no prefix and only one suffix: *-ene,* which is used in chemistry to form the names of certain unsaturated compounds. So what is the rest of the word composed of? The word base *ethyl,* which is also used in chemistry, and three combining forms: *poly-, tetra-,* and *fluoro-.*

Combining forms are word-building elements that are attached to prefixes, suffixes, word bases, and other combining forms either to change the meanings of words or to form new words. *Poly-,* for instance, does this in various ways, according to its various senses, all derived from the Greek word base meaning "much" or "many." In *polytetrafluoroethylene* it indicates that whatever follows is a "polymer of," that is, a special kind of naturally occurring or synthetic substance (as in *polyvinyl*). In its sense of "much, many, more than one," it forms words like *polyglot,* which refers to several languages (*glotta* means "the tongue" in Greek). In its sense of "more than usual, excessive," it forms words like *polyphagia,* which has to do with an extremely strong desire for food or with eating many kinds of foods. And in its sense of "in or of many kinds or parts," it forms words like *polymorphism,* which refers, among other things, to the very different forms and structures of a species of, say, insects.

Tetra-, from a Greek base meaning "four," appears in many words besides the long chemical one given above. A *tetrahedron,* for instance, is a solid figure with four triangular faces. The Latin-derived combining form *quadri-,* meaning "four times, fourfold," is even more commonly used, forming such words as *quadrangle, quadrennial,* and *quadriplegic.* These are a few of the other combining forms used in references to numbers:

centi- ("hundred or hundredfold," from Latin), as in centigrade and centi-pede. (Also "a hundredth part of," as in centigram.)

deci- ("one-tenth," from Latin), as in decibel and deciliter.

kilo- ("a thousand," from Greek), as in kilohertz and kilometer.

mega- ("a million," from Greek), as in megabyte, megaton, and the slang megabuck. (Also "large, great, powerful," as in megaphone.)

octo- ("eight," from Greek), as in October and octopus.

penta- ("five," from Greek), as in pentagon and pentameter.

The third combining form in *polytetrafluoroethylene* is the Latin-derived *fluoro-,* meaning both "fluorine" and "fluorescence." It appears, as well, in words like *fluorometer* and *fluoroscope.*

Combining forms, then, have no difficulty attaching themselves to other word elements to create new words. For example:

tele- ("at, over, from, or to a distance") + -graph ("something that writes or records") → telegraph

tele- + -phone ("a device producing or transmitting sound") → telephone

tele- + -scope ("an instrument for seeing or observing") → telescope

bio- ("life, of living things") + -graphy ("a process or method of writing, recording, or representing in a specified way") → biography

auto- ("of or for oneself") + biography → autobiography (and, with the addition of the suffix -ical, autobiographical) *semi-* (a prefix meaning "partly") + *autobiographical* → *semiauto-biographical*

SOMETIMES ENGLISH-SPEAKERS unconsciously reverse the word-forming process in which one or more affixes are joined to an existing word base. Thinking that one word is the base of another when in fact it is more recent, they add or remove an affix and end up creating a new word. (See BURGLARS BURGLE AND PEDDLERS PEDDLE, SO WHY DON'T JANITORS JANIT?)

Who would you turn to for help?

On page 16 of its monthly magazine, a public television station asked, "Whom Do You Trust More? Your Board of Supervisors or Your TV Set?" Though perhaps not politic, the headline was grammatical: when a relative or interrogative pronoun is the object of a verb or preposition, it should be in the objective form, or case; *who* is the object of the verb *trust;* the objective form of *who* is *whom.* But by the time the headline writer got to page 21, current usage had become more compelling than traditional grammar, so "Who Would You Like to See on the KQED Board of Directors?" turned up there. The mail to the magazine's editor was heavy that month—most of it critical of the use of *who* on page 21.

Mail is always heavy when the media trifle with *whom.* Whether out of principle or habit, many people still insist that it, not *who,* be used in the objective form, especially in formal usage. Yet the fact is that, in both speech and writing, *whom* is disappearing, especially at the beginning of a sentence or clause, because this is where a subject, not an object, usually goes. In other words, we are accustomed to constructions such as "They would like to see him on the board of directors," not "Them would like to see him on the board of directors."

When Jane Fonda said, in a London interview:

"So I did *California Suite,* which provided the challenge of playing a woman who I didn't like. . . ."

the only way she could have sounded more natural would have been by dropping the relative pronoun entirely, not just its *m* ("a woman I didn't like"). And the *Boston Globe* reporter who covered a speech by Vice President Bush also reflected current usage when he wrote:

"But to Bush last night, Loeb was 'a man of fierce and outspoken loyalty,' a crusading journalist who Bush compared with H. L. Mencken. . . ."

Nowadays *whom* is still often used as the object of a preposition, as in "It depends on whom you talk to" and "From whom would you take money?" Yet, except in set phrases like "To whom it may concern," even here *whom* is losing ground to *who.* A dairy company about to diversify asked in a newspaper advertisement:

"Orange juice from who?"

Y

"You're a goody-goody gumshoes."

In the 1970s a man named Kelly said in a newspaper interview:

> "People get the idea if you publicly state you're a Christian, you're a 'goody-goody gumshoes.' "

Was he using *goody-goody*, a reduplication of *goody*, to describe someone whose morality or piousness is perceived to be affected or insincere? Was "Goody Two-Shoes," the poor, virtuous, and resourceful heroine in the eighteenth-century nursery tale *The History of Little Goody Two-Shoes; Otherwise Called, Mrs. Margery Two-Shoes,* somewhere at the back of his mind? Was he remembering "Goody-goody gumdrops!," which children used to exclaim in delight? And did *gumdrops* somehow become *gumshoes*, whether rubber-soled sneakers or more than one detective? It doesn't matter. Without having the faintest idea what a *goody-goody gumshoes* is, most of us know, below the level of conscious reasoning, what Kelly intended to say. And we're tickled by his comment.

Another kind of illogical or incongruous mistake that strikes the reader or listener as ludicrous but usually goes unnoticed by the writer or speaker is called, among other things, a *bull* and a *Goldwynism*. This last name comes from the well-publicized bouts that were staged in Hollywood for more than half a century, with Sam Goldwyn in one corner and English in the other. Yet many of the colorful movie producer's misapplications of the language—whether his own or the invention of press agents and pranksters—are more than hilarious gaffes: though they turn logic upside down, in their own way they make sense. What, for example, can say more while seeming to say nothing than this statement attributed to Goldwyn:

> "He's overpaid but he's worth it."

Here are some of the often-quoted zanily compelling Goldwynisms that Arthur Marx includes in *Goldwyn: A Biography of the Man behind the Myth:*

> "I don't think anybody should write his autobiography until after he's dead."

> "Include me out."

> "I can tell you in two words: im possible."

> "A verbal contract isn't worth the paper it's written on."

> "I had a monumental idea this morning, but I didn't like it."

> "Our comedies are not to be laughed at."

"I never put on a pair of shoes until I've worn them at least five years."

"Yes, but that is our strongest weakpoint."

"I read part of it all the way through."

"What a wonderful day to spend Sunday."

Every day we hear and read statements that fall randomly from lips and pens while the minds that might have guided them are elsewhere. Like these:

We should not forget how far our limitations can take us.

Many consider him to be an avowed Communist.

With a great splash, the shark swirled silently out of sight.

Education must be aimed at health prevention.

Wear the life vest like an ordinary jacket: either side out.

New strategies were developed by antiabortion foes.

We've played only fifty minutes and we're already less than half through.

The fact is, people say funny things when they are inattentive, and sometimes when they are not.

Describing how the excitement in her first love scene with Robert Wagner was, as always, not in the kiss itself but in the communication, Elizabeth Taylor told *People* reporter David Wallace, "It happens between the eyes, like an umbilical cord."

Former secretary of state Alexander Haig, who was fond of "caveating it that way," hoped the Soviet Union would not "exacerbate the kind of mutual restraint both sides should pursue."

In calling for further study of the 1986 tax-overhaul plan, Senator Howard Metzenbaum, of Ohio, complained, "There is blatant concealment in this bill."

George Deukmejian, then governor-elect of California, softened his earlier hard-line campaign pledge of no tax increases this way: "I'm not one who uses words like 'never' or 'always'—those are absolute terms that I never use."

According to a CBS radio newscaster, "The shah's funeral is scheduled to begin two hours from now, Egyptian time."

A United Airlines pilot announced, "Time permitting, we will arrive in Cleveland at 7:55."

On a TWA flight an attendant announced that a passenger assigned to a seat in row 28 had requested a vegetarian meal. Then she said, "If you are on board, please identify yourself. If you are not on board, please ignore this."

SAM GOLDWYN, OR HIS STAND-INS, also got a lot of laughs by mixing metaphors, that is, by using in a single expression two or more inconsistent figures of speech containing an implied comparison. Arthur Marx cites these, among others:

"Keep a stiff upper chin."

"He treats me like the dirt under my feet."

"You've got to take the bull between your teeth."

"That's the trouble with directors. Always biting the hand that lays the golden egg."

Indeed, the air in Hollywood seems to be filled with mixed metaphors. For instance, the actor David Janssen gave his interviewer, Dwight Chapin, this reason for having spent lots of money:

"I was at a point in life where I needed to do it; the assumption that the grass is greener elsewhere is a monkey you've got to get off your back."

But not only in Hollywood. During an ABC television interview on the Jimmy Carter–Edward Kennedy primary race of 1980, an Iowa newspaper publisher said:

"It's anybody's ball game. The jury is still out."

Firings, whether done to or by one, are good occasions for mangling metaphors. On being dismissed as director of the National Park Service, William J. Whalen said:

"I stepped on a variety of toes. You run over the wrong dog, you have to leave town."

And following the layoff of six hundred Sprint employees, the president of the company said:

"We knew we needed to draw in our belt and get our costs in line. We decided to take a big bite now and get it behind us."

Here are a few more scrambled metaphors—the kind we frequently hear and probably say:

Every dog has its day in court.

Getting him to talk is like pulling hen's teeth.

The worm is on the other shoe.

You know which side your bread is buttered on, so lie on it.

Don't cross your bridges until they're hatched.

ANOTHER KIND OF BLOOPER involves idioms, that is, expressions whose meanings are different from the literal meanings of the words that make them up (see HOW COME THE CLOCK ISN'T GOING?). When a speaker or writer combines two idioms into one, in a syntactic blend, the effect is generally humorous. Such slips are made by native English-speakers as well as nonnative ones. For instance:

> In a letter to the editor of the *New York Times,* Lloyd M. Green, the assistant to the deputy director of the New York State 1984 Reagan-Bush Campaign Committee, criticized George Ball, the former under secretary of state, for having said that President Reagan was too old to be reelected. Mr. Green concluded:
>
> > "It is unfortunate that a man of Mr. Ball's age and stature is reduced to <u>grasping for straw men</u>."

The idiom *grasp* (or *clutch, catch*) *at a straw* (or *straws*) means "to try any measure, however unlikely, that offers even the least hope." In a political context *straw man* is used mainly in the sense of "a weak argument or opposing view set up by a politician, debater, etc., so that he may attack it and gain an easy, showy victory."

> Gilbert Highet noted in an essay on James Joyce:
>
> > "There is in Richard Ellmann's biography of Joyce a family portrait of James Joyce and Nora Barnacle and their son Giorgio and their daughter Lucia, <u>all dressed up to the nines</u> and facing the camera. . . ."

Two idioms are telescoped here: *dressed up,* which means "dressed in clothes more elegant than usual," and *to the nines,* which means "in the most elaborate or showy manner." The adverb *all* is often used before *dressed up,* for emphasis.

> In an article titled "Hollywood's Paranoia about Gays," the film critic Gene Siskel said:
>
> > "In the prison drama 'Fortune and Men's Eyes' (1971), inmate Zooey Hall <u>slits his wrists</u> with a razor."

English idiom gives us the choice of *slashing* our *wrists* or *slitting* our *throats.*

> A movie review in the *San Francisco Chronicle* carried this headline:
>
> > "Wedded Bliss Runs Amiss in 'Paso Doble' "

Something that *is* or *goes amiss* is done wrongly or improperly. Someone who *runs* or *goes amok* (or *amuck*) either rushes about in a frenzy to kill or loses control and does violence. Wedded bliss is more likely to *go amiss* than to *run* or *go amok.*

> A *Boston Globe* story on a television interview with Yitzhak Rabin noted that, in urging the United States to take a firm stand against terrorism, the defense minister of Israel had said:
>
> > " 'I've never tried to avoid responsibility. I've never <u>shrugged off my shoulders</u> the need to make a decision. . . .' "

The idiom *shrug off* means "to dismiss or disregard in a carefree way." *Shrug* conveys the notion of drawing up one's shoulders, as an expression of indifference, doubt, disdain, contempt, or the like.

Criticizing the "brutal, cruel" government of Nicaragua, President Reagan declared:

"I don't think the Sandinistas have a decent leg to stand on."

The informal idiom *not to have a leg to stand on* means "to have absolutely no defense, excuse, or justification." The adjective *decent* is sometimes applied to rules of conduct and the requirements of good taste, rarely to a leg.

For other kinds of boners, see "Kinkering Congs Their Titles Take" and Russian is written in the Acrylic alphabet.

SOME
TROUBLESOME
IDIOMATIC
PREPOSITIONS

The article on idioms, HOW COME THE CLOCK ISN'T GOING?, includes a general discussion of idiomatic prepositions. The following list gives, by key word (verb, adjective, or noun), some combinations of prepositions and other parts of speech that, though common, may trip up even native English-speakers.

The list is, of course, far from exhaustive. Besides, it deals only with current usage, for, like everything else in the language, idiomatic prepositions change over time. Nowadays, for example, most English-speakers would say or write "He is impatient *at* the delay," yet a few centuries ago "impatient *by* the delay" was common coin. So, too, some of the ways we now combine prepositions with other parts of speech will surely strike future speakers and writers as unfamiliar or even quaint.

ability	Some preschoolers show ability *with* computers.
	Technical schools develop ability *at* computer programming.
accommodate	The astronauts accommodated themselves *to* the lack of privacy.
	NASA accommodated them *with* flexible schedules.
accompanied	Children must be accompanied *by* their parents.
	Dessert was accompanied *with* a sweet wine.
accord (noun)	Accord *between* (*among*) the delegates was in sight.
	The meeting sought an accord *of* interests.
	Her driver's license was not in accord *with* her birth certificate.

accordance	All the work seemed to be *in* accordance *with* the civil code.
according	Uniforms were handed out according *to* size.
	Replacements were issued, according *as* they became available.
acquiesce	Did she acquiesce *in* (*to*) the divorce?
act (verb)	Will you act *on* (*upon*) your broker's advice?
	Is your broker free to act *for* you (*on your behalf*)?
adapt	The dialogue was adapted *to* American English.
	The dialogue was adapted *for* an American audience.
	The dialogue was adapted *from* a British play.
adept	One student proved adept *at* (*in*) windsurfing.
adequate	This violin is adequate *for* practice.
	This violin is adequate *to* (*for*) virtuoso playing.
admit	The junta's proclamation admits *of* no dissent.
	The junta admitted a colonel *to* (*into*) its inner circle.
advantage	As a member of long standing, he had the advantage *of* me.
	As a member of long standing, he had an advantage *over* me.
advise	Please advise us *of* (*concerning, regarding*) your summer plans.
affiliation	He denied an affiliation *with* (*to*) the mob.
affinity	There was a strong affinity *between* Paula and her stepmother.
	Paula had a strong affinity *with* her stepmother.
	Sodium has an affinity *for* chlorine, with which it forms sodium chloride, or table salt.
aggression	A charge of aggression *against* a Member State was brought before the Security Council.
agree	Both tenant and landlord agreed *to* an out-of-court settlement.
	These are the terms both parties agreed *on* (*upon, to*): reimbursement of . . .
	The tenant's lawyer considered the terms fair, and the tenant agreed *with* her.

agreement	An agreement *on* (*upon*) residuals was negotiated *between* the studio and the composer.
	The parties entered into an agreement *to* submit any differences to arbitration.
	The parties entered into an agreement *for* submission of any differences to arbitration.
aim (verb)	Congress aimed *at* an early adjournment.
	Congress aimed *for* the middle of June.
alienation	There was marked alienation *between* the newcomers and their classmates.
	The newcomers had feelings of alienation *from* their classmates.
all	See ALL OR ALL OF?
allied	China soon became allied *with* the Soviet Union.
	The onion is allied *to* the lily.
alongside	We pulled the kayak alongside (*of*) the pier.
ambitious	Ambitious *of* (*for*) fame, the actor moved to New York.
amenable	Fortunately, the illness was amenable *to* treatment.
amplify	The chairman amplified (*on, upon*) the treasurer's report.
amused	Queen Victoria is said to have been not amused *at* (*by*) her groom-in-waiting's imitation of her.
angry	I'm sorry you're angry *with* (*at*) me.
	I'm sorry you're angry *about* my decision.
annoyed	Tenants annoyed *by* (*at, with*) their neighbors formed a committee.
antipathy	A group of musicians expressed antipathy *toward* (*against, to*) the management.
	Did you notice the antipathy *between* the quarterback and the coach?
anxiety	Children show increasing anxiety *about* (*over, concerning*) nuclear war.
apply	Betty applied herself *to* the job.
	Betty applied *to* her boss *for* a promotion.
appropriate (adj.)	Is this book appropriate *for* a ten-year-old?
	His life style was appropriate *to* his new wealth.
approve	Many people approved *of* the state lottery. (BUT The legislature approved the lottery bill.)

arrive	We arrived *in* Mexico *by* car.
	Let's try to arrive *at* an understanding.
	The sheriff finally arrived *upon* (*on*, *at*) the scene.
ask	When you call, ask *for* Pierre.
	Tell your parents that I asked *about* (*after*) them.
astonished	We are astonished *at* (*by*) your sudden change of heart.
attack (noun)	The administration launched an all-out attack *against* (*on*, *upon*) drugs.
	He suddenly had an attack *of* dizziness.
authority	Take the matter up with someone *in* authority.
	Leon Edel is an authority *on* Henry James.
	Do you plan to use primary sources as the authority *for* your views?
	The warden has authority *over* the trusties.
averse	I am not averse *to* a nap in the afternoon.
aversion	Their aversion *to* (*toward*) potluck suppers was unmistakable.
back (noun)	A garage was built (*in*) back of the house.
base (verb)	Did you base your impression *on* (*upon*) that one visit?
	It was decided to base the survey team *in* (*at*) Bermuda.
blame (verb)	See BLAME FOR OR BLAME ON?
call (verb)	A group of supervisors called *on* (*upon*) the mayor.
	The supervisors called *upon* (*on*) the mayor to resign.
	The supervisors called *for* the mayor's resignation.
capable	The dormitory is capable *of* housing thirty students.
	The novel is capable *of* several interpretations.
capacity	The drum has a capacity *of* two hundred gallons.
	Is the grain elevator filled *to* capacity?
	The nuclear power plant is operating *at* capacity.
	Your capacity *for* sleep seems limitless.
	Please sign in your capacity *as* executor.
	Please sign in the capacity *of* an executor.
cause (noun)	A faulty valve was the cause *of* the leak.
	Your engagement is cause *for* celebration.

center (verb)	See CENTER AROUND.
charge (verb)	The defendant was charged *with* homicide.
	A nurse was charged *with* the care of the twins.
circumstances	See CIRCUMSTANCES, UNDER THE OR IN THE?
come	Let's try to come *to* an understanding.
commend	I commend you *on* (*upon*) your choice of wine.
compare	For compare <u>with</u> (<u>to</u>), see COMPARE OR CONTRAST?
compete	Four teams competed *with* (*against*) one another *for* the regional championship.
	Four teams competed *in* the play-offs.
complain	Many computer users complain *about* the glare from the screen.
	Some complain *of* headaches; others *of* eyestrain.
concern (noun)	Renters have little concern *with* (*in*) the management of condominiums.
	People throughout the world showed concern *for* the Cambodian refugees.
	Many parents expressed concern *over* (*about*) the decline in Scholastic Aptitude Test scores.
concur	I assume that you concur *with* the majority.
	I assume that you concur *in* the majority opinion.
conform	The architect's plan conforms *to* the building code.
	The wedding conformed *with* family tradition.
congratulate	I congratulate you *on* (*upon*) your taste in art.
consist	See CONSIST OF OR CONSIST IN?
consistent	The witness was consistent *in* her testimony.
	Today's testimony was consistent *with* yesterday's.
couple	For couple (<u>of</u>), see COUPLE, SEVERAL, OR FEW?
deal (verb)	Etiquette deals *with* behavior in polite society.
	The company deals fairly *with* its employees.
	Should schools deal *with* the drug problem?
	I like to deal *with* mom and pop stores.
	A store that deals *in* radiator caps opened next door.
debate (noun)	The debate *on* (*over*) a new downtown prison was postponed.

furnish	Can you furnish me (*with*) full information?
graduate (verb)	For *graduate* (<u>*from*</u>), see "SHOP MACY'S AND SAVE."
grateful	I am grateful *to* them *for* their support.
grieve	I grieve *at* (*for, over*) your loss.
hunger (verb)	Many latchkey children hunger *for* (*after*) affection.
identical	See IDENTICAL WITH OR IDENTICAL TO?
illustrate	The speaker illustrated his points *by* (*with, through*) graphic examples.
	Some writers illustrate their books *with* their own drawings.
	Is that edition of *Robin Hood* illustrated *by* N. C. Wyeth?
immigrate	Many unskilled workers immigrated *to* the United States *from* eastern Europe.
immune	Magazines are immune *from* import duty.
	Have the newlyweds become immune *from* (*to*) family interference?
	Many mosquitoes are now immune *to* pesticides.
impatient	I became impatient *at* the delay.
	I became impatient *with* them for being late.
	I am impatient *with* (*of*) tardiness.
	I was impatient *for* the party to begin.
inconsistent	Their behavior was inconsistent *with* their views.
incumbent (adj.)	It is incumbent *on* (*upon*) the candidates to attend.
independent	The candidate says he is independent *of* party pressure.
	The change occurred when India became independent *from* (*of*) the British Empire.
influence (noun)	Feudal lords exerted a great deal of influence *over* (*on, upon*) their fiefs.
	Do you have any influence *with* the headwaiter?
inquire	Reporters inquired *about* the President's health.
	Reporters inquired *after* the President.
	Whom shall I inquire *for*?
	You have no right to inquire *into* my personal life.

inquiry	A screening committee made inquiries *into* (*about, concerning*) the applicant's background.
inspired	Mary Cassatt was inspired *by* Manet and Degas.
	Many young people are inspired *with* a love of nature.
	Nijinsky was inspired *to* ever-greater virtuosity.
instruction	Extension courses offer instruction *in* woodworking.
	Were instructions *for* (*on*) assembling the shelf included?
intercede	An embassy official interceded *with* the local authorities *for* (*on behalf of, in behalf of*) the youth.
interfere	I hope you won't interfere *in* the management of the business.
	I hope you won't interfere *with* the managers.
intermediary	Will you serve as intermediary *in* the negotiations?
	Will you serve as intermediary *between* (*to, for*) the principals?
intervene	It's risky to intervene *between* quarreling couples.
	It's best not to intervene *in* other people's quarrels.
join	Join *with* us *in* the celebration.
	Join point A *to* (*with*) point B.
	The towns are joined *by* a canal.
labor (verb)	We labored *up* the hill.
	We labored *over* (*at*) the report all morning.
	We labored *in* (*for*) a good cause.
	We labored *under* a delusion.
lack (verb)	Ordinarily, he doesn't lack *for* words.
	He is lacking *in* direction.
mastery	One requirement is mastery *of* a second language.
	Champion chess player Gary Kasparov gained mastery *over* Anatoly Karpov.
means	We must find the means *of* (*for*) harnessing the sun's power.
	We have yet to find the means *to* harness the sun's power.
meddle	I wish you wouldn't meddle *in* my plans.
	I wish you wouldn't meddle *with* my tools.

mistake (noun)	The bill was sent to me *by* mistake.
mortified	They were mortified *by* the suggestion that they were poor hosts.
	They were mortified *at* being taken for poor hosts.
necessary	A food-supply system necessary *to* (*for*) life in outer space was developed.
need (noun)	You seem to have need *of* a rest.
	There is an urgent need *for* food and clothing.
occasion	Reopening the gym was the occasion *for* a week-long party.
	On the occasion *of* reopening the gym, we threw a week-long party.
occupied	He was occupied *with* (*by, in*) administrative details.
offended	I was offended *at* (*by*) their insistent questions.
	I was offended *with* them for questioning me.
opportunity	The role offered a good opportunity *for* (*of*) doing slapstick.
overlaid	The sculpture became overlaid *with* a bronze film.
	The basic plot is overlaid *by* (*with*) myth and anecdote.
overwhelmed	We're overwhelmed *by* (*with*) happiness.
parallel	She drew a series of lines parallel *to* (*with*) the equator.
pleased	Carl's parents were pleased *with* (*by, at*) his self-reliance.
possessed	She seems to be possessed *by* (*with*) the notion of immortality.
	Skiers are lucky to be possessed *of* good balance and strong legs.
prerequisite (noun)	Math is a prerequisite *for* (*of*) a course in statistics.
prerequisite (adj.)	Math is prerequisite *to* a course in statistics.
preside	Who will preside *over* the debate?
	The minister's wife presides *at* the organ.
prevent	Can you prevent the floor *from* sagging?
proficient	In no time they became proficient *in* (*at*) basketry.

proposal	The proposal *for* a new school was voted on.
	Did he accept her proposal *of* marriage?
protect	Companies try to protect themselves *against* industrial accidents.
	Most raincoats don't protect us *from* the rain.
protest (verb)	The employees protested (*against, about*) the company's promotion policy.
provide	Can you provide me *with* full information?
	Atlantic City has begun providing *against* the hurricane season.
	Atlantic City has begun providing *for* a heavy tourist season.
put	Put the dog *through* his tricks.
	Our troops put the enemy *to* flight.
	We put the cost *at* $150.
qualified	Will you be qualified *for* teaching this fall?
	Are you qualified *as* a kindergarten teacher?
reaction	By the mid-1980s a reaction *against* health foods was underway.
	What was his reaction *to* (*toward*) the news?
reconciled	Have you become reconciled *with* your parents?
	Jody appears reconciled *to* his lot.
regard	I am writing *in* regard *to* (*with* regard *to*, *regarding*, *as* regards) your ad for a drummer.
regardless	See "SHOP MACY'S AND SAVE."
regret (noun)	He expressed regret *for* his bad manners.
	He expressed regret *over* (*about, at*) his cousin's bad luck.
rejoice	We rejoiced *at* (*in*) the good news.
relation	The bank manager wrote *in* (*with*) relation *to* our overdrawn account.
replace	Just before curtain time the prima ballerina was replaced *by* her understudy.
	The bald tire was replaced *with* (*by*) a recap.
reprisal	For every act of sabotage, the conquerors took reprisals *against* (*upon*) the local residents.
	They will make reprisal *for* the attack.

resemblance	The resemblance *between* the twins was striking.
	Several people commented on your uncle's resemblance *to* John Barrymore.
resentment	Why do you feel resentment *against* (*toward*) her?
	Do you feel resentment *at* (*about*) her indifference?
respect (noun)	A breakthrough was reported *with* respect *to* (*in* respect *of*, *in* respect *to*) cancer therapy.
rest (verb)	Urban renewal rests *on* (*upon*) a four-point plan.
	Restoring the downtown area rests *with* the planning commission.
	Authorizing the work rests *in* his power.
result (verb)	The flooding resulted *from* a week of heavy rains.
	A week of heavy rains resulted *in* flooding.
revenge	Harold will surely take revenge *upon* (*on*) the company *for* his injury.
search (verb)	He searched everwhere *for* the letter.
	He searched (*through*) his briefcase.
	Psychiatrists searched *into* the refugee's mind.
	We searched *after* the truth.
	We finally searched *out* the truth.
seek	The scientists are desperately seeking (*after*, *for*) a cure.
	New guided missiles sought (*out*) their targets.
smile (verb)	Everyone in the park smiled *at* (*on*) the toddling twins.
	Luck certainly smiled *on* (*upon*) us that day.
solicitous	Thanks for being so solicitous *about* (*for*, *of*) my welfare.
strive	Many people strive *for* self-improvement.
	Many people strive *against* boredom.
substitute (verb)	Just before curtain time the understudy substituted *for* the prima ballerina.
suffer	Some artists suffer *for* their ideas.
	She suffers *from* a fragile ego.
	The people suffered *under* the dictatorship.
suitable	I doubt that the land is suitable *for* (*to*) cultivation.
supplement (verb)	Athletes usually supplement their diet *with* carbohydrates.
	Athletes usually supplement their diet *by* adding carbohydrates.

supply (verb)	Can you supply me (*with*) full information?
surprised	We were surprised *at* (*by*) your remarks.
sympathetic	The arts council is sympathetic *toward* (*to*) young graffiti artists.
talk (verb)	Charley can talk *to* (*with*) anyone.
	Charley can talk *on* (*about, concerning, regarding, to*) any subject.
	More and more people talk *by* signing (*in* sign language).
taste (noun)	This hollandaise sauce has a taste *of* mint.
	When did you develop a taste *for* jazz?
tired	They soon became tired *from* (*through*) the exertion.
	They became tired *of* board games.
	They eventually became tired *by* years of drudgery.
tolerance	She showed little tolerance *for* (*toward, of*) opposing views.
treat (verb)	The natives treated *with* the newcomers *for* a property settlement.
	The declaration treats *of* land rights.
trust (verb)	I don't trust *to* luck; I trust *in* your ability to raise the money.
	I trust you *with* my future.
	I trust my future *to* your care.
umbrage	Did the audience take umbrage *at* my remarks?
	I'm sorry that my remarks gave umbrage *to* my listeners.
unequal	Clearly, the two were unequal *in* debating skill.
	Both seemed unequal *to* their task.
unfavorable	The strong currents are unfavorable *for* swimming.
	The bank was unfavorable *to* (*toward*) my plans for a second mortgage.
united	We were united *by* (*in*) our common cause.
	We were united *with* (*to*) one another.
urge	Civil rights leaders urged caution *on* the group.
use (noun)	It was (*of*) no use arguing with them.
	There was no use (*in*) arguing with them.
variance	The group's actions are *at* variance *with* its goals.

want (verb)	Roy has never wanted *for* friends.
want (noun)	Roy has never been *in* want of friends.
	For want of company, Roy went to the movies.
worried	Everyone is worried *about* (*over, by*) the dry spell.
worry (verb)	In the wake of each storm we manage to worry *along* (*through*).
	As usual, Muffin was worrying *at* a bone.

GLOSSARY OF GRAMMATICAL AND LINGUISTIC TERMS USED IN THIS BOOK

Words or phrases printed in SMALL CAPITAL LETTERS within the following definitions appear as separate entries in this glossary.

abbreviation A shortened form of a word or phrase. For example: *univ.* for *university; lb.* for *pound; S.C.* for *South Carolina; ABC,* for *American Broadcasting Company.* The process of shortening a word or phrase by leaving out or substituting letters is also known as abbreviation.

absolute adjective or adverb An adverb or adjective that some say is beyond comparison, that is, cannot be modified to show the comparative or superlative degree. For example: *unique, perfectly.*

absolute construction A participle or gerund phrase that is grammatically independent of the rest of the sentence even though it modifies it in a general way and is therefore logically connected with it. For example: *"Dinner being late, we played another hand of bridge."*

abstract noun A noun designating a quality thought of apart from any particular material object. For example: *beauty, envy, enormousness.* Distinguished from CONCRETE NOUN.

acronym A word formed from the first, or first few, letters of a series of words. For example: *Benelux,* from *Belgium, Netherlands, Luxembourg; CARE,* from *Cooperative for American Relief Everywhere.*

active voice The form of a verb whose subject is shown as performing the action of the verb. For example: *"Who washes the car?"*

adjective Any of a class of words used to limit or qualify a noun or a word or word group functioning as a noun. For example: *"a hot drink."*

adverb Any of a class of words used generally to modify a verb, an adjective, another adverb, a phrase, or a clause, by expressing time, place, manner, degree, cause, or the like. For example: "They *seldom* watch television, and when they do it's *always* a *very* special occasion."

affix See PREFIX and SUFFIX.

agreement The correspondence between words in a sentence to indicate their relationship. A verb ordinarily agrees with its subject in number and person. For example, in "The actors are here," *are* is a plural third-person form of the verb *be,* to agree with the plural noun *actors.* A pronoun ordinarily agrees with the word, phrase, or clause to which it refers in number, person, and gender. For example, in "She takes her jogging shoes to work," *her* is a singular, third-person, feminine possessive pronoun, to agree with the singular, third-person, feminine personal pronoun *she.*

amelioration The same as MELIORATION.

analogy The process by which new or less familiar words, constructions, or pronunciations conform to the pattern of older or more familiar (and often unrelated) ones. For example, the verb *energize* is formed from *energy* by analogy with *apologize* from *apology.*

antecedent The word, phrase, or clause to which a pronoun refers. For example, in "Frank fed his cats their usual snack," *Frank* is the antecedent of *his,* and *cats* is the antecedent of *their.*

antonym A word that is opposite in meaning to another word. For example, *hot* is an antonym of *cold.*

appositive A word, phrase, or clause placed beside another to identify or explain it. For example, in "Robert Penn Warren, a poet, novelist, and essayist, was named the first official Poet Laureate of the United States," the phrase *a poet, novelist, and essayist* is an appositive of (or is in apposition with) *Robert Penn Warren.*

argot The specialized vocabulary and idioms of those in the same work, way of life, or so on, such as the secret language of criminals.

article See DEFINITE ARTICLE and INDEFINITE ARTICLE.

assimilation The process by which a sound, through the influence of a different, neighboring sound, becomes either identical with or more nearly like this other sound. For example, the *p* sound in *cupboard* has been lost by assimilation to the *b* sound.

attributive A modifier that is joined directly to (usually immediately before) the noun it modifies. For example, in "the black cat," *black* is an attributive adjective. In "a customs official," *customs* is an attributive noun.

auxiliary verb A verb, such as *have, be, may, can, must, do, shall,* or *will,* that is used with another verb, in a verb phrase, to indicate tense, mood, and voice. For example, in "The song was just recorded," the auxiliary *was* is the past-tense form of *be* in the third-person singular. It helps the main verb, *recorded,* show not only that the action took place in the past but also that the verb is in the indicative mood and the passive voice.

back-formation A word that is actually formed from another word but looks as if it were the base of that word. For example, the noun *greed* is a back-formation of the adjective *greedy,* and the verb *edit* is a back-formation of the noun *editor.* The process of forming such a word is also known as back-formation.

base Any of the smallest meaningful units or forms in the language to which one or more prefixes, suffixes, and the like have been or can be added. For example, *nonrepeating* is made up of three elements: the prefix *non-* (meaning "not"); *repeat,* a base word able to stand alone as a verb (the prefix *re-,* meaning "again," having already been attached to *petere,* a Latin word meaning "to seek, demand, or attack"); and the suffix *-ing,* which is used to form the present participle of verbs. A base is sometimes called a *stem* or a *root.*

blend A word formed by combining parts of other words. For example, *brunch* is a blend of *br(eakfast)* + *(l)unch.* Blends are sometimes called *portmanteau words.*

blooper The same as BULL.

borrowing The process by which one language adopts (and sometimes adapts) words and expressions from another. For example, English borrowed *operetta* from Italian, in which the word is the diminutive form of *opera;* it also borrowed the Algonquian word *askootasquash* but shortened it to *squash.* A word or expression taken into another language and naturalized is also known as a borrowing or, probably more often nowadays, as a *loanword.*

bull An illogical or incongruous mistake that strikes the reader or listener as ludicrous but usually goes unnoticed by the writer or speaker. For example: "I'm glad I hate onions, because if I liked onions I'd eat them, and I can't stand onions." Bulls are sometimes called *bloopers,* or *Goldwynisms* (after the Hollywood producer Sam Goldwyn).

buzzword A word or phrase used by members of some in-group; though it has little or imprecise meaning, it sounds impressive to outsiders. For example: *interface,* not in its computer sense of "the means of interaction between two devices or systems," but to convey the general notion of interacting with someone.

cant The distinctive stock words and phrases used by a particular sect, class, or the like. For example: "clergymen's cant." Also, insincere or almost meaningless talk used merely from convention or habit.

cardinal number Any number used in counting or in showing how many. For example: "two," "forty-seven," "634." Distinguished from ORDINAL NUMBER.

case The form of a noun or pronoun that indicates its grammatical relation to some other word or words in the sentence. Modern English has only three cases (or, as they are often called nowadays, *forms*). The *possessive* shows possession or a similar relationship. For example: "Roger*'s* garden," "women*'s* rights," "nobody*'s* business," "*my* shirt," "lives *of* politicians." The *subjective* shows mainly that a pronoun is being used as the subject of a verb. For example: "*They* always send him fruit"; "*Who* will get the prize?" The *objective* shows mainly that a pronoun is being used as the object of a verb or preposition. For example: "They like *him*"; "To *whom* it may concern." (Some people still use the traditional Latin-derived grammatical terms for the various cases, or forms: *nominative* for *subjective; genitive* for *possessive;* and *dative* and *accusative* for *objective.*) See also FORM.

catch phrase A phrase that catches or is meant to catch the popular attention. For example: "Never trust anyone over thirty."

catchword A word or phrase repeated so often that it comes to epitomize a certain group, movement, or the like, as a kind of slogan. For example: "the war to end all wars."

clause A group of words that contains both a subject and a predicate and is part of a sentence. For example: "*By the time the guest of honor arrived,* the party was nearly over."

cliché An expression or idea which, though once fresh and forceful, has become hackneyed and weak through much repetition. For example: "Here I am, *better late than never.*"

clipped word A shortened form of a word. For example: *chimp,* for *chimpanzee; pike,* for *turnpike.* Clipped words are also called *clipped forms, clippings,* or *clips.*

cognate Related through common ancestry, derivation, or borrowing; derived from a common original form. For example, the English *apple* and the German *apfel* are cognate words; and English and Flemish are cognate languages. Words or languages so related are known as cognates.

coinage The process by which a new word is invented or a new meaning is applied to an established word. For example, the word *humongous* (meaning "very large or great") is a twentieth-century coinage; so is the computer sense for the word *mouse* ("a small, hand-held device that moves or positions the cursor on a terminal screen"). A word or meaning created this way is known as a coinage. Another name for this process, and for a word or meaning so brought into the language, is *neologism.*

collective noun A noun that is singular in form but denotes a collection of individuals. For example: "a *crowd,*" "an *orchestra,*" "a *family.*" Whether a collective noun takes a singular or plural verb depends on the context.

colloquial Literally, "conversational." The term is applied mainly to the words, phrases, and idioms characteristic of informal speech and writing. It does not indicate nonstandard usage. In this book, *informal* is generally used in place of *colloquial.*

combining form A word form that can occur in compounds and derivatives and that can combine with affixes, suffixes, and the like to form other words. For example, the combining forms *cardio-* and *-graph* make up the word *cardiograph;* the combining form *odont-* and the suffix *-oid* make up the word *odontoid.*

comma splice The same as RUN-ON SENTENCE.

common gender See GENDER.

common noun A noun that refers to any of a group or class. For example: *house, strawberry, street.* Distinguished from PROPER NOUN.

comparative The second degree of comparison of adjectives and adverbs, expressing a greater degree of a quality or attribute than that expressed in the positive degree. For example: *softer* and *more expensive* (for adjectives); *more softly* and *more expensively* (for adverbs).

comparison The modification of an adjective or adverb to show the positive, comparative, and superlative degrees, or forms. For example: *tight, tighter, tightest* and *good, better, best* (for adjectives); *tightly, more tightly, most tightly* and *well, better, best* (for adverbs).

complement A word or word group that, with the verb, completes the meaning and structure of the predicate. For example: *manager* in "They made her manager"; *paid* in "He expects to get paid"; *green* in "The contestant turned green."

complex sentence A sentence consisting of a main clause and one or more subordinate clauses. For example, in "Once you get home, you'll forget that you've ever been away," the main clause is *you'll forget* and the two other clauses are subordinate.

compound predicate A word group consisting of two or more predicates whose subject is the same. For example: "The mail carrier *used to come early in the morning* and [*used to*] *drop my letters through the slot in the door.*"

compound sentence A sentence consisting of two or more independent, coordinate clauses. For example: "*Dick is always busy,* but *Jane keeps inviting him out.*"

compound subject A word group consisting of two or more subjects whose predicate is the same. For example: "*Dick* and *Jane* are now inseparable."

compound word A word which is made up of two or more other words that can stand alone and which expresses a single concept. Compound words (or, as they are more often called, *compounds*) may be hyphenated (*daughter-in-law*), written solid (*stomachache*), or written as separate words (*dining room*).

concrete noun A noun designating a thing or class of things that can be perceived by the senses. For example: "a *pineapple,*" "an *elephant,*" "four *trucks.*" Distinguished from ABSTRACT NOUN.

conditional clause A clause that, in expressing a condition, is introduced by *if, whether, unless,* or a similar subordinating conjunction. For example: "We plan to go, whether or not it rains."

conjugation A methodical presentation or arrangement of the inflectional forms of a verb according to tense, number, person, voice, and mood.

conjunction A word used to connect words, phrases, clauses, or sentences. The three kinds of conjunctions are COORDINATING, CORRELATIVE, and SUBORDINATING.

connective A word, such as a conjunction, a preposition, or a relative pronoun, that connects words, phrases, clauses, or sentences.

connotation An idea or notion suggested by or associated with a word or phrase, in addition to its explicit meaning. For example, the words *spinster* and *unmarried woman* have different connotations. Distinguished from DENOTATION.

consonant A speech sound produced by some kind of obstruction to the flow of breath. There are three kinds of consonants: those produced by stopping and releasing the air stream (as, for example, in the *p, b,* and *g* sounds); those produced by stopping the air stream at one point while it escapes at another (as in the *n, l,* and *r* sounds); and those produced by forcing the air stream through a loosely closed or very narrow passage (as in the *f, s,* and *h* sounds). A letter or symbol representing such a sound is also known as a consonant.

construction The arrangement and relation of words in a phrase, clause, or sentence.

contraction The shortening of a word or phrase by the omission of one or more letters or sounds. Also a word or phrase so shortened. For example: *can't* for *cannot; e'er* for *ever.*

conversion The same as FUNCTIONAL SHIFT.

coordinate clause A clause of equal structural rank as another, whether main or subordinate in the sentence. Coordinate clauses are connected by coordinating conjunctions like *and*, *but*, and *or*. For example: "Our guests had barely arrived when *it started to rain* and *the living room roof caved in.*"

coordinating conjunction A conjunction that connects words, phrases, clauses, or sentences of equal structural rank. For example: "The only flavors left were strawberry, lemon, *and* mocha"; "Joan wanted to go, *but* Phil didn't."

copula The same as LINKING VERB.

correlative conjunction One of a pair of words that connect words, phrases, clauses, or sentences of equal structural rank. For example: *either . . . or, neither . . . nor, both . . . and, not only . . . but also.* In a *correlative construction*, mutual relation is expressed by such conjunctions. For example: "*Neither* the fiddler *nor* the trumpet player auditioned."

counter word Any word freely used as a general term of approval or disapproval without reference to its more exact meaning. For example: *nice, terrible, lousy, terrific.*

count noun A concrete noun that has both a singular and a plural form and that names objects which can be counted as separate units. For example: "six *dollars*," "two *puppies*." Distinguished from MASS NOUN.

dangling participle A participle or participial phrase that lacks clear connection in qualifying another element in the same sentence. For example, in "Sitting in the movies, my mind began to wander," *sitting in the movies* seems to modify *mind.*

declarative sentence A sentence that makes a statement or assertion. For example: "It is raining."

definite article The function word *the*, which limits or specifies. For example: "This is *the* latest model." Distinguished from INDEFINITE ARTICLE.

degradation The same as PEJORATION.

degree See COMPARISON.

demonstrative adjective Any of the adjectives that point out or make reference to specific persons or objects. *This* and *these* generally refer to persons or objects that are near; *that* and *those*, to persons or objects that are farther away.

demonstrative pronoun Any of the demonstrative pronouns—mainly *this, that, these, those, so,* and *such*—that point out persons or things already mentioned or implied. For example: "*This*, then, is what I have to put up with!"; "They are friends and will remain *so.*"

denotation The direct, explicit meaning or reference of a word or term. For example, the denotation of *politesse* is "politeness" or "courtesy." Distinguished from CONNOTATION.

dependent clause The same as SUBORDINATE CLAUSE.

derivation The process of forming words from bases by adding one or more affixes other than inflectional endings, or by changing one or more of the sounds. For example, *childish (child + -ish), daily (day + -ly),* and *happiness (happy + -ness)* are all derivational, or derived, words, and so is *strength* (from *strong*).

Another meaning of *derivation* is "the origin and development of a word," or "etymology."

determiner A word, such as *the, a, an,* or *this,* which indicates the approach of a noun or a noun substitute without significantly modifying it.

dialect The form or variety of a spoken language peculiar to a region, community, social group, occupational group, or the like. Although the term *dialect* is sometimes restricted to varieties other than the standard one, actually every variety, including the standard, is a dialect of the language. Dialects differ from one another in such matters as pronunciation, syntax, and vocabulary.

diphthong A complex vowel sound made by gliding continuously from the position of one vowel to that of another within the same syllable. For example: the "ou" sound in *down,* the "ai" sound in *ride,* and the "oi" sound in *boy.*

direct address The use of a noun or pronoun to name the person or persons spoken to. For example: "Will you write, Sally?"; "Ladies and gentlemen, please give me your attention"; "Your Excellency."

direct object The word or words denoting the thing or person that receives the action of a transitive verb or is the goal or result of a verbal action. For example: "We put another *coat of paint* on the building"; "Do *a favor* for me, please." Distinguished from INDIRECT OBJECT.

direct quotation The reproduction or repetition of another's words, without change. For example: "Sally replied, 'Yes, I'll write.' " Also known as *direct discourse.* Distinguished from INDIRECT QUOTATION.

dissimilation A process of linguistic change in which one of two identical sounds within a word becomes unlike the other or disappears. For example, in *surprise,* the first of the two *r* sounds may not be pronounced because of dissimilation.

distributive pronoun A pronoun that refers to each member of a group regarded individually. For example, *each, every, either, somebody, everybody.*

double comparison The use of both forms for indicating the comparative or superlative degree of a single adjective—that is, adding the suffix *-er* or *-est* to the simple form and at the same time placing *more* or *most* in front of it. For example: *more handsomer* (instead of the usual *handsomer* or *more handsome*) and *most handsomest* (instead of the usual *handsomest* or *most handsome*).

double negative The use of two or more negatives in a single statement having negative force. For example: "I did*n't* hear *nobody* come in."

double possessive The use of both an *of* phrase and *'s* to indicate the possessive form, or case. For example: "Was Cassatt a student *of* Renoir*'s*?" This construction is also known as a *double genitive.*

double talk Ambiguous and deceptive talk.

elevation The same as MELIORATION.

ellipsis The omission of a word or words necessary for complete grammatical construction but understood in the context. For example, in "I shouldn't and therefore won't go," *go* is elided after *shouldn't.*

epenthesis A phonetic change which involves the insertion of an unhistoric sound or syllable in a word. For example: the *b* in *thimble* and the extra syllable in the pronunciation ath′ə lēt for *athlete.*

etymology The origin and development of a word, affix, phrase, or the like; the tracing of a word or other form back as far as possible in its own language and to its source in contemporary or earlier languages.

euphemism The use of a word or phrase that is less expressive or direct but considered less distasteful or less offensive than another. Also, a word or phrase so substituted. For example: *passed away* for *died.*

euphony A pleasant combination of agreeable sounds in spoken words. Also, such a combination of words.

exclamatory sentence A sentence that expresses surprise, strong feeling, determination, or the like. For example: "Is it ever raining!"

feminine gender See GENDER.

figure of speech An expression, such as a metaphor or a simile, that uses words in a nonliteral or unusual sense to add vividness, beauty, and the like to what is said. For example, "All the world's a stage" is a metaphor; "He's as gentle as a lamb" is a simile.

flat adverb An adverb that does not have the characteristic *-ly* ending. For example: "He drives *fast.*"

flat infinitive An infinitive that is not preceded by the sign *to.* For example: "Make them *go.*"

folk etymology A change that occurs in the form of a word over a period of prolonged usage so as to give the word an apparent connection with some other well-known one. For example: *coleslaw* is often called *cold slaw.* Folk etymology is also the popular but incorrect notion of the origin and development of a word. It is sometimes known as *popular etymology.*

form Any of the different appearances of a word in changes of inflection, spelling, or pronunciation. For example: *am* is a form of the verb *be.* The noun *form* is also used as a synonym of CASE. As a verb, *form* refers to building words from bases, affixes, and other word elements.

fragmentary sentence The same as SENTENCE FRAGMENT.

functional shift The ability of a word to serve as more than one part of speech. For example, *hand* is usually thought of as a noun, but in "He handed me the keys" it functions as a verb. Also called *function shift* or *conversion.*

function word A word that has little or no meaning when standing alone but that serves to relate parts of a sentence grammatically. For example, in "An apple and a banana have already gone into the salad," the articles *an, a,* and *the;* the conjunction *and;* the auxiliary verb *have;* and the preposition *into* are function words.

fused participle A construction in which a gerund has for its subject a noun or pronoun that is not in the possessive form, or case. For example: "Do you mind *Fred* traveling alone?" (instead of "Do you mind *Fred's* traveling alone?").

fused sentence The same as RUN-ON SENTENCE.

gender The formal classification by which nouns and pronouns (and often their accompanying modifiers) are grouped and changed in form, so as to show the relationship of certain sentence elements. Grammatical gender is not a formal feature of English, as it is of a number of other languages. However, according to what is usually called *natural gender,* some English nouns and the third-person singular pronouns are distinguished according to the sex or the lack of sex of whatever is named or referred to. For example, *boy* and *he* are said to be masculine; *girl* and *she,* feminine; and *door* and *it,* neuter. Words that may be either masculine or feminine (such as *child* and *you*) are sometimes described as having *common gender.*

generalization A kind of semantic shift in which a word or phrase comes to have a meaning regarded as more general, or broader, than the meaning it formerly had. For example, *pen* originally denoted a heavy quill or feather, but nowadays it refers to any of various devices used in writing or drawing with ink.

gerund A verbal noun ending in *-ing.* Having all the uses of nouns, gerunds retain certain characteristics of verbs, such as the ability to take an object, a complement, an adverb modifier, and even a subject. For example, in "Waving wildly is the best way to flag down a taxi," the gerund *waving* is modified by the adverb *wildly* and is the subject of the verb *is.* Gerunds are a kind of VERBAL.

ghost word A word created through misreading of manuscripts, misunderstanding of grammatical elements, and the like, but never really established in a language.

gobbledygook Pompous, wordy, and involved talk or writing that is usually associated with officialdom.

grammar The system of word structures and word arrangements of a given language at a given time; also, a body of rules for speaking and writing a given language. Grammar is generally subdivided into *morphology,* which has to do with the forms and structures of words, and *syntax,* which is concerned with the customary arrangement of words in phrases and sentences. It may also include *phonology,* which deals with the speech sounds of a language. Many people think of grammar as one's manner of speaking or writing as judged by prescriptive grammatical rules, so we see and hear statements like "She would do well in the job if her grammar weren't so poor."

homonym A word with the same pronunciation as another but with a different meaning, origin, and, usually, spelling. For example: *bore / boar* and *knight / night.* Homonyms are also called *homophones.*

idiom A phrase, construction, or expression that is accepted even though it goes counter to the way words are generally joined together to express thought. For example, nowadays the adverb *how* seldom precedes a form of the verb *come,* yet "How come?" is widely taken to mean "Why?" Also, an idiomatic phrase, construction, or expression is one whose meaning is different from the literal meanings of the words that make it up. For example, *sit on one's hands* ordinarily has nothing to do with resting the weight of one's body on the part of each arm below the wrist, but rather with failing to do what is needed or expected.

imperative mood See MOOD.

imperative sentence A sentence that expresses a command, strong request, or exhortation. For example: "Call the operator."

indefinite article The function words *a* and *an,* which do not limit or specify. For example: *"A* factory will be built here"; "Is this *an* eagle's nest?" Distinguished from DEFINITE ARTICLE.

indefinite pronoun A pronoun that does not indicate a particular person or thing but, instead, refers to any one or more of a class of persons or things. For example: *"Each* can take a guest to the party"; *"Many* have already voted."

independent clause The same as MAIN CLAUSE.

indicative mood See MOOD.

indirect object The word or words denoting the person or thing indirectly affected by the action of the verb. An indirect object generally names the person or thing to which something is given or for which something is done. For example: "Give *the building* another coat of paint"; "Please do *me* a favor." Distinguished from DIRECT OBJECT.

indirect question A statement that gives the substance of a question but not its exact words. For example: "I wondered *who had come in"*; "The passengers asked *when the plane was due."*

indirect quotation A statement of what a person said, without quoting his or her exact words. For example: "Sally said she would write." Also known as *indirect discourse.* Distinguished from DIRECT QUOTATION.

infinitive The form of a verb which expresses existence or action without reference to person, number, or tense and which can also function as a noun. An infinitive is usually in the form of the first-person singular in the present tense, either preceded by the marker *to* or by another verb form. For example: "They'll try *to go* tomorrow"; *"Make* them *try."* Because it is a VERBAL, an infinitive can take an object, a complement, an adverb modifier, and even a subject. For example, in "Do you plan to copy the letter exactly?," *copy,* an infinitive with the marker *to,* has *the letter* as its object and is modified by the adverb *exactly.*

inflection The change of form by which some words indicate certain grammatical relationships, such as number, person, tense, and case. For example, the inflectional ending *-s* forms the plural of most nouns (*rocks, toes*) and the third-person singular of verbs in the present tense, indicative mood (*gives, shows*). The inflectional ending *'s* forms the possessive case of many nouns and some pronouns ("the baby*'s* toy," "men*'s* shoes," "everybody*'s* favorite"). The suffix *-ed* forms the past tense and past participle of most verbs ("We *talked"*; "She had *talked"*); and *-ing* forms the present participle ("He is *singing"*). The suffix *-er* forms the comparative degree of many adjectives and adverbs (*later, faster*), and *-est* forms the superlative degree (*fastest, latest*).

informal The same as COLLOQUIAL.

intensive Giving force or emphasis. For example, in "It was too hot," *too* is an intensive adverb. In "He is the very man we want to see," *very* is an intensive adjective. In "She will do it herself," *herself* is an intensive pronoun. A word that strengthens or emphasizes the meaning of another word or words is sometimes called an *intensive* or an *intensifier.*

interjection An exclamation thrown in without grammatical connection. For example: *aha!, ouch!, well!*

interrogative sentence A sentence that asks a question. For example: "Are you coming?"

interrogative word A word used to introduce a question. The interrogative pronouns are *who, whom, whose, what,* and *which.* Other interrogative words include such adverbs as *why, when, where,* and *how.*

intonation Significant levels and variations in the quality or tone of sound in a spoken sentence or phrase. For example, certain questions are usually asked with a rising intonation. The term is also used to mean simply one's way of talking.

intransitive verb A verb that does not require an object to complete its meaning. For example: "He *smiles* a lot"; "Please *remember.*" Distinguished from TRANSITIVE VERB.

irregular verb A verb that does not form its past tense and past participle in the usual way—that is, the way a REGULAR VERB does. Instead of adding *-d* or *-ed* to the infinitive form (so that, say, *smile* becomes *smiled* and *talk* becomes *talked*), an irregular verb may be changed in any of several other ways. For example, the base may be radically altered (*be, was, were*); the suffix *-en* may be added to form the past participle (*write, wrote, written*); or the vowel in the base may be shortened or changed (*weep, wept, wept*). Regular verbs are sometimes called *weak verbs;* irregular verbs, *strong verbs.*

jargon The specialized vocabulary and idioms of those in the same work, profession, or the like—sportswriters or social workers, for instance. The term is somewhat derogatory, often implying unintelligibility. It refers, as well, to speech or writing that is full of long, unfamiliar, or roundabout words or phrases.

larynx The structure of muscle and cartilage at the upper end of the human trachea (windpipe), containing the vocal cords and serving as the organ of voice.

lexical Having to do with, or having the nature of, words as isolated items of vocabulary rather than as elements in a grammatical structure. Certain groups of words (mainly nouns, verbs, adverbs, and adjectives) are said to have "lexical meaning" in that they are definable, as in a dictionary, and, unlike function words, do more than grammatically connect words in a sentence.

lexicography The act, process, art, or work of writing or compiling a dictionary or dictionaries.

linking verb A verb that, instead of expressing action, functions chiefly as a connection between a subject and the noun or adjective that relates back to that subject. For example: *be* (as in "Faulkner *is* a writer"); *look* ("He *looks* tired"); *remain* ("The judge *remained* firm"). A linking verb is also known as a *copula* or a *copulative verb.*

loanword The same as BORROWING.

localism A word, meaning, expression, or pronunciation peculiar to one locality. For example, *tonic* is likely to be heard in the Boston area, but *soda, pop,* or *soda pop* in other parts of the United States.

locution A word, phrase, or expression.

long vowel A vowel sound of relatively long duration. In popular usage the term is often applied to a DIPHTHONG.

main clause In a complex sentence, a clause that can function as a complete sentence by itself (as distinguished from a subordinate clause). For example: "When daylight came, *the ship was far out to sea.*" A main clause is also known as an *independent clause* or a *principal clause.*

malapropism A ludicrous misuse of words, especially through confusion caused by resemblance in sound. For example: *progeny* for *prodigy* in "He is a child progeny."

masculine gender See GENDER.

mass noun A noun used to denote an abstraction or something that is uncountable. Mass nouns are not ordinarily preceded by *a* or *an*, and although they may be either singular or plural in form, they are typically used in singular constructions. For example: *money, love, oil, childhood, news.* Distinguished from COUNT NOUN.

melioration A semantic shift in which a word comes to have a meaning regarded as socially or culturally more favorable than the meaning it formerly had. For example, *marshal* originally denoted a groom or, later, a master of the horse in a medieval royal household; after being applied to a high official in such a household, the word came to refer to a holder of more prestigious positions, including that of officer of the highest rank in some armies. Melioration is sometimes called *amelioration* or *elevation.*

metathesis The transposition of letters or sounds in a word, or the result of this. For example, *clasp* was developed from Middle English *clapse* by metathesis.

misplaced modifier An adjective or adverb, or an adjectival or adverbial phrase or clause, that is so placed that it seems to qualify the wrong sentence element. For example, in "There were a dozen melons in the gunnysack, which we ate," the adjective clause *which we ate* seems to modify *gunnysack* instead of *melons.* Misplaced modifiers are sometimes thought to include a DANGLING PARTICIPLE.

modal auxiliary See AUXILIARY VERB and MOOD.

modifier A word, phrase, or clause that qualifies or limits the meaning of another word or word group. Adjectives and adverbs are modifiers.

mood A form of the verb that has to do with the speaker's attitude toward the action or state expressed. The *indicative mood* indicates that the action or state is regarded as an assertion (whether expressed as a fact or a question). For example: "It *snows* a lot in the Great Lakes region"; "*Does* the region attract skiers?" The *subjunctive mood* indicates that the action or state is regarded as a matter of supposition, desire, possibility, or the like. For example: "If I *were* President, things would be different"; "We wish he *were* home again." The *imperative mood* indicates that the action is regarded as a command. For example: "*Come* home at once!" In English, mood is often shown by auxiliary verbs, such as *should, may,* and *might. Mode* is synonymous with *mood.*

natural gender See GENDER.

neologism The same as COINAGE.

neuter gender See GENDER.

nonce word A word coined and used for a single or particular occasion.

nonrestrictive element A subordinate clause or a phrase or word that is felt to be purely descriptive, or not essential to the sense of the sentence. It is therefore usually set off by commas. For example: "Salem, *which is located on the Willamette River,* is the capital of Oregon"; "We got to the airport early, *with an hour to spare*"; "President Eisenhower and his wife, *Mamie,* retired to a farm near Gettysburg." Distinguished from RESTRICTIVE ELEMENT.

nonstandard Designating a word, grammatical construction, or pronunciation which differs from that of the language variety generally adopted by educated speakers. Nonstandard usage is not necessarily regarded as below standard usage (as SUBSTANDARD is).

noun Any of a class of words naming or denoting a person, thing, place, quality, or the like. For example: *Georgia, sculptor, garden, honesty.* Also, any word, phrase, or clause similarly used. For example, in "I like to swim," the infinitive phrase *to swim* serves as a noun, being the direct object of the verb *like.* A noun or any word group functioning as a noun is also called a *substantive.*

number A difference of form showing whether one or more than one is meant. In English, nouns, pronouns, and verbs have two numbers: singular and plural. For example, in "A big, nutritious breakfast is good for you," *breakfast* is a singular noun and *is* a singular verb. In "We prefer junk food," *we* is a plural pronoun and *prefer* a plural verb.

object A noun or noun substitute that receives the action of a verb or is governed by a preposition. The two kinds of objects are DIRECT and INDIRECT. For example, in "Give me the book," *book* is the direct object and *me* is the indirect object. In "Give the book to me," *me* is the object of the preposition *to.*

objective case See CASE.

ordinal number. Any number used to indicate order in a particular series. For example: "second," "forty-seventh," "634th." Distinguished from CARDINAL NUMBER.

parallel structure A balanced or coordinated arrangement of sentence elements, especially phrases and clauses. For example, "We like traveling nonstop and to carry our luggage with us" is not parallel. But "We like traveling nonstop and carrying our luggage with us" is, and so is "We like to travel nonstop and to carry our luggage with us."

parenthesis An additional word, phrase, or clause placed as an explanation or comment within an already complete sentence. It is usually marked off by parentheses, dashes, or commas. For example: "A national bank (which Madison finally approved after having argued against it) was expected to cure the ills of state banks." Or: "A national bank—which Madison finally approved after having argued against it—was expected to cure the ills of state banks." Or: "A national bank, which Madison finally approved after having argued against it, was expected to cure the ills of state banks."

parse To separate a sentence into its parts, explaining the grammatical form, function, and interrelation of each part. Also, to describe the form, part of speech, and function of a word in a sentence.

participle A verbal form basically having the qualities of both verb and adjective. The present participle ends in -*ing,* and the past participle most commonly ends in -*ed* or -*en.* Participles are generally used in verb phrases, with an auxiliary verb. For example: "It *is starting* to rain"; "She *has written* twice." They are also used as verbs (*"Seeing* the ad, he smiled"); as adjectives ("a *laughing* boy"; "the *beaten* path"); as nouns, that is, as gerunds (*"Seeing* is *believing"*); as adverbs ("He was *raving* mad"); and as connectives (*"Saving* those present, all voted yes"). Participles are one kind of VERBAL.

parts of speech In traditional English grammar, the eight classes into which words are grouped according to their form, function, meaning, and other characteristics. They are NOUN, VERB, ADJECTIVE, ADVERB, PRONOUN, PREPOSITION, CONJUNCTION, and INTERJECTION.

passive voice The form of a verb whose subject is the receiver, or object, of the action of the verb. For example: "The car *was towed* to the garage."

past participle See PARTICIPLE.

pejoration A semantic shift in which a word comes to have a meaning considered socially or culturally less favorable than the meaning it formerly had. For example, the Middle English word *huswife* meant simply "housewife," but the current contracted form *hussy* is a contemptuous or playful term for a woman, especially one of low morals. Pejoration is sometimes called *degradation.*

person The division of PERSONAL PRONOUNS and their corresponding verb forms into three classes to indicate whether the subject is speaking (first person), is spoken to (second person), or is spoken of (third person). For example: *I (we) go* (first person); *you go* (second person); *he (she, it) goes* (third person, singular); *they go* (third person, plural).

personal pronoun Any of a group of pronouns referring to the speaker(s), the person(s) spoken to, or any other person(s) or thing(s). There are three forms of personal pronouns.

> subjective (showing mainly that the pronoun is being used as the subject of a verb): *I, you, he, she, it, we, they*
> objective (showing mainly that the pronoun is being used as the object of a verb or preposition): *me, you, him, her, it, us, them*
> possessive (showing possession or a similar relationship): *my, mine; your, yours; his; hers; its; our, ours; their, theirs*

For example: "*We* take *our* car to visit *him,* and *they* take *theirs.*"

pharynx The muscular and membranous cavity of the alimentary canal leading from the mouth and nasal passages to the larynx and esophagus. The speech sounds known as VOWELS pass through the pharynx and opened mouth.

phrasal verb The same as VERB SET.

phrase A sequence of two or more words conveying a single thought or forming a distinct part of a sentence but not containing a subject and predicate. For example, in "We saw two noisy bluejays," *two noisy bluejays* is a noun phrase. In "I have been cleaning the garage," *have been cleaning* is a verb phrase.

pitch The quality of a speech sound as determined by the rate of vibration of the sound waves reaching the ear.

pleonasm The same as REDUNDANCY.

plural See NUMBER.

popular etymology The same as FOLK ETYMOLOGY.

portmanteau word The same as BLEND.

positive degree See COMPARISON.

possessive case See CASE.

predicate The part of a clause or sentence that makes a statement about the subject. A predicate is the verb and any complements, objects, and modifiers. For example, in "He took a bottle of wine to the dinner party," *took* is the verb and *took a bottle of wine to the dinner party* is the predicate.

predicate complement A word or word group used after a linking verb to complete the meaning. For example: "Fritz was *master of ceremonies*" (predicate noun); "The soup tastes *cold*" (predicate adjective). A predicate noun is also called a *predicate nominative*.

prefix A syllable, group of syllables, or word joined to the beginning of another word to alter its meaning or create a new word. For example, the word *nonessential* is made up of the prefix *non-,* meaning "not," plus the word *essential*.

preposition A relation or function word, such as *in, by, for,* or *with,* that connects a lexical word, usually a noun or pronoun, or a syntactic construction, to another element of the sentence. For example, in "They came from Atlanta," *from* connects the verb *came* to the noun *Atlanta*. In "Peals of laughter came from the next room," *of* connects the nouns *peals* and *laughter*. In "Good for her," *for* connects the adjective *good* and the pronoun *her*.

prepositional phrase A phrase consisting of a preposition and its object and used as an adverb, an adjective, or a noun-subject. For example: "We decided to go *on the spur of the moment*" (adverb); "She slipped on a cake *of soap*" (adjective); "*By the seashore* is where I want to live" (noun-subject).

present participle See PARTICIPLE.

preterit The past tense, that is, a verb tense expressing past action or state in a simple, or one-word, form. For example: "They *laughed*"; "I *broke* the jar." Also spelled *preterite*.

principal clause The same as MAIN CLAUSE.

principal parts The principal forms of a verb, from which the other forms may be derived. They are: present infinitive (*smile* and *creep,* for example); past tense (*smiled, crept*); and past participle (*smiled, crept*). The present participle, derived from the present infinitive with *-ing* added, is sometimes considered a principal part (*smiling, creeping*).

progressive verb A verb form that indicates continuing action. The main verb is a present participle (ending in *-ing*), and its auxiliary is a form of the verb *be*. For example: "I *am driving*"; "I *was driving*"; "I *have been driving*"; "I *had been driving*"; "I *will be driving*."

pronoun A word that generally takes the place of a noun, often so the noun need not be repeated. For example: "When Helen phoned, I told *her* the news," instead of "When Helen phoned, I told *Helen* the news." Pronouns are usually divided into eight classes: DEMONSTRATIVE, INDEFINITE, INTENSIVE, INTERROGATIVE, PERSONAL, RECIPROCAL, REFLEXIVE, and RELATIVE.

proper noun A noun that designates a specific person, place, or thing. It is ordinarily capitalized and not used with an article. For example: *Josephine, Oklahoma, Fifth Avenue.* Distinguished from COMMON NOUN.

pun A play on words. That is, the humorous treatment of a word or of words which are formed or sounded alike but have different meanings, in such a way as to put to use two or more of the possible applications. For example: "Airlines *fare* badly in the current price war."

quotation See DIRECT QUOTATION and INDIRECT QUOTATION.

Received Standard The dialect of British English spoken by the upper classes, especially by graduates of Oxford and Cambridge.

reciprocal pronoun A pronoun, such as *each other* or *one another,* which expresses mutual action or relation. For example: "Please share this program with each other."

redundancy The use of more words than are necessary to express an idea. For example: *essential prerequisites.* Also known as *tautology* or *pleonasm.*

reflexive pronoun A pronoun used as the object of a verb whose subject is the same person or thing: *myself, yourself, himself, herself, itself, ourselves, yourselves, themselves.* For example: "They hurt themselves skydiving."

reflexive verb A verb whose subject and direct object refer to the same person or thing. For example: "The dog *scratched* itself."

regionalism A word, meaning, expression, or pronunciation peculiar to one region. For example, *sack* is likely to be heard in the South, but *bag* in other parts of the United States.

regular verb A verb that forms its past tense and past participle by adding *-ed* or *-d* to the infinitive. For example: *jumped* from *jump; liked* from *like.* Such verbs are also called *weak verbs.* Distinguished from IRREGULAR VERB.

relative pronoun A pronoun that introduces a subordinate (adjective) clause and refers to an antecedent. *Who, whom, which, what, that,* and *whoever* are among the relative pronouns. For example, in "Leslie is the one who lives on a houseboat," *who* is a relative pronoun introducing the relative clause *who lives on a houseboat.*

restrictive element A subordinate clause or a phrase or word that is felt to limit the application of the word or words it modifies in such a way as to be essential to the sense of the sentence. It is therefore usually not set off by commas. For example: "One of the state capitals *that are located on a river* is Salem, Oregon"; "Please give me the book *with the green cover*"; "It's by the novelist *Elizabeth Bowen.*" Distinguished from NONRESTRICTIVE ELEMENT.

root The same as BASE.

run-on sentence Two or more complete sentences capitalized and punctuated as one. For example: "They are here, they came early." This construction is generally regarded as a fault.

schwa The neutral, uncolored, central vowel sound of most unstressed syllables in English. For example: the *a* in *ago,* the *e* in *agent,* the *i* in *sanity,* the *o* in *lemon,* the *u* in *focus.* In the International Phonetic Alphabet and in many dictionaries it is represented by the symbol ə (ə gō′, for example).

semantic shift Change in the meaning or meanings of a word or expression over time. The main patterns of semantic shift are GENERALIZATION, MELIORATION, PEJORATION, and SPECIALIZATION.

sentence A conventional unit of connected speech or writing that usually contains a subject and a predicate and that states, asks, commands, or explains something. In writing, a sentence ordinarily begins with a capital letter and concludes with an end mark of punctuation, such as a period, a question mark, or an exclamation mark. Sentences are usually classified in two ways: by structure (SIMPLE, COMPOUND, COMPLEX); and by the action of the principal finite verb (DECLARATIVE, INTERROGATIVE, IMPERATIVE, EXCLAMATORY).

sentence fragment Part of a sentence, such as a phrase or a subordinate clause, that is capitalized and punctuated as if it were a grammatically complete sentence (one with a subject and a predicate). For example: ''Out on the back porch.'' This construction is generally regarded as a fault.

short vowel A vowel sound of relatively short duration. In popular usage the term is often applied to the quality determined by the formation of the vowel at the front of the mouth. For example: the *a* sound in *fat* (as distinguished from the *a* sound in *fate* and *father*); the *e* sound in *ten* (as distinguished from the *e* sound in *scene*); and the *i* sound in *is* (as distinguished from the *i* sound in *time*).

simple sentence A sentence consisting of one main clause and no subordinate clauses. For example: ''Birds fly''; ''Every other Wednesday, a truck filled with pineapples pulls up to the school.''

singular See NUMBER.

slang Highly informal language that is outside of conventional or standard usage and consists of both coined words and phrases and of new or extended meanings attached to established terms. It develops from the attempt to find fresh and vigorous, colorful, pungent, or humorous expression, and generally either passes into disuse or comes to have a more formal status.

specialization A kind of semantic shift in which a word comes to have a meaning regarded as more specialized, or narrower, than the meaning it formerly had. For example, *deer* once denoted any wild animal or beast, but nowadays it refers to a member of a certain family of hoofed, cud-chewing animals, the males of which usually bear antlers that are shed every year.

split infinitive A construction in which the infinitive proper is separated from the marker *to* that often precedes it. For example: ''We were about *to* finally *reach* our goal.''

spoonerism An unintentional interchange of sounds, usually initial sounds, in two or more words. For example: *Lady Shane* for *Shady Lane.*

squinting modifier A misplaced adverb or other modifier than can be interpreted as referring to either the preceding or the following part of the sentence. For example: ''People who behave well *from time to time* are rewarded.''

standard Designating a level of usage in accord with that of educated, cultivated speakers of the language. It excludes vocabulary, constructions, pronunciations, and other items of usage considered too informal, vulgar, provincial, mistaken, or otherwise likely to detract from the dignity or prestige of the user.

stem The same as BASE.

strong verb The same as IRREGULAR VERB.

subject The noun, noun phrase, or noun substitute (usually a pronoun) in a sentence about which something is said in the predicate. For example: "*Madagascar* gained its independence from France in 1960"; "Where is *it* located?" A complete subject consists of the simple subject and its modifiers. For example: "*Madagascar, which is located off the southeast coast of Africa, gained its independence from France in 1960.*" In an imperative sentence the subject is implied, not stated. For example: "[*You*] come here!"

subjective case See CASE.

subjunctive mood See MOOD.

subordinate clause In a complex sentence, a clause that cannot function grammatically as a complete sentence (as distinguished from the MAIN CLAUSE). For example: "We pay taxes *whether we want to or not.*" Also known as a *dependent clause.*

subordinating conjunction A conjunction used to connect a subordinate word, phrase, or clause to some other sentence element. For example: "Two trucks had to move all the furniture, *because* the third was in the shop."

substandard Designating a language variety regarded as below the standards of the variety generally adopted by educated speakers. For example, the use of a singular verb with a plural subject is often said to mark substandard speech. Considering the term too judgmental, many linguists use NONSTANDARD instead.

suffix A syllable, group of syllables, or word added to the end of a word or word base to change its meaning, give it grammatical function, or form a new word. For example, the word *roller* is made up of the verb *roll* plus the suffix *-er,* meaning "a person or thing that." The present participle *snowing* is made up of the infinitive *snow* plus the suffix *-ing.*

superlative degree See COMPARISON.

syllable A unit of pronunciation (a word or part of a word) consisting of a single sound of great sonority (usually a vowel) and generally one or more sounds of lesser sonority (usually consonants). For example, *but·ter·fly* consists of three syllables. In written or printed material, a syllable is any of the parts into which a word is divided in approximate representation of its spoken syllables to show where the word can be broken at the end of a line. Some dictionaries use centered dots to separate the syllables of entry words.

syncopation A phonetic process in which sounds or letters are dropped from the middle of words. For example, *Gloucester* is pronounced gläs′tər or glôs′tər.

synonym A word having the same or nearly the same meaning in one or more senses as another. For example, *greedy* and *avaricious* are synonyms.

syntax The grammatical arrangement of elements (words, phrases, clauses) in a sentence to show their relationship to one another.

tautology The same as REDUNDANCY.

tense Any of the forms of a verb that show the time of its action or state of being. In accordance with Latin models, English tenses are usually listed as *present, past, future, present perfect, past perfect (pluperfect)*, and *future perfect.*

Tenses other than the simple present ("We *joke,*" for example) and the simple past ("We *joked*") are formed by using an AUXILIARY VERB with a PARTICIPLE or INFINITIVE form of a verb.

future: "We *will* (or *shall*) joke."

perfect (expressing a state or action completed at the time of speaking or at the time indicated): present (or simple) perfect ("We *have joked*"); past perfect (or pluperfect) ("We *had joked*"); and future perfect ("We *will* (or *shall*) *have joked*").

The progressive verb forms are used to show continuing action. For example: "We *are* (*were*) *joking.*"

transitive verb A verb expressing an action that is thought of as passing over and taking effect on some person or thing. It takes a direct object to complete its meaning. For example: "I *collect* my mail in the afternoon." Distinguished from INTRANSITIVE VERB.

usage The customary manner of using the words of a given language in speaking or writing; more particularly, the way in which a word, phrase, construction, or the like is used to express a certain idea. Usage is what ultimately determines the meaning, pronunciation, spelling, and other aspects of a term or construction.

utterance The act of uttering, or expressing by voice. Also, that which is uttered, especially a word or words uttered, whether written or spoken.

verb Any of a class of words expressing action, existence, or occurrence, usually as the main element of a predicate. A verb may also be an AUXILIARY VERB or a LINKING VERB. For other characteristics of verbs, see TRANSITIVE VERB, INTRANSITIVE VERB, MOOD, TENSE, VOICE, NUMBER, PERSON.

verbal A word that has all the uses of a noun, together with certain characteristics of a verb. A verbal cannot be altered to show number, person, or tense, and it would not make sense as the principal verb in a sentence or clause. Yet, like verbs, it can take an object, a complement, an adverb modifier, and even a subject. A verbal may be an INFINITIVE, PARTICIPLE (past or present), or GERUND. Another name for *verbal* is *nonfinite verb.*

verb phrase A word group consisting of a verb form (such as *swum*) and an auxiliary verb (such as *have*). For example: "The ducks *have swum* across the pond."

verb set An idiomatic phrase consisting of a verb form followed by an adverb. For example: *make up* (meaning, among other things, "to become friendly again after a disagreement or quarrel"). A preposition may be tacked on as well. For example: *make up to* ("to flatter, or try to be agreeable to, in order to become friendly or intimate with"). Also called a *phrasal verb.*

vocabulary The entire word stock of a given language. *Active vocabulary* refers to all the words used by a particular person, class, profession, or the like. *Passive* *vocabulary* refers to all the words recognized and understood, though not necessarily used, by a particular person.

vocal cords Either of two pairs of membranous cords or folds in the larynx, consisting of a thicker upper pair (*false vocal cords*) and a lower pair (*true vocal cords*). Voice is produced when air from the lungs causes the lower cords to vibrate. Pitch is controlled by varying the tension on the cords, and volume is controlled by regulating the air passing through the larynx.

vogue word A word or expression that is used widely for a relatively brief period and then falls from fashion.

voice In grammar, any of the forms of a verb showing the connection between the subject and the verb, either as performing (ACTIVE VOICE) or receiving (PASSIVE VOICE) the action.

In phonetics (the branch of language study dealing with speech sounds), *voice* denotes the sound made by vibrating the VOCAL CORDS with air forced from the lungs, as in pronouncing all vowels and such consonants as *b, d, g,* and *m.* Sounds made this way are called *voiced,* whereas those made without vibration of the vocal cords (*p, t, k,* and *s,* for example) are called *voiceless* or *unvoiced.*

vowel A voiced speech sound produced by air passing in a continuous stream through the pharynx and opened mouth, with relatively little constriction of the speech organs. In most syllables, the vowel sound has greater prominence than the consonant sound or sounds. The letters representing vowel sounds (*a, e, i, o, u,* and sometimes *y*) are also known as vowels.

weak verb The same as REGULAR VERB.

weasel word A word or remark that is equivocal or deliberately ambiguous or misleading.

word A speech sound, or series of such sounds, that can stand alone in communicating meaning. A word is also a letter or group of letters representing such a unit of language, written or printed usually in solid or hyphenated form.

word order The arrangement of words in a phrase, clause, or sentence.

PRONUNCIATION SYMBOLS USED IN THIS BOOK

As in *Webster's New World Dictionary of the American Language,* the pronunciations shown in this book are those used by cultivated speakers in normal, relaxed conversation. They are symbolized in as broad a manner as is consistent with accuracy so that speakers of every variety of American English can easily read their own pronunciations in the symbols used.

Symbol	Key Words
a	asp, fat, parrot
ā	ape, date, play
ä	ah, car, father
e	elf, ten, berry
ē	even, meet, money
i	is, hit, mirror
ī	ice, bite, high
ō	open, tone, go
ô	all, horn, law
o͞o	ooze, tool, crew
oo	look, pull, moor
yo͞o	use, cute, few
yoo	united, cure, globule
oi	oil, point, toy
ou	out, crowd, plow
u	up, cut, color
ʉr	urn, fur, deter

ə	**a** in **ago**
	e in **agent**
	i in **sanity**
	o in **comply**
	u in **focus**
ər	perh**aps**, murd**er**
b	**b**e**d**, fa**b**le, du**b**
d	**d**ip, bea**d**le, ha**d**
f	**f**all, a**f**ter, o**ff**
g	**g**et, ha**gg**le, do**g**
h	**h**e, a**h**ead, **h**otel
j	**j**oy, a**g**ile, ba**dge**
k	**k**ill, ta**ck**le, ba**k**e
l	**l**et, ye**ll**ow, ba**ll**
m	**m**et, ca**m**el, tri**m**
n	**n**ot, fla**nn**el, to**n**
p	**p**ut, a**pp**le, ta**p**
r	**r**ed, po**r**t, dea**r**
s	**s**ell, ca**s**tle, pa**ss**
t	**t**op, ca**tt**le, ha**t**
v	**v**at, ho**v**el, ha**v**e
w	**w**ill, al**w**ays, s**w**ear
y	**y**et, on**i**on, **y**ard
z	**z**ebra, da**zz**le, ha**z**e
c/h	**ch**in, cat**ch**er, ar**ch**
s/h	**sh**e, cu**sh**ion, da**sh**
t/h	**th**in, no**th**ing, tru**th**
t/h	**th**en, fa**th**er, la**th**e
z/h	a**z**ure, lei**s**ure
ŋ	ri**ng**, a**ng**er, dri**n**k
'	(see explanatory note below)

Although the qualities of most of the above symbols can be readily understood from the key words in which they appear, a few explanatory notes on some of the more complex of these symbols follow.

ä   This symbol represents essentially the low back vowel of *car*, but may also represent the low central vowel sometimes heard in New England for *bath*. Certain words shown with ä, such as *alms* (ämz), *hot* (hät), *rod* (räd), etc., are heard in the speech of some persons with vowel variation, ranging all the way to ô (ômz), (hôt), (rôd), etc. Such variation, though not generally recorded, may be assumed.

e   This symbol represents the mid front vowel of *ten*, and is also used, followed and hence colored by *r*, to represent the vowel sound of *care* (ker). For this sound, vowels ranging from ā (kār or kā'ər) to a (kar) are sometimes heard and, though not recorded, may be assumed as variants.

ē This symbol represents the high front vowel of *meet* and is also used for the vowel in the unstressed final syllable of such words as *lucky* (luk′ē), *pretty* (prit′ē), etc. In such contexts, reduction to i (luk′i), (prit′i), etc, is often heard. Such variations, though not recorded, may be assumed.

i This symbol represents the high front unrounded vowel of *hit* and is also used for the vowel in the unstressed syllables of such words as *garbage* (gär′bij), *goodness* (good′nis), *preface* (pref′is), *deny* (di nī′), *curate* (kyoor′it), etc. In such contexts, reduction to ə is commonly heard: (gär′bəj), (good′nəs), (pref′əs), (də nī′), (kyoor′ət), etc. Such variants, though not recorded, may be assumed. This symbol is also used, followed and hence colored by *r*, to represent the vowel sound of *dear* (dir). For this sound, vowels ranging to ē (dēr or dē′ər) are sometimes heard and, though not here recorded, may be assumed as variants.

ô This symbol represents the mid to low back vowel of *all*. When followed by *r*, as in *more* (môr), vowels ranging to ō (mōr or mō′ər) are often heard and, though not here recorded, may be assumed as variants. Certain words shown with ô, such as *cough* (kôf), *lawn* (lôn), etc., are heard in the speech of some persons with vowel variation ranging all the way to ä (käf), (län), etc. Such variation, though not generally recorded, may be assumed.

ʉr and ər These two clusters of symbols represent respectively the stressed and unstressed r-colored vowels heard successively in the two syllables of *murder* (mʉr′dər). Where these symbols are shown, some speakers, especially in the South and along the Eastern seaboard, will, as a matter of course, pronounce them without the r-coloration, that is, by ''dropping their *r*'s.'' Such pronunciations, though not generally recorded, may be inferred as variants.

ə This symbol, called the schwa, represents the mid central relaxed vowel of neutral coloration heard in the unstressed syllables of *ago, agent, focus*, etc. The degree and quality of the dulling of such vowels vary from word to word and from speaker to speaker. In many contexts, as for *-itis* (īt′əs), the vowel is often raised to i (īt′is). Such variants when not shown may be inferred.

t This symbol represents the voiceless alveolar stop of *tap* or *hat*. When it appears between vowels, especially before an unstressed vowel, as in *later* (lāt′ər), or before a syllabic *l* as in *cattle* (kat′′l), it is often heard as a voiced sound that approaches the sound of *d* in *ladle*. Although such variants are not shown, the symbol (t) is generally placed in the same syllable with the preceding vowel to help the reader infer the voiced alternative.

ŋ This symbol represents the voiced velar nasal sound indicated in spelling by the *ng* of *sing* and occurring also for *n* before the back consonants *k* and *g*, as in *drink* (driŋ) and *finger* (fiŋ′gər).

′ The apostrophe occurring before an *l*, *m*, or *n* indicates that the following consonant is a syllabic consonant; that is, that it forms the nucleus of a syllable with no appreciable vowel sound accompanying it, as in *apple* (ap′′l) or *happen* (hap′′n). In the speech of some persons, certain syllabic consonants are replaced with syllables containing reduced vowels, as (hap′ən). Such variants, though not entered, may be inferred.

REFERENCES

For its definitions of words and phrases, etymologies, and pronunciations, this book draws mainly on *Webster's New World Dictionary of the American Language,* Second College Edition (New York: Prentice Hall Press, 1986). *The Oxford English Dictionary* (Oxford: Clarendon Press, 1933), together with its *Supplements* (1972–1986), is cited from time to time. The sources of other quotations that appear in this book are listed below, by entry.

a or *an?*
Associated Press. "Airline President Cut Up by Bomb" (syndicated article), June 1980.

about or *around?*
Wood, Frederick T. *Current English Usage: A Concise Dictionary.* London: Macmillan, 1962, p. 23.

ain't
Ayres, B. Drummond, Jr. "Senate Votes, 81–15, Talmadge Criticism on Handling Funds," *The New York Times,* October 12, 1979.
"Mudd Leaving NBC for PBS," *San Francisco Chronicle,* January 30, 1987.

all or *all of?*
Flesch, Rudolf. *The ABC of Style: A Guide to Plain English.* New York: Harper & Row, 1964, p. 19.

alternate or *alternative?*
Copperud, Roy H. *American Usage: The Consensus.* New York: Van Nostrand Reinhold, 1970, pp. 13, 37.
Copperud, Roy H. *American Usage and Style: The Consensus.* New York: Van Nostrand Reinhold, 1980, pp. 19, 56.
Hurt, Peyton. *Bibliography and Footnotes: A Style Manual for Students and Writers.* 3d ed., revised and enlarged by Mary L. Hurt Richmond. Berkeley: University of California Press, 1968, p. 37.

among or *between?*
Salm, Peter. "Virginia Woolf: Wrestling with Chaos," *Pinpoint of Eternity: European Literature in Search of the All-Encompassing Moment.* Lanham, Md.: University Press of America, 1986, p. 94.
Simon, John. "*Dictionary Johnson: Samuel Johnson's Middle Years,* by James L. Clifford," *The New York Times Book Review,* October 14, 1979, p. 45.

and **or** *or?*

United Press International. "GOP Halts Its Probe of 'Bugging' " (syndicated article), June 1980.

"And so it goes."

Ellerbee, Linda. *And So It Goes: Adventures in Television.* New York: Putnam's, 1986.

Graves, Robert, and Alan Hodge. "The Present Confusion of English Prose." Chap. 2 in *The Reader over Your Shoulder: A Handbook for Writers of English Prose.* 2d ed., rev. and abr. New York: Vintage Books, 1979, p. 26.

Guerard, Albert J. "The Ivory Tower and the Dust Bowl," in *New World Writing: Third Mentor Selection.* New York: New American Library, 1953, p. 345.

Leslie, Paul. "Exits," in George E. Murphy, Jr., comp. *The Editors' Choice,* vol. 3. Toronto: Bantam Books, 1987, p. 149.

Orwell, George. "Raffles and Miss Blandish," *A Collection of Essays.* Garden City, N.Y.: Doubleday, 1954, p. 150.

and/or

Highet, Gilbert. "Learning a Language," *Explorations.* New York: Oxford University Press, 1971, p. 100.

Apologize, **sí;** *finalize,* **no.**

The American Heritage Dictionary of the English Language, Second College Edition. Boston: Houghton Mifflin, 1982, p. 504.

Flesch, Rudolf. *The ABC of Style: A Guide to Plain English.* New York: Harper & Row, 1964, p. 123.

Gilmore, Tom. "Giants near Cable-TV Deal," *San Franciso Chronicle,* February 11, 1986.

Harvard Educational Review. Form letter to prospective authors, 1986.

Hersey, John, "A Reporter at Large—Hiroshima: The Aftermath," *The New Yorker,* July 15, 1985, p. 37.

Mitchell, Richard. *Less Than Words Can Say.* Boston: Little, Brown, 1979, p. 130.

Morris, William, and Mary Morris. *Harper Dictionary of Contemporary Usage.* 2d ed. New York: Harper & Row, 1985, pp. 223, 224.

Oxford American Dictionary. New York: Oxford University Press, 1980, p. 241.

Partridge, Eric. *Usage and Abusage: A Guide to Good English.* Harmondsworth, Eng.: Penguin Books, 1973, p. 119.

Pritchett, V. S. "The Fig Tree," *On the Edge of the Cliff.* New York: Random House, 1979, pp. 152–153.

Sayers, Dorothy L. "The Entertaining Episode of the Article in Question," *Lord Peter.* Compiled and with an introduction by James Sandoe. New York: Avon Books, 1972, p. 27.

"Sir Roy Strong: Strong by Name but Certainly Not Strong by Nature," *The Sunday Times,* London, February 1, 1987.

Strunk, William, Jr., and E. B. White. *The Elements of Style.* 3d ed. New York: Macmillan, 1979, p. 47.

Wood, Frederick T. *Current English Usage: A Concise Dictionary.* London: Macmillan, 1962, p. 95.

as . . . as **or** *so . . . as?*

Percy, Walker. *The Moviegoer.* New York: Noonday Press, 1961, p. 67.

as well as or *and*?
Goleman, Daniel. "What Makes Beauty Beautiful?" (a *New York Times* syndicated article), August 1986.

Rich, Frank. "English Musical Goes Over in New York" (a *New York Times* syndicated article), August 1986.

bad or *badly*?
Percy, Walker. *The Second Coming.* New York: Pocket Books, 1980, p. 8.

Truman, Margaret. *Murder in Georgetown.* New York: Fawcett Crest, 1986, p. 139.

The ball dropped between he and the left-fielder.
Cooke, Alistair. Introduction to "Lillie," *Masterpiece Theatre*, Public Broadcasting Service, 1979.

Didion, Joan. *A Book of Common Prayer.* New York: Simon & Schuster, 1977, p. 100.

Eliot, T. S. "The Love Song of J. Alfred Prufrock," *The Complete Poems and Plays.* New York: Harcourt, Brace, 1952, p. 3.

Garchik. Leah. "Personals," *San Francisco Chronicle,* June 23, 1984.

McMurtry, Larry. *All My Friends Are Going to Be Strangers.* New York: Simon & Schuster, 1972, p. 242.

Nolte, Carl. "Mayor's Old House Sold for $825,000," *San Francisco Chronicle*, December 22, 1984.

Nott, Kathleen. "Books [review of *Growing Up in a London Village*, by Phyllis Willmott]," *The Observer*, London, May 13, 1979.

Van Buren, Abigail. "Dear Abby" (syndicated column), September 1980.

Williams, Roger M. "Paradise for Two: A Weekend at the Forêt de Fontainebleau," *Vis à Vis* (Allegis Corporation), March 1987, p. 57.

Wilson, Earl. "It Happened Last Night" (syndicated column), September 1975.

B.C.; A.D.
Carmody, John. "The TV Column," *The Washington Post,* August 7, 1986.

Vonnegut, Kurt. *Galápagos.* New York: Dell, 1985, p. 3.

belabor or *labor*?
Adams, J. Donald. *The Magic and Mystery of Words.* New York: Holt, Rinehart and Winston, 1963, p. 64.

Betsky, Celia. "*Victoria Ocampo: Against the Wind and the Tide*, by Doris Meyer," *Smithsonian*, August 1979, p. 115.

Mayes, Herbert R. "London Letter," *Saturday Review*, November 14, 1979, p. 6.

Zinsser, William. *On Writing Well: An Informal Guide to Writing Nonfiction.* New York: Harper & Row, 1976, pp. 18–19.

Zinsser, William. *On Writing Well: An Informal Guide to Writing Nonfiction.* 2d ed. New York: Harper & Row, 1980, p. 20.

Zinsser, William. *On Writing Well: An Informal Guide to Writing Nonfiction.* 3d ed., rev. and enl. New York: Harper & Row, 1985, p. 19.

bemuse or *amuse*?
Bernstein, Richard. "On Language: Gallic Gall," *The New York Times Magazine,* August 17, 1986, p. 8.

bi- or *semi-*?

Associated Press. "A Homosexual Father Gains Custody of Son" (syndicated article), July 1986.

Garino, David P. "In Times of Stress, Avoid Violence; Try Unvoiced Fricatives Instead," *The Wall Street Journal*, March 25, 1981.

The Horn Book Magazine, Boston.

IDP Report, White Plains, N.Y.

LMP 1987—Literary Market Place: The Directory of American Book Publishing. New York: Bowker, 1986, pp. 576–579.

Ulrich's International Periodicals Directory: A Classified Guide to Current Periodicals, Foreign and Domestic, 1986–1987, vol. 1. 25th ed. New York: Bowker, 1986, p. 470.

blame for or *blame on*?

Bernstein, Theodore M. *The Careful Writer: A Modern Guide to English Usage.* New York: Atheneum, 1965, p. 76.

"Los Angeles Times" Stylebook: A Manual for Writers, Editors, Journalists and Students. Compiled by Frederick S. Holley. New York: New American Library, 1981, p. 47.

"The New York Times" Manual of Style and Usage: A Desk Book of Guidelines for Writers and Editors. Revised and edited by Lewis Jordan. New York: Times Books, 1976, p. 26.

"The Washington Post" Deskbook on Style. Compiled and edited by Robert A. Webb. New York: McGraw-Hill, 1978, p. 59.

bring, take, or *fetch*?

Kanner, Bernice. "Gaffe Riot," *New York,* August 4, 1986, p. 20.

Kennedy, Eugene. *Himself! The Life and Times of Mayor Richard J. Daley.* New York: Viking, 1978, p. 16.

Burglars burgle and peddlers peddle, so why don't janitors janit?

Bremner, John B. *Words on Words: A Dictionary for Writers and Others Who Care about Words.* New York: Columbia University Press, 1980, p. 56.

Claiborne, Robert. *Saying What You Mean: A Commonsense Guide to American Usage.* New York: Norton, 1986, p. 115.

Faulty Diction, As Corrected by the "Funk & Wagnalls New Standard Dictionary of the English Language." New York: Funk & Wagnalls, 1915, p. 28.

Flesch, Rudolf. *The ABC of Style: A Guide to Plain English.* New York: Harper & Row, 1964, p. 103.

Orwell, George. "Inside the Whale," *A Collection of Essays.* Garden City, N.Y.: Doubleday, 1954, p. 228.

Strunk, William, Jr., and E. B. White. *The Elements of Style.* 3d ed. New York: Macmillan, 1979, p. 45.

"Burnett goes dramatic as a gaunt Iowa wife."

Barzun, Jacques. "A Writer's Discipline." Chap. 1 in *On Writing, Editing, and Publishing: Essays Explicative and Hortatory.* 2d ed. Chicago: University of Chicago Press, 1986, pp. 11, 14.

Boyd, L. M. "The Grab Bag" (syndicated column), February 1986.

Colford, Paul D. "MacNeil and Lehrer, the Other Two Anchors" (a *Newsday* syndicated article), June 1986.

Fowler, H. W. *A Dictionary of Modern English Usage*. Oxford: Clarendon Press, 1926, p. 176.

"Just Plain Justices" (a *New York Times* syndicated article), November 1980.

"Manguage" (editorial), *The New York Times*, June 2, 1985.

McCabe, Charles. "Himself," *San Francisco Chronicle*, February 5, 1980.

Public Broadcasting Service. "Adventures of Sherlock Holmes II: The Greek Interpreter," *Mystery!*, February 1986.

Robertson, Stuart. *The Development of Modern English*. New York: Prentice-Hall, 1946, p. 1.

Smith, Cecil. "Burnett Sticks Her Neck Out," *Los Angeles Times*, March 18, 1979. (Reprinted in *San Francisco Sunday Examiner & Chronicle*, April 22, 1979, under the headline "Burnett Goes Dramatic As a Gaunt Iowa Wife.")

United Press. "Roget's Rubs Out 'Mankind' " (syndicated article), April 1982.

Who's Who in America. 44th ed., 1986–1987, vol. I. Wilmette, Ill.: Marquis Who's Who, 1986, p. 396.

Can I borrow your lawn mower? Not if you might keep it.

Brown, Michael. "Robert Oppenheimer: *Letters and Recollections*," *Saturday Review*, June 1980, p. 78.

Faulty Diction, As Corrected by the "Funk & Wagnalls New Standard Dictionary of the English Language." New York: Funk & Wagnalls, 1915, p. 21.

McCartney, James. "Carter's Shake-up 'Botched' " (a Knight News Service syndicated article), July 1979.

Strunk, William, Jr., and E. B. White. *The Elements of Style*. 3d ed. New York: Macmillan, 1979, p. 42.

care less

Van Buren, Abigail. "Dear Abby" (syndicated column), December 1980.

center around

Johnson, Wendell. "You Can't Write Writing," in S. I. Hayakawa, ed. *The Use and Misuse of Language*. New York: Harper & Row, 1962, p. 111.

McMurtry, Larry. "*Charlie Boy*, by Peter S. Feibleman," *The New York Times Book Review*, April 20, 1980, p. 14.

Morsberger, Robert E. *Commonsense Grammar and Style*. 2d ed., rev. and exp. Based on *Commonsense Grammar*, by Janet Aiken. New York: Crowell, 1972, p. 23.

"Prospects for Survival: A Conversation with Robert Penn Warren," *San Francisco Sunday Examiner & Chronicle*, September 14, 1980.

circumstances, under the or *in the*?

Bernstein, Theodore M. *The Careful Writer: A Modern Guide to English Usage*. New York: Atheneum, 1965, p. 101.

Fowler, H. W. *A Dictionary of Modern English Usage*. Oxford: Clarendon Press, 1926, pp. 77–78.

Cold slaw on my new chaise lounge!

Isbister, J. N. *Freud: An Introduction to His Life and Work*. Cambridge, Eng.: Polity Press, 1985, p. 80.

Weschler, Lawrence. "Profiles: Boy Wonder—I," *The New Yorker*, November 17, 1986, pp. 54–55.

West, Rebecca. *The Thinking Reed*. London: Macmillan, 1966, pp. 268–269.

compare or *contrast?*

Hogan, William. "World of Books," *San Francisco Chronicle,* February 22, 1980.

Lawrenson, Helen. "Jackie at 50," *San Francisco Sunday Examiner & Chronicle,* July 29, 1979.

Morsberger, Robert E. *Commonsense Grammar and Style.* 2d ed., rev. and exp. Based on *Commonsense Grammar,* by Janet Aiken. New York: Crowell, 1972, p. 12.

comprise or *compose?*

Barker, Barbara. "The Marriage That Astounded Spain," *People Weekly,* April 2, 1979, p. 120.

Dessauer, John P. "Books in Education," *Publishers Weekly,* October 29, 1979, p. 37.

Landau, Sidney I. *Dictionaries: The Art and Craft of Lexicography.* New York: Scribner's, 1984, p. 283.

A concept-oriented framework may effectuate a consensus of opinion in terms of the maximization of a meaningful continuum of program factors.

Anderson, Jack. "Merry-Go-Round" (syndicated column), September 1980.

Associated Press. "Anderson Defends 'Rhythm' Comment" (syndicated article), June 1980.

Associated Press. "TV Anchor Injured in N.Y. Attack" (syndicated article), October 1986.

"Bank's 'Gobbledygook' Spurs Suit," *The New York Times,* June 26, 1980.

Betzina, Sandra. "Sew with Flair" (syndicated column), January 1987.

Christian Child Care, Inc., Gaithersburg, Md. "Speedgram," April 1987.

City of Palo Alto (Calif.), Department of Public Works. Letter to residents, August 1986.

Goren, Charles, and Omar Sharif. "Bridge" (syndicated column), April 1987.

"Jargon Control Program," *Harper's Magazine,* August 1957, p. 28.

Liebert, Larry. "Brown Signs the Budget," *San Francisco Chronicle,* July 7, 1978.

McCarthy, Eugene J., and James J. Kilpatrick. *A Political Bestiary: Viable Alternatives, Impressive Mandates, and Other Fables.* New York: McGraw-Hill, 1978, p. 44.

Mohr, Charles. "Lexicon," *The New York Times,* May 2, 1985.

"Nader vs. Beetle," *San Francisco Sunday Examiner & Chronicle,* September 12, 1971.

Olson, Elder. "An Outline of Poetic Theory," in R. S. Crane, ed. *Critics and Criticism: Essays in Method.* Abr. ed. Chicago: University of Chicago Press, 1957, p. 6.

Roth, Steve. "Hardware Review," *Personal Publishing,* June 1986, p. 38.

"State General Election Measures Detailed," *Hollywood Independent,* Los Angeles, October 22, 1980.

Stein, Rob. "Study Casts New Doubt on Heart Bypass Surgery" (a United Press International syndicated article), April 1987.

Teachers Insurance and Annuity Association/College Retirement Equities Fund. *The Participant,* New York, January 1987, p. 3.

Tovey, Donald Francis. *The Main Stream of Music and Other Essays.* Cleveland: World, 1966, p. 268.

United Press. "Cut Out Cliches, Brezhnev Advises" (syndicated article), April 1980.

United Press. "How Careers Cut Down on Sex" (syndicated article), June 1985.

United Press International. "Commerce Secretary Tries to Lop the Gook off the Gobbledy" (syndicated article), May 1981.

Weinraub, Bernard. "The Reagans Won't Take Manhattan," *The New York Times,* June 30, 1986.

contact
>   Evans, Bergen, and Cornelia Evans. *A Dictionary of Contemporary American Usage.* New York: Random House, 1957, p. 116.
>   Follett, Wilson. *Modern American Usage: A Guide.* Edited and completed by Jacques Barzun in collaboration with others. New York: Hill & Wang, 1966, p. 105.

Covered with onions, relish, and ketchup, I ate a hot dog at the ballpark.
>   Bawden, Nina. *Familiar Passions.* New York: Morrow, 1979, p. 83.
>   "Dick's Health Hints," *Paris Express–Progress,* Paris, Ark., September 13, 1979.
>   "Doctor Who Treated Sen. East Linked to a Rehnquist Problem" (a *Washington Post* syndicated article), August 1986.
>   Gordon, Lyndall. *Virginia Woolf: A Writer's Life.* New York: Norton, 1984, p. 210.
>   Lessing, Doris. *The Grass Is Singing.* New York: Popular Library, 1976, p. 16.
>   Ryan, Patrick. "A Suspect Philosophy of Lawn-Mowing's Joys," *Smithsonian,* August 1979, p. 124.
>   Updike, John. "Books: The Bear Who Hated Life [a review of *The Letters of Gustave Flaubert, 1830–1857,* selected, edited, and translated from the French by Francis Steegmuller]," *The New Yorker,* February 25, 1980, p. 127.

Dancing to a samba beat.
>   Angelou, Maya. "No Longer Out of Africa: My Sojourn in the Lands of My Ancestors," *Ms.,* August 1986, p. 37.
>   Bell, Madison Smartt. "Zero DB," in George E. Murphy, Jr., comp. *The Editors' Choice,* vol. 3. New York: Bantam Books, 1987, p. 44.
>   *The New Yorker* advertisement, in *Fortune,* September 10, 1979.
>   Warren, Robert Penn. *All the King's Men.* New York: Harcourt, Brace and Co., 1946, p. 102.

Dear Mr. Webster.
>   Associated Press. "Ted Kennedy Jr.'s Plea for Disabled" (syndicated article), June 1985.
>   Ferris, Richard J. "Capturing Corporate Creativity" (editorial), *United,* January 1987, p. 7.
>   Harry and David. "Good Grief, Mr. Webster! Have You No Soul?" Medford, Oreg., 1986.
>   "Jargon Control Program," *Harper's Magazine,* August 1957, p. 28.
>   "Outtakes: Entertainment Sidelights" (a *Los Angeles Times* syndicated article), June 1986.
>   Thomas, Ron. "Warriors Do It Again—Rout Lakers," *San Francisco Chronicle,* February 12, 1986.

different from, different than, **or** *different to*?
>   Gordon, Lyndall. *Virginia Woolf: A Writer's Life.* New York: Norton, 1984, p. 104.
>   Partridge, Eric. *Usage and Abusage: A Guide to Good English.* Harmondsworth, Eng.: Penguin Books, 1973, p. 330.
>   Strunk, William, Jr., and E. B. White. *The Elements of Style.* 3d ed. New York: Macmillan, 1979, p. 44.

disinterested or *uninterested*?

Huxley, Aldous. "Propaganda under a Dictatorship," *Brave New World Revisited*, in *Brave New World and Brave New World Revisited*. New York: Harper & Brothers, 1960, p. 51.

Pater, Walter. "Conclusion," *The Renaissance*. New York: The Modern Library, [n.d.], p. 198.

Don't she know it'll be dark soon?

Blumenthal, Karen. "Pickens Ends Bid for Diamond Shamrock Corp.," *The Wall Street Journal*, February 10, 1987.

Buckley, William F., Jr. "The Sporting Scene: Racing through Paradise—I," *The New Yorker*, February 9, 1987, p. 40.

Gordon, Mary. *Men and Angels*. New York: Ballantine Books, 1985, p. 15.

Malamud, Bernard. *The Fixer*. New York: Dell, 1966, p. 100.

Peter, John. "Theatre: Low Comedy Raised to High Drama," *The Sunday Times*, London, February 1, 1987.

Roosevelt, Franklin D. "Inaugural Address" (March 4, 1933), in Richard N. Current, John A. Garraty, and Julius Weinberg, eds. *Words That Made American History*. Vol. 2, *Since the Civil War*. 3d ed. Boston: Little, Brown, 1972, p. 407.

"A Summit of Substance," *Time*, May 19, 1986, p. 16.

due to

Capote, Truman. *Music for Chameleons*. New York: Random House, 1980, p. 53.

"Getting Testy: A Rebellion Gathers Steam," *Time*, November 26, 1979, p. 114.

Hall, Robert A., Jr. *Linguistics and Your Language*. 2d rev. ed. New York: Doubleday, 1960.

Hazzard, Shirley. *The Transit of Venus*. New York: Viking, 1980, p. 3.

Scott, Foresman and Company. *Annual Report, 1978*, p. 23.

"What Was On . . . ," *Evening News*, London, May 15, 1979.

each other or *one another*?

The Associated Press Stylebook and Libel Manual. Edited by Christopher W. French, Eileen Alt Powell, and Howard Angione. Reading, Mass.: Addison-Wesley, 1980, p. 65.

Calisher, Hortense. *On Keeping Women*. New York: Arbor House, 1977, p. 129.

Drabble, Margaret. *The Middle Ground*. New York: Knopf, 1980, p. 2.

Greenfield, Edward. "RPO/Dorati/Menuhin," *The Times*, London, May 29, 1981.

Kohl, Herb. "Listening to Each Other," *Teacher*, September 1979, p. 14.

"The New York Times" Manual of Style and Usage: A Desk Book of Guidelines for Writers and Editors. Revised and edited by Lewis Jordan. New York: Times Books, 1976, p. 67.

Partridge, Eric. *Usage and Abusage: A Guide to Good English*. Harmondsworth, Eng.: Penguin Books, 1973, p. 101.

"Electric shaver for women with delicate floral design on the handle."

Bernstein, Theodore M. *Miss Thistlebottom's Hobgoblins: The Careful Writer's Guide to the Taboos, Bugbears and Outmoded Rules of English Usage*. New York: Farrar, Straus and Giroux, 1971, p. 68.

Boyd, L. M. "The Grab Bag" (syndicated column), November 1979.

Cheever, John. *Oh What a Paradise It Seems*. New York: Ballantine Books, 1982, p. 1.

" 'Deep Throat' Star Getting New Liver," *Chicago Sun-Times*, March 6, 1987.

Drewes, Caroline. "Writer Edna O'Brien's 'Fanatic Heart,' " *San Francisco Sunday Examiner & Chronicle,* October 13, 1985.

Enright, D. J. *A Mania for Sentences.* Boston: Godine, 1985, p. 172.

Gilliatt, Penelope. *A State of Change.* New York: Random House, 1967, p. 101.

"Lady Sunbeam Rascal." Advertisement in *San Francisco Chronicle,* February 13, 1980.

Marx, Arthur. *Goldwyn: A Biography of the Man behind the Myth.* New York: Norton, 1976, p. 4.

"News Summary: Israel Agrees to Submit a Dispute," *The Boston Globe,* January 14, 1986.

Percy, Walker. *The Second Coming.* New York: Pocket Books, 1980, p. 26.

Schutze, Jim. "Keeping Anticipatory Eyes on New DART Leadership," *Dallas Times Herald,* November 22, 1986.

Shakespeare, William. *The Merchant of Venice* (act 2, scene 7), in George Lyman Kittredge, ed. *The Complete Works of Shakespeare.* Boston: Ginn, 1936, p. 270.

"Student Jailed," *Iberian Daily Sun,* Madrid, January 20, 1982.

Tuchman, Barbara. "Quality and Non-Quality," *San Francisco Sunday Examiner & Chronicle,* November 16, 1980.

Wills, Garry. "Introduction," in Lillian Hellman. *Scoundrel Time.* New York: Bantam Books, 1976, p. 23.

Woolf, Virginia. *Jacob's Room,* in *Jacob's Room. The Waves.* New York: Harcourt, Brace, 1950, p. 162.

Zinsser, William. *On Writing Well: An Informal Guide to Writing Nonfiction.* New York: Harper & Row, 1976, p. 9.

Eliot was born in Missouri, however, he spent most of his life in England.

Bernstein, Theodore M. *Miss Thistlebottom's Hobgoblins: The Careful Writer's Guide to the Taboos, Bugbears and Outmoded Rules of English Usage.* New York: Farrar, Straus and Giroux, 1971, p. 78.

Doctorow, E. L. *World's Fair.* New York: Ballantine Books, 1985, p. 366.

The Random House College Dictionary. Rev. ed. New York: Random House, 1984, p. 567.

Thornton, Lesley. "British Grail Guide," *Observer* magazine, London, August 3, 1986, p. 7.

enormity or *enormousness*?

Curry, Bill. "Houston's Murderous Dilemma" (a *Washington Post* syndicated article), September 1979.

equally or *equally as*?

Garraty, John A., and Peter Gay, eds. *The Columbia History of the World.* New York: Harper & Row, 1972, p. 23.

O'Connor, John J. "TV View: A Fond Cheerio to 165 Eaton Place," *The New York Times,* May 1, 1977.

Ever so funny jokes can be quite amusing.

Conway, John A., ed. "Trends," *Forbes,* July 14, 1986, p. 8.

Fowles, John. "The Irish Maupassant [a review of *The News from Ireland,* by William Trevor]," *The Atlantic,* August 1986, p. 90.

Hillmore, Peter. "Grave Crisis at Heart of Empire," *The Observer,* London, August 3, 1986.

Mathews, Mitford M. "Dictionaries Contain Surprises," in Leonard F. Dean and Kenneth G. Wilson, eds. *Essays on Language and Usage.* New York: Oxford University Press, 1959, p. 47.

Nessen, Ron. *It Sure Looks Different from the Inside.* New York: Playboy Paperbacks, 1979.

Sledd, James. "Something about Language and Social Class," *Halcyon 1986: A Journal of the Humanities,* pp. 35–36.

Fish and chips is on the menu again.

Hechinger, Fred M. "Far Right Steps Up Effort to Control Classrooms," *The New York Times,* April 16, 1985.

Lindsey, Robert. "Sinatra, Long a Friend of Politicians," *The New York Times,* January 2, 1981.

Nabokov, Vladimir. *Lectures on Literature,* vol. I. New York: Harcourt Brace Jovanovich, 1980. (Quoted in V. S. Pritchett, "Books," *The New Yorker,* January 19, 1981, p. 111.)

Niesewand, Peter. "Gandhi Plummets On in Pursuit of Vision of Glory," *The Guardian,* London, May 22, 1979.

Trilling, Diana. "The Liberated Heroine," *The Times Literary Supplement,* London, October 13, 1978.

flaunt or *flout?*

"Carter Calls On U.N. to Vote Economic Sanctions to Halt Iran's 'Arrogant Defiance,' " by Bernard Gwertzman, *The New York Times,* December 22, 1979.

"Carter Will Ask U.N. for Sanctions on Iran," *San Francisco Chronicle,* December 22, 1979.

Freidel, Frank. *America in the Twentieth Century.* New York: Knopf, 1960, p. 260.

Hunnicutt, C. W.; Jean D. Grambs; and William F. Benjamin. *The Great Adventure: Teacher's Manual.* 2d ed. New York: Singer, 1967, p. 17.

Klanwatch (The Southern Poverty Law Center, Montgomery, Ala.), March 1980, p. 2.

Povey, Terry. "Anti-Khomeini Forces Take To the Street," *Financial Times,* Frankfurt, September 10, 1981.

former, ex-, or *late?*

Logan, Andy. "Around City Hall," *The New Yorker,* August 4, 1986, p. 67.

former; latter

Liebert, Larry. "Tax-Reform Goof: Words Fail Hayakawa," *San Francisco Chronicle,* February 10, 1981.

get

Bernstein, Jeremy. "Personal History: The Life It Brings—1," *The New Yorker,* January 26, 1987, p. 35.

Eliot, T. S. "Sweeney Agonistes," *The Complete Poems and Plays.* New York: Harcourt, Brace, 1952, pp. 77, 83.

Flately, Guy. "It Looks like the Year of the Melvyn Douglas Renaissance," *San Francisco Chronicle,* June 3, 1979.

Secter, Bob. "Town Tickets Residents for Weeds, Peeling Paint," *Los Angeles Times,* June 10, 1979.

Grampa got his strenth back last Febuary.
Grant, Hank. "Hollywood Reporter" (syndicated column), July 1979.

The headwaiter asked if I were alone.
Bernstein, Theodore M. *Dos, Don'ts & Maybes of English Usage.* With the assistance of
Marylea Meyersohn and Bertram Lippman. New York: Times Books, 1977, p. 73.
Jespersen, Otto. *Growth and Structure of the English Language.* 9th ed. Garden City,
N.Y.: Doubleday, 1955, p. 3.
Kraft, Joseph. "Only the Voters Won" (syndicated column), January 1980.
Moncreiffe, Sir Iain. "The Expectancy and Rose of the Fair State," in Richard Buckle,
ed. *U and Non-U Revisited.* New York: Viking, 1978, p. 97.
Public Broadcasting Service. *Republican Presidential Debates from Iowa,* January 5,
1980.
Raines, Howell. "Both Sides Use Many Tricks to Bring Out Florida Voters," *The New
York Times,* October 14, 1979.
Weinraub, Judith. "After the Crazy Winter of '79, the Top U.S. Weatherman Warns:
Spring Won't Be Any Picnic," *People Weekly,* April 2, 1979, p. 57.

hopefully
Kaiser, Robert G. " 'Verification'—Slippery Key to Salt" (a *Washington Post*
syndicated column), June 1979.
Morris, William, and Mary Morris. *Harper Dictionary of Contemporary Usage.* New
York: Harper & Row, 1975, p. 311.
Morris, William, and Mary Morris. *Harper Dictionary of Contemporary Usage.* 2d ed.
New York: Harper & Row, 1985, p. 291.
Pooley, Robert C. *The Teaching of English.* Urbana, Ill.: National Council of Teachers
of English, 1974, p. 175.

How come the clock isn't going?
Montoya, Sarah. "Print Pollution," *Word Watching,* August/September 1979, p. 44.
Veríssimo, Érico. Personal conversation (Washington, D.C., 1958).

human or *human being?*
Baky, John S., ed. *Humans and Animals.* New York: Wilson, 1980.
Dowdall, Mike, and Pat Welch. *Humans.* New York: Simon & Schuster, 1985.
*Faulty Diction, As Corrected by "The Funk & Wagnalls New Standard Dictionary of the
English Language."* New York: Funk & Wagnalls, 1915.
Fuller, R. Buckminster. *Humans in Universe.* Hawthorne, N.Y.: Mouton, 1983.

hung or *hanged?*
National Public Radio. *All Things Considered,* October 4, 1985.

Hurricane David left devastation in her wake.
Carson, Luella Clay. *Handbook of English Composition: A Compilation of Standard
Rules and Usage.* Rev. ed. Yonkers-on-Hudson, N.Y.: World Book Company, 1911,
p. 130.
Cooper, Wyatt. *Families: A Memoir and a Celebration.* New York: Harper & Row,
1975, p. 59.
Dictionary of American Regional English. Cambridge: Harvard University (Belknap)
Press, 1985, pp. lxxiii, lxxiv.

Ebbit, Wilma R., and David R. Ebbit. *Perrin's Index to English.* 6th ed. Glenview, Ill.: Scott, Foresman, 1977, p. 257.

Lakoff, Robin. *Language and Woman's Place.* New York: Harper & Row, 1975, pp. 17, 43.

Landau, Sidney I. *Dictionaries: The Art and Craft of Lexicography.* New York: Scribner's, 1984, p. 3.

Lapham, Lewis H. "Gilding the News," *Harper's,* July 1981, p. 39.

Lapham, Lewis H. "Notebook: Social Hygiene," *Harper's,* November 1986, p. 8.

Seawell, Mary Ann. "Hey Man, Here're a Few Words about Women," *The Peninsula Times Tribune,* Palo Alto, Calif., July 1979.

Strunk, William, Jr., and E. B. White. *The Elements of Style.* 3d ed. New York: Macmillan, 1979, p. 60.

van Leunen, Mary-Claire. *A Handbook for Scholars.* New York: Knopf, 1979, pp. 4, 10.

I cannot but love that man of mine.

"Can't Help Lovin' Dat Man." From *Show Boat*, adapted from Edna Ferber's novel of the same name. Book and lyrics by Oscar Hammerstein II. Music by Jerome Kern.

Cleaver, Eldridge. *Soul on Ice.* New York: McGraw-Hill, 1968, p. 82.

Collins, Monica. "TV Preview—'Sakharov': A Tale of Hopeless Heroism," *USA Today,* June 20, 1984.

Drabble, Margaret. *The Middle Ground.* New York: Knopf, 1980, p. 86.

Frugé, August. "Lectures into Books," *Scholarly Publishing,* January 1981, p. 160.

Schaer, Sidney C. "What Goes into a Humongous New Dictionary" (a *Newsday* syndicated article), November 1980.

Will, George. "When Art Becomes Absurd" (syndicated column), August 1981.

"Ice cream your kids today with Rocky Road."

Blake, Nicholas. *End of Chapter.* New York: Harper & Brothers, 1957, p. 84.

Colgate television commercial, 1980.

Foremost Food Company. So-Lo brand milk carton, 1979.

Gilliatt, Penelope. *A State of Change.* New York: Random House, 1967, pp. 27–28.

Hatfield, Julie. "*Victorian Revival in Interior Design,* by Jim Kemp," *The Boston Globe,* December 13, 1985.

Kennedy, John F. "Inaugural Address" (January 20, 1961), in Richard N. Current, John A. Garraty, and Julius Weinberg, eds. *Words That Made American History.* Vol. 2, *Since the Civil War.* 3d ed. Boston: Little, Brown, 1972, p. 568.

Lazarus, Emma. "The New Colossus," a sonnet (1883) inscribed on the base of the Statue of Liberty.

O'Hara, John. "Hope of Heaven," *Hope of Heaven and Other Stories.* London: Faber and Faber, 1939, p. 85.

Pall Mall advertisement, 1960.

Panter-Downes, Mollie. "Our Far-flung Correspondents: Charleston, Sussex," *The New Yorker,* August 18, 1986, p. 63.

Pepsodent television commercial, 1956.

Shakespeare, William. *The Life of King Henry the Fifth* (act 4, scene 3), in George Lyman Kittredge, ed. *The Complete Works of Shakespeare.* Boston: Ginn, 1936, p. 651.

"If someone could make your child a genius, would you let them?"

Davies, Robertson. *The Manticore.* New York: Viking, 1972, p. 98.

Garchik, Leah. "Personals," *San Francisco Chronicle,* July 10, 1980.

Hellman, Lillian. *Scoundrel Time.* New York: Bantam Books, 1976, p. 82.

Kael, Pauline. "The Current Cinema," *The New Yorker,* July 15, 1985, p. 70.

Medwick, Cathleen. "Norman Mailer on Love, Sex, God, and the Devil," *Vogue,* December 1980, p. 269.

Public Broadcasting Service. Advertisement for "Monkey Monkey Bottle of Beer, How Many Monkeys Have We Here?," *Theater in America.* In *San Francisco Chronicle,* April 9, 1975.

The Quality of Spoken English on BBC Radio: A Report for the BBC. By Robert W. Burchfield, Denis Donoghue, and Andrew Timothy. London: British Broadcasting Corporation, 1979, p. 22.

Stutz, Terrence. "Rights Group to Monitor Campaigns," *The Dallas Morning News,* April 1, 1986.

Wilde, Oscar, *Lady Windermere's Fan,* in J. S. P. Tatlock and R. G. Martin, eds. *Representative English Plays from the Miracle to Pinero.* 2d ed., rev. and enl. New York: Appleton-Century-Crofts, 1926, p. 864

Woolf, Virginia. *Jacob's Room,* in *Jacob's Room. The Waves.* New York: Harcourt, Brace, 1950, pp. 30–31.

imply or *infer?*

Sullivan, Pat. "Good-by Clambake, Hello AT&T," *San Francisco Chronicle,* January 29, 1986.

In one year and out the other.

Associated Press. "Washington Post Blames Its Editors for Pulitzer Fiasco" (syndicated article), April 1981.

Chamberlin, Anne. "Caribbean Retreats: To Get Lost, Hurry Up," *The Saturday Evening Post,* March 14, 1964, p. 36.

Fowler, H. W. *A Dictionary of Modern English Usage.* Oxford: Clarendon Press, 1926, p. 697.

Fowler, H. W. *A Dictionary of Modern English Usage.* 2d ed. Revised by Sir Ernest Gowers. Oxford: Clarendon Press, 1965, p. 684.

The New York Times, October 25, 1964.

Nicholson, Margaret. *A Dictionary of American-English Usage, Based on "Fowler's Modern English Usage."* New York: Oxford University Press, 1957, pp. 632–633.

irregardless or *regardless?*

Dixon, Jeane. "Horoscope" (syndicated column), July 1979.

Editorial, *The Star-Progress,* Berryville, Ark., September 27, 1979.

Is it me you like better than her?

Bowen, Elizabeth. *The Death of the Heart.* New York: Vintage Books, 1955, p. 8.

Calisher, Hortense. *On Keeping Women.* New York: Arbor House, 1977, pp. 14, 203.

Columbia Broadcasting System. *60 Minutes,* March 9, 1986.

People Weekly, cover, March 24, 1980.

Public Broadcasting Service. *The Royal Heritage,* 1979.

Shakespeare, William. *Twelfth Night* (act 2, scene 5), in George Lyman Kittredge, ed. *The Complete Works of Shakespeare.* Boston: Ginn, 1936, p. 413.

Jobbed in a humongous scam, the tweaked-out mobster exclaimed, "Peachy-keen!"

Ace, Goodman. "Top of My Head: The Baloney Syndrome," *Saturday Review*, August 1979, p. 16.

Associated Press. "Blumenthal Sees 8½% Inflation" (syndicated article), May 1979.

Associated Press. "VA Uses Computer to Hunt Deadbeats" (syndicated article), February 1981.

Drucker, Peter F. "How to Manage the Boss," *The Wall Street Journal*, August 1, 1986.

Flanigan, James. "General Motors on the Move" (a *Los Angeles Times* syndicated article), August 1980.

"Keister II" (editorial), *The Washington Post*, March 23, 1983.

Mansfield, Stephanie. "Now Everyone Can Shmooz with Oprah" (a *Washington Post* syndicated column), November 1986.

Norman, Geraldine. "Getting at the Roots of Holbein's Horseman," *The Times*, London, October 20, 1980.

Quindlen, Anna. "A Royal Wedding Ritual: The Pig-out in Front of the TV," *The New York Times*, July 30, 1986.

Royko, Mike. "The Real Irsay?" (a *Chicago Tribune* syndicated column), December 1986.

"Stuffing Farmers, Stiffing Peasants" (editorial), *The New Republic*, August 11 and 18, 1986, p. 5

White, Donald K. "Everything Is 'Peachy-Keen,'" *San Francisco Chronicle*, September 19, 1980.

"Kinkering Congs Their Titles Take."

Bartlett, John. *Familiar Quotations*. 14th ed., rev. and enl. Edited by Emily Morison Beck. Boston: Little Brown, 1968, p. 807.

Brewer's Dictionary of Phrase and Fable. Centenary edition, revised by Ivor H. Evans. New York: Harper & Row, 1981, p. 1062.

The Independent News (INN), November 12, 1986.

like or *as, as if*?

Associated Press. "Americans Eat like There's No Time for Home" (syndicated article), June 1979.

Barnett, Chris. "The Movie Mogul and 'That Cosmo Girl,'" *Mainliner* (United Airlines), July 1980, p. 61.

Davis, Kenneth C. "*PW* Interviews: Gay Talese," *Publishers Weekly*, April 11, 1980, p. 6.

Didion, Joan. "In Hollywood," *The White Album*. New York: Pocket Books, 1979, p. 152.

Downie, Leonard, Jr. "Thatcher Is Dead Set on a Quick British Victory" (a *Washington Post* syndicated article), April 1982.

Evans, Bergen, and Cornelia Evans. *A Dictionary of Contemporary American Usage*. New York: Random House, 1957, pp. 276, 277.

Fogarty, John. "Sen. Hayakawa Feels Jilted," *San Francisco Chronicle*, February 4, 1982.

Gilchrist, Ellen. "Rich," *In the Land of Dreamy Dreams*. Boston: Little, Brown, 1981, p. 10.

McMurtry, Larry. *All My Friends Are Going to Be Strangers*. New York: Simon & Schuster, 1972, p. 207.

Shales, Tom. "Television: Troubled CBS Will Lay a Basket Full of Prime-Time Eggs" (a *Washington Post* syndicated column), September 1986.

Winston (R. J. Reynolds Tobacco Company) slogan, 1954.

likely, apt, or *liable?*

Balliett, Whitney. "Jazz: Bob's Your Uncle," *The New Yorker*, February 23, 1987, p. 126.

Gilliatt, Penelope. *A State of Change*. New York: Random House, 1967, p. 30.

"Los Angeles Times" Stylebook: A Manual for Writers, Editors, Journalists and Students. Compiled by Frederick S. Holley. New York: New American Library, 1981, p. 137.

Maslin, Janet. "The Screen: Pavarotti Is the Star of 'Giorgio,' " *The New York Times*, September 24, 1982.

The Oxford Paperback Dictionary. Oxford: Oxford University Press, 1979, pp. 367, 638.

Reston, James. "Reports" (syndicated column), October 1979.

"The Washington Post" Deskbook on Style. Compiled and edited by Robert A. Webb. New York: McGraw-Hill, 1978, p. 70.

Lo and behold, it's man's best friend.

Dessauer, John P. *Book Publishing: What It Is, What It Does*. 2d ed. New York: Bowker, 1981, p. 14.

Dickens, Charles. *David Copperfield*. London: Macmillan, 1964, pp. 465, 538.

Dickens, Charles. *A Tale of Two Cities*. New York: Grosset & Dunlap, 1948, p. 3.

Eliot, T. S. "The Hollow Men," *The Complete Poems and Plays*. New York: Harcourt, Brace, 1952, p. 59.

Fallada, Hans. *Little Man, What Now?* Chicago: Academy Chicago Publications, 1938.

Lewis, Sinclair. *It Can't Happen Here*. New York: New American Library, 1970.

Newman, Edwin. "Royal Wisdom?" (a Kind Features Syndicate article), October 1986.

Rossetti, Christina. "Song," in Marya Zaturenska, ed. *Selected Poems of Christina Rossetti*. New York: Macmillan, 1970, p. 25.

Sarton, May. *The Bridge of Years*. New York: Norton, 1985, p. 287.

Scobie, William. "Texas in Crisis," *The Observer*, London, August 3, 1986.

Shakespeare, William. *The Complete Works of Shakespeare*. Edited by George Lyman Kittredge. Boston: Ginn, 1936, pp. 305, 789, 1017, 1155.

Shawe-Taylor, Desmond. "Books: Exuberance [a review of volume 3, *Bernard Shaw: Collected Letters, 1911–1925*]," *The New Yorker*, December 23, 1985, p. 88.

"What, No B'ar?" (editorial), *Seattle Post-Intelligencer*, August 16, 1986.

Wolfe, Thomas. *You Can't Go Home Again*. New York: Harper & Row, 1973.

loan or *lend?*

Martin, Judith. "Miss Manners" (syndicated column), May 1985.

lot; lots

Faulty Diction, As Corrected by the "Funk & Wagnalls New Standard Dictionary of the English Language." New York: Funk & Wagnalls, 1915, p. 45.

Whipple. A. B. C. "The Raccoon Life in Darkest Suburbia," *Smithsonian*, August 1979, p. 84.

Love from Buddy and myself.

Christie, Agatha. *A Caribbean Mystery*. New York: Pocket Books, 1964, p. 135.

Cleaver, Eldridge. *Soul on Ice*. New York: McGraw-Hill, 1968, p. 4

Flanner, Janet. *Darlinghissima: Letters to a Friend*. New York: Random House, 1985, p. 6.

Lewis, J. Windsor. "Prefatory Note," in *A Concise Pronouncing Dictionary of British and American English*. Oxford: Oxford University Press, 1972, p. xv.

Trilling, Diana. "The Liberated Heroine," *The Times Literary Supplement*, London, October 13, 1978.

Waugh, Evelyn. Letter of December 27, 1945, in *Letters*. Edited by Mark Amory. (Fragment quoted in Robert Burchfield, *The English Language*. Oxford: Oxford University Press, 1985, p. xiii.)

manor or *manner*?

Shakespeare, William. *The Tragedy of Hamlet, Prince of Denmark* (act 1, scene 4), in George Lyman Kittredge, ed. *The Complete Works of Shakespeare*. Boston: Ginn, 1936, p. 1154.

"Today BBC 1," *The Sunday Times*, London, October 5, 1980.

"The Washington Post" Deskbook on Style. Compiled and edited by Robert A. Webb. New York: McGraw-Hill, 1978, p. 71.

"Me carrying a briefcase is like a hog wearing earrings."

Didion, Joan. *A Book of Common Prayer*. New York: Simon & Schuster, 1977, p. 73.

Gilliatt, Penelope. "The Current Cinema," *The New Yorker*, May 7, 1979, p. 141.

Lurie, Alison. *Foreign Affairs*. New York: Random House, 1984, p. 16.

"Sayings," *San Francisco Sunday Examiner & Chronicle*, June 1979.

Vonnegut, Kurt. *Galápagos*. New York: Dell, 1985, p. 39.

Modor, we've got company.

"An English Patio" (letter to the editor), *The Times*, London, May 19, 1981.

nauseated, nauseous, or *nauseating*?

The Plain Dealer (Cleveland), June 28, 1984.

"Neither fish nor flesh nor good red-herring."

Blake, Nicholas. *End of Chapter*. New York: Harper & Brothers, 1957, p. 173.

Faulkner, William. *Sartoris*. New York: Random House, 1956, p. 278.

Reston, James. "Reports" (syndicated column), December 1979.

No time to scan the newspaper? Well, then, just scan it.

Judis, John B. "The Conservative Wars," *The New Republic*, August 11 and 18, 1986, p. 18.

normalcy or *normality*?

Hofstadter, Richard; William Miller; and Daniel Aaron. *The American Republic*. Vol. 2, *Since 1865*. Englewood Cliffs, N.J.: Prentice-Hall, 1959, p. 427.

Not for nothing does Paris claim to be the world's most beautiful city.

Crittenden, Ann. "Jamaica Is Not a Happy Place" (a *New York Times* syndicated article), August 1979.

Didion, Joan. *A Book of Common Prayer*. New York: Simon & Schuster, 1977, p. 61.

Hofmann, Paul. "Hand Kissing: Guide for the Perplexed," *The New York Times,* June 17, 1979.

Kraft, Joseph. "Washington Insight" (syndicated column), July 1980.

Leroux, Charles. "A Loving Response to Emily Dickinson from One Well-versed in Her Work," *Chicago Tribune,* December 11, 1980.

Serfaty, Meir. "Political Pragmatism in Spain," *Current History,* November 1986, p. 379.

Now, that's something to write home about.

Espy, Willard. *Words to Rhyme With: A Rhyming Dictionary*. New York: Facts on File, 1986.

Gordon, Mary. *Men and Angels*. New York: Ballantine Books, 1985, p. 67.

Once children retire, they spend more time with their parents.

Fury, Kathleen. "Jack & Meryl & Carl & Nora: 'Heartburn' at the Movies," *Ms.,* August 1986. p. 12.

One should not tell secrets if you want to be told any.

Buckley, William F., Jr. "Cries about Whispers," *The Washington Post,* August 22, 1984.

Kempster, Norman, and Lee May. "Kalb Quits State Dept. in Disinformation Row," *Los Angeles Times,* October 9, 1986.

"Understanding: Coming to Grips with Moments of Inadequacy, Neurosis, Isolation, Depression, Masochism, Frustration, by Ann Dally," *Publishers Weekly,* May 28, 1979, p. 49.

The Oval Office which is in the White House symbolizes the Presidency.

Hall, Robert A., Jr. *Linguistics and Your Language*. 2d rev. ed. Garden City, N.Y.: Doubleday, 1960, p. 4.

Morris, William, and Mary Morris. *Harper Dictionary of Contemporary Usage*. 2d ed. New York: Harper & Row, 1985, pp. 578–579.

Percy, Walker. *The Second Coming*. New York: Farrar, Straus, and Giroux, 1980, pp. 5–6, 359.

Roth, Philip. *Goodbye, Columbus (and Five Short Stories)*. Cleveland: World, 1959, pp. 46, 62, 63.

Simon, John. *Paradigms Lost: Reflections on Literacy and Its Decline*. New York: Clarkson N. Potter, 1980, p. 60.

over or *more than?*

The Associated Press Stylebook and Libel Manual. Edited by Christopher W. French, Eileen Alt Powell, and Howard Angione. Reading, Mass.: Addison-Wesley, 1980, p. 147.

Faulty Diction, As Corrected by the "Funk & Wagnalls New Standard Dictionary of the English Language." New York: Funk & Wagnalls, 1915, p. 53.

"Los Angeles Times" Stylebook: A Manual for Writers, Editors, Journalists and Students. Compiled by Frederick S. Holley. New York: New American Library, 1981, p. 145.

There's no home like Eaton Place.

BBC Pronouncing Dictionary of British Names. Oxford: Oxford University Press, 1971, p. vi.

Bowen, Elizabeth. *The Death of the Heart.* New York: Vintage Books, 1955, p. 218.

Christie, Agatha. *The Clocks.* New York: Dodd, Mead, 1963, p. 155.

"Financial Times to Make 200 Redundant," *The Times,* London, May 29, 1981, p. 15.

Murdoch, Iris. *The Time of the Angels.* New York: Viking, 1966, p. 36.

Quirk, Randolph. *The Linguist and the English Language.* London: Edward Arnold, 1974, p. 144.

Strauss, Henry (Lord Conesford). "You Americans Are Murdering the Language," *The Saturday Evening Post,* July 13, 1957, p. 71.

"To err is human; to really foul things up requires a computer."

Didion, Joan. *A Book of Common Prayer.* New York: Simon & Schuster, 1977, p. 74.

Drew, Elizabeth. "A Reporter at Large—1980: The President," *The New Yorker,* April 14, 1980, p. 121.

Joos, Martin. *The Five Clocks.* New York: Harcourt, Brace & World, 1967, pp. 7–8.

Marshall, John. "Lesson from Injury: There Is Life after Football," *Seattle Post-Intelligencer,* August 16, 1986.

Minow, Newton N. "Program Control: The Broadcasters Are Public Trustees" (speech delivered to the 39th Annual Convention of the National Association of Broadcasters, May 9, 1961), in *Vital Speeches of the Day,* June 15, 1961, p. 535.

"On the Defence: Reagan Has to Watch As Congress Takes Over," *The Sunday Times,* London, February 1, 1987.

Reddicliffe, Steven. "The Strange Truth about Fat Albert" (a *Dallas Times Herald* syndicated article), June 1984.

Ridgeway, James. "The Scalia-Nixon Connection," *The Village Voice,* New York, July 1986.

Schickel, Richard. Letter to the editors, *The New Republic,* August 11 and 18, 1986, p. 2.

"Sir Roy Strong: Strong by Name but Certainly Not Strong by Nature," *The Sunday Times,* London, February 1, 1987.

Us TV watchers have strong convictions.

Drane, James. "Repent! Who, Us?" *Arkansas Times,* Little Rock, July 1980.

Henniger, Paul. "TV People" (a *Los Angeles Times* syndicated article), October 1982.

Kitman, Marvin. "Networks, Not Pledges, Should Finance Public TV" (a *Newsday* syndicated article), September 1986.

Noble, Valerie. *The Effective Echo: A Dictionary of Advertising Slogans.* New York: Special Library Association, 1970, p. 71

United Press. "How Billy Said 'No' to President" (syndicated article), July 1980.

United Press. "Nancy Mildly Anemic" (syndicated article), November 1984.

The Walrus and the Carpenter weeped like anything.

Carroll, Lewis. *Through the Looking-Glass,* in *Alice's Adventures in Wonderland, and Through the Looking-Glass.* Cleveland: World, 1946, p. 210.

"War is peace."

Associated Press. "Winds Could Push Big Slick on Texas Beaches" (syndicated article), August 1979.

Isaacs, Arnold R. *Without Honor: Defeat in Vietnam and Cambodia.* Baltimore: Johns Hopkins University Press, 1983, p. 195.

NCTE (National Council of Teachers of English) news releases.

"Newsbeats," *San Francisco Sunday Examiner & Chronicle,* November 8, 1981.

Orwell, George. *Nineteen Eighty-four.* New York: Harcourt, Brace & World, 1949, pp. 17, 215–216.

"Transcript of the President's [Carter's] News Conference on Foreign and Domestic Matters," *The New York Times,* April 30, 1980.

Washing down pillows takes a strong stomach.

Carroll, Lewis. *Alice's Adventures in Wonderland,* in *Alice's Adventures in Wonderland, and Through the Looking-Glass.* Cleveland: World, 1946, p. 139.

Christie, Agatha. *The Sleeping Murder.* New York: Bantam Books, 1976, p. 2.

Daily Express, London, May 21, 1979.

Johnson, Samuel. "Preface to the Dictionary," in E. L. McAdam, Jr., and George Milne. *Samuel Johnson's Dictionary: A Modern Selection.* New York: Pantheon Books, 1964, p. 23.

Murdoch, Iris. *A Fairly Honourable Defeat.* New York: Viking, 1970, p. 83.

Murray, K. M. Elisabeth. *Caught in the Web of Words: James A. H. Murray and the "Oxford English Dictionary."* Oxford: Oxford University Press, 1979, p. 9.

Quirk, Randolph. *The Linguist and the English Language.* London: Edward Arnold, 1974, p. 148.

Schiff, Bennett. "Fresh Perception of Impressionism's Vibrant Successor," *Smithsonian,* June 1980, p. 58.

Strauss, Henry (Lord Conesford). "You Americans Are Murdering the Language," *The Saturday Evening Post,* July 13, l957, p. 71.

Wedding bells are breaking up that old gang of me.

Blakey, Scott. "Christine Craft's Appeal Rejected," *San Francisco Chronicle,* March 4, 1986.

Commager, Henry Steele. "Letting Children Be Children," *Mainliner* (United Airlines), September 1979, p. 77.

Cook, Don. "Duchess of Windsor, 89, Dies in Paris," *Los Angeles Times,* April 25, 1986.

"Deaver Lobbying Case—New Probe Sought" (a *New York Times* syndicated article), April 1986.

Gill, Brendan. "The Theatre: Happy Liar," *The New Yorker,* June 30, 1980, p. 55.

Hirsch, Julia. "Why Is There No German Refugee Novel?," in Carolyn Toll Oppenheim, ed. *Listening to American Jews: Sh'ma, 1970–1985.* Port Washington, N.Y.: Sh'ma, 1986, p. 172.

"A Meese Link to Wedtech Payments" (a *New York Times* syndicated article), May 1987.

"Well, I'll be a drity brid!"

Delaplane, Stanton. "Postcard" (syndicated column), May 1979.

whether or *whether or not?*

Faulty Diction, As Corrected by the "Funk & Wagnalls New Standard Dictionary of the English Language." New York: Funk & Wagnalls, 1915, p. 78.

Who would you turn to for help?

Calisher, Hortense. *The New Yorkers.* Boston: Little, Brown, 1969, pp. 23–24.

Focus (KQED magazine), San Francisco, September 1979, pp. 16, 21.

Janos, Leo. "Black Sheep of the Fondas," *Sunday Telegraph Magazine,* London, May 13, 1979.

Knudsen Foods orange juice advertisement, 1979.

Robinson, Walter V. "Bush Honors an Old Foe—Loeb," *The Boston Globe,* December 12, 1985.

Serafín, David. *Saturday of Glory.* New York: St. Martin's Press, 1981, p. 17.

VerMeulen, Michael. "The Real Thing," *TWA Ambassador,* July 1986, p. 40.

whose or *of which*?

Murdoch, Iris. *The Time of the Angels.* New York: Viking, 1966, p. 75.

Naipaul, V. S. "The Engima of Arrival," *The New Yorker,* August 11, 1986, p. 28.

Quirk, Randolph. "Charles Dickens, Linguist," *The Linguist and the English Language.* London: Edward Arnold, 1974, p. 30.

"You're a goody-goody gumshoes."

ABC television news, San Francisco, January 10, 1980.

Bancroft, Ann. "Deukmejian Softens Stand on Tax Boost," *San Francisco Chronicle,* November 20, 1982.

CBS radio news, San Francisco, July 28, 1980.

Chapin, Dwight. "Alone at the Ending," *San Francisco Chronicle,* February 17, 1980.

Cline, Alan. "Parks Chief Tells Why He Was Ousted," *San Francisco Sunday Examiner & Chronicle,* May 18, 1980.

Green, Lloyd M. "Reagan Isn't Too Old for a Second Term" (letter to the editor), *The New York Times,* July 10, 1984.

Guthmann, Edward. "Wedded Bliss Runs Amiss in 'Paso Doble,'" *San Francisco Chronicle,* July 15, 1986, p. 42.

Highet, Gilbert. "The Personality of Joyce," *Explorations.* New York: Oxford University Press, 1971, p. 145.

"Israel Sticking to Release Timetable," *The Boston Globe,* June 21, 1985.

"Loopholes in Tax Bill Challenged," *San Francisco Chronicle,* June 7, 1986.

Marx, Arthur. *Goldwyn: A Biography of the Man behind the Myth.* New York: Norton, 1976, pp. 3, 4, 5, 9, 36, 113, 225.

"People get the idea if you publicly state you're a Christian . . ." Untitled article in an unidentified U.S. newspaper, around 1979.

"Reagan Lashes Out at 'Brutal' Sandinistas," *San Francisco Chronicle,* February 22, 1985.

Siskel, Gene. "Hollywood's Paranoia about Gays" (a *Chicago Tribune* syndicated column), December 1981.

Southwick, Karen. "Sprint to Lay Off 600," *San Francisco Chronicle,* August 14, 1985.

Toohey, Brian. "General Haig Bludgeons the English Language," *The National Times,* February 1–7, 1981.

Wallace, David. "Heart to Heart with Liz and R.J.," *People Weekly,* October 6, 1986, p. 111.